Urban Design

The American Institute of Architects

Urban Design:

THE ARCHITECTURE
OF
TOWNS
AND CITIES

Written and Illustrated by

PAUL D. SPREIREGEN, AIA

For The American Institute of Architects

McGraw-Hill Book Company

New York   San Francisco   Toronto   London   Sydney

URBAN DESIGN

ISBN 07-060380-4

101112131415 HDBP 76543

Foreword

THE IMPORTANCE OF URBAN DESIGN IN AMERICA

Charles A. Blessing, FAIA

This book is addressed to all the design professions and to all students of cities. It is a challenge and a guide to those who would save the city and the metropolis from itself during the fateful decades of explosive urbanization which lie just ahead. Recognizing that all of man's works, including the cities man builds, must respect nature or suffer the consequences, the first chapter of this book skillfully evokes the often prodigious achievements of the city builders of the past. On this solid foundation the chapters which follow develop with clear logic and convincing visual language an outline of basic principles and techniques of urban design.

In the building of the cities of America there has been a long and sad record of failure to understand, respect, and respond to nature, with consequent destruction of essential qualities in the landscape of cities. This volume calls on those who aspire to be the true designers of tomorrow's environment to combine a deep appreciation of nature in all its aspects, a sophisticated use of today's complex and fast-expanding computerized technology, and a creative design talent rooted in the history of cities and of design.

This study, to a responsive mind and eye, offers a deep and abiding emotional involvement in the ever-varied, frequently rich, and evocatively beautiful physical results of man's interaction with nature in the building of cities.

These related essays on the history, principles, and practices of urban design call on one to recognize the unfinished epic that is the building of America; to see the future as an extension of the past with the discerning eyes and concerned sympathy of a George Perkins Marsh, the father of American conservation; of a Lewis Mumford, the historian of the life, culture, and evolution of cities; of a Benton McKaye, prophet of regionalism in America.

Reading this book will suggest to the perceptive designer that every village, town, city, and great urban region on this continent, whatever its inherent natural characteristics of site and terrain or man-made problems, has a potential which stems from its own natural form, its sense of place, its sense of history, its spirit, its ethos. It urges us never to forget man's fundamental yearning for the beauty of nature. It also urges a respect for nature by man when he reshapes it for his own uses.

If we will but accept the inspiration of the natural setting as we work to build a better human environment, we will find a compelling logic in the sense of regional identity of New England with its beautiful hills and valleys and its richly varied coastal lands; of the Great Lakes states with their gently rolling glacial morraine with its thousands of lakes and streams; of the Mississippi Valley, with its surprisingly varied terrain; of the great plains, the land of vast distances enriched by the indigenous architecture of the ubiquitous grain elevator; of the stupendous grandeur of the Rocky Mountain region; of the red butte lands of the great Southwest; and of the strikingly beautiful Pacific coastal area.

The most important field of inquiry to the future of architecture and of all the design professions is the creative design of the city itself. To design cities we must first learn to visualize—to see— cities as they are in their natural setting and as they could be in the future. The vision of the creative architect, the extent to which he has perceived the shape of the world today, is the crucial factor in the building of better cities. The architect must build his potential for imaginative creativity by perceiving acutely the world of nature and cities around him. The architect and designer of cities must learn to see, to perceive, to imagine on a scale never before faced by designers. Some help can be offered by the richness of his vision of form in nature and of the stored images of the great architectural and urban compositions from the past 6,000 years. The architect and all other designers of the environment must resolve the dilemma of reconciling in their designs all the implications of a vast technological revolution in building and in transportation and of the overwhelming change in rate of growth and scale in cities.

The quality of environment of the city of the future will rest upon the creative imagination and intellectual vigor of the skilled and sensitive designer of cities. The education of architects and others for the design of cities must be perfected rapidly if we are to reverse the progressive formlessness and ugliness which is undeniably threatening to engulf the civilized world. The design of cities can be advanced only when all architects throughout the nation and world make it their greatest concern. The tremendous increase in awareness of the importance of the design of cities in recent years must be still further encouraged. Both architectural educators and the majority of practicing architects realize that the design of cities is of overwhelming importance today.

How to educate the architect for the design of cities is basic to the future of architecture itself. This book represents a great step forward in the provision of well-organized visual material on the form and design of cities. It provides a much-needed supplement to the present great variety of documentation on urban design, much of which is too cumbersome, too poorly organized, and too uninspiring to be of convenient and practical value to the busy practicing architect or the overly pressured teacher and student in the architectural school. Its rich visual treatment with sketches and plans of many examples of good design make it ideal for use both by students and by practicing architects.

As an introduction to the rapidly growing field of urban design, this work should stimulate the provision of detailed studies of the design of cities on the basis of major regions of the world and of the great number of nations which are becoming so rapidly urbanized.

As a professional contribution of The American Institute of Architects this book sets a high standard of public and professional service toward the better understanding of the design of cities and toward increasingly effective solutions to this problem which is so central to the welfare of the urbanized world.

VII

Acknowledgments

This book fulfills a long-standing dream dating back well before the inception of the AIA's current urban design program which began with the establishment of the Institute's Committee on Urban Design in 1957. The twelve chapters in this book were originally published as a series of twelve articles in the *AIA Journal,* from December, 1962 to November, 1964. They have been revised—and in some cases, entirely rewritten—for publication in this book.

Both this book and the original articles reflect the architectural profession's reborn awareness of the design of the American city and its encompassing region. The pressing problems of our urban areas require the attention of every citizen, professional and non-professional alike. Indeed professional status carries a greater obligation for personal involvement.

Concern for the design of the urban environment is by no means new to architecture. Historically the art of architecture and town design proceeded hand in hand. One spurred the other. Each was elevated by the other's excellence. While this book is a product of architects, it is by no means intended for their eyes alone. It has been our intent to produce a book on urban design understandable and meaningful to all.

This book is a product of the AIA's Committee on Urban Design, a committee which dates back a half-century and which produced in the early 1920s a series of articles, in significance not unlike those recently concluded. Over the years the AIA's Urban Design Committee has been made up of men whose names represent their century's accomplishments in American architecture and town planning. In the late 1950s this Committee renewed its efforts. By the early 1960s the Institute had appropriated funds from its supplementary dues to finance the twelve urban design articles in the *AIA Journal* as well as to support a program of urban design seminars at AIA regional chapter meetings throughout the country.

The articles were written and illustrated by Paul D. Spreiregen under the guidance of the Urban Design Committee's members and others. The Committee members were: Edmund N. Bacon, Frederick Bigger, FAIA, Charles A. Blessing, FAIA, Kenneth W. Brooks, Henry Churchill, FAIA (deceased), Vernon DeMars, FAIA, Carl Feiss, FAIA, Robert L. Geddes, George N. Hall, Donald H. Lutes, Albert Mayer, FAIA, Matthew L. Rockwell, Archibald C. Rogers, Nicholas Satterlee, Clarence Stein, FAIA, Harry M. Weese, FAIA, Arch R. Winter, Gordon G. Wittenberg.

The Committee expresses its deep gratitude for the advice and counsel of the following: Hans Blumenfeld, Lester Collins, FASLA, E. H. Holmes, Morton Hoppenfeld, Patrick Horsbrugh, ARIBA, Francis D. Lethbridge, George Mayer, FAIA, Roger Montgomery, Elbert Peets, Robert J. Piper, John O. Simonds, FASLA, Joseph Watterson, FAIA, Robert C. Weinberg, Samuel B. Zisman.

At AIA headquarters the Institute's Urban Design Programs and the production of the articles were directed by Matthew Rockwell, Robert J. Piper, and Paul D. Spreiregen. The original articles and the book were edited by Joseph Watterson, FAIA. We are most grateful for the research assistance of Mrs. Mary Osman of the Octagon library and for the secretarial assistance of Miss Nana May, Mrs. Betsy Heide, Miss Lilli Vincenz, and Miss Caroline Feiss.

William H. Scheick, FAIA

Contents

1

The Heritage of
Urban Design

The Beginnings

In the long history from camp to village a handful of innovations accelerated the art of settlement design. In agricultural societies such an innovation may be symbolized by the plow, for it boosted food production enough to free some people from tilling the soil and enabled them to attend to other pursuits. With the plow, man put his first lines on the earth's surface. On the flat riverside floodlands—civilization's first tilled soil—the plow etched parallel furrows which added up to a number of plots, more or less rectangular in shape. Agricultural societies needed a system of easy land division for crop planning and land ownership. They also needed a system of land plotting for redivision and reapportionment after a flood, an annual event on the Nile, the Tigris, and the Euphrates Rivers. Rectilinear plotting suited all these needs perfectly. It enabled men to plan the use of land.

As the logic of the plow led to rectilinear plotting in the field, the geometry of mud-brick house construction, as well as the need for easy land division, led to rectilinear plotting in the town. Village dwellers, too, had to be able to measure and record land plots for ownership, transferral, or rudimentary planning. They also had to divide their urban lots into squares, yards, or gardens. Mud

Air view of rectilinear land division in a farming area.

A village of rectilinear mud-brick houses.

1

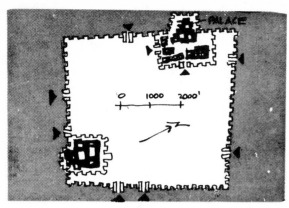

Khorsabad, Iraq, 8th century, B.C.
An example of rectilinear town layout.

A circular village. Air view of Ba Ila Village in Northern Rhodesia. Small huts form the outer circle. The chief's compound is in the center. Cattle pens line the outer circle of huts.

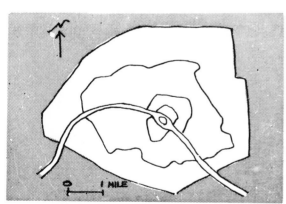

Successive walls built around Paris from its founding to the 19th century.

The Temple of Poseidon at Cape Sounion, as seen approaching the Attic mainland.

brick, convenient lengths of roofing lumber, and house planning were all combined in the logic of rectilinear town plotting. Rectilinear layout is found in the entire history of town building. It was used in ancient and later Greek towns; in Roman colonial outposts; and in the Indian, Chinese, and pre-Columbian cities. Our early colonial settlements employed this basic idea and its many variations. Indeed, the biggest application that has ever been made of the rectilinear or gridiron configuration was the division of the entire Western United States as prescribed by land ordinances dating back to our national independence. But the rectilinear was not the only geometric system used in the history of town planning.

The grid layout was accompanied and probably preceded by an equally important layout system: the circular form of settlement. The grid had been the product of the farmer; the circle was originally the product of the herdsman, the descendant of the hunter and the ancestor of the warrior. In the circle was found an ideal form for fencing in cattle, for it enclosed a maximum of land with a minimum of fence. That, however, was not its only advantage, for a fence could, besides keeping cattle in, also keep an enemy out. The major role of the circular form of town layout was to be a defensive one. Early fortified towns, usually built on hilltops or on islands, had protective walls which were more or less circular enclosures.

The immediate descendant of the circular form was the radiocentric, the means by which circular settlements enlarge. The radiocentric pattern develops from the circular by first growing outward along the radial routes; the wedge-shaped areas between the radials filling in gradually. Fortress cities, for example, developed small settlements around their gates and along the roadways. Eventually these settlements grew enough to require a second encircling wall, and then a third and fourth. This process kept repeating itself, from ancient Athens or Rome to nineteenth-century Paris or Vienna. But this gets us a little ahead of our story.

While there is much to learn from all the lessons of the past, both East and West, we do best to concentrate on the history of urban design in Western civilization, starting with ancient Greece. From there, in spite of many interruptions, we can trace a definite continuity. In ancient Greece the ideas and ideals upon which Western civilization is based were brought to first maturity. There, too, first matured a humanist basis for urban design and the skills to go with it.

Ancient Greece

The sunlight in Greece is brilliant and revealing; the air is clear and the land form is rocky and hilly. The landscape of Greece is powerfully assertive. Its presence is keenly felt at all times. At night the clear air allows the stars, too, to present themselves in brilliant array.

This inspiring landscape roused the ancient Greeks to wide intellectual speculation. They ascribed values to particularly prominent or unique pieces of land, as did many early civilizations. The high places in the land became sacred. In Athens the high place was originally a fortified hilltop, which, with the later growth of the city, became the sacred precinct, the Acropolis. It was a site for the temples of the gods, their treasures, and their attendant artifacts. Athens proper developed below the

2

Acropolis, starting at the entrance to the fortress hill and expanding along the major routes as a circular concept of settlement. The agora developed at the foot of the Acropolis along the route leading to Athens' port, Piraeus, and was the city's political and commercial heart.

The attitude of the ancient Greeks toward town design stems from their sense of the finite, the idea that all things should be of a definite size to be comprehensible and workable. Aristotle described the ideal size of a city, or polis, noting that less than 10,000 people are too few to constitute a viable political entity and more than 20,000 are too unwieldy. The early Greek cities were quasi-rectilinear, the houses being small cubicles and the early towns a jumbled mass of irregular rectangular cells. The street was not treated as a principal design element but as the minimal leftover space for circulation. The meeting place was neither in the house nor in the street, but in the agora. In time the agora became the marketplace as well as the place of assembly—in effect, the downtown area of ancient Greek society. The climate of the Mediterranean, too, had great influence on town design.

The Greek stress on the finite is clearly seen in the design of their buildings and towns which never attempted to overwhelm nature but, rather, asserted themselves graciously as another component. The temple of Sunion at the headlands of Attica as seen from the sea embodies this harmony—as do the Greek towns in their total natural settings. Because Greek architectural massing and detailing were made to man's measure, Greek buildings always gave a sense of human measure to the landscape. Often the landscape lacked completely any objects for dimensional reference. Such man-made objects are conveniently called "parameters." It is this sense of human measure that architects call "scale."

Three examples of Greek design illustrate these qualities: the Athenian Acropolis; the Athenian agora; and the Greek colonial towns.

The Acropolis

The buildings of the Acropolis were once believed to exemplify the Greeks' preoccupation with limited entities. Sited on the sacred spots of the Acropolis, the component buildings were once thought to lack visible design relationships with each other. Such evaluations would have insulted the ancient Greek architect. For while the buildings of the Acropolis do not have a geometrical axial relationship, they do have a very definite visual relationship. This is evident when one approaches them from afar, from middle viewing distance, and from close up. The buildings of the Acropolis were not designed according to any drafting-table geometry. They were conceived, built, and rebuilt over a long period of observation and reflection—to be seen by the human eye and experienced by people moving on foot. Their design discipline was not the abstract plan: it was the real experience of people.

The Acropolis group consisted of buildings which, individually and together, gave measure to surrounding space. They articulated the space of nature as a series of purposefully sculptured masses. The visual sophistication of the Parthenon's design is only too well known—so well known that it has obscured the design sophistication of the entire Acropolis group. From the Acropolis proper, for example, there was a striking panoramic view of the

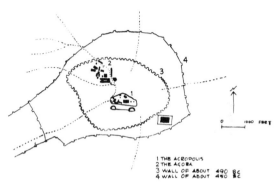

A Greek temple at Segesta, Sicily. An example of the Greeks' skill in setting a temple in nature.

Ancient Athens ca. 400 B.C., showing the agora and the Acropolis in relation to the city's walls and hills.

The Acropolis of Athens.

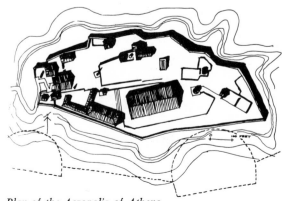

Plan of the Acropolis of Athens.

3

The Parthenon from the Propylaea.

The Athenian agora with the Odeon against a background of stoas. In the distance, the Acropolis.

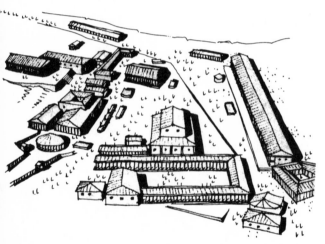

The Agora of Athens as seen looking down from the Acropolis.

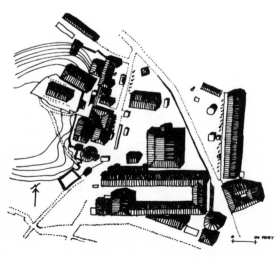

Plan of the Athenian agora, 2nd century B.C.

surrounding hills and mountains. The sacred character of the Acropolis itself may very likely have derived from this stirring visual relationship. This panorama was dramatically accented by the foreground of man-made temples. They added man's work to nature's. Lesser designers might have blocked these vistas by placing buildings squarely on axis with the features of the overall view. The Greeks placed their buildings to relate faraway vista to nearby temples, keeping all in clear, visible relationship.

The buildings of the Acropolis and their siting illustrate one concept for grouping buildings. A considerable amount of Athens' public wealth was spent on them. Below the Acropolis, however, a rather different concept evolved, one which nobly sufficed for less lavish buildings and which employed exactly the opposite concept of grouping.

The Agora

Whereas the Acropolis consisted of masses articulating space, the buildings of the agora served as facades to form an enclosed urban space. The agora, too, was built over a long span of time. Its early buildings were small and unified visually by their smaller shapes, details, and sizes. The later buildings were longer and more regular. All were grouped around a central open space. Small gaps between the buildings led to smaller peripheral spaces and to pathways to various parts of the city.

Because they were low, the buildings created a comfortable sense of spatial enclosure. Statues and other sculptural details accented the central open space here and there. The buildings, being regular and architecturally horizontal, gave a sense of stable repose. A pediment seen outlined against the sky here was balanced by other pediments elsewhere, repeating a theme similar to a range of mountain profiles. The smaller buildings were symmetrical and on varying ground levels. Combining all structures was their similar detailing—the visual composition of the whole group being one of asymmetrical balance. The cohesive design elements gave a sense of visual stability to what would otherwise have been a chaotic assemblage.

Essentially, though, it was the idea of massing buildings to form spatial enclosure that bound the parts into the whole. The agora was, first and foremost, an urban space. Its buildings were constantly being changed to alter the character of the space, but the space prevailed. In later days the Romans built a bulky music hall at one end of the agora, somewhat out of scale with the existing buildings. The agora then became a spatial setting for this one focal building. But it was still a space.

The lesson of the agora as an urban space is that urban space is flexible. Like the gridiron plan it allows many changes in its component buildings. Unity is maintained as long as the buildings are reasonably sympathetic in scale. Because space is the essential experience, the component buildings do not have to be lavishly detailed. Indeed, the more modest the buildings, the more successfully they function as supporting elements. Here, contrasted with the concept of the Acropolis, is a technique for achieving distinction in a modest group of buildings and giving them a place of common focus—even though they house quite different activities.

Like all lessons from other times or places, this one must be carefully understood. Designers of urban spaces have to understand fully how people actually use them. The agora was con-

4

stantly abuzz with people meeting, moving, talking, or just being present. In no small measure this was due to the variety of functions which the many buildings generated. The idea of the agora as both a *place* and as a *space* is one of the most useful concepts of urban design.

Greek Towns

Except for the Acropolis, the agora, and a series of enclosing walls, Athens as a city was a cluster of irregular cells. By the time Greek architects developed a design concept for whole towns, the form of Athens was immutable. It could not be torn down and rebuilt. However, Greek architects had ample opportunities to build entire towns elsewhere.

The design ideas which they used came from long experience and observation. Its principles are credited to a lawyer named Hippodamus, who lived in the fifth century B.C. He proposed regular street layouts along gridiron patterns. Some of his inspiration probably derived from ancient Babylonia, where open plazas were interspersed throughout the grid layout. The plan of Athens' harbor, Piraeus, is attributed to Hippodamus and is an example of this concept.

The Greeks thought of cities as areas of finite size, comprehensible to the eye and politically workable. They built them as a series of rectangular blocks or cells, all adding up to a whole town, designed from the inside out and ending against a steep hillside or along a shore. The town sites were quite often built on irregular topography. The harbors of such towns were enclosed by walled quays with the agora located alongside the harbor.

When a town reached its largest practical size—this largely determined by the capacity of surrounding farmland to feed the population—growth was terminated and a new town started at another propitious site, usually not too far away. The new town was called a "neopolis," and when that in turn reached its maximum size, they started another one. The first neopolis was then called a "paleopolis" or old town. Miletus, the hometown of Hippodamus, is said to have spawned some seventy or more new towns.

The perfection of this form and the way of life it represented is best visualized by studying the plan of Miletus, Priene, or Alexandria. The world of these little towns was the world of the Mediterranean, many of whose societies built towns based on the general design concepts perfected by the Greeks. Not the least of them were the Romans, who adopted and enlarged upon the ideas of Greece and added a few of their own.

Urban Design in Ancient Rome

Whereas the Greeks were motivated by a sense of the finite in their towns and buildings, the Romans were motivated by political power and organization. The proportions and sizes of Greek architecture—its scale—were based primarily on human measurements. Once established, these standards determined the size of a whole building. The Romans, on the other hand, used a set of proportions that would harmoniously relate the various parts of a building to each other but not necessarily to human measure. The size of a column determined, by rules of proportion, the sizes of all other elements. The basic dimension in such

The Greek colonial town of Miletus, illustrating the principles of Hippodamus, although built before his time.

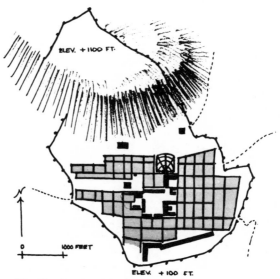

The Greek colonial town of Priene, illustrating the principles of Hippodamus, but planned after his time.

The facade of the Colosseum, Rome. Classic orders in tiers, an example of absolute architectural scale.

5

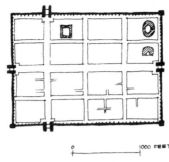

Aosta, a typical Roman military town.

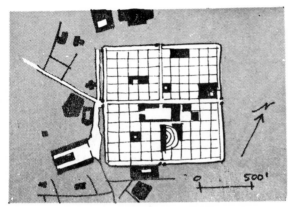

Timgad, North Africa. Built A.D. 100–117. A Roman colonial town.

The Republican Forum. The Curia (Assembly) is the center building.

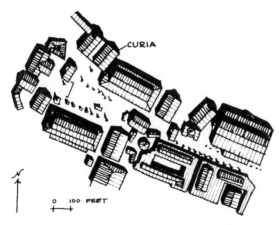

The Republican Forum in Rome. The buildings were erected one by one along an irregular axis.

a system of proportions is called a "module." For their buildings the Romans usually chose large modules in order to achieve a sense of overpowering grandeur. In their towns they chose another kind of module, one for relating all the parts of the town. The Greeks had done this, too, in a sense. Their urban module was a house but the Roman urban module was more abstract. They chose to think of the basic pattern of a town, not as houses made to human scale, but as overall street patterns made for military government.

A Roman colonial town was a system of gridiron streets enclosed by a wall. The wall was built first; the buildings came later. Traditionally, they used a plow in the ceremony to lay out the town walls, perhaps symbolically recalling the origin of the rectilinear town form. The Romans, with their emphasis on street layout, introduced the idea of major and minor streets—two main streets at right angles. They were called a "cardo" and a "decumanus" and divided the town into four quarters.

This system of town design was a simple but well-organized framework for a town's many buildings. The places of public assembly were the theater, the arena, and the market. However, they were not placed axially on the streets, as one might expect from such a highly organized society. The public buildings, too, were treated as elements subordinate to the street layout rather than as monumental features. The development of fully monumental design concepts came in ancient Rome in its cluttered central area.

The Republican Forum in Rome

Developing alongside the Tiber River at a point that could be crossed, Rome's early settlement was atop one of its seven hills, the Capitoline. The base of this hill became a marketplace and eventually, as in Athens, the commercial and administrative heart of Rome—the Old or Republican Forum.

Because the level area was small, only about five or six acres, buildings were crowded close together. They were conceived as individual objects with no formal relationship between each other except for their location along a common narrow space, about a thousand feet long on an east-west axis. Each of the Forum's buildings, big or small, was in effect a monument to its sponsor, commemorating him or some event associated with him. As an architectural group it had the character of a permanent carnival. So exhibitionist were all these buildings that the Romans resorted to a novel method to give prominence to the Republican Forum's most important building, the Senate's assembly house, or "Curia." The Curia was a small blocklike building amidst a horde of giants. Its exterior walls were left practically bare. Its distinction lay in being the only plain building among many highly decorated ones, and in being smaller than any of them—actually a good design approach. Time has brought about somewhat the same scale relationship between New York's old City Hall and its modern skyscraper neighbors.

The buildings of the Republican Forum (509 B.C.–27 B.C.) represent the development of steadily increasing political power. Successive buildings were ever larger than their predecessors. Gradually, Roman architects realized that the solution to designing grand arrays of buildings lay not in the superlatives of massing or detailing, but in grouping the buildings to form urban spaces. Perhaps they saw the design utility of enclosed architectural or

6

urban space as they sat in their hippodromes, their theaters, or in the Colosseum. Or perhaps they recognized this concept in the many ancient cities of the Mediterranean world which they had conquered, particularly those in Greece and Egypt. At any rate, they recognized the utility of the concept of enclosed space, architectural and urban, and they perfected its use.

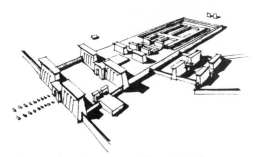

The temples of Ammon at Karnak in Egypt. Processional avenues, accented by pylons and court spaces, lead a religious inner sanctum.

The Imperial Forum

The extension of the Forum during the period of the Empire (27 B.C.–476 A.D.) demonstrates this skill. Like the Republican Forum, it was built along an axis determined by the space left between hills in the central city. This axis started about midway along the Republican Forum's axis and proceeded in a northwest direction for over a thousand feet. The design concept of the Imperial Forum was as different from that of the Republican Forum as Athens' Acropolis is from its agora. Here, again, architectural and urban masses were made subordinate to spaces.

The Imperial Forum was composed of square, rectilinear, and semicircular plazas, each formed by a colonnade and acting as a setting for a key focal building: a temple or basilica at the end of the space. Such a configuration had many advantages. In particular, it created distinct places within a still larger place. Further, individual plazas could readily be connected by a colonnade, which acted as both transition and link.

The Imperial Forum. The buildings were designed to form large regular spaces.

Perhaps the Romans were fortunate in having two completely different forums so close together. What complements they must have been to each other: the old one full of odd corners and places, cool and informal; the new one, spacious and open, brilliant with sunlight and order! The Imperial Forum was a work of great clarity, of immense regular spaces framed by colossal buildings. In contrast, the Republican Forum was a jumble of buildings, arranged incidentally along an irregular spine of space. The modern visitor can no longer discern the concept of the Imperial Forum, for its enclosed spaces disappeared when its buildings vanished. In contrast, the Republican Forum, now an array of stones, still suggests its original character: that of architectural masses.

The Roman architects continued to develop their ideas of enclosed space. They designed buildings to be contained in the centers or on the sides of larger spaces, at the ends of long spaces, and facing each other across spaces. The Imperial Forum was nearly a textbook of all types. The ultimate refinement of their space concepts can be seen in the large baths of Rome, which consisted of immense building masses in immense architectural spaces. A colonnade marked the edge of the complex and the space in which the main bath building sat. The colonnade served a very useful purpose, too, for it housed many shops. While readily accessible to the bathers, the shops with their profusion of goods were not visually distracting or unharmonious for they were screened by the colonnade's columns. The Renaissance architect Andrea Palladio was to employ the same idea much later in designing the service buildings of villas.

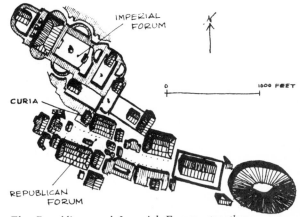

The Republican and Imperial Forums together.

Hadrian's Villa

Hadrian's country villa, 10 miles from Rome, manifests the skill of late Roman architects in arranging complex groups in natural settings, utilizing *both* spatial and mass concepts. Hadrian's villa consisted of many regular court spaces connected at irregular

Roman temples at Baalbek, Lebanon.

7

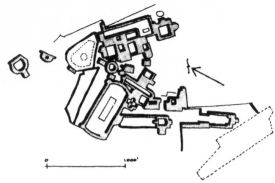

Hadrian's villa near Rome. Main axes were bent at special joints to adjust to the hilly site.

Hadrian's villa. Even in ruins, the principle of the joints which connected major axes and spaces can be discerned.

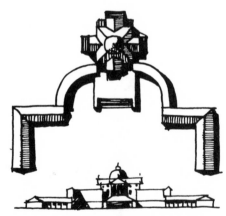

A villa in Meledo, Italy, by Palladio.

Fortified portal to a castle town, site of an early market.

angles. The major court spaces were located to fit the topography and their interconnection was achieved through the careful bending of the architectural axes. The links where the axes bent were usually small openings or small chambers. By passing from a large space into a small chamber and then into another large space at a different angle, the effect of irregularity was nearly canceled. The observer, rather than having his orientation confused, was comfortably summoned from one space to another. Thus the courtyard spaces were strongly related to each other, and the whole complex well adapted to the dramatic topography.

All of these design ideas were to inspire the architects of the Renaissance a few centuries later, for they were models for all architects to see. To the Roman architect Vitruvius can be attributed the foundations of theoretical design thinking. In his *Ten Books of Architecture* he related the experience of Roman architecture and town design. His writing includes many practical suggestions, such as the location of streets in relation to prevailing winds, the siting of public buildings, the testing of drinking water by examining the entrails of local animals, and the design of plazas.

To make their cities habitable, the Romans became great civil engineers: they built long aqueducts, and a road system to tie their empire together; they perfected arch and dome construction; and in Rome they built the ancient world's greatest sewer system. These brilliant engineering feats allowed Rome to function, but did not make it more livable. With the transport of water and food from distant sources, the Romans introduced an imbalance into the harmonies of nature. Raw sewage was dumped into the Tiber, whereas in earlier or smaller cities it would have been used to fertilize surrounding farmland. The sewer was an ingenious device to solve a problem that should have been avoided completely. The Greeks with their sense of the finite never had to face such dilemmas; they avoided them. The new towns of the Greeks were envisioned as self-sufficient and balanced communities in the Mediterranean world. So were some of the Roman towns, such as those in North Africa, serving as old soldiers' homes. So, too, were some of the major outpost towns, like Nîmes. But Rome, the main center of administration, was never made livable except for a privileged few.

To speak of real success in such a complex and large civilization—and to speak of fine cities in such civilizations—one must deal with planning at a regional and even national level. And then one must recognize that engineering can only go so far in solving a city's problems. The best city planning avoids these problems, for the most brilliant engineering can also serve to make a bad situation only slightly more tolerable and so prolong it. But the world would have to wait until well into modern times for a regional and humanist outlook that would take this point of view.

Urban Design in Medieval Times

The decline of Rome's power left many outpost settlements all over Europe which became the nuclei of new societies. Some, because of their opportune locations, thrived as influential towns. In the tenth century these nuclei began to grow into viable towns. In addition some castle towns also began to enlarge.

First they had been military strongholds—like Athens' Acropolis and Rome's Capitoline Hill. Throughout the centuries, mon-

8

asteries, often complete towns in themselves, had dispensed healing, nurtured the crafts, and acted as citadels of the world's learning. The monasteries were often laid out in rectilinear pattern. The castle towns, built atop hills, were enclosed by circular walls. The growth of a town around either monastery or castle was a natural growth starting at gateways, extending along roadways and then fanning out. This growth logically assumed a radiocentric pattern.

The transition of castle stronghold to caste-dominated town has an interesting portrayal in medieval paintings. The early fortress towns were dominant symbols for the people, a symbol which they served and supported by their labors. In early medieval illustrations, paintings, or manuscript drawing, the castle was portrayed as an object in the landscape—dominating and aloof. Later, as the castle became a town filled with merchants, tradesmen, and craftsmen, its portrayal changed from a thing in the distant landscape to an environment for people.

As an environment the town had much to recommend it. The houses were small, but had gardens and privacy. Craftsmen lived and worked at home. The town was fairly clean and modestly, though reasonably, spacious. Medieval towns were the centers of agricultural domains, whose boundaries could be reached in half a day's journey. This was a natural deployment, growing from the practicality of having a town center as the nucleus of an area which could be readily traversed.

Like ancient Greek towns, the early medieval town was small, of finite size and not enlarged beyond practical limits. These limits were largely determined by the capacity of a particular land area to support its dependent population. The town could be enlarged to accommodate an increasing population—and new walls built to encircle the town's expansion—but eventually growth reached a practical limit based on supply. It was not uncommon, therefore, to establish new towns in unsettled areas—or to go to war to gain land. In many ways medieval society was repeating the customs of the ancient Greeks and a number of other societies of history. Medieval townsmen relied heavily on the security derived from their protective town walls and the various fraternities that developed in such towns. Eventually, the bonds of Christianity welded the separate guild fraternities into a community spirit. The guild and burgher mentality developed in the home and was motivated by mutual materialistic interests. In the Greek polis the meeting place had been the agora, which nurtured a worldly political and social mentality. But just as the ancient Greeks' sense of the finite led to scale in their town design, the medieval burgher's need for reassuring surroundings resulted in a similar sense of human scale in his towns and buildings.

As the efficiency of this medieval society increased, so did its powers. The medieval towns became parts of larger territorial states. Growth in population and trade soon created the need for marketplaces. Marketplaces had not been necessary before because the burghers had their own small gardens and food merchandising was modest. An exception is found in certain cattle market towns. The marketplace of the medieval town became the counterpart of the agora or forum.

Intellectualized or abstract theories of urban design help little in understanding the medieval town. Geometric drawings scarcely portray them. These towns were too immediate, tangible, and personal. Even the smallest, with its winding streets, is full of

A castle stronghold commanding a water route in Corsica.

A fortress that grew into a city. Siracusa, Sicily.

A medieval Italian town on the Amalfi drive.

*A medieval Italian plaza.
The Piazza S. Croce in Florence.*

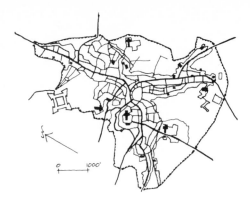

Siena, Italy. The Piazza del Campo is at the center. The cathedral is to its northwest.

The Piazza del Campo. An outdoor living room for the entire town.

The Piazza del Campo.

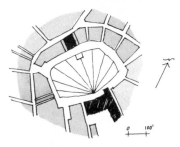

The Piazza del Campo in Siena climaxes the minor plazas and the entire street network of the town.

The main cathedral of Siena climaxes the architectural massing of the town.

a minutiae of sights and sounds. The winding streets preclude long vistas and thus direct one's attention to immediate details. In walking through a medieval town, one catches glimpses of a church tower in sequential views—or one may even keep it continuously in sight. Either way, one never feels lost, for the town is small and gives constant assurance of its human scale in visible construction and human activity. The Italian hilltown of Siena is a good example of these characteristics.

Siena

Siena is composed of several political sections, each occupying prominent topography, each with its local small square, but together focusing on one of the finest piazzas in the world and, a short distance from the piazza, on a central dominating cathedral. The city of Siena has a pattern of streets which follow the most logical topographical lines, converging on the central Piazza del Campo, a large outdoor living room for the whole town. The streets are all quite narrow, and the passage from them into an open piazza is dramatic. The main streets are those which are most regular. Lined with shops, they run from the town gates to the main piazza and consequently bear the greatest volume of traffic. As in most Northern Italian towns, the entrance views of a piazza were determinants in the placing of towers, and obviously the detailing of an important public building was strongly influenced by how it was seen from various places in the piazza. Since town form and building form are so related, it is certain that Siena's builders must have been thinking of both simultaneously.

The variety of sights of the town is enormous, yet the overall impression is unified by the constant interplay of basic themes: open space and closed space; narrow, winding streets lined with shops and opening into private courtyards; simple stone architecture; characteristic roof overhang on the houses; similar doors and windows; the relatively small size of the town; the frequent and dazzling vistas into the surrounding countryside; and, not the least, the flow of familiar people everywhere.

Medieval Town Design

In medieval times the practice of architecture as an art revolved principally about fortifications, churches, guild halls, and burghers' houses. The design of building facades reveals a particularly sensitive appreciation of how they were actually viewed. Seldom was a building seen as an isolated whole from nearby, and some facades were only partially seen. The front facade of a church was generally the only part fully in view. Even then the observer had to look up to see it. These conditions induced architects to design the visible exteriors of their buildings to best suit the total viewing conditions of small spaces. Vertical emphasis on French Gothic church facades was a result of close viewing conditions as well as a logical consequence of the structural system. Medieval architects did not prefer irregular forespaces as the settings for their works. These were the spaces they were given to work in. The striking results they achieved resulted from a realistic acceptance of settings which were largely foreordained and unchangeable.

Likewise, the fine siting of towns derived largely from the consideration of vista for military defense. This, coupled with the generally human scale of medieval buildings, made the towns fine accents in the landscape. They were proudly portrayed in paintings, tapestry, and sculpture.

The design elements of the medieval town were its houses and gardens, its walls, its plazas, its church, its public buildings, and, most important, its streets. Although a plan of a medieval town usually appears to be like a maze with no logical form (because it lacks pure geometry), the street layout was actually very functional. The early medieval towns had no differentiation of street types because they needed none. However, as the towns grew and as traffic increased, the different types of traffic found their logical way along different types of streets. Traffic from town gate to central plaza sought a direct and convenient course. The streets that led to houses were narrower and more irregular, and often dead-ends. The remnants of this differentiation are still in evidence in the street nomenclature of Italy, France, Germany, and England. The Renaissance had a different role for its streets to play, one that would neglect the essential differentiation between streets that serve houses and those that carry noisy traffic. Centuries were to pass before this problem was duly recognized. It still remains a problem for us to resolve today.

The familar geometry of the grid layout is sometimes found in medieval towns, usually in those built as colonial outposts. Aigues Mortes, in Southern France, was built either by an English king to establish his power there or by crusaders as a stop on the trip eastward. It is a simple rectangle with defensive wall, moat, and circular stronghold tower at one corner. The streets are a grid and there is a plaza at the center, but the streets do not lead directly from the gates to the plaza, probably to confuse an enemy who might break in. The walls of Aigues Mortes and those of several other fortress towns were built by Genoese contractors who had become world-renowned specialists in such work.

Medieval society was advancing in a direction which would bring a new age. Its growing capabilities led to the growth of powerful political states. In these states, certain towns enjoyed advantages because of the contributions they could offer a ruler or simply because of strategic position. In the guild hall there grew a spirit which molded the *bourgeoisie* into a strong political force, eventually culminating in what we now call a laissez-faire philosophy. Knowledge, skills, and materials gained through the early crusades and explorations added further to the capabilities of medieval society. In the skill of builders, in the wealth of the *bourgeoisie* and the nobility, in the organization of the military, in the new and persuasive force of gunpowder, in the development of political powers and expertise, in the new organizations of the medieval world, in the scholarly knowledge of the church—in all these elements lay the foundations of a new society that would need and would develop a whole new system of urban design.

The advance into that new era, the Renaissance, was only gradually felt. Western historians cite three major events to mark the moment of transition: the dawn of science; the fall of Constantinople; and the discovery of the New World. All occurred toward the end of the fifteenth century. The new era was to pit for centuries the forces of one group against another. It was also to test the strength and validity of many new institutions. In this conflict the design of cities was to become an instrument of political administration and many of the gains of medieval urban design were to be discarded, particularly the sense of scale and

Gothic verticality on a church facade. Amiens Cathedral.

Typical roof overhangs and massing of buildings in a medieval Italian town. The house of Dante in Florence.

The walls of Aigues Mortes in southern France, 13th century.

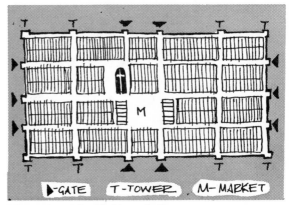

Monpazier. A fortified town built by the English in southern France in 1284.

11

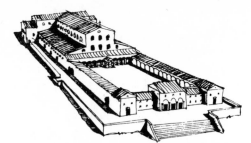

An early Christian church. Old St. Peter's in Rome.

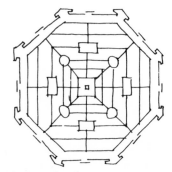

Plan for an ideal city by the younger Vasari.

Plan of an ideal fortified city by G. Maggi.

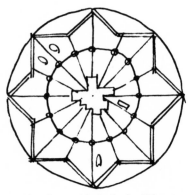

Plan for an ideal city by Filarete.

the intimate relation between house and street.

In spite of its constant lack of ease and assurance, the medieval world had produced a system of town design that was truly livable. That human element of urban design was bound to be lost, for the main purpose of town design ceased to be the comfort of its inhabitants. A principal lesson in medieval urban design is its humanist basis, but we must proceed with caution in searching for its expression in the form and design of the medieval town. For we are of an age that examines things in the abstract. We design our towns and buildings on paper, in small-scale models and by policy—not on foot. We have conditioned ourselves to see town and building concepts as functional abstractions. Of course, this is necessary because the scale of our design is so large, but we must remember that representations are only separate aspects of a larger condition. We must always be wary of the representation of ideas in plan form, be they ideas for towns or buildings. The experience itself must always be kept foremost in mind, and plans must be regarded only as instruments for realizing human purposes.

With the change to the Renaissance the role of the individual as a builder of his town was lost—with some exceptions, as in the New England town of colonial times. That role was assumed by many groups of individuals who were to hold power for several centuries. Their attitude was one of suiting ends to purposes at hand, the well-being of the populace usually being of secondary concern. It is difficult to imagine that the medieval world could develop the benefits which we now enjoy while maintaining its personal way of city building. With the growth of the power groups that shaped the modern world went the power to design cities. The links they forged are the roots of our present thinking, and these achievements stand among the Western world's highest accomplishments.

Urban Design Principles in the Renaissance

Ideal Cities

The year 1440 marks the beginning of the Renaissance. In architecture and urban design, Leon Battista Alberti is regarded as the foremost early theoretician. His book, *De Architectura,* like the books of his Roman precursor Vitruvius, treats architecture and town design as a single theme. Vitruvius had summed up Roman building knowledge. Alberti reminded his colleagues of the world's earlier knowledge and stimulated them to new ideas. Actually, Alberti stood with one foot in the medieval world and the other in the Renaissance. As a theoretician, some of his ideas are rather fanciful, particularly in urban design, but they are important in that they sparked other architects.

As an urban designer, Alberti is chiefly remembered for his "ideal" cities, star-shaped plans with streets radiating from a central point, usually proposed as the location for a church, palace, or possibly a castle. Many architects at this time were absorbed with the design possibilities of perfectly symmetrical compositions. Alberti's designs on this theme are as varied as the snowflakes they resemble, but they were not entirely abstract. He devised designs for ideal cities on hillsides as well as flat land. The hillside designs usually had curved streets to conform to the topography. He wrote that a curved street can seem to be longer than it really is because its ends are out of sight, and monumental buildings are magnified in importance when seen only in part.

Many architects tried their hand at the design of ideal star-shaped cities. They found that the polygon was an advantageous shape for fortifications and that converging streets were a useful means of focusing on an important central building. Some designers, like Filarete, were preoccupied with the military possibilities of the star shape. It was much better for laying out earth walls than a rectangular plan with right angles, because the corners of the wall could better accept the impact of cannonballs. Later on, the points formed by the wall became the locations of bastions, from which covering fire could be directed against an enemy attempting to scale the walls. The priest Fra Giaconda saw artistic possibilities in a central layout. He sketched an ideal city plan with a tall central building whose vertical is echoed in each of its peripheral bastions. Still another variation was a star city whose interior is divided up into special quarters, one for each trade and craft. Many designers realized that the radiating street pattern would cause great difficulties in the design of buildings, particularly where sharp corners occurred. Vincenzo Scamozzi designed an ideal city with a gridiron interior street layout. Albrecht Dürer in Germany designed a rectangular city, with zones for each activity.

The surviving fortification walls of Renaissance cities are the remnants of these ideal designs. There are still a few colonial forts in the United States which were laid out according to these principles, but they were built as forts rather than fortified towns. The shape of the Pentagon in Washington recalls a long military tradition. As interesting as these ideal cities are in the history of urban design, their very attractions have obscured a far more important accomplishment of the early Renaissance: public works and civic improvement projects. Well before 1440 efforts were made in Milan, Bologna, Siena, and Ferrara to improve circulation, sanitation, and defense. Of these programs, Ferrara's is the most interesting.

Rebuilding Ferrara

About the time that Columbus was sailing toward America, a powerful and self-important ruler ascended the throne of Ferrara. He called himself Hercules I and found the city-state he inherited far from his liking. Lying between two rivers, it was a mean medieval town, a scramble of narrow streets surrounded by an obsolete wall. Fortunately for Hercules, he had in his court a very able architect and town planner, Biaggio Rossetti.

Rossetti is remembered for his Palazzo Diamanti, a fortress-like palace in Ferrara whose rusticated stonework was cut in the shape of diamonds, hence the palace's name. But this was by no means Rossetti's major accomplishment: that lay in the redevelopment of Ferrara, a work in three parts.

Rossetti *first* prepared a plan for rebuilding old Ferrara, providing for street widenings, the erection of new buildings in the old town, and the improvement of the encircling wall. *Second,* he made a plan for enlarging Ferrara, more than doubling its size, specifying new walls, gates, main roads, plazas, and key buildings. *Third,* he spent the remainder of his career carrying forward the major elements of his plan. The importance of Rossetti's three-pronged approach lies in the logic of his original plan, for it suited perfectly the realities of town building in his day.

Rossetti's plan was not a detailed concept of every building

Fra Giacondo's sketch of an ideal city. The central church and gate towers accentuate the main terminals of the city.

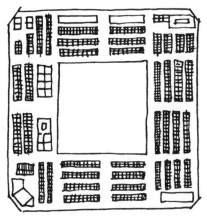

Plan of an ideal city by Albrecht Dürer.

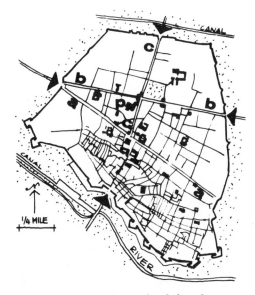

Ferrara. The original town lies below the street marked a-a. b-b and c-c are the two main crossing streets of Rossetti's plan. The Palazzo Diamenti is marked p.

13

The Palazzo Diamenti at the main intersection of Ferrara.

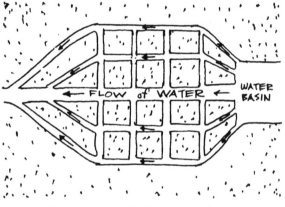

Leonardo's sketch of a water and sewage system for a spindle-shaped river city.

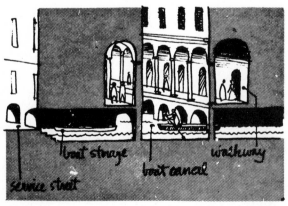

One of Leonardo's many ideas for multilevel circulation separations.

and street in Ferrara but only of those new elements that were most important. He furnished the bones and vital organs of the new town's design, around which the supporting flesh could grow in a logical and organized way—and with ample variation.

Rossetti planned three new broad streets for the extension of Ferrara. One of these ran east-west and would connect the new city with the old. The other two were at right angles and divided the city into four quadrants. At their intersection he designed a new palace for Hercules, the Palazzo Diamanti. In Rossetti's day there was no assurance that a proposed street would come into being just because it was designated on a plan. A more compelling force was required—which Rossetti provided by the sheer logic of his plan. All main streets connected vital points of the town to each other: gates to palace; gates to old fortress; plazas to plazas; and important buildings to each other.

Rossetti may be regarded as one of the Western world's earliest modern urban designers. He, like ourselves, had to repair an existing city and plan for its enlargement. He, like ourselves, had to decide where to concentrate his efforts, not being able to build either on a totally clear site or build everything at once. His genius lay in conceiving a plan that was logical and realizable, one that concentrated on essentials and provided a framework for others to build upon. Indeed, when Jacob Burckhardt visited Ferrara in 1860, he wrote: "Ferrara is the first modern city in Europe."

Leonardo da Vinci as a Town Planner

Less than a century after Rossetti's work in Ferrara, Leonardo da Vinci pondered the same problems but from a still larger point of view. Upon entering Milan, Leonardo was struck by the general squalor and unhealthful crowding. No doubt he had seen much the same symptoms of urban disease elsewhere, but he thought of ways to cure them and described, in his *Codex Atlanticus,* a new concept of urban planning.

Leonardo sketched a city straddling a river. Upstream, the river was diverted into six or seven branches, all parallel to the main stream and rejoining it below the city. These streams were to supply water and carry away waste. The city itself would have three levels: the lower for water and sewage; the middle for baggage and functional circulation; the upper for the "gentlemen" of the city. He suggested hydraulic devices to vary water levels so that the lower levels could be cleansed by moving streams. Multilevels would also relieve traffic congestion and facilitate circulation.

Leonardo's thinking went even further. He proposed movable wooden houses for workers so that they could live in the countryside during the period of crop raising, at the same time improving their health. This idea anticipated the greenbelt concept as an open space around a city. He also proposed satellite towns for workers around Milan. Of course only those parts of Leonardo's designs which suited the needs of his time were used—his fortification and canal plans. Leonardo's logic also embraced the idea that neither urban growth nor functional improvement is necessarily an advantage. Enlargement can prolong a bad situation, and the improvement of function can allow basic problems to remain unsolved. Leonardo's thinking along these higher lines had, unfortunately, little influence. The chain of urban design adds its next link not from Leonardo, but from the popes in Rome, where

14

the sphere of the Renaissance expanded in the early 1500s.

Rebuilding Rome

Like the cities of Northern Italy, Rome was confronted with problems of growth, but in a city of old ruins. Problems of circulation, defense, water supply, and sanitation prompted the popes to undertake civic improvement projects. These were rather like those of the Northern Italian cities, with one great difference: Rome was a place of pilgrimage and its important centers were the shrines of Christianity. The pilgrims who came to Rome came to see and partake in religious ceremonies at the sacred spots in the city. The popes realized that the improvement of churches and shrines—for instance, St. Peter's—or secular buildings, such as the Campidoglio, Rome's city hall, was not enough. The connections between these sites were as important as the sites themselves. In other words, urban design and architecture had to proceed hand in hand.

To connect the special sites and shrines, Pope Sixtus V commissioned architect Domenico Fontana to prepare a street plan. A mural in the Vatican shows Fontana's general concept. In developing it, Fontana undoubtedly employed the ideas of street design that had been tried in other old cities, but he hit upon an idea that advanced the technique into the realm of art. He marked out the key points in the city with tall obelisks left over from the days of the Roman Empire. Fontana "staked out" his design for all to see. In this way he introduced the idea that the new streets of the city would not only connect key hubs—the streets could also be visually accented. Fontana was a good observer and an imaginative architect. He realized that the jumble of Rome's hills and stone ruins needed a system of strong visual accents to mark out the overall street design concept. The obelisks provided a ready answer.

Equally an influence in this design decision was the limited means at Fontana's disposal. Sixtus V, as it turned out, was pope for only five years, 1585 to 1590. During this period only the preliminary execution of the plan could be initiated, by placing the design stakes, the obelisks. As fortune would have it, this turned out to be a wise first move. The obelisks were to act as guideposts for the whole city plan, as well as scale reference points for successive designers. The popes, like other temporal rulers, were not above jealousy. Succeeding popes were never anxious to complete the unfinished work of a predecessor, preferring to undertake a project to memorialize their own papacies.

Sixtus' achievements perfectly suited this situation. He established both a general framework of design for the whole city and a series of design opportunities which later popes could fulfill to their ego's content. The overall plan required the attention of individual architects working on individual sites for several centuries. Sixtus had set up a network of hubs. Now the hubs themselves had to be completed. The principle of their design had its roots in the architecture of ancient Rome and in the new design concepts of the early Renaissance.

Renaissance Building Groups

Bramante, for example, had drawn designs for symmetrically composed buildings in ideal symmetrical settings. Bramante also produced a plan for St. Peter's across the Tiber. He proposed a Greek or symmetrical cross as the basis of the church's plan, the

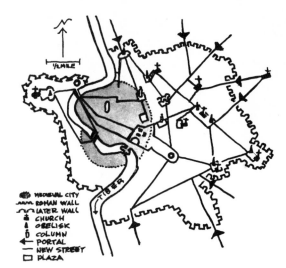

Fontana's plan for Rome.
His intent was to connect the shrines of Christianity and other monuments by a network of streets. In so doing he established a framework for the city's growth.

St. Peter's Square in 1660.

San Tempietto in Rome, designed by Bramante.
A circular building designed for an "ideal" circular setting, the latter never built.

15

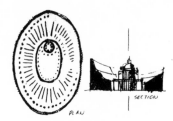

*Carlo Fontana's proposal
for remodeling the Colosseum.*

*The Villa Rotunda in Vicenza, Italy, by Palladio.
The building was symmetrical about two axes.
It was set on top of a rounded hill and could be
approached from four axial directions.*

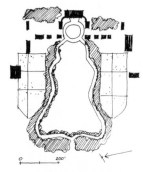

*Mount Vernon, designed by George Washington.
Palladian arrangement with an English garden
entrance.*

*San Giorgio Maggiore, a church in Venice
by Palladio illustrating the use
of the colossal or gigantic order.*

San Giorgio Maggiore seen from afar.

whole set in a large symmetrical square. The Tempietto (little temple) near the Vatican is a miniature version of Bramante's larger vision. Along similar conceptual lines but on a grander scale, Carlo Fontana proposed that the Colleseum be rebuilt as an elliptical setting for a great basilica within.

The Renaissance architects, in looking to the classical past, found design ideas which answered many of their own design problems. The classical orders and ornaments, with their finely proportioned details, offered a broad palette of design possibilities. Of course these details of architecture had never entirely vanished from the art of medieval builders, but the Renaissance architects used them to much greater advantage. Indeed, they took classic details as a starting point and created a wide range of innovations, just as the Romans had advanced the architectural ideas of the Greeks fifteen hundred years before.

The Northern Italian architect Andrea Palladio was particularly influential in promulgating these design sources and their possibilities for innovation. Palladio studied old Roman buildings, built many villas in Northern Italy, introduced many variations on basic classical themes, and developed precise theories of proportion and module. He also saw in the building groups of ancient Rome two superb prototypes: the Roman country villa as a composition in nature and the Roman Forum as a model urban building group. Both of them were, in effect, civic centers—the one in a rural setting, the other in an urban setting.

In copying and adapting these models, Palladio and his colleagues were more Roman than the Romans themselves. The classical villas he designed were intended for refined life in natural surroundings and influenced many future designers, including George Washington and Thomas Jefferson. Palladio's villas were the perfect adornments of nature under man's control. The Villa Rotunda, for example, is symmetrical about both axes and crowns the top of a rounded hill. Other country villas were designed with outreaching one-story colonnades housing many service elements while creating a forecourt for the villa itself. Palladio's opportunities to design villas far outmatched his opportunities to design urban forums, but his famous and influential *Four Books of Architecture* (1540) are full of examples of plazas—the forum brought up to date.

Palladio was also highly imaginative in using Roman classical detailing on buildings seen from great distances. His villas with porticoes modeled after the front facades of Greek and Roman temples were several stories high and could be seen distinctly at great distances. In his church of San Giorgio Maggiore in Venice, he developed this idea into the "colossal" or "gigantic" order. Huge engaged columns were used as parts of an enormous facade at a scale that would have amazed the Romans. San Giorgio Maggiore was designed to be clearly seen across an expanse of open water, a distance of about a third of a mile—hence the gigantic columns. Of all the applications made of classical architectural motifs, the idea of the colossal order was undoubtedly the most ingenious. It recognized in the broad possibilities of classical architecture the visual conditions under which buildings are really seen, from afar and from close up. Palladio was not the only architect to advance this valuable technique, a technique that would soon prove essential to large-scale urban design work.

16

The Campidoglio in Rome

Michelangelo faced a similar challenge in one of his finest architectural works, the Campidoglio. Atop a small hill, this group could be seen at a distance as a whole composition. Close up it would be a series of minute architectural details. The project was actually a remodeling job. Two buildings sat atop the hill at a slightly acute angle to one another. Pope Paul III, a predecessor of Sixtus V and collector of Roman art, had placed a fine equestrian statue of Marcus Aurelius in the space formed by the two buildings. Michelangelo's design was essentially the completion and adornment of a spatial setting for the statue. The statue was the centerpiece or guidepost for Michelangelo's remodeling work. He started by proposing a grand staircase behind it, which acted as a backdrop. Simultaneously he saw that a third building was needed to form a spatial enclosure with the statue at the center. This use of the statue as a controlling device may have suggested to Fontana that obelisks could be used in a similar way, but on a larger scale.

The Campidoglio is best understood by taking an imaginary walk toward it. At a distance, the group forms an enclosed space centered on an equestrian statue. A long, ramped stair leads up to the plaza on axis with the three main buildings. The facades of the buildings are unified visually by the gigantic order—flat pilasters. The two side buildings have two stories. The Palazzo del Senatore at the rear has three stories—the bottom, a strong rusticated base and the upper two stories unified by gigantic pilasters.

The entrance ramps are not parallel but actually widen toward the top. This divergence creates a perspective effect and makes the stair appear shorter. Similarly the two side buildings are not parallel but diverge toward the rear, creating an effect that lends more depth to the enclosed space. As one approaches the plaza proper, fine sculptural details begin to capture interest, heightening the sense of expectation. The visitor is enticed and rewarded by the discovery of ever-finer details. Then the corners of the plaza are seen to be open and so beckon the visitor to views out over the old Roman Forum. From the top of the Senatore's entrance stairway a fine panorama, framed by buildings and sculpture, presents itself—the city from which the approaching visitor has come.

Probably no architect in history ever achieved as much success in as many aspects of a single work as Michelangelo. Every step of the way, every view, every moment of looking is a rich visual experience. Together these individual moments reinforce each other as in a symphony. It is most significant that this was a remodeling job, for architects of the next centuries were to be working largely on urban remodeling. Their dreams were to stretch far beyond their real accomplishments, perhaps illustrated best of all in Piranesi's imaginative reconstruction in ancient Rome of the Campus Martius, in which individual buildings and spaces are stressed as the prime elements of city design. The Campus Martius is a piling of huge complex against huge complex, with neither axes to relate them nor ordinary houses to separate them. The city was seen as a world for heroes and the plaza and building group as the ideal means for making it so.

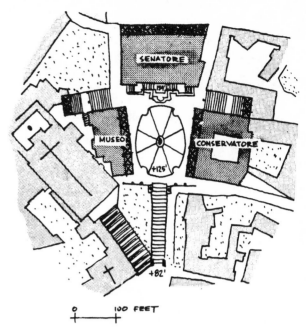

The Campidoglio in Rome.
Michelangelo's masterpiece of urban design.

Approaching the Campidoglio via the ramped stair.
The gigantic order unifies the facade
from this viewing distance.

The rusticated basement and stair elevate
the Senatore building. The stair forms a backdrop
for the equestrian statue.
From below, these could not be seen.

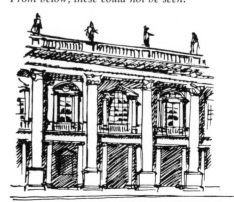

The facade design of the flanking Museo
and Conservatore buildings.

17

Du Cerceau's concept for the Pont Neuf in Paris.

Place Dauphine, Paris.

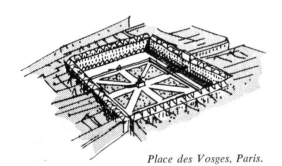

Place des Vosges, Paris.

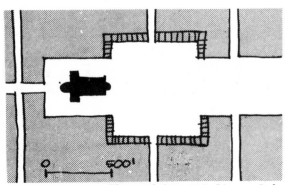

The arcaded square in Livorno, Italy.

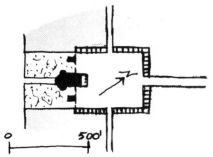

*Covent Garden, designed by Inigo Jones
and modeled after the plaza in Livorno.*

Urban Plazas in France and England

The urban design concepts of Italy were not long in reaching France and England, whose principal cities were rapidly expanding. The French architect Jacques Androuet du Cerceau visited Rome and is credited with bringing to Paris many ideas for designing urban plazas. His English counterpart, Inigo Jones, brought the Renaissance plaza to London. The growth of Paris and London was conditioned by rather opposite factors: the French tried to restrain the growth of Paris, while London was allowed to spread horizontally. Nevertheless, the urban plaza was perfectly suited to conditions in both cities. The plaza, wherever it became an element of urban design, had its incipient form in the barnyard and its more developed form in the central open space of a castle or a fort. The first Renaissance plazas in Paris were actually the courtyards of palaces built on the edge of the city. The city was so crowded that room for gardens could only be found outside the city walls.

The rulers of Paris maintained a firm policy of restriction on Paris' growth to facilitate tax collection and population control. Henry IV was the first king who tried to improve Paris with public plazas and a bridge. Henry was fond of promenading in the streets. During his reign, a fine plaza, the Place Dauphine, was built at the apex of the Ile de Cité. Triangular in shape, two of its three sides faced out across the river to both sides of the city. At the apex, a new bridge, the Pont Neuf, spanned the two branches of the Seine; here stood a statue of the Dauphin, Henry's heir—later to be Louis XII. The Place des Vosges, originally called Place Henry IV, was another plaza built in his time. Although Renaissance in layout, its buildings were Gothic in design—individually and vertically treated units set side-by-side to form the four containing walls of the plaza. The plazas of France were convenient compromises between the city's urge to grow and constraining royal decrees. If the city could not be enlarged, it could be improved. A *place* built in honor of the king was a clever subterfuge for a real estate venture. In London no such subterfuge was needed.

Inigo Jones's Bedford Square was the contemporary of the first of the French plazas, but it was more advanced. It was started in 1631 as a means of rescuing the finances of the Duke of Bedford. Although only three of its four sides were ever completed, its design was more classical than Henry IV's plazas. Inigo Jones had, in fact, copied the arcaded plaza of Livorno, Italy, in which the facades were horizontally unified rather than articulated as individual houses. The portico of St. Paul's church projects into Bedford Square, similar to a Roman temple projecting into its forecourt or forum space.

The lesson of Bedford Square was quickly appreciated, and not mainly for its esthetics. Residential squares could be highly profitable in a society that went in for extraordinary speculation. Leicester Square was started in 1635 and Bloomsbury Square in 1665, the year of a great plague. Before the year 1700 another six were built, of which St. James Square was the most regular in shape.

The Renaissance plaza is one of the elements of urban design par excellence. Every architect of stature from Palladio to Wren thought about the plaza's design problems and details. Brilliant theories of proportion were advanced on the basis of practical

18

experience. A plaza, for example, should not be too long in relation to its width; otherwise the cornice at the far end would be too far below the eye's field of vision. Statues should be placed at heights, so that they would be seen silhouetted against the sky, above cornice lines. A plaza could also be very large, Renaissance architects reasoned, but at the upper end of the acceptable scale of sizes, fountains should be introduced to attract observers to particularly fine vantage points. Plazas could be built as series, connected by such transitional devices as narrow streets, *bosques,* column screens, or arches. They could also be made in different shapes—circles and ellipses—and shapes could be combined.

The plaza suited the needs of urban design in sixteenth-century cities, because it furnished a place of spatial repose amidst what was often a sea of urban squalor. It could be applied to rather large areas of the city, but it fell short of solving one very serious problem: tying the whole city together. Rossetti had accomplished this in Ferrara, and Fontana had done it in Rome—Rossetti with a street system according to the realities of building in Ferrara, and Fontana according to the exigencies of Rome's topography. But neither Rossetti's nor Fontana's experience was drawn upon in dealing with the problems of Paris or London. The problems there were similar but the opportunities were different. A plaza was ambitious enough, a palace and garden a colossal venture. The techniques which later Renaissance architects would apply to their cities as a whole were to come not from design experience in the city, but from experience in parks and gardens.

Renaissance Landscape Architecture

In the Renaissance a garden was the extension of the house. Villa and garden were the rural counterpart of the city's palace and plaza. Garden art and landscaping are obviously conditioned by climate much more than are buildings. In Italy, for example, gardens were never too large. Most Italian gardens were built as terraces because the land was hilly. Besides, the climate was hot and the comforts of an airy garden with shady trees and trickling water were to be preferred to a huge expanse of open field. The early French castles and gardens followed this theme. But the exuberant nature of the French, the more moderate summer climate, the urge to command vista, and the gentler rolling topography led the French to a much more elaborate system of landscape design. The roots of their ideas stem from their large hunting forests.

The French nobility, quite fond of hunting, found that by cutting long straight clearings in the forests they could spot game running from one wood to another. Such vista pathways intersecting at acute angles at certain places in the hunting forest enabled a hunter, standing at an intersection, to scan two or more pathways simultaneously. High ground was chosen for the intersections, for it afforded a better view. Some hunting forests eventually became intricate spider webs of intersecting pathways, and the intersections, or *rond points,* places of social meeting.

It remained for the perceptive eyes of artists to see the esthetic potential of these pathways and *rond points.* If the pathways could be directed toward a prominent hill, they could be directed toward a prominent building. If the *rond points* could be social gathering places in the woods, they could also be focal points in the landscape for a palace.

The outstanding early application of this idea is the town and

Covent Garden by Inigo Jones.
All but one side was completed.

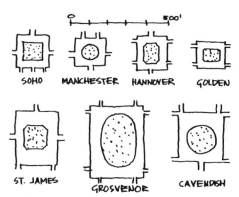

18th century squares in London.
The centers were landscaped.

Belvedere Gardens in the Vatican. Gardens as terraces.

Plan of a French hunting forest with rond points.

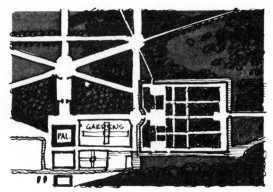

Richelieu, the palace to the left, the town on the right.

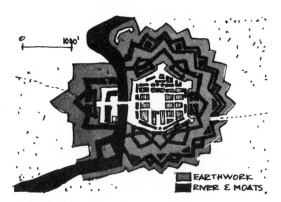

Saarlouis, France, planned by the military engineer Vauban in the late 17th century.

EARTHWORK
RIVER & MOATS

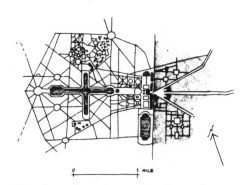

Versailles, the park, gardens, main palace and town.

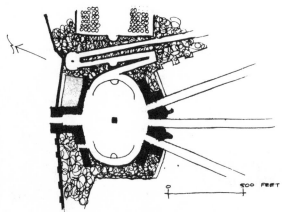

The Piazza del Popolo, main gateway to Rome. The final plan was made by Valladier.

park of Richelieu. In addition to his Paris residence, Cardinal Richelieu wanted a country residence, after the custom of the earlier kings of France who had built castles on the Loire River. Richelieu wanted an estate in his home province for receiving the King and impressing the court. The design of Richelieu's new palace brought together in perfect artistry the arts of architecture, landscape architecture, and urban design. The Richelieu project was started about 1630 and consisted of palace, gardens, park, and town. This was not a new combination; it repeated the form of the earlier châteaux on the Loire. However, it put these elements in a carefully designed and totally conceived relationship. Designing whole towns was not new to France either; many towns had been built as military outposts by the French architect Vauban. The innovation of Richelieu, however, was the inclusion of a designed town as an element in the total landscape. The Cardinal's architect for his palace was Jacques Lemercier. His landscape architect is far better known: André Lenôtre, the Western world's master of landscape architecture.

Lenôtre and Versailles

Lenôtre's talents were matched by his opportunities, for his major client was Louis XIV, the "Sun King" of France. In successive designs he perfected the art of tailoring the landscape to the complete and orderly comprehension of the human eye by making the features of the landscape visible and distinct. He achieved this by aligning principal axes with main landscape features. In his greatest work, the layout of Versailles, he related a town, a palace, gardens, and a huge park to each other. Work on Versailles commenced about 1670 and was substantially complete by about 1710. The palace is the center of gravity of the whole composition, being the apex of the town and a main feature at the edge of the park. From the town side, three main roads converge at the palace entrance at an angle of about 20 to 25°. This three-road configuration was a principal means of bringing vista-roads together at one point. Three roads at angles of about 20 to 25° comprise a total viewing field of about 50°, well within the human range of vision. Thus the three roads could be embraced as a single view, as in the hunting forests. This configuration, often used by French landscape architects, was given the name *patte d'oie* or "goose foot," and is found extensively in Versailles. One of the best-known examples of the *patte d'oie* intersection is at the entrance to Rome and appeared almost accidentally as a result of Fontana's plan. Three roads branch out from the Piazza del Popolo creating the framework for a *patte d'oie* that was not formally finished until the early nineteenth century—by a French architect, incidentally.

The park of Versailles is a veritable encyclopedia of vista axes—some long, some short, some single, some multiple. The main axis is the center line of the park itself and scans a vista from the center of the palace to the distant horizon. The foreground of this axis, at the foot of the palace, is a series of terraces and fountains. From there it continues as a grassy slope. This drop in elevation allows its distant surface to be better seen, part of which is a cruciform reflecting pool. Even the sky was tied into the composition.

The principal design advantage of this art was that it related an unlimited variety of buildings and places. The park of Versailles contains a zoo, a children's playground, a few adult playgrounds, several small palaces, classical temples and statuary, a mock dairy village, gardens, lakes, innumerable woods, and other features. Lenôtre's system of landscape design was a huge visual framework for tying the landscape together by making it completely comprehensible to the human eye and mind. While it has been criticized from a social standpoint for its extravagant cost and oppressive monarchical symbolism, this system can also be defended—from a design, as well as a social, standpoint. As a system of design it was highly flexible and adaptable. The focal places could as well be the centers of a democratic society as of an aristocratic one, depending on how the concept is used. Indeed, the concept of Versailles was to be used for centuries after by many different societies for many different reasons, just like the grid. The system of land design perfected at Versailles had tremendous influence, and its application can be found throughout the world. As a system for designing the total landscape it was unequaled, though there have been other, highly useful systems.

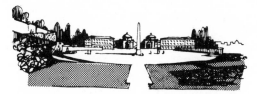

A schematic view of the Piazza del Popolo with the entrance gateway and the wall removed.

French, English, and Italian Landscaping Compared

The French regarded landscape in its natural state as barbarian. They did not hesitate to remake nature and transform its trees and shrubs into man-made, preferably geometric, creations. At Versailles they moved huge quantities of earth to make hills; built great pump works at Marly le Roi (still in operation) to supply Versailles with water; cut trees spherically or square and trimmed bushes to perfect conical shapes. Absolute command of nature was the underlying philosophy.

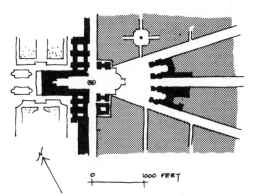

The Place d'Armes at Versailles.

The English were at first enchanted by the French concepts and attempted to copy them. The English have always tried ideas from many different sources—French, Dutch, Chinese. Sometimes they were very formalistic, sometimes very naturalistic. Their willingness to experiment is an indication of their dedication to landscape, which, despite all their experiments, is characterized by an attitude of sympathy with nature. It is an attitude best summed up by their practice of *taming* nature, clarifying its inherent features rather than altering them to some man-made design.

A fine cluster of trees, for example, would be freed of undergrowth so that it could stand alone and be seen for all its beauty. A sloping hillside might also be cleared of bushes so that its surface form would not be cluttered. A tree might be removed to allow a glimpse of a distant church steeple, and a pavilion placed in the landscape as an accent. The grounds of Prior Park near Bath, a work of John Wood about 1800, best exemplifies this approach to design. However, the Italian, French, and English garden all had important roles to play in urban design.

The Italian terrace garden is the model par excellence of gardening in a limited space. The essence of such designs is the variation in shape, sculpture, paths, walls, and plant types. The terrace garden is intended first to be seen from above as a pattern in plan. The higher the location of the observer, the better. It must then be seen by walking through it and delighting in the rich contrasts of sculpture and balustrades against dense green foliage. If there is room on the site, a second or even a third terrace garden at successively lower levels can be created, as at the Villa d'Este. After seeing one terrace, another terrace with perhaps totally different design is presented, and after that another.

The Italian garden was the prototype for gardens which extended from palaces. Examples of this concept in history range

Versailles, looking westward to the gardens and park from the palace.

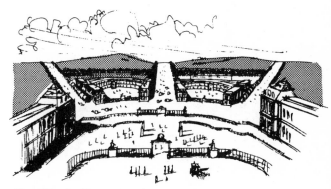

Versailles, looking eastward across the Place d'Armes from the palace.

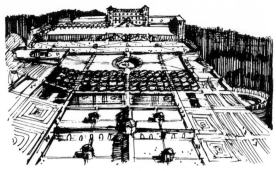

Villa d'Este, near Rome.
Nature terraced into geometric plots.

Prior Park, England.
Nature tamed and its highlights accented.

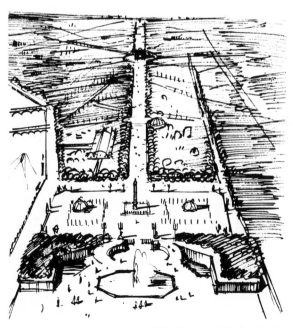

The Champs Elysées, Paris.
Nature employed to accent geometric layout.

from the terraced Tivoli gardens near Rome to the recently completed Constitution Plaza gardens in Hartford, Connecticut. Examples in Paris are the gardens of the Palais Royal, the Luxembourg gardens, and the Tuileries gardens of the Louvre. English manor houses also had such gardens. The obvious limitation of such a garden in an urban setting was size, for like the urban plaza they could exist only as spatial islands in the city. However, both the English and the French systems of park design overcame this limitation.

The English attitude toward gardening, or rather landscape treatment, brought nature right into the city. If one loves nature, what can be better than to have it close at hand? If one is a city dweller, then one must have nature in the city. The love and creative use of open space for recreation underlies the design and building of English towns. The love and need of green space for recreation pervaded the creation of England's squares and its large natural parks. Introducing nature into towns has been the goal of urban designers for centuries and is ever more vital today, as we need complements and contrasts to the built-up city. The English landscape, in the city, is a complement to urban form. The concept of the English landscape could be easily applied, for it was not geometrically rigid. How obvious to allow swaths of natural landscape to flow right through a city! Such a "landscape" could be a large urban park, or simply an area of land left unbuilt. It could also be a swath of land following a river or stream. Or it could be a series of swaths—connecting, narrowing, enlarging—together forming a park system for the whole city.

French land design is perhaps the most ambitious, in scale and intent. The characteristic attitude has been to command the landscape by making it entirely comprehensible and, further, by imposing on it a clear and logical geometry. The concept of Versailles could be transferred to the city by substituting blocks of houses for *bosques* of trees. Grand axes through landscape could become grand avenues through the city. The French concept offered a comprehensive system for traffic circulation, symbolic focusing, and grand vista. There is one important difference between the English and the French systems, however. Nature, brought into the city, can complement urban form and divide it into workable sections or quarters. The design of the quarters themselves, however, still remains to be done. The French concept —if fully used—does everything simultaneously; green areas, roads, squares, and the urban quarters can all be designed integrally.

The vista in an Italian landscape is a combination of views— terrace gardens in the foreground and countryside in the distance. English landscape presents an overall view of carefully tailored land: nature tamed and tidied up. French landscape consists of rationally located vista axes aimed at prominent features. Of course it is an oversimplification to reduce gardens and landscape to three prototypes. There are numerous combinations and variations which form far larger classifications. These three concepts, however, are the principal contributions of landscape architecture to the art of urban design. When the lessons of landscape design were added to those of architecture, plaza design, and the techniques of urban redevelopment—plus a modicum of concern for the public's well-being—the Renaissance had its basic urban design palette.

Applying the Palette in London

Although these design ideas were applied to a number of small cities and parts of larger ones, they had yet to be tested on the total scale of a large city. The first attempts to do this took place in London. A crowded medieval city of narrow streets and flimsy buildings, its chaotic form hindered busy commerce. The plaza was a ready but limited answer for developers in the face of these conditions. In 1661 John Evelyn wrote *Fumifugium,* a treatise dealing with air pollution, in which he proposed a permanent greenbelt around London to absorb smoke and gases. A few years later, in 1666 and 1667, came the great plague and the great fire, nearly razing the city.

This catastrophe furnished London with the opportunity to rebuild itself along modern functional lines. Several designers produced plans to show how this might be done. The most ambitious were those that reflected the concepts of French landscape design applied to the city and of these the most famous was offered by Christopher Wren. He proposed a network of avenues connecting the main features of the city. The largest intersections were to be treated as plazas. One sector of the city was to be laid out as a kind of ideal city—a radial pattern focusing on a center. Robert Hooke proposed a somewhat similar plan, as did John Evelyn, author of *Fumifugium,* whose design, if adopted, would have resulted in more ample plazas. These baroque conceptions, however, all have similar defects, for they would have created overly large blocks between the grand avenues with the inevitable result of crowded and unhealthy masses of houses. The grand avenues and plazas might have formed a fine organizational network for the city's more aristocratic life, but the humbler needs of the workingman were largely overlooked. Further, none of these designs were particularly well adapted to the topography. It is significant, however, that some nonarchitects could try their hand at this baroque system of urban design.

Less spectacular was a plan proposed by an obscure soldier, Valentine Knight. While lacking the artistic refinements of Wren, Hooke, or Evelyn, Knight proposed a highly functional grid of streets. A dozen or so main streets were to run from the river northward, as main spines of movement between river and hinterland. They would be the location of the principal facilities of business and commerce related to river traffic and trade. Perpendicular to these and parallel to the river would be several additional main streets running east-west, together with a number of secondary or side streets for houses. Knight's plan was accompanied by a detailed description of street widths, rental values, and financing. Had Knight's plan been followed, it would have resulted in both a functional and livable city with more light, air, and open space throughout—open spaces not only for grand avenues and squares but for every house.

Because of the complications of land ownership and the radical changes that any of these plans required, none of them were officially adopted. London's growth is characterized by the development of its squares and the spreading of the city outward into the countryside. Horizontal spreading was favored by the fresh memory of the plague and fire. One result of the fire was the enactment of laws between 1707 and 1709 restricting the use of combustible materials on building exteriors, which led to the extensive use of brick. Plazas were developed individually or some-

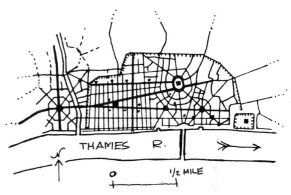

Sir Christopher Wren's plan for rebuilding London.

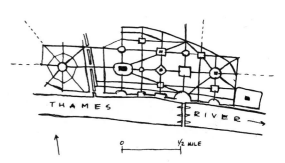

John Evelyn's plan for rebuilding London.

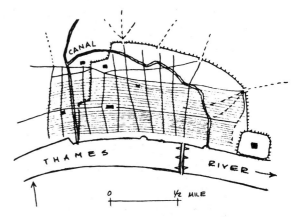

Valentine Knight's plan for rebuilding London.

23

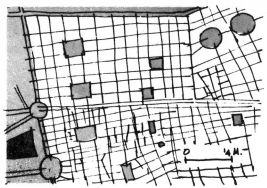

Detail of John Gwynn's plan for London, 1760, which inaugurated the creation of new quarters in the city.

Adam's Adelphi Terrace, London.

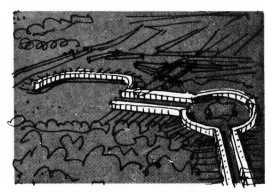

The Royal Crescent and Circus at Bath, England, 18th century. John Wood the Elder and the Younger, architects.

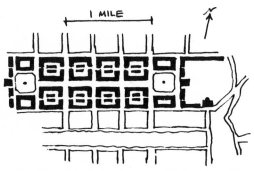

Craig's original plan for central Edinburgh, 1767.

times in groups. The streets connecting them were also built as ensembles and enjoyed the distinction of being near a fine square. While none of the plans of 1666 were followed, they may have injected the idea of planning London as a whole city. This itself was an accomplishment that was to bear fruit a century later.

In 1766 John Gwynn produced a remarkable plan called *London and Westminster Improved*. Here was a whole plan for London's growth and redevelopment, showing embankments, lighting, paving, squares, streets, bridges, and new quarters. Gwynn's plan heralded a Golden Age of building in Georgian London. Many of the ideas of his plan were actually carried out over the next century. The Golden Age encompassed a thirty-year period and is highlighted by the work of the Adam brothers. In 1768 they started their Adelphi Terrace, a real estate speculation of Gargantuan proportions and risk. Unlike a plaza which could be built in modest pieces, Adelphi required a heavy outlay at the beginning, for it was a complex multilevel design. It was to be built along the Thames as a combination dock, warehouse, and residential area. The lower levels consisted of Piranesi-like arches housing the warehouses and dock facilities. Above, were terrace houses. Adelphi came close to faltering financially but the Adam brothers were saved from ruin when elements of their Adelphi venture became prizes in a lottery.

Such daring speculations were more and more the mode. At the fashionable resort city of Bath the architects John Wood, Sr., and Jr., had created superb residential groups. Originally a Roman spa, Bath's modern popularity dates from 1702, when it was "discovered" by the aristocracy. In 1727 Wood built a rectangular plaza called the Queen's Square, and a great circle known as the King's Circus in 1754. The Woods' finest achievement was the Royal Crescent, started in 1767. It followed the topography along a large curve and looked out across a wide expanse of park. Plazas and streets were connected to form a large urban area. This had been done piecemeal in London but with considerable artistry by the Woods in Bath.

The idea of interconnected plazas was used deftly by a young Scottish architect, James Craig, to win a competition for the enlargement of Edinburgh in 1767. Craig proposed a grid of houses and open spaces combined on a high plateau overlooking the city. The interconnected plazas of Nancy, France, and the Amalienborg Plaza in Copenhagen are better known examples of this idea. All date from the mid-1700s. The Bloomsbury area of London was developed between 1800 and 1860, following the lessons of the builders of the earlier interconnected residential squares.

In 1811, however, architect John Nash attempted to introduce a more ambitious concept in London. Nash made a plan for Regent Street, Regent Park, and Park Crescent and worked on its implementation for nearly twenty-five years. He wanted to create a fine group of buildings around a park, all at the edge of the city, connected to the center of the city by a grand avenue. In essence it was a satellite town for London. The park and the residential area turned out admirably, but the avenue suffered from a number of compromises which resulted in awkward bends and conflicting architecture.

The coming of the industrial and railroad era brought the London plaza era to an end. The niceties of the urban square were swept aside by the pressures for massing a large working population. Fortunately, this was relieved to some degree by large city parks accessible by public transportation. Hampstead Heath is an outstanding example of this. It is simply a piece of nature in the city, and one regrets that London does not have more parks like it. The lesson of London is not that a city has no need for a comprehensive plan. Nor is it that a detailed plan is of no value. London had all kinds of plans and tried many of them—from square to park to baroque street. The lesson of London is that everything known was tried and many attempts were successful. In Ferrara and Rome architects had shown plans which made real sense—and so they were carried out. In London the much-publicized plans of 1666 did not have this fortune because no instrumentality existed to carry out such a plan and the public could not be persuaded to create one. But Gwynn's plan of 1766 did have the logic that was needed. While his concept was not followed to the letter, it was followed in intent. The ideas he proposed were as realizable as they were desirable and so his plan —really a plan of practical ideas—was carried out.

London's expansion is a lesson in the use of plazas and open spaces and the energy of speculative enterprises which had an ample stock of design ideas to feed on. Had the later development of the various public transportation systems been accompanied by commensurate open space creations, London's lessons would be of very great value to modern cities. In the eighteenth century, its influence in city design extended to the shores of colonial America. But a far more influential system of design for the cities of the modern world evolved across the Channel, in Paris.

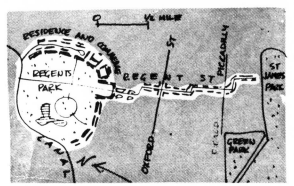

John Nash's concept for Regent's Park and Regent Street, London. Early 19th century.

View in Regent's Park.

Applying the Palette in Paris

As in London, the plaza played an important role in Paris. Here, too, efforts were made to introduce the grandiose concepts of French landscape design into the city. Louis XIV attempted to create a large *patte d'oie* at an entrance to Paris, focusing on the rear of the Louvre—now the Place de la Concorde—the largest plaza in Paris. Louis was no lover of Paris, as his predecessors had been, for his life had been seriously threatened by a mob uprising when he was a child. He chose to concentrate on building a new palace city for himself rather than rebuild an unruly and undeserving Paris. Nevertheless, Paris does have souvenirs of Louis XIV's artistic urban enterprises.

In 1667 work commenced on the rebuilding of the eastern end of the Louvre, one of the Louvre's many remodelings, but by far the most significant one from an urban design standpoint. The Italian architect Lorenzo Bernini came from Rome to prepare designs, but his concepts were rejected for those of a court physician, Claude Perrault, who recognized some particularly important facade problems which Bernini had overlooked.

The east facade of the Louvre. The use of the gigantic order in Paris, designed by Perrault, a court physician.

Bernini proposed a sumptuous and highly sculptured facade. Perrault proposed a more orderly facade and took cognizance of the actual viewing requirements of this facade: it was to be seen both from afar and from close up. As a matter of fact, its viewing conditions raised the same design questions that confronted Palladio in San Giorgio Maggiore and Michelangelo in the Campidoglio. Perrault's solution was as brilliant as those of his precursors. He conceived the facade as a horizontal composition with porticoes to accent the ends and the center. The first-floor facade was treated as a strong horizontal base. The facades of the upper two floors were recessed behind double columns. The

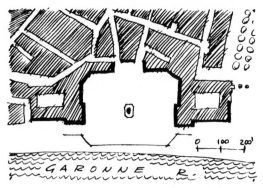

Place Royale in Bordeaux, France, 1733. A plaza built "in honor" of the king.

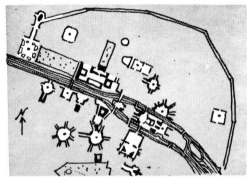

Pierre Patte's compilation of the proposals for royal plazas in Paris, mid-18th century.

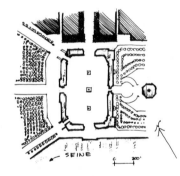

The Place de la Concorde designed by Gabriel. One of the largest of French squares formed by ground surface, buildings, water, landscaping, and sculpture.

Place de la Concorde, Paris, looking northeast.

Place Vendôme, Paris.

windows with their fine details were in shadow to allow the double columns to stand out. From a distance one would see a solid-looking base surmounted by columns and cornice, accented by three porticoes—all very simple and cohesive from afar. From close up, the finer details came into visual play. Of course many French architects were busy refining and adapting the classic orders for ever-larger buildings. Perrault's work paved the way for designing buildings for grand plazas.

The pressures to enlarge Paris met with strong and generally successful resistance on the part of the monarchy. In 1665 François Blondel made a plan to enlarge the city in a limited way. In 1675 Louis' minister, Colbert, concluded agreements to restrain city growth, adding to the edicts that were in effect between 1638 and 1784. However, when the city was enlarged, new walls were built and the old ones torn down. The land recovered from the fortifications was broad, long, fairly straight, and useful for creating wide streets, which were called "boulevards" (the term derived from the Dutch word for bulwark).

In 1748, however, perhaps from the examples of London, proposals for new plazas were submitted to King Louis XV. These were regarded as ways of relieving the squalid crowding of Paris —less to make the city livable for the populace than to make it habitable for the aristocracy. The plazas would be built where land was available or could be cleared. They would be large quadrangles, not the residence of independent individuals, but the collective residence of courtiers. The plazas were built "in honor" of King Louis XV. A second series of proposals was made a few years later. Pierre Patte recorded all these designs in a book by drawing all of them together on a large map of Paris. Had they been built as Patte showed, they would have transformed Paris into a city of large plazas with minimal connections, for only a few had avenues radiating from them. This was a natural consequence of inviting individual proposals for a whole city.

The most spectacular result of this competition was the Place de la Concorde, started in 1757 and finished about 1770, originally called Place Louis XV. It was surrounded by a moat and its northern facade, actually twin buildings, was modeled after Perrault's Louvre concept. Another impressive *place* was the Place Vendôme. Originally conceived as a forum of the arts, the project ran into financial difficulties. The facade was built first, the lot depth behind being sold off by the measure—a practice which amazes a contemporary architect but which actually made quite a bit of sense in its time. For the French Renaissance architect was primarily interested in creating an urban space and its architectural embellishment. Even though the buildings would take time to finish, the distinctive space itself would prevail, its completion awaiting the participation of investors. Had this not been done, there would never have been any Place Vendôme. One might well conjecture on the possibilities of applying this procedure to the large-scale creation of open spaces in metropolitan areas today—without building the facades, of course. The open space could be established and the frontages reserved for private development regulated by a design plan.

In 1775, fourteen years prior to the French Revolution, the restrictions on Paris' growth were relaxed as a concession to the restless population. It was as if a dam of houses had burst open. Buildings shot up all around the city. By the time of the Revolution in 1789, Paris had a raw ring of helter-skelter streets and urban squalor. In 1793 a new plan was made for Paris, called the *Plan des Artistes*.

It provided for streets, public improvements, sanitation, markets, and other practical necessities. The particular significance of this plan was that it recognized the need for providing broad circulation arteries throughout the congested city. Unlike the proposals of the plan of 1748 which emphasized the plaza, the plan of 1793 emphasized the street. This plan also possessed considerable artistic merit and was supported and followed by Napoleon I. Among his accomplishments were the improvement of the Champs Elysées and the Arch of Triumph, built at an elevated end of the avenue. He also built the highly regular Rue de Rivoli with its arcaded facade, which runs alongside the Louvre. In essence, the plan was a proposal to apply the principles of French landscape design to the city, substituting stone for vegetation—an undertaking of such Gargantuan proportions that it would necessitate an absolutist government to carry it out, not to mention huge financial resources and the concurrence of the more powerful members of the aristocracy and *bourgeoisie*. However, the extreme crowding of Paris and the years of following a policy that had restrained the city's growth favored an ambitious public works program on the scale of the entire city. The plan of 1793 mapped out the surgery and Napoleon I performed the first operations. But a half century was to pass before the patient received the full treatment.

The Champs Elysées in Paris, the Renaissance vista axis in its grandest example. It was started by Louis XIV and completed by Napoleon III.

That came with the accession of Napoleon III in 1853. France was then in a state of moral and financial depression and the new Emperor was regarded as somewhat of a weakling. He sought to remedy France's sad situation and with it transform his own reputation. He put Baron Georges Eugène Haussmann in charge of rebuilding Paris. Accountable to the Emperor alone, Haussmann had been chosen because he was without scruples and extremely bold. He concentrated his efforts on the creation of new boulevards. These would constitute a badly needed road system for Paris as well as opportunities for private real estate ventures. A still-popular conception of Haussmann's reasoning is that he thought the boulevards could be used by troops to shoot up and down streets to control citizens' riots. This is somewhat exaggerated. The boulevards certainly would facilitate the movement of troops and the isolation of an unruly quarter, but the main reasons for the boulevards was financial speculation in which the government worked hand-in-pocket with entrepreneurs. The city razed the houses and planted the trees, while the speculators built the houses along the new boulevards according to uniform designs. The uniform designs, with the trees, gave an air of urbane distinction. But the poor were ruthlessly crowded into ever smaller and ever more expensive dwellings. Two large parks at either end of the city were transformed into romantic gardens by Haussmann's landscape architect, Jean Charles Adolphe Alphand.

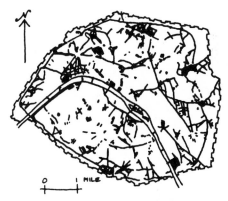

Haussmann's transformations in Paris.

The artistic quality of Haussmann's work was mediocre. For example, the architect of the Paris Opera House, Charles Garnier, complained bitterly about his building's bad siting. Haussmann paid no attention to him. Once Haussmann wanted to build houses in the Luxembourg Gardens. Only a concerted citizens' protest saved a portion of it. In all, Haussmann tore down three-sevenths of the houses of Paris in history's largest public works project. Haussmann's name has become nearly synonymous with ruthless

Alphand's design for the "Buttes Chaumont" in the Bois de Vincennes, Paris.

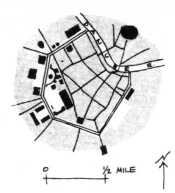

The Ringstrasse in Vienna. Originally it was the outer fortification wall of the city. In concept, it is a curved axis with architectural accents and landscaping.

Karlsruhe, from a plan of 1715.

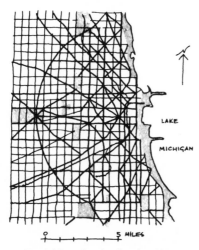

Daniel Burnham's plan for Chicago.

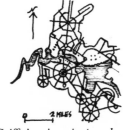

Walter Burley Griffin's prize-winning plan for Canberra, Australia.

and heartless urban speculation and corruption. Actually, he was no worse than any person in a comparable position in most of the cities of the world at that time. He was just more successful. With a few exceptions, some of them significant, nineteenth-century cities were resources to be exploited.

Paris' Influence

The rebuilding of Paris and the centuries of urban design lessons which it portrayed for better or worse all stood in the bright spotlight of world attention. Indeed, Paris was known as the "City of Light." Haussmann proved, in brutal fashion to be sure, that all the ideas of urban design could be applied to a modern city. If they could be realized in Paris, they could be realized in any other city, particularly new cities that were just beginning to grow. These design ideas could also be employed to lay out whole new towns as had been done in the past. The partial rebuilding of Vienna confirmed this thesis.

In 1857 the Ringstrasse was started on the site of Vienna's old city wall. After a military victory, Napoleon I had the walls torn down, and they were left where they fell. When they were eventually cleared away, the city found itself with a big ring of open space between the new suburbs and the old medieval heart. Elaborate plans were made to make a grand circular boulevard lined with plazas and grand public buildings. To a large extent, this plan was carried out, but not without unfortunate compromises; the same greedy practices that were rampant in Paris.

The early application of these design concepts had, of course, a long history. Karlsruhe in Germany had been laid out as an application of the Versailles design in 1715. Jean Baptiste Alexandre Le Blond used these concepts in laying out St. Petersburg, Russia, in 1717—with probably the most successful results even though his plan was much modified. Jacques François Blondel used them in laying out Strasbourg in 1768. Pierre Charles L'Enfant adapted them to Washington, D.C. in 1791. They were used in Berlin, Turin, Athens, Mexico City, and innumerable small cities. They were models for the American "City Beautiful Era." Daniel Burnham adapted them to the American city; Otto Wagner to the Austrian city. In 1911 the young American architect Walter Burley Griffin used these principles to win an international competition for the design of Canberra, capital of Australia.

Many copies of the Haussmann boulevards were better than the originals. Commonwealth Avenue in Boston, for example, was laid out as a grand landscaped avenue. The house designs were well coordinated and followed a prescribed roofline. Many American cities have such broad landscaped streets. In some cases, of course, these urban design concepts were also copied poorly.

Perhaps the greatest tragedy of Haussmann's work is one proposal he failed to accomplish: a greenbelt encircling Paris. It would have had a circumference of over twenty miles. He may have been thinking of the welfare of the people or of the additional value it would add to speculative lots as a result of limiting the market. But Haussmann never got his greenbelt, because a minister whose vote was needed to approve the idea was out of town. Undoubtedly the minister would have agreed to the proposal. Had this been achieved, the Paris greenbelt may have been as influential a model for the world to copy as its dazzling boulevards. Urban design, too, has its sorrows—most of all when its ideas are not put to use.

The Roots of
Our Modern Concepts

Background

The Greeks had created an urban form made for people. The Romans built upon their theories but not without discarding some of Greece's most important urban ideals. In medieval times ideas parallel to those of ancient Greece found a new expression. Again these more humane concepts were discarded by the Renaissance, whose aims were loftier and of considerable artistic quality. The design of cities in the Renaissance had been an instrument of state control. In the eighteenth and nineteenth centuries it became a technique for greedy speculation. At the same time, however, a new breed of design theorists entered the scene. Sometimes their thinking was quite practical, like Valentine Knight's. Sometimes it was utopian. Sometimes it relied on extravagant mechanical concoctions. Sometimes it rejected all semblances of engineering technology as unnecessary, proposing instead a return to nature. But all of these ideas strove toward one objective: the design of cities as a place to live for all, with particular emphasis on the needs of the working classes.

There is no distinct line of separation between the architects of the grand baroque cities and those oriented toward the well-being of the general population. By way of illustration, John Wood

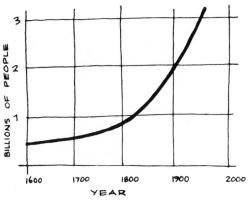

World population: 1600–1950.

John Wood's design for a duplex workers' cottage.

29

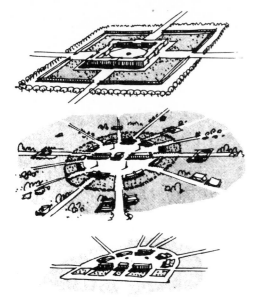

Ledoux's three plans for Chaux.

Robert Owen's "Village of Unity and Mutual Cooperation."

New Lanark, Scotland. Started in 1785 and, in 1799, operated by Robert Owen as an enlightened social and manufacturing community. Owen left in 1825. The mills are still in use.

François Fourier's "Phalanstery."

the younger, architect of the Royal Crescent at Bath, also produced a book of designs for workers' houses in the healthful open countryside. But the French architect Claude Nicolas Ledoux is best remembered as one of several late eighteenth and early nineteenth-century theorists who brought intense analysis and rationale to the design process. He also launched a new era of urban design, one that gave as much attention to workers as it did to society's ruling classes.

Ideal Towns and Worker Towns

The principal urban work of Ledoux was the design of Chaux, a town for salt workers in France. Its construction dates from 1776. In all, Ledoux made three plans for Chaux. The site was in open countryside between two villages, with a pair of overland roads intersecting at right angles at the center. In the first version of his plan, a quadrangle of buildings—workers' homes, common buildings, and allotment gardens—was arranged as a 1,000-foot square formed by tree-lined avenues. In later revisions of his plan, Ledoux changed the square to an ellipse and, finally, to a semiellipse with roads radiating into the surrounding countryside. He may have preferred the semiellipse for better sunlight orientation. Along the roads Ledoux envisioned informal groupings of houses. This was one of the first plans to advocate informal grouping as part of an overall design concept. Ledoux thought of his design as an ideal plan "wherein everything is motivated by necessity." The workers would even grow their own food. He published all his plans in an influential book called *Architecture* in 1804.

Implicit in Ledoux's thinking was the self-sufficiency of the worker towns. Ledoux was an architectural visionary, soon to be followed by men of similar inclinations. In 1799 the English social reformer Robert Owen started construction of an industrial village at New Lanark mills near Manchester. Owen pondered deeply the question of the worker community. His thoughts led him to theories which he expounded and which proved highly influential. Owen's ideal was a community of 800 to 1,200 people on at least 600 to 1,800 acres. Each community would be self-sufficient and there would be no child labor. The community would have recreational and educational facilities. Several Owenite communities were set up in England and the United States. Owen's son started one in Indiana, called New Harmony. A group of New England transcendentalists created Brook Farm in Massachusetts. A Frenchman named Cabet was one of the more adventuresome Owenites. He proposed a utopian settlement to be called "Icarus" on the Red River in Texas. When it failed, he joined with the Mormons in their search for their promised land and helped lay out Salt Lake City.

In 1829 the French social reformer François Fourier published *The New World of Industry and Society*. His visions were far more rigid than Owen's, for Fourier would put 1,620 people, 400 families, into one large palace-like building which he called a "Phalanstery." The building he pictured resembled a Renaissance palace. A succession of "ideal" proposals followed. In 1849 James Silk Buckingham published *National Evils and Practical Remedies* and proposed "Victoria," a glass-roofed town like the Crystal Palace. Robert Pemberton planned "Happy Colony" for New Zealand, a series of ten circular town-districts laid out along the lines of Chaux.

In the United States, Dr. Benjamin Richardson proposed

"Hygeia," a town spaciously laid out for fresh air and health. Thomas Jefferson had advocated a simple expedient to achieve this. Jefferson's favorite city plan was a simple grid in which every other block was a park—a grid city built as a checkerboard. Jefferson felt that this grid variation could easily be adapted and several were actually built. By leaving alternate blocks empty, the city would be more spacious, would have more light and air, the danger of the spread of fire would be lessened, and the town be more handsome. Unfortunately, the towns laid out in this way sold their public squares to developers when municipal finances were depleted.

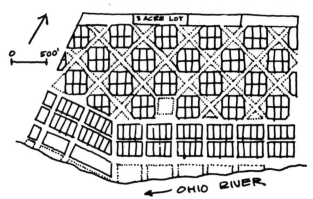

1802 plan of Jeffersonville, Ind. The upper portion "laid out after the plan suggested by President Jefferson."

Planned Industrial Towns

Several planned industrial towns were built in the nineteenth century. The scale of organization of large manufacturing operations necessitated a well-organized corps of workers. The English were the main developers of these large-scale operations in their textile plants, and the Americans were quick to learn their lessons. A small mill village of workers' houses was erected as early as 1812 in Georgiaville, Rhode Island. Francis Cabot Lowell perfected mill operations in Waltham, Massachusetts, and in 1816 built a mill town in Harrisville, New Hampshire. In 1822 he built another one, Lowell, Massachusetts, in which he tapped a hitherto unused source of labor: young New England farm girls who came to work for a few years in order to earn a dowry.

In 1859 the town of Vésinet was started in France. Designed by an architect named Olive, its plan was a remarkable combination of classical French landscape architecture and English parks. Olive laid out an artful network of axial streets for the houses and interspersed the whole town with meandering swaths of green space. This design anticipated, by half a century, the design of the twentieth-century garden city.

Around the Krupp factories of Essen, Germany, a number of communities were built starting in 1863. Called *Siedlungen,* or worker colonies, by 1925 they amounted to 25,000 houses in about a dozen communities. In 1879 Pullman, Illinois, was started as a town for factory and workers. The overly paternalistic management held the employees in all but feudal bondage which resulted in a famous strike. By 1890 the town numbered 11,000 people. In 1887 the W. H. Lever Soap Company built Port Sunlight, a worker community near Liverpool. In 1889 the Cadbury Chocolate Company built Bournville, a garden community near Birmingham. In 1906 Gary, Indiana, was laid out by a steel corporation, a "made to order" city. Kohler, Wisconsin, is a descendant of these nineteenth-century towns.

While many towns were rather good in design, they were almost insignificant in comparison to the enormous workers' agglomerations being built in the world's expanding industrial cities. Only large and wealthy companies could afford to build them, and even then they were considered rather risky.

The idealization of the industrial city was expressed by a young French architect, Tony Garnier, in designs he made between 1901–1904 while on a scholarship at the French Academy in Rome. Garnier designed a hypothetical industrial town which he called *Une Cité Industrielle.* He created an imaginary site consisting of high plateau and level valley, all alongside a river. The plateau would be used as the residential portion of the city; the valley for the factories. The total population of the city, including

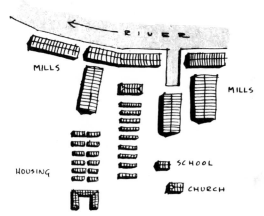

Schematic plan of Lowell, Mass.

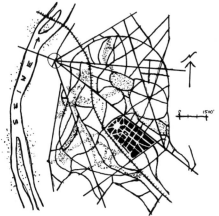

The village of Vésinet, France, built in a former hunting forest. The curved paths were 19th-century alterations.

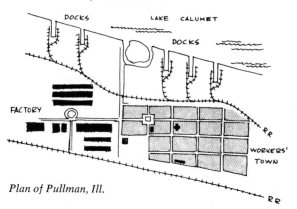

Plan of Pullman, Ill.

31

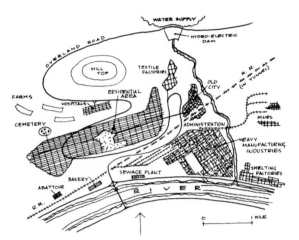

Tony Garnier's Cité Industrielle.

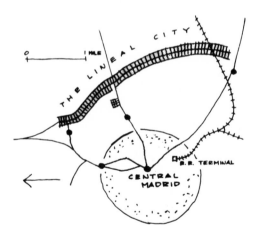

Soria y Mata's Ciudad Lineal.

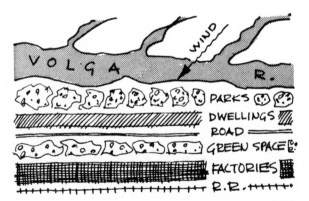

*Stalingrad, Russia. An example of
an actual linear city based on linear communication.*

an imaginary existing old town incorporated in the plan, was to be about 32,000. A dam would furnish hydroelectric power. Garnier's separation of the city's parts anticipated modern zoning but with considerably more wisdom, for he first decided where things should be most suitably located and then laid out areas according to those decisions. He also located complementary urban facilities together where they belonged—a relationship sometimes denied by improper zoning ordinances.

In this respect Garnier's plan is incredibly detailed. A hospital is on a high hill. Cemeteries have fine natural vistas. Smelting factories and mines are at respectful distances. The plan included detailed locations for sewage plant, abattoir, bakery, and civic center. Garnier showed testing grounds for cars and even airplanes! He used a grid plan for the residential area with 100- by 500-foot blocks; the short cross streets would accommodate major circulation, thus diverting through traffic from the long residential streets. He drew working drawings for many buildings, utilizing the newly developing technique of reinforced concrete. Garnier returned from Rome to his native Lyons, where he spent his career trying to carry out his ideas on individual buildings.

Not many years later the Dutch architect J. J. P. Oud built a small worker colony near Rotterdam which is reminiscent of Garnier's plans. As a matter of fact it comes closer to embodying Garnier's ideals than any other town plan built. In the world of letters George Bernard Shaw suggested that such planned industrial towns had their merits, as in his play *Major Barbara*.

Urban Design and Machines

Practical inventions have always fascinated designers. For example, the complexities of Renaissance fortification design eventually found their way into the design of villas. In the nineteenth century, mechanical inventions grasped the imagination of many designers, as they still do to a large extent. The Spanish businessman and engineer Don Arturo Soria y Mata was of such a mind. He had created Madrid's first streetcar and telephone system. In 1882 he suggested the idea of *La Ciudad Lineal,* or the "Linear City," in which he proposed that the logic of linear utility lines should be the basis of all city layout. Houses and buildings could be set alongside linear utility systems supplying water, communications, and electricity. Soria y Mata thought that linear cities could crisscross the entire globe and actually built a linear city on the outskirts of Madrid. Stalingrad is the outstanding example of a planned linear city.

In 1899 the Russian-born geographer, author, and revolutionary Peter Kropotkin published a book called *Fields, Factories and Workshops: or Industry Combined with Agriculture, and Brainwork with Manual Work*. In it he suggested the use of electricity to allow towns to be built anywhere. He advocated minimal government and maximum individual self-sufficiency, for he saw only tyranny in large organization. The idea of freeing town development and locale by the use of electricity was important to town designers of this era, like Garnier.

Among the inventions of the nineteenth century which influenced urban form, the railroad stands foremost. Railroads for long distances or short commuter runs were highly profitable. They opened up large land areas for speculation. The possibilities of transportation technology extended well beyond the railroad, and

32

were fascinating. The 1893 World's Fair in Chicago had a moving sidewalk which carried footsore tourists along a long pier projecting into Lake Michigan. A world's fair in Paris had a moving sidewalk to connect its exhibits. The world's first monorail system was built in Wuppertal, Germany, around the turn of the century and is still in operation.

After the turn of the century, Edgar Chambless, an American, proposed a city with all vehicles running on the rooftops of a continuous building. Undoubtedly he was influenced by Soria y Mata. The same idea keeps popping up in different guises. It was recently proposed in England under the name "Motopia," this time with the rooftop roads laid out as a grid. In 1910 an inventive Frenchman, Eugène Hénard, published *Les Villes de l'Avenir* (The Cities of the Future), in which he proposed buildings on stilts, traffic circles, underpasses, and airplanes landing on rooftops. Hénard may have influenced Le Corbusier's early urban concepts.

View of Sant'Elia's Città Nuova.

The Italian futurist architect Antonio Sant'Elia provided a new, perhaps frightening vision of what might come: an enormous metropolis—*La Città Nuova*—based on motion, with every element of its design implying either horizontal or vertical circulation. Sant'Elia was inspired by the complex plans for the Grand Central area of New York City, a horizontal skyscraper with buildings connected above ground by pedestrian walks and vehicular roads. Many contemporary urban scenes are living examples of Sant'-Elia's vision. Such an example is the approach road to the George Washington Bridge in New York City with its air-rights apartment towers above.

Just recently a French book called *Où Vivrons-Nous Demain?* (Where Will We Live Tomorrow?) was published with many illustrations of visionary urban design. Most of the illustrations would be at home in science fiction magazines. Some Japanese architects who call themselves the "Metabolism Group" have produced underwater cities, biological cities, cities that change their own forms, and cities that are built as pyramids.

Concept of a floating city from a sketch by Kiyonori Kikutake.

The possibilities of modern science and engineering in the improvement of the city are vast, but there are dangers also. This potential, and its concomitant pitfalls, has been the theme of much literature, most notably *Looking Backward, 2000–1887* by Edward Bellamy, published in 1887, and several books by H. G. Wells that were published between 1902 and 1911.

Visionary thinking is to be expected in a society which depends so much on science and machines. Most of the ideas cited here are fanciful. Many of them are still frequently proposed, and some of them have actually been put into highly useful operation. Visionary thinking is inevitable in any growing society. In a society that depends heavily on machines, visionary thinking naturally takes a mechanistic approach to solving problems. Some of the mechanical devices proposed for modern cities have been highly useful. Others have simply allowed undesirable conditions to worsen. For example, a rail rapid-transit system can cause further crowding in an already crowded city. It can also be the principal transit means for organizing satellite cities around a central metropolitan core. Any judgment of a visionary idea with mechanical overtones is twofold: We must evaluate its possibilities for improving the quality of urban life and we must be sure that we have the means to achieve proper usage of a new device. Otherwise it can simply make things worse in the name of expedience or in the guise of progress.

A New Attitude toward Nature

The technological advances of the nineteenth century were not all greeted as signs of progress. The nineteenth-century industrial city was all too horrible evidence of technology at work. While some designers saw possibilities for innovation that could harness technology to human purposes—the designers of industrial towns and self-sufficient communities—there were others who saw in it only disaster. The chief spokesmen of this point of view were the Frenchman Viollet-le-Duc, the Englishman John Ruskin, and the American Henry David Thoreau.

Viollet-le-Duc and John Ruskin popularized a return to the simpler Christian virtues of the Gothic period. In England their sentiments found expression in a crafts movement led by William Morris. Between 1875–1881, with architect Norman Shaw, he succeeded in creating Bedford Park, a picturesque residential area on the outskirts of London, linked to the city by rail—which, incidentally, heralded the commuter suburb. The Gothic revival of the nineteenth century in churches, in houses, and later in American college campuses was evidence of the popularity of Ruskin's and Viollet-le-Duc's outlook. Thoreau, meanwhile, sought complete refuge in nature where he conducted a personal experiment in independent existence. The ideals of these men still have considerable appeal. Frank Lloyd Wright, for example, once commented that the Gothic period was the last original architectural era, and Le Corbusier wrote a book nostalgically titled *When the Cathedrals Were White*.

The Conservationists and the Park Movement

Of all nineteenth-century thinkers, perhaps the most profound is the one least known, at least by the general public: the American, George Perkins Marsh. Marsh was dismayed at the wasteful land practices around his native New England. A man of brilliant mind—he mastered twenty languages by the age of thirty—he was a naturalist, humanist, historian, geographer, and practical politician. In overgrazing and overcutting he saw major causes of land erosion and river flooding, the foolish despoilment of the land. He, too, had his predecessors, including such men as conservation-minded John Quincy Adams, ornithologist James Audubon, naturalists William Bartram and Henry David Thoreau. In 1849 Marsh was appointed minister to Turkey, and in 1861 Lincoln appointed him minister to Italy. These travels gave him an opportunity to see the geography of Europe and the Middle East, which deepened his thinking and confirmed his practical ideas for using the land's resources in ways that would not destroy its bounties. In 1862 his thoughts were collected in a book called *Man and Nature*.

Marsh's book was widely read. It was an introduction to ecology, an encyclopedia of land facts, depicting the deterioration of land as a result of man's ignorant disregard of the laws of nature. Marsh also explained the interrelationship between plant and animal life. He assailed the myth of superabundance and described how despoiled land could be restored. Marsh, in short, was the founder of modern conservation, putting man in the position of cooperation with nature. He had a considerable influence on America's great conservationists, including Carl Schurz, Theodore Roosevelt, John Wesley Powell, Gifford Pinchot, George Norris, John Muir, Rachel Carson—people associated with our national parks and preservation measures, exercised or advocated.

Marsh's ideas applied to land at regional and continental scale. It is one of the principal contributions to the art and knowledge of the use of the earth. However, it was not the only major American contribution. In the more specific area of urban design stands the American park system. The foremost name in this enterprise is that of Frederick Law Olmsted.

Olmsted came to the public's attention prior to the Civil War as a social reformer through articles on slavery published in the *New York Times*. He was aware of the increasingly rapid urbanization of the United States, noting that urban population doubled between 1840 and 1860, mostly because of immigration. He felt that the improper use of both land and labor was damaging to democracy. He was concerned as well with the moral disintegration that large formless cities engender—formless in physique and social community. Olmsted, also a farmer, saw in landscape design a solution to these ills. Disdaining aristocracy, he nevertheless admired the landscaping of English estates. The urban park could be an aid to social reform, giving the downtrodden city dweller uplifting communion with nature.

Olmsted's first opportunity came with the design of Central Park in New York City. A plan had been drafted by an Army officer for a large city park, but it was little more than a military drill field and drew stinging criticism. In the face of public clamor, a competition was held, and won by Olmsted in 1859. His notes on the design of Central Park, and the thoughts that ran through his mind as the plan proceeded, are brilliant insights into the creative mind of an artist at work in a city.

Olmsted designed several other parks in the New York City area and throughout the United States. The original park plans for San Francisco, Buffalo, Detroit, Chicago, Montreal, and Boston are his work. He also had a hand in the Yosemite Park bill during Lincoln's presidency. He believed that cities should plan for two generations ahead, maintain sufficient breathing space, be constantly renewed; and that urban design should embrace the whole city. The city should exist to serve its inhabitants. His attitudes toward comprehensive park planning were summed up in 1870 in his book *Public Parks and the Enlargement of Towns*.

Olmsted was followed by other great urban park designers—notably, Charles Eliot, who completed Olmsted's Boston park system; George Kessler, who laid out the Kansas City park system; and Jens Jensen, who designed Chicago's original park system. This gave many American cities fine urban parks, but the practice, regrettably, has not been maintained as Olmsted insisted it must. To be successful a park and open space program must be continuous. The present misuse of metropolitan open space might not exist had we followed Olmsted's advice. Olmsted had many colleagues here and abroad. Haussmann's landscape architect, Alphand, has been called "the French Olmsted." In Germany an interesting and widely adopted idea was advanced by Daniel Schreber, a physician and educator. Schreber proposed small gardens for children, for healthful play and exercise; later *Schrebergärten* were also used by the elderly, to raise vegetables. In effect, he popularized the idea of the urban playground in Europe.

Reviewing the Past

The nineteenth century was also an age of exploration into the past. Archeology was becoming a science. The architectural academicians kept an eager eye on the discoveries, for they were busily

The Boston Metropolitan Park System. Originally planned by Frederick Law Olmsted, it was enlarged by Charles Eliot. The city of Boston is shown shaded.

The Public Gardens, Boston, Mass. A central feature of the Boston park system.

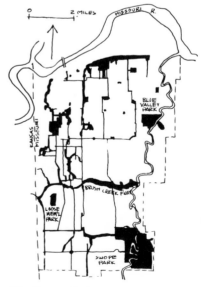

The Kansas City, Mo., park system. Parks, parkways, and boulevards. It was originally planned by George Kessler.

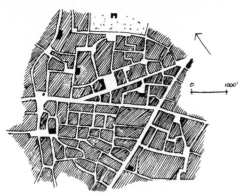

Informal plan of Camillo Sitte.

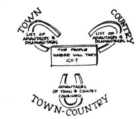

Formal plan of Camillo Sitte.
Three buildings on a small site forming six plazas.

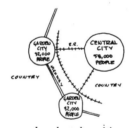

Ebenezer Howard's diagram
of the "three magnets."

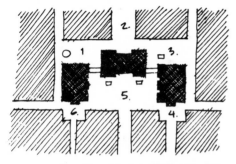

Howard's central and garden cities.

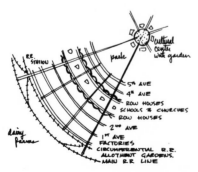

Ebenezer Howard's schematic diagram
of a garden city.

engaged in classifying and dispensing the sum of the world's architectural knowledge. Much of this knowledge was improperly applied.

In 1889 a Viennese architect, Camillo Sitte, published *An Architect's Notes and Reflections upon Artistic City Planning.* His book provided deeper understanding of the various modes of urban design of the past, and so became an invaluable guide to contemporary design. Sitte may have been influenced by a German colleague, J. Stübben, who in 1880 published a book called *Städtebau,* in which he advocated the careful preservation of old cities as they are enlarged—possibly in reaction to Haussmann. Sitte described the design of medieval and Renaissance cities, delving into the principle of arrangement, proportion, scale, and purpose with clarity and objectivity. His book has sometimes been regarded as a defense of the contrived, the irregular, and the picturesque— qualities of the Gothic and medieval towns which Ruskin had popularized. At a deeper level, however, Sitte's work was an argument, not for superficial style, but for underlying principle. In his city designs, Sitte applied these principles with sensitive appropriateness. His designs for civic centers were classically formal in layout. His plan for a small village, on the other hand, is rustically informal, with winding streets following the terrain. Sitte regarded no design element as sacred and inveighed against "paper architecture," formal or informal, which failed to fulfill its design promise.

The Garden City Movement and a Scientific Approach

In his influential book *Tomorrow: A Peaceful Path to Social Reform* (1898), Ebenezer Howard, an English parliamentary stenographer, showed how workable and livable towns could be formed within the capitalist framework. He started with discussions of the optimum size for towns—a subject frequently debated by theorists—and concluded with a cluster concept: a central city of 58,000 people surrounded by smaller "garden cities" of 30,000 people each. Permanent green space would separate the city and towns, serving as a horizontal fence of farmland. Rails and roads would link the towns, which would have their own industries, the nearby farms supplying fresh foods. All increases in land values would accrue to the town and its "stockholders," the townspeople.

Howard's proposal was accompanied by diagrams showing the attractions of the town, the country, and then of both, when ideally combined. The functional relations between the central city and its surrounding garden cities were also depicted, as well as the overall concept of a garden city and its internal layout. Howard's detailed thinking was not limited to physical design or to studies of optimum population sizes. He also made a precise financial analysis of what it would cost to build a garden city and how its operating costs would be met. Therein lay the strength of his proposal. He showed how it could be accomplished.

The idea received great acclaim, and in 1902 a garden city was started, Letchworth, about thirty-five miles from London. It was planned by architects Barry Parker and Raymond Unwin. Unwin, an exponent of low-density planning, had demonstrated his design principles in the Hampstead Gardens suburb, also near London. The plan of Letchworth was a combination of landscaping, informal street layout to suit topography, and a main axis focusing on a town center. Sports fields, a train station, houses, and factories were all included.

36

The factories failed to materialize at the outset and Letchworth became a satellite for London, thus revealing the principal difficulty of Howard's ideas. It was a risky venture depending on coordination between homebuilders and industry—which was not easy to bring about. Nevertheless the idea prevailed and in 1920 a second garden city was started, Welwyn. It was designed by architect Louis de Soissons and was more successful than Letchworth in terms of Howard's original concept. Today it is a center of the British film industry.

Howard's analytical approach was an indication of the almost scientific study that modern city building requires. The city is so large and its operations so complex that its proper understanding can only be gained by the full application of precise analysis. The Scottish city planner Patrick Geddes was the man who established this tool. His approach was not only analytical and comprehensive but also stressed the social basis of the city. The analytical survey was the principal groundwork from which any plan would be conceived.

Geddes was a prolific writer, lecturer, and planner. His writings include reports on park development, cultural institutions, applied sociology, the function of a civic museum, and the actual techniques of an urban survey. His most widely read book, *Cities in Evolution,* was published in 1915. In this work he coined the term "connurbation" to describe the waves of population inflow to large cities, followed by overcrowding and slum formation, and then the wave of backflow—the whole process resulting in amorphous sprawl, waste, and unnecessary obsolescence. As a planner he laid out some fifty cities in India and Palestine. Geddes' contributions to the understanding of the city stand alongside Marsh's contributions to the understanding of land. Geddes was concerned with the relationship between people and cities and how they affect one another. Marsh's concern had been with the interrelationship between man and nature.

Thus, just after the dawn of the twentieth century, the foundation of ideas for building the modern city were in place. From Ledoux to Geddes extends a course of ideas a hundred years in the making. From the days when the plow first broke the soil and the herdsman built a fence there has been an unbroken tradition of designing cities, a tradition as old as civilization itself. Beset with mighty thoughts, mighty experiments, and mighty deeds, an encyclopedia of urban design experience was the heritage given to our era. It remains only to know of this experience, to put it to use, to adapt it to particular conditions, and, where necessary, to build upon and expand it.

The American Experience

Two world wars, a major depression, waves of immigration, and a host of major and minor crises have erased from the public's mind the fact that this country once enjoyed what might well be called a golden age of urban design: the years between about 1890 to the Great Depression. Often narrowly termed the "City Beautiful Era," this period drew upon almost every idea in the history of designing cities. In many cases the ideas were enlarged upon significantly. Emphasis on formal design distinguishes the period somewhat unfairly, for there were broad social motives underlying the purposes of the ambitious designs.

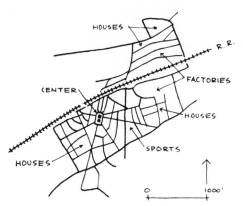
Letchworth, the first garden city.

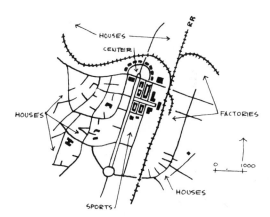
Welwyn, the second garden city.

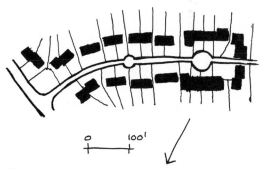
Grouping of houses in Welwyn.

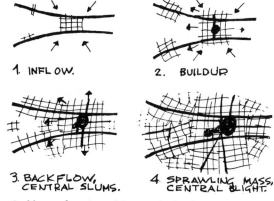
Geddes explanation of "connurbation."

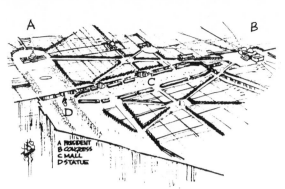

L'Enfant's concept for central Washington, 1791.
(After Elbert Peets.)

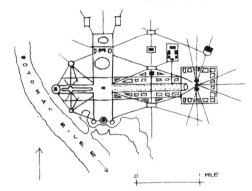

McMillan Commission plan for central Washington.

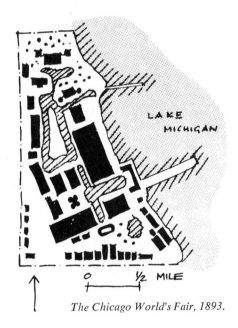

The Chicago World's Fair, 1893.

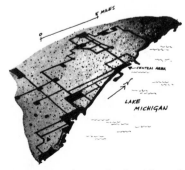

Concept of the parkways, boulevards, and Lake Shore parks of Burnham's plan for Chicago.

In our world's fairs of the late nineteenth century, we proclaimed a new hope and a fresh image for our cities. They could be far nobler than the small towns of our many farming regions, and the ugliness of our large industrial cities could be displaced by handsome works of civic art. The world's fairs were living examples of civic art to match any of the wonders of modern Europe or ancient Rome. Their design took advantage of our latest technology, from moving sidewalks to the spanning of large interior spaces with iron trusses. Although facade architecture was decried by Louis Sullivan, who saw in it only sham and a denunciation of his own search for an original American architectural expression, the buildings were, in fact, harmoniously designed as groups. There were ample pedestrian places with fountains, trees, and places to sit and relax. Here, in elegant, albeit, foreign clothes was the promise of America come to life.

The fairs were sometimes designed as renewal operations. The land upon which they were built became a new quarter of the city after the fair was over. For example, Jackson Park in Chicago was the site of its world's fair of 1893, and San Francisco's Marina district as well as Treasure Island were originally fairgrounds.

In 1901 the AIA held a national conference on city beautification in Washington, D.C. The McMillan Commission was then formed to prepare a plan for the improvement of central Washington. Some of the country's foremost artists constituted the group, including Daniel Burnham, Augustus St. Gaudens, and Frederick Law Olmsted. They toured Europe for inspiration and returned to propose a grand classical concept of landscape architecture with axes, mall, focal points, and pools—in effect reviving the original L'Enfant plan for the city. This, together with the example of the world's fairs, initiated a country-wide program of civic improvement efforts: the City Beautiful Era.

A city hall, a county court house, a library, an opera house, a museum, and a plaza were employed as the building blocks of civic centers the country over. A dome for the city hall was an essential article of pride and architectural accent. The movement spread to embrace public works of all sorts. Bridges were designed by architects as pieces of sculpture. River embankments were made into classical garden terraces. The vision of the classical world, neatly arranged, became a chief architectural concept for many a college and university: Columbia, M.I.T., the University of California at Berkeley, and the University of Washington in Seattle. The American railroads, at their zenith, built Roman basilicas and baths as grand portals to Chicago, New York, Washington, and many other cities. In 1917 the AIA published a book of all the projects, proposed or accomplished, throughout the land.

The City Beautiful Era was by no means limited to civic centers or fine public buildings. Daniel Burnham made plans for the whole of Chicago, San Francisco, Manila, and several other cities. Burnham is regarded as the father of American city planning, and his remark: "Make no little plans . . . they have no power to stir men's blood . . ." still rings. Burnham's concept of a city was a totally designed system of main circulation arteries, a network of parks, and clusters of focal buildings. In his plans are to be seen the last use of French Renaissance principles applied at the largest scale possible.

There was considerable activity in the creation of planned residential communities. Roland Park in Baltimore was started in

1892 as a garden suburb for commuters. Its lessons of finance and design were copied in many similar developments throughout the country. All the large cities with flourishing economies and well-to-do families were only too ready for such commuter suburbs. The Country Club area in Kansas City is one of the more famous. Indeed, the image of the green American suburb became the ideal of all urban American families. Forest Hills Gardens in Long Island was built as a commuter suburb for Manhattan in 1911, financed by the Russell Sage Foundation.

American architects promptly rose to the problems of burgeoning cities. From these beginnings, the American city planning profession came into being. In the early twenties city planning was very popular and plans were made for almost all our cities. Zoning was introduced in 1916 and generally adopted within a decade or two over the entire country as a means for enforcing city plans. From abroad came many lessons, too, particularly from England and the garden city movement. English architect-planners lectured in the United States and the early English books on city planning had an avid audience here. Low-density planning and grouped housing designs were advocated and acclaimed. Tempering this activity was an atmosphere of social reform. The civic center and commuter suburbs were handsome indeed, but what of the residential needs of the average man? Among those who felt that we could produce not only better homes but better communities was a group that included several deep-thinking architects.

The New Communities Movement

In the early twenties, discussions were held on community problems in meetings in New York City. Among the participants were Clarence Stein, Frederick L. Ackerman, Lewis Mumford, Henry Churchill, Henry Wright, and Alexander Bing. Some of these names are still remembered; some, unfortunately, are not. They all felt that the piecemeal development of residential communities on endless gridiron tracts was wasteful and unnecessary —worse still, it did not produce the kind of housing and communities we were capable of creating. The common practice of laying out block-pattern streets long before the builder arrived on the scene prevented clustered community design and the interspersal of open and built-up spaces, as the English planners had been advocating and as we ourselves had done. Other built-in restrictions, too, prevented us from building well-designed communities. These men set out to show how this situation could be corrected. By forming home building corporations, financed by prosperous companies seeking long-term investments, well-designed communities could be built, like Roland Park, the Country Club district, and Forest Hills Gardens. The English experience furnished ideas, and Sunnyside Gardens, Long Island, heads the list of accomplishments that resulted.

The designers of Sunnyside had to contend with an inefficient and unchangeable block pattern. They could overcome this difficulty only partially by siting the houses as row-house quadrangles with common garden space inside. The basic problem was that the blocks were too long and narrow and that there were too many through streets. The block pattern had been platted by an engineer who had spent his life laying it out. He refused to allow any alterations. This was typical of platting practice throughout the country—municipalities laid out plats and sometimes entire utility systems as an inducement to speculators. Wright and Stein decried

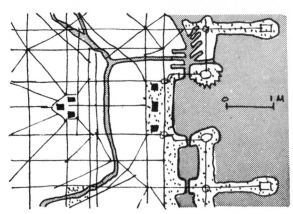

Concept of central Chicago, from Burnham's plan.

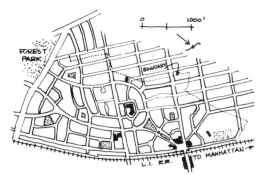

Forest Hills Gardens, L.I. Curvilinear streets, parks, public buildings, and a commuter railroad. Note the difference in street layout within the project boundary from the typical layout of blocks.

Typical block development in Long Island in the 1920s. Duplex houses; narrow side yards; poorly lit and poorly ventilated side rooms; no common play space.

The Sunnyside idea. Row houses eliminating useless side yards; well-lit and well-illuminated rooms; useable private yards, plus ample common play space.

39

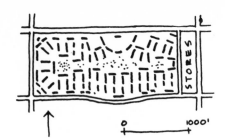

Baldwin Hills Village, Los Angeles.

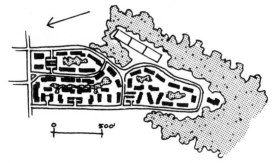

Chatham Village, Pittsburgh.

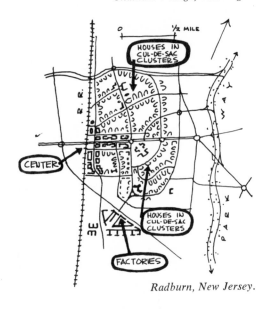

Radburn, New Jersey.

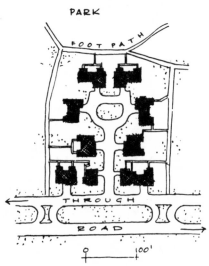

Radburn, New Jersey.
Site planning of houses around a cul-de-sac.

this practice and proposed carefully considered alternatives. Henry Wright's *Rehousing Urban America* (1934) and Clarence Stein's *Towards New Towns for America* (1951) tell the full story of this group's work.

The early residential communities, such as Roland Park, had curvilinear road layouts which suited their generally rolling topography. However, all houses fronted on a through street. By the twenties, automobile traffic was recognized as a formidable fact of urban life, for no landscaped street, however pastoral and winding, was free of the annoying intrusions of through traffic. The solution was the creation of traffic-free groupings of houses. Auto traffic should be made to serve the houses without despoiling the whole neighborhood. The answer to this problem was the "superblock," an island of green, bordered by houses and carefully skirted by peripheral automobile roads. Parking areas were conveniently located along the peripheral roads in carefully sited clusters. Chatham Village in Pittsburgh and Baldwin Hills Village in Los Angeles are among the best examples of the idea. However, a superblock was not a whole community or a whole town. What of the larger community? Indeed, what of a whole town?

The opportunity to demonstrate a design concept to answer this larger problem came at Radburn, New Jersey, less than an hour's travel time from Manhattan. The Radburn idea was to create a series of superblocks, each around an open green with the greens themselves interconnected. Within the greens, pathways led to schools, shopping, and other centers. The greenways were pedestrian ways. Where they crossed a street they bridged over it or passed under it. The automobile circulation did not interfere with, or endanger, the pedestrian. Auto access to houses was by means of a short dead-end road. Hence the houses were arranged as cul-de-sac clusters around a stub service drive. The main circulation streets were also kept generally free of parked cars to allow unhindered flow of through traffic.

Unfortunately Radburn was never entirely completed because of the Depression. It is one of the most important designs ever conceived for the modern residential community. Essential to the Radburn idea was the scheduling and coordination of its construction. No town can be built as a whole overnight—unless it is built for a special purpose or by one large company. In Radburn, industries were to be established to create jobs for the inhabitants—as in Howard's garden cities. As new industries furnished new jobs, new houses would be built, of course in carefully designed cluster communities. Through coordinated town development—industries and houses—investors in both would be assuring each other's investment.

An essential aspect of the Radburn idea was the organization of the town into cohesive neighborhoods, described by Clarence A. Perry, in 1929, in a book called *The Neighborhood Unit*. The idea would be applicable not only to new towns but to large city areas. One of the objectives of replanning old cities became the creation of neighborhood centers and the physical delineation of neighborhood groups. The "Radburn idea" was a new town idea. Of course, all American towns had been new towns originally. The nineteenth-century commuter suburbs were a form of "new town" in their time. Gary and Pullman were new industrial or satellite towns, as the American G. R. Taylor observed in two books: *Satellite Cities, A Study of Industrial Surburbs* (1915) and *The Building of Satellite Towns* (1925). Taylor's reasoning

40

reinforced Ebenezer Howard's belief that metropolitan growth could and should be directed into a colonization movement.

Regional Planning

However, these concepts of community planning were part of a far larger picture, namely, the city or town in its total physical and economic region. A town thrives because its region is healthy; it dies as its region declines. America had, by the twenties, more than one impoverished region and more than one ghost town. Bad soil practices in farming or in lumbering could wipe out a whole area's economy. The decline of small towns and the growth of large cities were both outcomes of the same regional picture. In many cases, however, growth and decline were caused by conditions that could be altered. Small town demise and large city expansion could be checked within significant limits. Howard and Taylor had shown that satellite colonization was an alternative, and Radburn was a living demonstration of that alternative. The real answer to the larger questions could be found only in a regional outlook. That outlook had its roots in the thoughts of Marsh and Geddes and its champions in Henry Wright and Benton MacKaye.

Working under a commission chaired by Clarence Stein, Henry Wright produced the *Report of the Commission on Housing and Regional Planning for the State of New York*. Wright, with a simple group of drawings, showed how the towns of New York State had first been small trade centers for an agricultural society. Western expansion and the development of Midwestern farms, producing food more cheaply, caused New York's farms to dwindle. Simultaneously, however, industrialization took hold, favoring towns that lay along streams and roads; streams were the early sources of power and roads facilitated distribution of industrial products. Thus the small farm towns declined, and the Hudson River and Mohawk River valleys became the spine of New York's industrial economy. New York City became a world port for distributing the products of the American industrial belt. It also became its financial and managerial heart. Henry Wright's plan explained these phenomena and proposed channeling these forces into a better development pattern. The former farm hinterlands could become recreational and dairying lands. The industrial spine would improve transportation, and New York City would be a strong central core for a constellation of smaller communities like Radburn. Wright's plan is still one of the finest models of regional planning ever produced. The evidence of its validity is that while it was not officially adopted, its key recommendations were eventually realized, in some cases at the hands of people who had never known of the plan. The regional approach to planning led to the formation of the Regional Planning Association of America (RPAA).

In the late 1920s another significant regional plan was made for the New York City metropolitan area by the Regional Planning Association of New York. RPAA and RPA of New York are sometimes confused. The latter was a study which embraced 22 counties, 500 municipal districts, 10 million people and parts of New York State, New Jersey, and Connecticut. This plan, however, was far smaller in scope than Wright's. In 1928 an eight-volume survey was produced, two volumes of which were plan proposals. All of this was done under the direction of the Scottish planner Thomas Adams. This was the most complete plan study

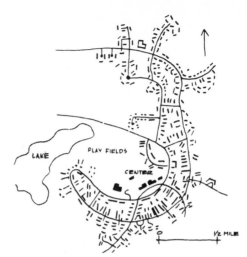

Greenbelt, Maryland.

New York State. "M" is the Mohawk Valley; "H" is the Hudson River Valley.

I. New York State, 1840–1880. Rapid development of natural resources; small towns economically independent; industry served by water power and canals. Near the end of this period the drift toward the new rail lines had started.

II. New York State, 1880–1920. Development of central rail routes; concentration along main-line transportation; use of steam power; agricultural competition with the West. Town growth is in the central valley belts and the towns off the main line decline.

III. New York State, the future. New forces of influence are the automobile, good roads, and electric power transmission. Rather than a return to the past dispersion and distribution pattern, it is possible to make a more effective use of all economic resources, to divert growth from New York City, and to develop areas in accord with their most favorable use—industry, agriculture, recreation, water supply, and forest reserves.

41

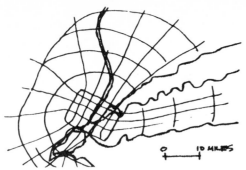

Concept of highways from the regional plan of New York.

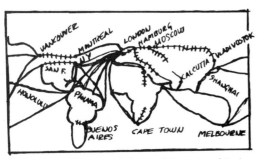

MacKaye's diagram of the U.S. stream of industrial productive flow through the Port of New York. He compared this to the flow of streams and rivers in a watershed area.
(From "The New Exploration.")

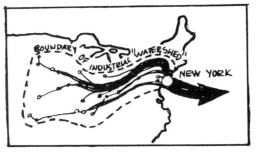

MacKaye's diagram of the world's major shipping and rail routes—the main arteries of flow between the modern world's metropolitan areas.
(From "The New Exploration.")

MacKaye's diagram of the relative strength of the world's civilizations in terms of population.
(From "The New Exploration.")

MacKaye's diagram of the relative strength of the world's civilizations in terms of resources.
(From "The New Exploration.")

ever done for an American metropolitan area, but it was criticized by the RPAA which felt it was too limited in its physical scope.

Planning, if it is to be successful, must start at the beginning. The beginning, according to Wright's approach, is the total situation of a village or a metropolis in its statewide and multistate region. Benton MacKaye was to go even further.

MacKaye was originally a forester, a man in the tradition of the great American conservationists. He saw the nation as a series of component parts whose natural divisions were river drainage areas, not state lines. For him the Connecticut and Colorado River basins were truer pictures of our country's component parts than its political lines. The country, to MacKaye, was really a number of natural "flow systems." MacKaye also saw towns and cities as part of these flow systems—determined, to be sure, by natural resources but built by men. If the two systems did not operate in harmony, either the land would be ruined or the towns fail. MacKaye's greatest accomplishment was the Appalachian park and trail system. MacKaye realized that the entire Eastern seaboard's population needed a system of open spaces commensurate with its continuing growth. Indeed, he titled his plan *An Open-space System for Appalachian America*. Incidentally, MacKaye proposed this idea in an article in the *AIA Journal* in 1921. In 1928 MacKaye published *The New Exploration, A Philosophy of Regional Planning*. Along with Geddes' and Mumford's writing it is one of the best statements of the regional outlook. A second edition was published in 1962. MacKaye also realized the necessity of separating through traffic from residential areas. He spoke of the "townless highway" (today's interstate system which bypasses cities) and the "highwayless town" (like Radburn), as mutually interdependent.

MacKaye, like his colleague Wright, also used simple sketches to explain these ideas. But where Wright sketched New York State, MacKaye sketched maps of the entire world. He discussed the world's resources, climates, history, and major routes of trade and ports. He showed how all were inseparably related. In a page or two he summed up all the economic theories of the past. He showed New York City as the entry and exit portal for the entire American industrial empire; how Boston, Philadelphia, and Baltimore were portals on this main stream of flow with New York City; and how Pittsburgh, Detroit, and Akron were ancillary parts of the industrial stream. In short, he showed how the country worked as a combination of man's cities on nature's land.

In the twenties, the battle of conservation was far from won, but it had gained a strong foothold. The campaign for conservation had been initiated by George Perkins Marsh and those men, like MacKaye, who followed him. MacKaye, however, started a new campaign. The exploration of the wilderness and conservation practices had to be expanded to include cities. That was the "new exploration" that MacKaye advocated so eloquently in his book.

The Depression furnished us with the manpower and opportunities to expand on the urban design ideas which had been proposed so far. Through WPA projects many urban parks, playgrounds, pools, and bathing beaches were created. Their design often derived from the old City Beautiful concepts, and the "greenbelt" towns built during this time were patterned after the Radburn idea.

Regional studies were also undertaken by the National Resources Planning Board, according to the outlook of Henry Wright and Benton MacKaye. The Tennessee Valley Authority put these ideas into practice and remains the greatest accomplishment ever achieved on this scale. MacKaye conceived the "multi-use programs" of TVA, and he proposed numerous programs which could be put into operation to the benefit of the TVA region, ranging from fish breeding to rural electrification. These were the side effects of a regional enterprise.

The American story of urban design of the last fifty years is little known on a popular level and often misunderstood where it is known. By far it is one of the richest stories in the annals of urban design—even though its accomplishments were not too numerous. The men who authored its deeds were part of a world-wide fraternity. Throughout continental Europe similar stories were unfolding.

Achievements Abroad

Several garden cities were built in France—not long after Howard had proposed the original idea in England. The first, Dourges, was built in 1919 by a railroad. It was followed by Longueau, Tergnier, and Lille-la-Déliverance.

In England, Raymond Unwin had written *Nothing Gained by Overcrowding* (1903) and *Town Planning in Practice* (1909). F. J. Osborne's *New Towns after the War* (1918) advocated garden cities balanced with a central metropolis. The titles of these books indicate the kind of discussion held in England since Howard. In 1940 Sir Anthony M. Barlow headed a commission which studied urban problems and produced *The Report of the Royal Commission of Distribution of Industrial Population,* which encouraged industry to locate away from large cities in planned communities. In 1943 Sir Patrick Abercrombie and J. H. Forshaw published *The County of London Plan.* The Barlow report paved the way for the British New Towns policy, and the Abercrombie plan showed how London could be improved while retaining a large bulk of the population.

The English New Town movement has produced about twenty new towns to date. The early ones were rather spread out with large open spaces, indeed sometimes far too large. Some towns lacked cohesiveness and convenience, the spaces being distances to overcome rather than amenities. A radical change in New Town design was introduced in the 1950s in the plan for Hook, wherein houses were very closely grouped along a multilevel linear spine. This decreased distances and all communal facilities could be reached by a short walk. The open countryside was right at the edge of town, just as accessible to the pedestrian as was the town center. The circulation concept of Hook, in fact, was that of an ocean liner. Because of a political controversy it was not built, but a second one, Cumbernauld, was planned and is proceeding toward completion at this writing. Recently a vast new plan for Southwest England was drafted as a further attempt to check London's growth.

An attempt to incorporate the demands of the automobile in modern town building is exemplified in London's Barbican area. Actually there are two Barbican areas, or projects. One is a 63-acre area cleared by wartime bombings. The second is a 28-acre zone along the Thames just east of London Bridge. Both are high-density projects with tall towers. Their main design significance is their multilevel circulation system. Elevated walkways

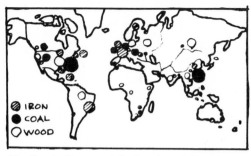

MacKaye's diagram of the location of the prime natural resources of modern industrial civilizations: iron, coal, and wood.
(From "The New Exploration.")

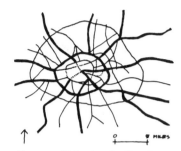

Abercrombie's plan for London. Radiocentric road system.

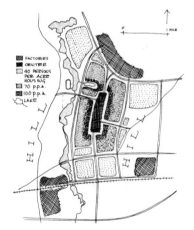

Plan of Hook. A proposed "new town" for 100,000 set in a valley. Though not built, it was a radical design departure which paved the way for Cumbernauld.

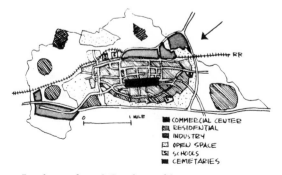

Land use plan of Cumbernauld.

43

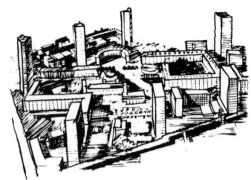

The Barbican Development, London.

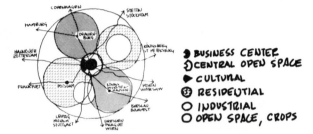

- ● BUSINESS CENTER
- ◗ CENTRAL OPEN SPACE
- ► CULTURAL
- ⊕ RESIDENTIAL
- ○ INDUSTRIAL
- ○ OPEN SPACE, CROPS

Martin Mächler's plan for Greater Berlin, 1920.

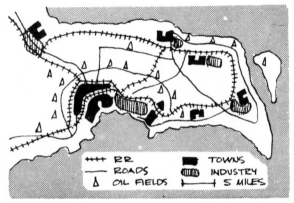

+++ RR		■ TOWNS	
— ROADS		▦ INDUSTRY	
△ OIL FIELDS		├─┤ 5 MILES	

Baku. Plan for a satellite-city group in Russia, 60,000–80,000 people in each town.

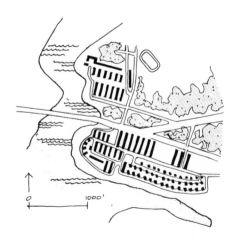

Part of West Kungsholmen, Stockholm.

link various parts of the projects. The Barbican scheme attracted the attention of the world's planners not because it was a new idea—da Vinci had proposed it, the Adam brothers had used it, and Rockefeller Center was based on it—but because it was being built in response to the postwar pressures of the automobile, pressures which every modern city was feeling.

Traffic congestion became a main concern of the English planners. The automobile was making intolerable instrusions into cities and towns. A report published in 1963, *Traffic in Towns,* deals with the long-term problems of traffic in urban areas. It designates traffic as a servant, not a wanton force to wreak havoc in cities. The town is foremost a place to live, with traffic playing a service role. Many old towns have a limited capacity for traffic, which should not be exceeded. Other towns can be reshaped to advantage with increased traffic, but only up to a point. New towns, like Cumbernauld, can be designed with totally new circulation concepts. This kind of investigation is sorely needed for the United States.

The story of Germany would repeat many ideas so far outlined, as would those of Italy, Holland, Switzerland, the Scandinavian countries, the Soviet Union, and Israel. In the early twenties, the Berlin architect Martin Mäckler produced a typical diagram of basic metropolitan planning, showing the fundamental relationships between the central core, its cultural facilities, outlying residential and industrial areas, open space, and circulation. Sweden's story traces a history of planning that goes back centuries. Its new towns are based on Howard's original concepts, much advanced and refined. In Finland, Tapiola is a new satellite town of Helsinki, and in Holland, Amsterdam South is a satellite of Amsterdam. Many of their lessons and innovations are pertinent to our problems here in the United States.

Men of Modern Architecture and Planning

Foremost in these years of search have been the ideas and writings of modern architects. Eliel Saarinen, for example, produced a prize-winning plan for Helsinki in 1911. He proposed orderly and distinct subcommunities, open space, and an overall circulation pattern to suit Helsinki's island and bay topography. At Cranbrook, where Saarinen taught for many years, the teaching of architecture and urban planning were closely allied. Walter Gropius came to the United States from his Bauhaus school in Germany via England and took the same approach in his teaching at Harvard. In 1943 Saarinen wrote *The City,* proposing the decentralization of large cities. E. A. Gutkind discussed this concept in detail in *The Twilight of Cities,* published in 1962. The idea of at least articulating urban segments is of great importance. Ludwig Hilbersheimer proposed that cities be laid out in relation to prevailing winds so as to avoid the smoke of factories. He later modified his ideas to include avoidance of atomic fallout particles—before the destructive effects of larger bombs invalidated any such defensive possibilities. Richard Neutra wrote *Rush City Reformed,* in which he showed how a modern city could use modern transportation technology to avoid congestion. Le Corbusier fused the ideas of modern architecture and city form with modern technology. In 1922 he unveiled *Une Ville Contemporaine,* a hypothetical plan for a city of 3 million people —not an abandonment of the congested industrial city, but, rather,

44

a rearrangement of its form exploiting the new technology. His ideas are traceable to Eugène Hénard's *Les Villes de L'Avenir* and Tony Garnier's *Une Cité Industrielle.*

Le Corbusier's proposed rearrangement would create three distinct areas: a central business city with 400,000 inhabitants in twenty-four tall skyscrapers; an encircling residential zone of 600,000 occupying multistory continuous slabs; then garden houses for 2 million. The plan had a crisp geometric form, with roads creating large rectangles interwoven with major diagonals. Le Corbusier had four major objectives: to decongest the center city; increase density; improve circulation; and, all the while, provide more natural verdure, light, and air.

Three years later came his *Plan Voisin* (Neighborhood Plan), embodying the same goals but applied to a large section of Paris. Eighteen sixty-story towers replaced the crammed-in houses of central Paris, freeing the ground for high-speed circulation, parks, cafés, shops—and people. The vitality of the streets of Paris was to be released from its traditional corridor setting to extend freely in all directions.

In 1935 he proposed *La Ville Radieuse,* refining many of his earlier concepts. Long rectilinear buildings meandered in zig-zag fashion to cover only 12 per cent of the ground surface. And in 1937 came *Le Plan de Paris,* an even more advanced development, showing how all of Paris could be rebuilt without destroying its magnificent old architectural monuments. Le Corbusier felt that the old role of the street as an artery for pedestrians and vehicles was no longer possible. The two had to be separated. If, as he proposed in his designs, the road were elevated and connected directly to buildings, the ground would then be free for omnidirectional pedestrian movement. It would also be free for recreational use. High urban density, essential to the modern city, would be realized through the use of multistory skyscrapers and multistory buildings, meandering as slabs in a fret pattern across the landscape. From the ground level they would barely be visible despite their size, for they would be screened by dense groves of trees. Through the years, Le Corbusier had been applying his ideas—on paper—to many cities of the world, punctuated in a handful of places by a few accomplishments. As his sketches increased, his fame multiplied. He became the leading spokesman and fountainhead of the "International Movement."

Not until the last decade did he get the opportunity to design an entire city: Chandigarh, in India. His plan, done in collaboration, followed the earlier and brilliant concepts of Matthew Nowicki, himself strongly influenced by Le Corbusier. Its great significance is its regional flavor—its embrace of local Indian culture in decidedly modern terms. It is a series of neighborhood enclaves, arranged in a grid pattern and interconnected by a carefully articulated circulation system.

Le Corbusier also showed how massive design problems could be handled by large groups of high and low buildings; in effect, he brought cubism to large-scale architectural compositions. Coupling these concepts of architectural mass to modern construction, his ideas have been followed the world over. Le Corbusier's influence and popularity stem from his use of modern forms and designs in his architecture and the convenience of his large block-like compositions for planning large-scale developments. His architecture and town planning were in tune with modern technology and administrative organization.

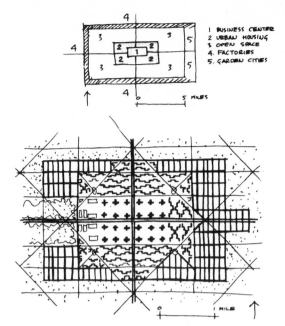

Le Corbusier's plan for a city of 3 million people (whole city above, central portion below).

Le Corbusier's Plan Voisin *for Paris.*

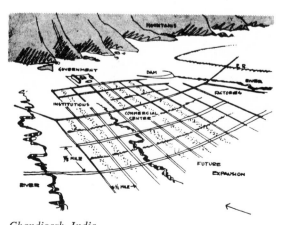

Chandigarh, India.

45

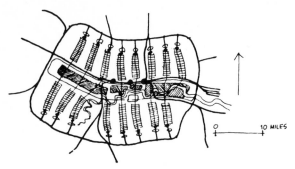

1938 MARS plan for London. An east-west spine of commerce and industry with sixteen residential corridors.

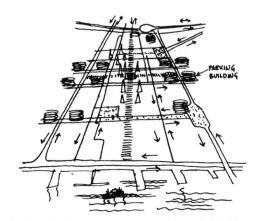

Louis Kahn's movement pattern for Philadelphia.

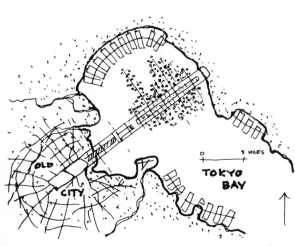

Kenzo Tange's plan for Tokyo.

His writing on architecture includes much discussion of city design in particular. *When the Cathedrals Were White* (1947) is a brilliant essay on modern technology as well as on American life generally, and on New York City particularly. *Concerning Town Planning* (1948) emphasizes urban housing. Lewis Mumford has been critical of Le Corbusier, feeling that his designs are spectacular rationalizations of gigantism of the modern metropolis. Mumford would prevent the giant from getting so big and, where it has, cut it down to size. Mumford would start with a regional approach. But so, too, would Le Corbusier. His urban studies include sketches and discussions of countries as a whole and show their "flow systems" and urban hubs in a style almost identical to MacKaye's. Le Corbusier recognizes large cities as a fact of life but has never denied the village or the region in which both operate.

Le Corbusier was instrumental in organizing the Congrès International d'Architecture Moderne (CIAM), an international group of architects and planners who discussed the urbanization problems that were appearing in all the world's cities. In their Athens Charter of 1931 they proclaimed their dedication to the service of urban planning. The English CIAM organization, the MARS group, proposed a plan for rebuilding London. The whole population would be redistributed in sixteen finger corridors all connected by a major circulation spine and encircling circulation loop. Le Corbusier conceived the CIAM grid—a graphic file system for recording pertinent information in an urban study and for explaining a plan. The grid had four component sections: work, residence, circulation, and leisure.

Great study has been concentrated on the problems of circulation and urban design. For example, Louis Kahn has made important designs for central Philadelphia showing circulation—main arteries, stop-and-go streets, and parking towers—as key determinants of urban form, all organized into a symphony of circulation.

One of the most profound designs to appear for the modern city is Kenzo Tange's plan for Tokyo. Like Kahn, Tange puts great emphasis on the role of circulation as a determinant of urban form. Kenzo Tange's proposal is based on penetrating analysis which casts light on our own problems. Setting out to make a plan for Tokyo, he concluded that the primary problem of large cities (Tokyo has 10 million people) is circulation. The very life of a city of 10 million depends on the ability of its inhabitants to communicate with each other face-to-face. Through careful study, Tange saw that once a city grew beyond 2 or 3 million inhabitants this vital communication became very inefficient in a radiocentric city form created by spontaneous growth. He examined every possible alternative. Tower buildings in large open spaces were no solution, he felt, because they still caused congestion in circulation systems. Overall densities are not altered by a tower pattern. His proposed solution envisioned the construction of a new Tokyo over Tokyo Bay, hung on a series of suspension bridges. Vehicular circulation would be segregated according to speed, and dwelling and work areas stacked in several levels. Tange developed detailed cost estimates and concluded that they would not exceed the construction outlays contemplated for Tokyo in the next several decades.

Frank Lloyd Wright, in contrast to Le Corbusier or Tange, showed the way for abolishing the city. He followed Howard,

Geddes, and the social reformers in their distrust of the modern monster city and, especially in his early years, echoed the views of his great teacher Louis Sullivan, who built his most important works in the city but had no affection for it. In 1932 Wright published *The Disappearing City* and later *Broadacres*—proposing that every family live on an acre of land. Present-day American suburbs are crude microcosms of what Wright would have made into art.

But at the end of his career, perhaps in recognition of the difficulties of land supply and logistics in applying the Broadacres plan to an America grown immense in population, Wright (possibly with tongue in cheek) unveiled a scheme for a superskyscraper a full mile high. Ten or so of these could replace all of Manhattan's buildings and free the land for greenery. Wright's site design for the Marin County Civic Center north of San Francisco is a slice out of his old Broadacres plan.

Among the world's foremost urban theorists today are Constantine Doxiadis, Charles Abrams, and Buckminster Fuller. Their thinking could be categorized along the lines of MacKaye, Le Corbusier, and the other regionalists. Doxiadis has addressed himself to the problem of urbanization on a worldwide scale and his major designs have been made for countries where the economy and productive system can be coordinated by policy and decree. Doxiadis' best work is in the newly developing nations of Africa and the Middle East, where this is possible. In *Architecture in Transition* (1963), he explains his total view. Case studies in his magazine *Ekistics* show many of his plans—also including detailed programs and schedules. He recently published his Ekistics grid, a system for recording planning data and ordering the planning process. It is reminiscent of the old CIAM grid. Doxiadis's contribution—and it is not a small one—has been to state the problems of modern urbanization with scientific clarity and to propose a rational method for addressing those problems. He approaches town planning as a science which includes planning and design as we traditionally know it, as well as the contribution of the sociologist, geographer, economist, politician, social anthropologist, ecologist, demographer, etc. All this he assembles into a total rational and human approach which he calls "ekistics"—the science of human settlements.

Charles Abrams sees housing as one of the prime fields of endeavor for solving urban problems. In *Man's Struggle for Shelter in an Urbanizing World* (1964) he discusses the prime role of housing in urban development and in national policy. Abram's experiences and thought extend from highly developed to completely underdeveloped nations. Buckminster Fuller continues the internationalist train of thought best of all. His *Inventory of World Resources—Human Trends and Needs* (1963) is a work par excellence in assessing the current state of the world's production and productive energy—and in suggesting how it can be turned to man's complete advantage.

No modern thinker, however, has surpassed the scope and depth of Lewis Mumford, who has seen fit to devote his energies to writing. His all-embracing views have been consistently confirmed over the last forty years, in which time he has authored some twenty books and innumerable articles. Mumford has been urging that the fundamental needs of society be the basis for the judicious use of our technological power, a power whose wonders obscure the better ends they might bring. These ends are the

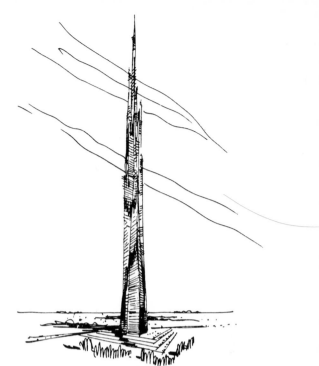

Frank Lloyd Wright's mile-high skyscraper.

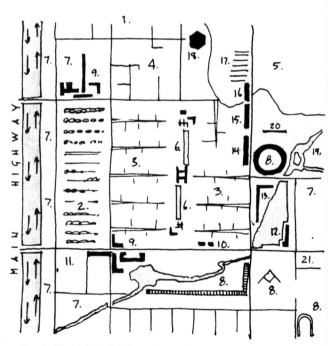

Frank Lloyd Wright's Broadacres.

 1. *Small farms*   11. *Tourists' hotel*
 2. *Orchards*   12. *County seat*
 3. *Small houses*   13. *Arts*
 4. *Medium houses*   14. *Arboretum*
 5. *Large houses*   15. *Aquarium*
 6. *Schools*   16. *Zoo*
 7. *Small industries*   17. *University*
 8. *Sports and recreation*   18. *Community church*
 9. *Markets*   19. *Sanitarium*
10. *Clinics*   20. *Hotel*
                        21. *Airport*

harmonious life of civilized social groups in ecological balance with the particular place occupied—a notion too readily, and incorrectly, dismissed as latter-day romanticism. Inherent in Mumford's thinking is the need for recognizing the physical limitations of human settlements. One of his most eloquent and, at the same time, concise expressions of his philosophy was the speech he delivered in June, 1965 in Washington, D.C., at the AIA national convention. The great summary of his thought is contained in his largest volume, *The City in History,* published in 1961.

Conclusion

The vastness of current urban problems confounds the average mind. It occupies a large fraternity of theorists who may have produced in the last five years more books on cities than in the whole history of civilization. Indeed the complexity of the problem has spawned a complexity of language which raises some doubt as to usefulness—but no doubt as to expenditure of energy in behalf of a vital human problem.

In this book we will try to acknowledge some of these ideas, but we will follow one main theme. That is, that the city is as much a physical object in three dimensions as it is anything else. As a physical object it can be designed—perhaps as artfully as the gardens of Versailles, as practically as the town of Ferrara, and as humanely as the towns of the ancient Greeks. Indeed, for those who do not care to look in those directions we can draw encouragement from our own history of accomplishments. After all, it is the physical city which is the result of all planning efforts, whether dealing with economy, sociology, or transportation. It is the physical city we have to live in. It is the physical city we must design.

With this sketch of the history of urban design, we can examine with some understanding the current state of the art as it applies to us. It is an extremely rich state at present, one which asks now, as it has asked throughout history, to be put to use. If our problems seem vast, we must remember that our means are greater than those of any society in the past. Our problems are compounded by the multiplicity of actions needed to yield a decision to act. Here the history of urban design is helpful because it gives us ideas as to what we can act on, the things we can decide to do.

For today's city dweller, a history of urban design is an insight into the current state of things as well as a suggestion of better alternatives. For the politician, it is a demand for administrative techniques and actions that will realize the vast store of urban design possibilities. For every urban administrator and engineer, the history of urban design insists on responsible and considered decisions. For the designer, the merits of studying the history of urban design may go further. A knowledge of its store of ideas is not so much a matter of correct interpretation, for interpretations and even acknowledgments of historical events will vary from person to person and from era to era. The value of this knowledge is that it stimulates one's thoughts toward a deeper understanding of his own period. It enables him to act with far greater depth of understanding and scope of vision. And, not the least, it sharpens his taste for excellence as nothing else can.

3

Making a Visual Survey

A Working Vocabulary of Urban Form

Architectural design begins with the preparation of a building program and site analysis. So, too, do plans for designing or redesigning a portion of a city. In the case of a city, the analysis is a diagnosis of the city's component pieces, to see the relations between these pieces and to assess their condition. A visual survey in urban design is an examination of the form, appearance, and composition of a city—an evaluation of its assets and liabilities. A visual survey also enables us to see where the city needs reshaping.

A visual survey can be made of any city or town, regardless of size. It can also be made at different scales—a neighborhood, the center, a suburban area, or a small group of buildings. Furthermore, it can be made for a built-up part of the city which is going to be altered very slightly or for a part of the city which is going to be rebuilt entirely. The process of making a visual survey is not complicated, nor need it be done with a high degree of precision. As a matter of fact, it is best done in general terms, for to deal with the city on a large scale we must think broadly.

To conduct a visual survey, one must have a basic idea of the elements of urban form. These necessitate a descriptive vocab-

A visual survey discerns a city's assets . . .

. . . and its liabilities.

49

ulary. Next, one must examine the city and describe it in terms of this vocabulary. It is also necessary to relate the elements, in order to understand its workings, its form, and its consequent appearance.

While making a visual survey, it is important to constantly evaluate. Certain discordant elements must be noted as faults to be corrected; certain appropriate elements must be noted as assets to be protected. A good urban design survey will also disclose a number of specific ideas for improving, correcting, or replacing parts of the city, for a good survey leads to ideas for action.

The Image of the City

People's impressions of a building, a particular environment, or a whole city, are, of course, more than visual. Within the city lie many connotations, memories, experiences, smells, hopes, crowds, places, buildings, the drama of life and death, affecting each person according to his particular predilections. From his environment each person constructs his own mental picture of the parts of the city in physical relationship to one another. The most essential parts of an individual's mental image, or map, overlap and complement those of his fellows. Hence we can assume a collective image-map or impressions-map of a city: a collective picture of what people extract from the physical reality of a city. That extracted picture is the image of the city.

Every work of architecture affects the details and often the whole of the collective image. The collective mental picture—the image of the city—is largely formed by many works of architecture seen in concert or in chaos, but definitely seen together.

Several years ago, Prof. Kevin Lynch conducted a study of what people mentally extract from the physical reality of a city. He reported the results in a book called *The Image of the City,* and his findings are a major contribution to understanding urban form and to architecture as component parts of that form. Professor Lynch is one of the country's leading investigators of urban form. Many of the ideas in this book were derived from his studies. In his examination of the form of the city, Professor Lynch found that there are five basic elements which people use to construct their mental image of a city:

Pathways: These are the major and minor routes of circulation which people use to move about. A city has a network of major routes and a neighborhood network of minor routes. A building has several main routes which people use to get to it and from it. An urban highway network is a network of pathways for a whole city. The footpaths of a college campus are pathways for the campus.

Districts: A city is composed of component neighborhoods or districts; its center, uptown, midtown, its in-town residential areas, trainyards, factory areas, suburbs, college campuses, etc. Sometimes they are distinct in form and extent—like the Wall Street area of Manhattan. Sometimes they are considerably mixed in character and do not have distinct limits—like the midtown area of Manhattan.

Edges: The termination of a district is its edge. Some districts have no distinct edges at all but gradually taper off and blend into another district. When two districts are joined at an edge they form a seam. Fifth Avenue is an eastern edge for Central Park. A narrow park may be a joining seam for two urban neighborhoods.

Paths.

Districts.

Edges.

Landmarks: The prominent visual features of the city are its landmarks. Some landmarks are very large and are seen at great distances, like the Empire State Building or a radio mast. Some landmarks are very small and can only be seen close up, like a street clock, a fountain, or a small statue in a park. Landmarks are an important element of urban form because they help people to orient themselves in the city and help identify an area. A good landmark is a distinct but harmonious element in its urban setting.

Nodes: A node is a center of activity. Actually it is a type of landmark but is distinguished from a landmark by virtue of its active function. Where a landmark is a distinct visual object, a node is a distinct hub of activity. Times Square in New York City is both a landmark and a node.

These five elements of urban form alone are sufficient to make a useful visual survey of the form of a city. Their importance lies in the fact that people think of a city's form in terms of these basic elements. To test them, sketch a map of your own city, or better still, ask someone else to do it, taking only a few minutes. The result will be twofold: a picture of the most salient features of a city's form—its image—and a map of the sketcher's particular interests as they relate to the city. The result will also be akin to the cartoon maps of the United States as seen through the eyes of a Texan or a New Yorker. The features will be distorted and probably exaggerated, the degree of distortion reflecting the hierarchy of values of the sketcher.

The more "imageable" a city, the easier it is to find one's way about in it, even if its street pattern is not clear. In designing a city, it is important to consider how a new development will affect the total urban image. A new development can be made to tie visibly into a city's path system; to form or help reinforce a district; if on an edge, to strengthen the edge; and if at a seam, to maintain continuity. It can also become a good landmark and an active node.

Paths, landmarks, nodes, districts, and edges are the skeletal elements of a city form. Upon that basic framework hangs a tapestry of embellishing characteristics which all together constitute the personality of a city. To build a broader vocabulary upon this basic framework we must consider landform, natural verdure, climate, several aspects of urban form itself, certain details and several lesser facets of form.

Landform and Nature

Every city is built on a piece of land. The form of this land and its features are the foremost determinants of a city's form. In speaking of landform, we are speaking primarily of topography.

In looking at landscape, we are seeking its character. As urban designers we observe the form of the terrain—flat, gently rolling, hilly, mountainous—in relation to the architecture and the cities which are set in it. A flat site may suggest either vertical architecture or assertive horizontals. A slightly hilly site may call for vertical architecture at the summits with a flow of cubes on the slopes, or may suggest a termination of architecture just below the crests. A steep hillside or valley may lend itself to terracing, with orientation to the sun. In every case we must assess the qualities of the terrain, including the design relationships they express.

The prominent features of a landscape should be carefully noted—cliffs, mountain peaks, ranges of hills on the horizon,

Landmarks.

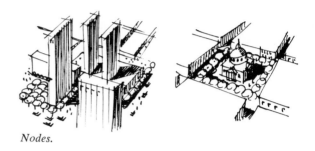

Nodes.

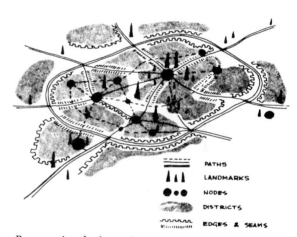

Representing the form of a city with abstract *symbols.*

PATHS
LANDMARKS
NODES
DISTRICTS
EDGES & SEAMS

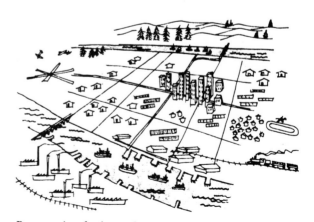

Representing the form of a city with representational *symbols.*

51

Topography.

Form and character.

Characteristic features.

Classification of native trees.

Architectural form in relation to terrain.

The city in nature; nature in the city.

plateaus, rivers, or lakes. These are accenting landscape features which can be employed actively as sites or passively as vistas, supplementing architectural and urban form. They can be used as major vista objectives from points within the city or as special sites for buildings. Some are better left in their natural state.

Indigenous greenery should be assessed in terms of shape, size, character, practicability, and seasonal change. An urban designer needs a working knowledge of the local flora and its suitability in various uses. A thickly foliated tree, formally shaped, might be proper for lining a road to shield the automobilist from a low sun. A spreading shade tree of informal shape, might be quite appropriate as a restful sitting place in the bustle of the city.

Characteristic detail of the landscape should be considered for possible use as architectural and urban design embellishment: a native rock or gravel, a characteristic earth color, the form of local streams, characteristic stands of trees. Indigenous architecture should also be noted, particularly in older towns. These are the result of evolution and may have achieved a mature relationship with their environment.

Certain areas of landscape should not be touched, but preserved in their natural state. A survey of the natural landscape may disclose areas which are better left as wilderness. These might well be chosen with relation to nearby cities and towns so that they are accessible as necessary complements to urban life, but not menaced by it.

Buildings and small towns can often be seen in their entirety in the framework of nature. As such, they are accents or counterpoints to their natural settings, elements of vitality in a setting of repose. A larger town, however, can seldom be seen in its entirety, but only in part, from various viewing places. Here we have a one-to-one relationship, nature being less a setting than a major component of the whole scene—balancing the sight of the city rather than acting as a setting for it. Raw nature sometimes exists within large cities in the form of streams, rivers, shore lines, cliffs, etc. Here the city is the setting for nature. Nature, in this circumstance, becomes a foil or counterpoint to the urban surroundings.

Thus, we might regard a small town as an object in the embrace of nature, a larger town as being hand-in-hand with nature, and finally, the large city as assuming the role of nature and becoming the embracer.

A visual survey of nature in relation to achitecture and urban design is threefold in scope. We first try to determine the character of the surrounding landscape to which our architectural and urban forms must respond esthetically and functionally. Second, we evaluate the degree to which our existing architecture and cities enhance nature. Third, we must decide what natural areas are to be left alone to act as complements to urban form. Throughout this process we search for assets and liabilities, preserving and enlarging upon the one and noting corrections to be made on the other.

Every work of architecture affects the natural landscape either positively or negatively; so does every structure and human settlement. Nature, in turn, as a setting for our constructions, is a visual framework to which all our constructions must respond.

Local Climate

While on the subject of the natural features of the terrain, it is wise to check on local climatological conditions. Local climate determines much of the character and appearance of the landscape and buildings. The following aspects of climate can be readily found in United States Weather Bureau publications.

Temperature: Seasonal temperature and humidity as averages and extremes which indicate the periods of relative comfort, the extremes which must be ameliorated, and which therefore determine architectural and urban form.

Light: The number of clear, partly cloudy, and fully cloudy days, which conditions the light affecting the appearance of the city and of buildings.

Precipitation: The amount of precipitation in the form of rain and snow.

Sun: The angles of the sun in different seasons, which affects viewing conditions and, thus, design. It is useful to make a simple three-dimensional model to study these angles.

Winds: The prevailing seasonal winds including the direction and intensity of cold winter winds, gentle or severe fall and spring gusts, and cooling summer breezes. These affect design considerably.

In addition to these quantitative factors there are a number of qualitative aspects of climate which are as important in urban design. Some cities are well oriented toward the rising sun or the setting sun. Some cities have forms that derive almost directly from their climates—arcaded cities in the sun, for example. Considerable research or experimentation might be done to determine how cold winter winds could be slackened and cooling summer breezes induced. The quality of light—sharp and clear or cloudy and dull —should be a determinant in the design of building facades including their degree of intricacy and their coloring. These are always a matter of artistic consideration but a careful appraisal of actual conditions can help a decision.

Shape

Every city has a general overall shape. There are several classifications of shape.

Radiocentric: The most frequently found urban form is the radiocentric, a large circle with radial corridors of intense development emanating from the center.

Rectilinear: A variation on radiocentric form is the rectangle, which usually has two corridors of intense development crossing at the center. This variant of the radiocentric form is found in small cities rather than large. It is the radiocentric form with right angles.

Star: A star shape is a radiocentric form with open spaces between the outreaching corridors of development.

Ring: A ring shape is a city built around a large open space. The San Francisco Bay is such an open space for the cities of the bay area. A ring and star may be found in combination, particularly where a loop road is built around the outskirts of an expanding metropolis.

Linear: The linear shape is usually the result of natural topography which restricts growth or the result of a transportation spine. Stalingrad in the Soviet Union was planned as a linear city. The megalopolis on the East Coast has become a vast metropolitan area with a linear configuration.

Branch: The branch form is a linear spine with connecting arms.

Sheet: A vast urban area with little or no articulation.

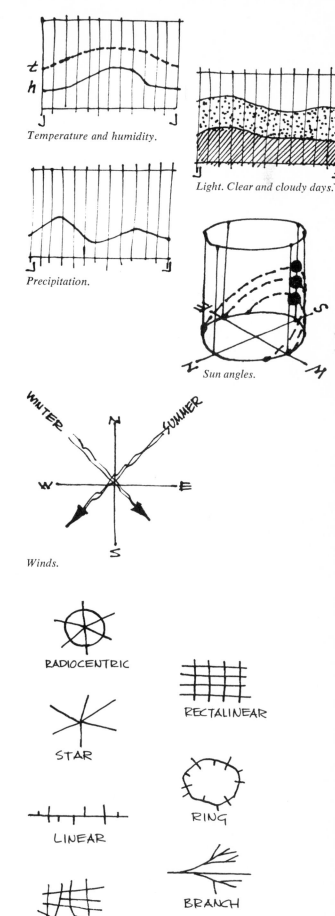

Temperature and humidity.

Light. Clear and cloudy days.

Precipitation.

Sun angles.

Winds.

RADIOCENTRIC

RECTALINEAR

STAR

RING

LINEAR

BRANCH

SHEET

53

ARTICULATED
SHEET

CONSTELLATION

SATELLITE

Articulated Sheet: The articulated sheet form is accented by one or more central clusters and several subclusters.

Constellation: The constellation is a series of nearly equal-size cities in close proximity.

Satellite: The satellite is a constellation of cities around a main center.

These classifications of form have definite implications for a city's function. They have advantages and disadvantages related to circulation, proximity to open space, and articulation of neighborhoods or districts. Further, these classifications may be applied to the city as a whole or to parts of the city, isolated for study, like open spaces or circulation. The open spaces of a city may be linear or branched; or they may form a radiocentric pattern. The circulation networks may likewise be described as one or another shape.

Size and Density

Closely related to a city's shape is its size, a quantitative aspect which can be approached several ways. We first of all think of the physical extent of a city: so many miles across or so many miles from center to outskirts. We can also describe size in terms of the number of inhabitants. The relation between size and density is important, for it indicates the distribution of people and the city's urban massing.

Density can be computed mathematically in several ways: the number of people per square mile; the number of houses per acre or square mile; or the amount of building floor area in a given section. It can also be expressed in terms of automobile population. In 1962 Los Angeles, the country's most auto-oriented city, had 2,220 cars per square mile and Washington, D.C., had 4,100 cars per square mile. This comes as a surprise to most people. One would think that those figures are reversed—which suggests a note of caution in judging aspects of quality from statistics of quantity.

The gross size of a city in terms of its population is also revealing. Classifications according to size alone are quite useful. A basic population of about 200,000 to 300,000 is necessary to support basic public cultural facilities. Amsterdam, Holland, with a population of about a million people, is of the maximum size that can be traversed on foot by a hearty walker, from center to outskirts.

Unless a city is evenly built-up, studies of density are best made on separate sectors of a city. Density figures indicate the relationship between built-up and open land; therefore they can describe almost graphically the image of a suburban residential area or an in-town row-house area. Densities have definite implications for various forms of transportation. In making a visual survey, it is helpful to determine the density of various areas and to relate the density figures to physical patterns of land and buildings and, hence, the visible form of the area.

Pattern, Grain, and Texture

Urban areas have distinct patterns. Usually these are seen in their block and street layouts. Most American cities have rectilinear block and street patterns. On rolling terrain, in outlying areas, curvilinear streets and blocks form another type of pattern. A cul-de-sac system forms a third pattern. Mixtures of open space and built-up space constitute still another pattern. A basic design

Anchorage, Alaska. A rectilinear pattern on flat land in the lap of a mountain range.

54

pattern can be very helpful in planning a residential area or a campus area. An urban pattern is the geometry, regular or irregular, formed by routes, open spaces, and buildings.

Grain is the degree of fineness or coarseness in an urban area. Texture is the degree of mixture of fine and coarse elements. A suburban area with small houses on small plots has a fine grain and a uniform texture. With small houses on varying size lots, it could still have a fine grain but an uneven texture. In the city, large blocks with buildings of varying sizes could be described as having a coarse and an uneven texture. If the buildings are uniform in size, they could be described as having a coarse grain but a uniform texture.

Such distinctions are easily indicated on a sketch map. They are useful in evaluating an area's form and in making decisions about a design treatment for it. For example, a coarse-grained unevenly textured area may be impersonal and repellent and could be treated with some fine scale and unifying design elements. An extensive and uniformly-grained area might well be treated with relieving accents.

Urban Spaces and Open Spaces

Urban shape, pattern, grain, size, density, and texture are primarily aspects of solid form—the building masses of the city. In architecture it is rather helpful to conceive of a building not only as a solid but as spaces modeled by solids. It is also helpful to consider a city this way. The spaces of the city range from the space of the street to the space of a park system and, ultimately, to the vast space in which an entire city exists. It is helpful to think of these spaces as two generic types: formal or "urban spaces," usually molded by building facades and the city's floor; and natural or "open spaces," which represent nature brought into, and around, the city.

Basically an urban space must be distinguished by a predominant characteristic, such as the quality of its enclosure, the quality of its detailed treatment or outfittings, and the activity that occurs in it. An urban space should, ideally, be enclosed by surrounding walls, have a floor which suits its purpose, and have a distinct purpose to serve. If, however, any one of these qualities is sufficiently strong, it alone may establish the sense of urban space.

A group of office buildings may contain a space around a poorly designed plaza or a complex road intersection, the floor space being devoted entirely to traffic. This is an urban space which has a sense of place in the city. It is both a landmark and a traffic node, as well as an office node. An urban square may be beautifully landscaped as a restful urban park, but it may lack entirely the peripheral building facades which are needed for a sense of enclosure. Here we have a poorly enclosed space, but a space nevertheless. In another instance, a particular place in the city may function as the locale of an important activity while possessing neither physical enclosure nor appropriate floor. Times Square in New York is such an example.

In all these examples we have a sense of space. Such spaces are islands or oases in the city. But urban spaces can also be linear corridors. Avenues and streets are linear urban spaces if they are enclosed on two sides or have some element of unifying character —trees or uniform buildings. Corridor spaces are spaces for linear movement. Island or oasis spaces are stopping places. Of course the two can be interconnected. In fact, a spatial structure for an

Fine-grain and uniform texture. Row houses in Philadelphia.

Coarse-grain and uniform texture. Yonkers, New York.

Coarse-grain and uneven texture. Lower Manhattan.

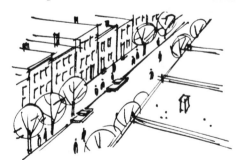

A corridor space.

An enclosed space. The University of Virginia Quadrangle, designed by Thomas Jefferson.

A spatial setting for a key building. A court house square in Missouri.

Urban spaces formed by building masses.

Routes traverse the countryside in many ways.

Routes can approach architecture or cities in many ways.

entire city is exactly such an arrangement at the city's total scale.

Open spaces, being nature brought into the city or open expanses allowed to remain in their original state, cannot be described in quite the same manner used for urban spaces. Their scale is given by the trees, shrubs, rocks, and ground surface rather than their gross width and length. Their appearance is characterized by the sight of natural verdure rather than surrounding buildings. However, a vista of a distant building may accent a particular spot and a bridge or pathway may complement nature's forms. Open spaces in the city have a wide variety of purposes. They are a complement and foil to urban form. They are also reservoirs of land for future use. For an urban design survey, one should study the spaces of the city as an overall structure. In doing this it is helpful to classify spaces according to their actual use and to consider formal urban spaces and the natural open spaces together.

For example, one could start by mapping all the recreational parks in the city, then the interconnected stream parks. The center city urban parks could be mapped, and the main corridor spaces that lead to them or connect them. The nodal spaces as well as the connector spaces all together would form the spatial network. Such a survey would disclose a need for creating spaces in certain areas, a need to improve existing spaces, and some possibilities for connecting all of them. The survey of spaces should disclose a hierarchy of spaces for rest and repose to spaces for meeting and bustling activity.

A city's entire system of public lands—roadways, schools, parks, civic buildings, libraries, etc.—could be thought of as an open space network possibly complemented here and there by public buildings. In an urban design survey we look for the location, quality, and amount of open space in relation to the city's built-up areas.

Routes

Landscape, architecture, and cities are seen as sequences as we travel along routes of movement. Routes of movement affect considerably the appearance of the landscape through which they pass and the architecture and cities which they serve. Routes of movement are a principal determinant of urban form. In making an urban design survey of the routes of a city, one should begin with the area well beyond the city limits, far out in the country. The primary function of a highway is to allow traffic to move, but a large part of that job depends on how clear the route is in relation to the city. This aspect of highway engineering—the "image-ability" of the highway—is a matter of revealing its clarity of form and direction to the user. Too many highways have very poor physical relationships to the areas they serve. Rather than helping to define these areas, they often slash through them, actually acting as a blighting and disintegrating force.

Routes in the Countryside

In the open landscape, existing and proposed routes should be examined and assessed with a view to how well they relate to the natural terrain. How artfully or awkwardly do routes traverse the landscape, revealing its prominent features? Are vistas taken advantage of, or ignored? Some vistas might well be presented with dramatic suddenness; others might be introduced gradually, or be seen only in part.

Are there dull areas which require embellishment? Perhaps the introduction of a curve or rows of trees and shrubs could give more visual interest. Are there obstructions to the enjoyment of the prominent natural features? Does the road itself and its furniture mar the landscape or add beauty to it?

The outlying routes of your city are the first introductions which approaching visitors receive, giving them their major impressions. In making a visual survey of routes, the routes should be charted, noting the character of the terrain and the adaptation of the roads to it, the artful dramatization of landscape features, the quality of added features, the accenting of the route, its faults and possibilities for improvement or correction. Every new route should be examined and designed on these bases as a matter of sound road engineering.

What is the quality of the furnishings of a route?

Approach Routes and Surface Arteries

Approach routes present cities to us. They must satisfy the visual requirement of presenting architecture and cities in their best light, while enabling us to find our destination readily. The two requirements go hand in hand. An approach route must both inform us and conduct us.

The major routes through the city are surface arteries—high-volume traffic streets which carry buses and autos. They can be evaluated according to how they tie into the expressway pattern, their clarity of form, their relation to the cityscape, the shape of the building sites they pass by, and the way they pass through existing districts.

Another consideration is the street furnishings of the major surface streets. Can their design be improved and a program for improving signs and traffic furniture be started? How well do the through arteries tie into the pattern of slower-speed local streets? How well do they tie into major garages and parking areas? How easy is it to find a garage near your destination and to get into and out of it? Most important of all, we must examine the relation between a street's traffic and buildings. A good index is the degree to which street traffic is actually serving the buildings on the street, in contrast to traffic which is merely passing through on the way to some other destination.

Modulating the approach route by screening a portal.

Local Streets

The through arteries serve an intricate network of small streets, along which cars, buses, and delivery trucks stop and go. These streets carry a mixture of vehicles and people. In surveying them, we examine whether vehicular and pedestrian movement are in conflict with each other or aiding one another. Where do they belong together and where not? Are pedestrians forced to wait for long periods of time to cross streets, or are pedestrians free to cross streets anywhere? Is safety achieved by the use of stoplights or by grade-separated pedestrian crossings?

Is the vehicular traffic strictly local, or is much of it through traffic? Can this through traffic be relocated? How can existing small streets be protected against the intrusions of through traffic? What is the dimensional scale of the intimate local streets? How do they relate to the size of their districts? Can these patterns be improved and strengthened?

These comments illustrate that an inquiring survey raises many questions and stimulates many ideas. As we elaborate on the path-district-edge-landmark-node framework, we find that some of them require more attention than others. Degree of emphasis on one

A clear route with its own strength of character aids orientation.

The foreground of a city should reinforce a view, not distract from it.

Recording the visual sequence of a route.

A small town may have only a few districts; a large city, very many.

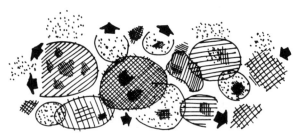

Districts may be expanding or shrinking. They may have clear edges or overlap. They may be uniform or complex.

Surface arteries may reinforce districts or slash them.

Strength of character—degree of identity —varies from one district to another.

Regularly occurring elements give cohesiveness. Small squares or trees.

aspect or another will depend on the size of the city or the urban sector being surveyed. On the large-scale survey of the whole city, its paths, districts, and open spaces, for example, may be the predominant elements. However, at all levels, the examination of the *districts* of the city will probably require the greatest effort.

The Districts of a City

Every city consists of a series of parts which we refer to as districts or enclaves or sectors—or perhaps as quarters, precincts, or areas. They are distinguishable in that they have dominant and pervasive characteristic features. Our mental images of cities consist, to a large extent, of the arrangement of these parts. Some are distinct, some overlap others, some are uniform, some are very complex. Almost all are in a process of change, which further affects their appearance and their size. A very small town has at least several distinguishable areas; a metropolis may have fifty or a hundred.

The pattern of districts is closely related to the pattern of routes. The size of a district may be determined by the nature of the internal routes serving it. A commercial center, for example, can usually be traversed on foot or by a short cab ride. A residential section may often have local community facilities which can be reached on foot, although its gross size may be far beyond the limits of pedestrian traverse.

The districts of a city vary considerably in their strength of character. Districts which do have very strong characters often develop identifying names—Wall Street, Georgetown, Beacon Hill, Greenwich Village, the Loop. Other districts with less assertive character often bear names related to their historic origin—Market Street or Main Street, Foggy Bottom, Silver Spring, Brookline.

American cities, like most cities of the world, reflect their characteristics of culture, growth, and development in an urban nomenclature. In the United States this nomenclature includes: "downtown," the original center; "uptown," the enlargement of the original center; "midtown," an offshoot of both; "Chinatown" and "Harlem," ethnic areas; "the other side of the tracks," characterizing poor residential areas in the shadow of factories; "the waterfront"; "the outskirts."

Basically, there are two things to look for in discerning the various districts of a city: physical form and visible activity. For example, in a commercial center the types of buildings, the signs, the demolition and construction activity, the crowds of rushing people, the cabs and buses, the parking facilities—all these identify the place for us. On the other hand, in a residential area we have the houses, their spacing, the trees, the milk wagons, the parked cars, the children playing, the occasional neighborhood stores and schools. The sum impression of the individual parts and their relationships conveys to us the existence of a particular district of a city—a part in relation to a whole.

Few, if any, cities can be neatly compartmentalized in this way. The most prominent enclave may dissipate visually at its periphery. Most urban enclaves lack outstandingly prominent characteristics. Further, complexity in an urban enclave should not be mistaken for confusion. Urban complexity—the intense intermixture of complementary activities—is one of the major reasons for cities and the spice of urban life. One must also distinguish between uniformity amounting to dullness, and unifying architectural and landscape elements constituting visual cohesiveness, especially in the face of great variety. We should search for answers to the following:

Components: What are the principal component districts of the city? Where do they begin and end? What are their characteristics, physically and as defined by activity? How apparent are they?

Size: What is the size of a district—its shape, density, texture, landmarks, space?

Appearance: Regarding their physical appearance, what are the characteristics of building forms, building density, signs, materials, greenery, topography, route-pattern landmarks? What is the nature of the mixture of different building types?

Activity: Regarding visible activity, what are the principal clues of the activity of an area—the kinds of people, when and how they move about? What are the key visual elements—the things principally seen—which establish the character of a district?

Threats: What are the threats to a district? What external elements, such as a through road, threaten the health and survival of district? How is the district changing? Is it changing its position? Is an edge decaying? Is an edge advancing, perhaps into a peripheral district?

Emergence: Are there latent districts struggling to emerge, such as a new in-town residential section?

Relation: How do all these parts relate to each other and especially to the route patterns of the entire city? Finally, what are the areas in a city that cannot be classified easily, that lack cohesion in form and character? Are some of these targets for urban design work?

The Anatomy of a District

Having distinguished the separate parts of the city, it remains to go one step further and survey the parts individually—to diagnose the districts, the parts which constitute the whole. In surveying the visual aspects of a district or enclave we should be asking:

Form: What is the physical form of the place—form and structure in three dimensions and in broad outline? What is the density and character of the buildings? What is the spacing of the buildings? How does it vary? What is the greenery of the place? How would you describe the paving, the signs, the night lighting? How uniform or how varied is the whole, or sections of it? Can a district be further dissected into meaningful places within it? What are these places like? What are the physical patterns of the place? What are the patterns and the linear and focal points or urban spaces within the district?

Activity: What do people do there? How well does architecture and the district serve people? What are the natural groupings of different activities within the district? How does the activity pattern change according to the time of day, week, or season? How lively are the central city areas? How does the local climate affect life in the areas? What are the detrimental aspects of the place?

Features: What are the features of the district—the major hubs or nodes, landmarks, and vistas? What are the major magnets, generators, and feeders? In a busy center-city area, what are the oases, the places of repose? In a quiet residential section, what are the hubs, the places of community focus?

Paths: What are the principal paths of movement in a district? How are they differentiated? How well do they serve the people

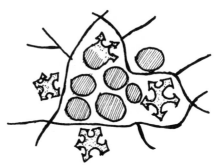

Are there new districts struggling to emerge or old ones struggling to enlarge?

Particular sights characterize particular districts.

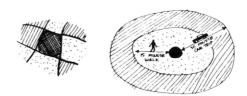

Patterns of routes help define a district; scales of distance help determine its size.

Some districts have unique unifying features.

What are the major vistas of a district?

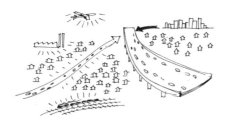

What are the blighting threats to a district?

How lively is the city core at different times of the day and week?

Active areas also need places of repose.

there? How well do they connect to the larger network of paths? Are the actual physical dimensions of the paths adequate or excessive? How do they determine the physical limits of the districts?

Centers: What are the features of a district that serve a symbolic civic role? What are these places like? Are they lively or lifeless? How can they be made lively? Are they integral parts of the areas around them? Are they part of the life of the community, or are they inanimate symbols?

Intrusions: What are the intrusions and detrimental features of a district? What are the blighting features? Here again one must be careful to distinguish between enlivening intermixtures and truly harmful elements. How much traffic can be tolerated on a street before it is impaired? How little before it is dead?

Change: How is the district changing, both in internal character and the adjustment of its periphery to change? Is there a direction of growth? In which direction is the center of gravity moving? Is the edge decaying? How can a decaying edge be invigorated? How can a district be stabilized?

Improvement: Finally, how can the formation of a new district be aided? What are the new elements of the city that are struggling to emerge? Which marginal districts can be protected and improved as part of the complementary complexity of the whole city? How would you analyze and depict the important districts in your city? What strengths do you discern, what weaknesses? What differences do you find between districts? Is there significance in their relative positions and character?

Activity Structure

An examination of districts and nodes reveals that there are certain spots in the city that have characteristic functions. Generally speaking, these districts fall into such categories as places of living, working, shopping, traveling, leisure, recreation, and learning. There is a logic to the location of these activities and there are definite visual results in their deployment and interrelationships. Density, topography, and transportation routes all affect an urban activity structure.

For example, a high-density residential area will have a central shopping cluster which many of its clients can reach on foot. A low-density residential area will more likely be served by a shopping center reached by automobile, its use shared with other low-density areas. Topography can dictate the location of routes and therefore the location of centers and subcenters. Topography can also dictate the location of hospitals and airports.

New transportation patterns can alter an existing urban structure by causing the relocation of facilities which depend on a high degree of public access. Shopping centers on a city's periphery are in large measure a consequence of circumferential expressways. Small neighborhood shopping centers on radial routes are approximate indicators of the centers of residential districts.

A large-scale study of activity structure will reveal the general centers of work and residence and a physical correspondence between activity and district. When tied into an examination of major routes of movement, the relation between activity and circulation access becomes clear. So do points of conflict and areas in transition.

Orientation

If there is logic in the arrangement of a city's anatomy and if that arrangement is visibly evident—articulated—the sense of orientation will be strong. If there is logic but little or no visible articulation, a city can be confusing even to the point where it arouses a high degree of frustration and anxiety, and the feeling of being lost.

Landmarks are a prime aid to orientation. On the overall scale of the city, prominent landmarks are tall verticals like central skyscraper groups, natural features such as rivers or shores, district edges, unique vistas, clear routes which lead to and from a known place, and districts with strong visual characteristics.

Orientation studies should be made on the scale of the whole metropolis as well as small enclaves such as shopping areas, commercial areas, or institutional groupings. Design programs to improve the sense of orientation are particularly important where there are many visitors, as at an airport, or downtown, or at a shopping center. The logic of arrangement and its visible evidence, achieved through design, is the prime device for improving orientation. Signs are a secondary device. Where signs are relied on too heavily, they may add to the confusion or go unheeded.

Orientation studies can be made by the urban design surveyor himself if he is unfamiliar with the area, but they are best made by an interview-map technique.

An old landmark. The Flatiron Building in New York.

Details

The appearance of small details, such as cracks in the pavement, parking meters, tree trunks, doorways, are major factors that characterize an area. They tell us of the area's age, purpose, upkeep, or decay. Signs are an important urban detail. A visual survey should examine the types of signs in an area: for advertising a product; for giving directions; and for marking a building, shop, theater, or hotel.

It is important to ascertain the intended audience of a particular sign. If the signs in a shopping area—store names, goods on sale, etc.—are scaled entirely to the pedestrian shopper, they will usually be appropriate. The signs on a highway should be designed for the fast-moving automobilist. On an expressway, signs other than traffic signs may be confusing, especially when seen together with traffic signs. The signs in a busy commercial area that relate to driving should be designed to be readily seen and to give information quickly and clearly. Confusion with signs arises when an area has too many conflicting uses. The solution to these conflicts lies not so much in trying to control the signs as it does in removing the reasons for their mixture.

A visual survey of urban details should, therefore, include sign studies. More broadly, it includes the quality and conditions of park benches, wastebaskets, streetlamps, pavements, curbs, trees, fences, doorways, shopwindows, etc.—the street furniture and hardware of the city.

Consider the quality of details.

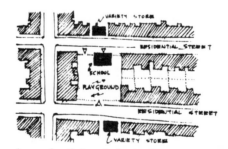

A very detailed analysis of a district can be helpful.

Pedestrian Areas

A large part of the difficulty in our cities arises because we have neglected the pedestrian. Walking will always remain a prime mode of transportation. Some areas of the city depend on it almost entirely as a means of communication and intermovement. Many new shopping centers and college campuses are models of design for pedestrian circulation. Older areas in the city need similar treatment.

We must be careful, however, in concluding that all the trouble

Central areas should be designed to accommodate pedestrians.

Bus terminals below, pedestrian area above. From the plan for Hook, England.

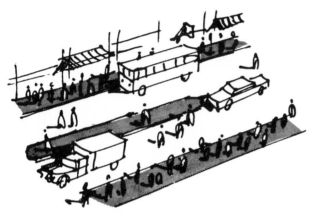

Pedestrian and vehicular circulation can be mixed if traffic is kept slow and islands provided.

In every city the pedestrian should be given primary consideration.

Vista from a tall building. Boston.

comes from the mixture of pedestrians and cars. Many city streets would be lifeless without cars. The problem comes when cars prevent the free flow of pedestrians. It is possible to have both—cars and pedestrians—in busy urban centers if the cars operate at very low speeds and if through traffic is reduced to the utmost.

A good way to check the quality of pedestrian movement in a busy area is first of all to examine the sidewalks for their adequacy—width, paving, condition, protection from rain and hot sun, and sidewalk outfittings such as benches. Second, one should walk through a pedestrian area taking several different paths to locate the main points of interrupted movement, generally speaking the intersections and crossovers. Too many intersections in city centers are designed to allow a maximum flow of traffic and to subjugate the pedestrian to long and annoying waiting periods. An answer to this problem is pedestrian safety islands and reduced-speed traffic. Pedestrian crossings should be frequent and convenient. A shopping street which is difficult to cross cuts the pedestrian-shop contact in half.

The ideal answer to this problem is the separation of cars and people onto different levels, the cars below and the people above. But this is impossible in most cities. In smaller towns it is possible to make the downtown area a pedestrian-oriented zone by providing a convenient bypass road for through traffic and by providing adequate parking garages around the downtown area itself. The essential approach to this problem lies in regarding a downtown area, or any center for that matter, as a stopping place and not a place for through traffic.

In outlying areas the same principles of pedestrian flow can be studied, to examine the pedestrian linkages between neighborhoods and their centers. Children should not have to cross busy streets, and the centers themselves should be at the center of a convenient walking as well as auto-shopping radius.

Vista and Skyline

Every city has a few striking vistas—of it and from it. Approaching Dallas, Texas, from the west, one sees a towering cluster of skyscrapers rising from the plains. The approach to Chicago along Lake Shore Drive is a dramatic urban entrance, as is the approach to New York City from the West Side Highway, and Salt Lake City through a pass in the Rockies. These are the major vistas of the city, and they must be protected from intrusion.

From the city, too, there are always a few dramatic outlooking vistas. Sometimes these vistas are modest, but still of great importance in characterizing the city. The slot views down the sloping streets of San Francisco afford fine vistas of the bay. Similar slot views down the side streets of Richmond, Virginia, afford glimpses of the surrounding countryside across the river.

The views into and out of a city are precious assets. They are an important part of an urban design plan. Some views of the city are in need of legal protection, like the shores of the Potomac across from Mount Vernon. Other views can be complemented by well-poised pieces of architecture, like the buildings of West Point on the palisades of the Hudson River.

An urban design survey should note the major views of the city and different points around the city, particularly points of approach. It should also note the major aspects of vista out of the city from points within. Evaluations should be made of improvements needed in both types of vista.

A further study can be made of a city's skyline. The city's skyline is a physical representation of its facts of life. But a skyline is also a potential work of art. An urban skyline is its collective vista. It is often the single visual phenomenon which embraces the maximum amount of urban form. Every building that alters the urban skyline should be studied for its effects on the overall view. Many skylines can be improved, particularly by adding a small counterpoint tower at an outlying location.

It is interesting to compare the visual effect of a cluster of towers with a single tower. A prominent single tower must be designed as a *chef d'oeuvre* if it is to be admired. It is too much on display to be mediocre. However, a cluster of towers, like a group of statues, can tolerate less distinguished design. If a tower is to be built at a prominent outlying location, it may be helpful to consider double or triple towers rather than a single shaft. Twins or triplets can be more modestly designed, and their profile as an ensemble can then be more assertive than the single shaft. On the other hand, an elegant profile may be easier to achieve with the single shaft.

Another aspect of vista and skyline is night lighting. Few cities are more dramatic as overall views than when seen at night. Twilight heightens the experience for it adds the drama of sunset to the unified view of the three-dimensional forms of the city. Colored beacons and the shafts of searchlights accent the scene with dots and thrusting lines. A new tower, particularly if it stands alone, should be studied from this aspect of appearance. The buildings of central Detroit are interesting examples of just such studies.

The night scene of the city, particularly its lights, is to a large extent within the control of the public. Every city that is building urban highways has a fine opportunity to add a ribbon of unifying illumination to the city's general appearance. The island of Manhattan is one of the most interesting cities to study from this point of view.

Manhattan can be seen on its two long sides and from the south across large expanses of water. It can be seen as a whole composition of masses and lights. At night the highways that ring the city are marked out by their evenly spaced and specially hued dots of highway lighting—ribbons of dotlike lights against a splash of electric stars. Further, Manhattan's several suspension bridges now have their catenary cables strung with lights. On a clear night several bridges can be seen simultaneously. The random lights, the even ribbons, and the gracefully curved bridge lights are one of the wondrous urban sights of the world. This illumination theme could well be used as a model in principle for every city. A visual survey of a city at night could suggest just when and how new lights could be added to achieve a similar composition.

Nonphysical Aspects

There are many nonarchitectural aspects of urban character: the New Year's Day parade in Philadelphia, the Rose Bowl parade in Los Angeles, Mardi Gras in New Orleans. These are a very large part of the image of a city and a large part of its personality. Architects can do much to improve the appearance and urban quality of cities by recognizing them and making better provision for them.

Every city has a history, linking it to its origin, and present in the minds of its population. Visible signs of that history can constitute a major aspect of its appearance. Architectural provision can be made for public ceremonies and events. In new areas the

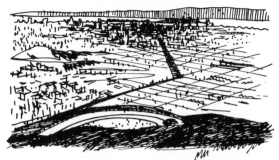
Vista from a mountain. Twin Peaks, San Francisco.

Manhattan at night. The outlined bridges are nocturnal landmarks.

Nonphysical aspects. An annual parade.

A problem area.

inclusion of some visible symbols of the old city's personality give continuity and character to the new. Every city has a particular purpose which should be expressed architecturally. Boston is a center of learning as well as commerce. New York is a center of culture as well as finance. Miami is a center of leisure. Pittsburgh is a center of steel production. Detroit is our automobile manufacturing center.

Problem Areas

As a result of the visual survey, it is helpful to map the problem areas of a city alone. This map would stand as the urban design diagnosis of ills. It would show points of conflict between pedestrians and automobiles, areas with little or no sense of orientation, nondescript or gray areas, ugliness, communities lacking form and definition, areas with confusing signs, confusing circulation elements, incomplete routes, marred vistas, etc. As a diagnosis of ills, such a map would be a direct source of ideas for action programs.

Some Personal Techniques for Surveying

Anyone who attempts a visual survey of his city will undoubtedly develop his own technique and, very likely, a personal vocabulary. In our discussion of this subject we mean primarily to suggest the many different aspects of form that can be examined. But it is also important to be able to link all of the separate aspects of form into a chain of related aspects. One observer, therefore, might want to assemble his vocabulary of form elements into a coherent whole, such as the following: Paths, landmarks, nodes, districts, and edges are the skeletal elements of a city form. On that basic framework stand embellishing characteristics which all together constitute the personality of a city.

Size.

Suppose that we think of urban form in the following way: A city or town is generally thought of in terms of *size*—its population and physical extent. Size is closely linked to *shape*—the physical outline in horizontal plan form and vertical profile or contour. Size and shape are qualified by *pattern*—the underlying geometry of city form. Size, shape, and pattern are further modified by *density*—the intensity of use of land by people and buildings. Density is determined by urban *texture* and *grain*—the degree of homogeneity or heterogeneity of use by people or buildings.

Shape.

We can usually identify the parts of a city by their *dominant visible activities*. Often these activities are complementary, yet sometimes they are conflicting. It is important not to mistake complexity for conflict; complexity is the spice of urban life. The bustling urban centers are *magnets* of the city. People are the *generators* which require magnets around which to rally. *Feeders* are the links and paths which connect the two.

Pattern.

These areas of dominant visible activity exist in sequence as linked *accents*. The periodic occurrence of accents in sequence is rhythm. The disposition in a sequence has, of course, visible manifestations. Thus, accents in a sequence produce a *modulation of visual intensity*—varying degrees of richness of visual experience.

Density and grain.

Our use of the various parts of a city depends upon their degree of accessibility. Demands for accessibility produce channels of flow. Channels of flow vary in intensity, according to the time of day, week, or season, and thereby establish *patterns of movement*. Patterns of movement help define *districts* and act as links.

Visible activity, road signs, store signs, building signs, and symbolic objects are messages to us which convey purpose. They are *clues* to the organization of urban form.

The visual experience of a city is enriched by major *vistas*—views of large portions and major elements of the city, and of contrasting natural scenery. We are highly conscious of the nature of *land surface* (generally thought of as topography). We are aware of going up, going down, and the quality of the surface upon which we move. Natural landscape features form important *borders* or *edges* in cities.

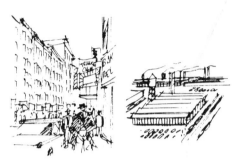

Rhythmic sequence of accents.

Buildings are the immobile *masses* of a city. Arrangements of buildings form *patterns of mass.* Arrangements of buildings also form *urban spaces* which exist as *patterns of channels and reservoirs.* Entrances to a city can be accented by *portals,* the doorways to a city or a district in it. Pauses or relaxations in an intense area are *oases*—places inducing repose. They are passive accents which complement intense activity. Districts in a city are characterized by a pervading *continuity* of use, purpose, and appearance. Some districts are oriented to particular types of people or particular age groups. A fine distinction can even be made between masculine and feminine districts.

Our knowledge of these visible phenomena, the presence of visible landmarks, pattern, shape, etc., imparts a sense of *orientation*—a sense of where we are and where things are in relation to us. A sense of orientation is basic to our understanding, familiarity, and well-being in a city. We are conscious of the *age* of a city and its parts, the newness and oldness in buildings and places. We must avoid the danger of equating oldness with decay, or newness with amenity. In his work, the urban designer must transcend time and relate all parts of the city to each other. A major objective of urban design is to relate different kinds of buildings, regardless of differences in architectural style, age, or use.

Dominant visible activity.

Magnets and generators.

Recording the Results

Visual surveys are most readily recorded as simple maps accompanied by sketches, photographs, and brief notes. The maps can be base maps of the city, at the scale or scales of the survey. The sketches, photographs, and notes can be attached to the maps and the whole study put on display or published as a report. The maps and their notations are best done in a cartoon style and notations of certain features best indicated as a graphic symbol.

Routes of movement can be indicated by arrows, parking garages as a spiral, landmarks as large X's, vistas as sector lines, points of conflict in red, "gray areas" in gray, etc. One map should show the sum total of the general form of the city and its features. The remaining maps should complement this as a series of detailed aspects of the city's form.

A full set of survey maps might include the following:
1. Topography
2. Microclimate—sun, wind, and storm directions
3. Shape
4. Patterns, textures, and grains
5. Routes
6. Districts
7. Landmarks and nodes
8. Open spaces

9. Vistas
10. Magnets, generators, and linkages
11. Special activity centers and overall activity structure
12. Hubs of intense visual experience
13. Strong and weak areas of orientation
14. Sign areas
15. Points of conflict
16. Historic or special districts
17. Community structure
18. Areas for preservation, moderate remodeling, and complete overhaul
19. Places needing clarifying design elements
20. Sketch maps produced by the "man on the street" to discern the urban features and forms prominent in the public's eye.

Each of these maps should be illustrated by a few salient sketches or photos that show exactly what a map symbol represents and also a series of pictures which characterize the area.

Conclusion

Music can be described and discussed with considerable precision and insight because it has a vocabulary and a body of literature. At present painting also enjoys this advantage. So does architecture, to an extent. Up to now the complex modern city has lacked a precise vocabulary for discussing its form and appearance. If we formulate such a vocabulary we will be able to discuss urban form with clarity. We will also be able to discuss the effects of various actions and policies that affect the city in terms of its buildings, parks, streets, and places. Therefore we will be better able to discuss its design.

While developing this language and engaging in conversations on urban form, we must avoid overly abstract terms. Unlike the complexities of modern music or painting, the city is familiar to everyone and can always be described in simple terms. That may be the best test of any vocabulary.

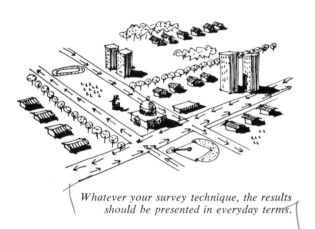

Whatever your survey technique, the results should be presented in everyday terms.

4

Some Basic Principles and Techniques

The moment an architect undertakes the design of a house, certain design requirements implant themselves in his mind's eye. He knows that he will have to consider a particular site with its special conditions, common and private areas for the family, space for storage and circulation, overall form, and mechanical equipment. The moment an architect undertakes to design an office building, a factory, or a school, a similar array of design conditions becomes apparent to him—all, of course, posed by the design problem at hand. The architect then proceeds to ascertain the exact nature of his client's requirements. He defines and digests the design program.

Simultaneously his creativity is activated, as he mentally arranges the elements of the program into a building. Depending on experience and skill—and the complexity of the problem—each architect arrives at a design with more or less difficulty and more or less success. Actually, the creative process of designing a building is not unlike planning a formal dinner, a vacation, or a business venture. First the problem is defined, then its elements are put in an order of importance, then into a context of relationships, and, finally, synthesized into a design that resolves the problem.

The creative design process, the synthesizing operation, can be facilitated by the judicious selection of a *modus operandi*. For ex-

The purpose of urban design is to make the extent of the city comprehensible . . .

. . . to make the city humane . . .

. . . to relate urban forms to natural settings . . .

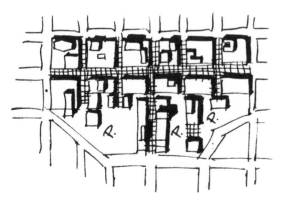

. . . to weave new centers into the urban fabric . . .

ample, in designing a house it is very helpful to think in terms of activity areas, indoors and out. By thinking in terms of activity areas, the architect simultaneously correlates spaces, functions, circulation, site, and orientation.

Another helpful *modus operandi* is to think of the spaces of the building. At other stages one may choose to think in terms of structure or of mechanical equipment. Of course, their positions and relationships are implied in the first conceptual stages. But their careful consideration fills out the design and usually prompts some revisions.

In urban design, likewise, it is helpful to make use of a design *modus operandi*. As in architectural design there are as many of these as there are design types. Again, the design methods are chosen directly in response to the nature of the design problem. Here is where urban design enlarges upon the methods of architectural design. Most buildings are designed to be built at once. Cities are built over long spans of time. A building has one client. A city has a collective client. A building is designed in its every detail, including the furniture—at least so the conscientious architect hopes. The city is designed primarily in skeletal outline—in such a way that its later flesh proves workable and amenable—so hopes the conscientious urban designer. A building is designed according to the state of the building arts, building economy, and technology. A city is designed according to the state of an informed public consciousness, which is reflected in government's general attitude, public desire, and a detailed capital improvements budget.

In sum, the conditions of urban design are: the size of the urban design project; the time span over which realization is contemplated; the degree of activity regarding the area's use; the degree of completeness possible; and the public and private tools at hand.

The size of an urban design project is as much a matter of practicality as obligation. We ought to be designing our cities and their outlying districts at the same scale at which we use them. In fact, we should be designing our entire country as regional areas. We should be designing for time spans and schedules that are practical and coordinated. A long-term plan can be subdivided into a series of smaller coordinated programs. We can design areas whose future use is not completely known by working with a broad framework of reasonable assumptions. Then we can take steps to achieve the essential design elements which will allow all likely future uses to function well. Similarly, we can work with some basic elements of urban design in an area where we cannot be sure of the degree of development. And, finally, the tools of realization —laws, programs, budget, policies, etc.—help us formulate our approach in any one of these circumstances.

In short, the approach to any urban design program lies in understanding clearly the nature of the problem, and, once the problem itself is posed, the *modus operandi* in any particular program becomes apparent. Urban design, like architecture, has a few techniques that facilitate the conceptualizing process. For example, it is very helpful to think in terms of activity areas in urban design in much the same way we would think of them in architectural design. It is also helpful to conceptualize in terms of urban spaces, urban mass, circulation patterns, urban scale, or the process of urban growth and change.

These conceptualizing factors aid not only the design process, but they are, at heart, the components of urban form stated a bit in the abstract. The physical city, after all, is a system of activity areas, spaces, masses, and circulation systems which are constantly undergoing change.

The arrangement of the physical, and thus perceived, form of the city is the objective of urban design. Thus the proper application of the elements of urban design may be thought of as principles—the proper array of urban masses, the proper deployment of urban spaces, the functional deployment and mixture of urban activities, and the functional arrangement of patterns of movement. Above all, the visual and perceived results of any of these efforts must be human in scale.

In urban design there is one constant factor whose importance cannot be overestimated. In any city, in any time, moving at any speed, that factor has given a constancy to the objectives of urban design. That factor is man himself with his abilities to comprehend his surroundings. Every man's actions are conditioned by the twenty-four-hour daily cycle and by his abilities to absorb information and correlate it—his abilities, in short, to make use of the city. Over the ages, men's minds have pondered the sights around them and have slowly advanced toward an understanding of their environment. The concept of space as held by an ancient Greek may seem remarkably naïve when compared to that held by today's astronaut. This slowly enlarging understanding amounts, at present, to an enlarged ability to perceive. However, it has not changed at all the mechanics of seeing nor our basic physiological needs while looking—or while doing anything else, for that matter.

The physiological needs of men are constant. His God-given abilities to see are constant. His abilities to understand and perceive are a slow accumulation built upon his basic mechanical limitations as a human being. One of the contributions of modern artists has been to show us how to perceive more deeply what we see. One of the facts of life in the modern world is that we are given much more to see and to comprehend. We necessarily have to perceive more deeply.

Today it is most important to acknowledge the basic mechanical abilities and physiological needs of man—which is paramount to acknowledging limitations—in a discussion of urban design principles and techinques. For we live in a world of mechanical wonders which, every day, are offered as solutions to all sorts of urban ills.

These innovations can enlarge the scale of our daily world, and so our thoughts about the world in general. But they cannot change our fundamental abilities to see the sizes of things and to feel at ease in a particular urban place. Mechanical innovations, including mechanized cities, can add to our experience and stimulate our perceptive capacities, but they do not eradicate the mechanisms of human physiology.

The proper size of a bedroom has not changed in thousands of years. Neither has the proper size of a door nor the proper size of a community. If cities have become immense, so much more is the need for subdividing them into comprehensible sections. Transportation systems may render the outlying parts of the city more accessible, but communities must remain individual entities whose size and appearance are comprehensible. The physical *fact* of scale must also be *visually* apparent.

When these principles are violated the results are cities without human form, cities without sympathy, cities without pride. Worse still are the effects on the spirit and human sensitivities of its people. At that point the city is a failure. A large reason for en-

. . . to complement the monumental with the mundane . . .

. . . to complement the urbane with nature . . .

. . . to create key focal sites . . .

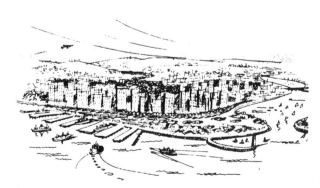
. . . and to make the city a harbor of diversity.

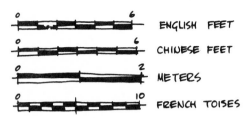

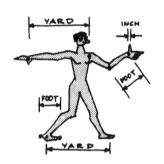

A scale is any convenient system of measurement.

The human body is the basis of the English system of measurement.

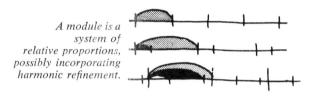

A module is a system of relative proportions, possibly incorporating harmonic refinement.

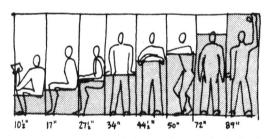

Le Corbusier's "Modulor" made man the basis of a system of measurement and harmonic proportion combined.

Scale in architecture *is a quality that relates* buildings *to our human abilities of comprehension and keeps the component parts in the same context.*

gaging in a nationwide urban design effort today is to rescue many of our cities from just this malady.

To discuss urban design in practice we best begin by considering these principles—principles of scale, of masses, of spaces, of activity areas, as well as several related incidentals. We can then go on to examine how these principles are applied to the many different kinds of urban design programs that we must currently develop—in other words we can outline the different *modi operandi* of urban design and the application of principles therein.

Scale in Urban Design

A scale is any system of measurement convenient to us and whatever it is we are measuring. For example, a quart or a liter is an amount of liquid which we can lift with an outstretched arm across a dinner table—or drink at a normal meal. An acre developed as the amount of land a man could till in one day. Inches, feet, and yards—the English system—started as a convenient method for measuring length. In effect, everyone carried his own ruler around with him. The thumb measured an inch, the forearm measured a foot, and a pace measured a yard. The English system was originally quite suited to buildings. Not only did it match the measurements of the human body, it suited the objects being measured as well. The details of buildings could be conveniently measured in inches, the size of rooms in feet, and outdoor spaces in yards.

Another aspect of measurement is relative proportion or "module." The full extent of a building or a city whose design is based on a module consists of elements occurring at regular intervals. This allows us to imagine the parts which we cannot see. A few readily visible elements, such as towers at key terminations, tell us where things begin or end, and where important hubs are. A module may or may not be related to human dimensions. Gothic architects, like ancient Greek architects, used modules based largely on human dimensions. Renaissance architects, however, used modules sometimes based on abstract proportions alone. The sizes of modern building components are largely based on our technology and modern requirements for handling and shipping. A four-by-eight sheet of plywood is such an example.

In design there is an additional way of measuring which is not as absolute or simple as inches, feet, and yards. It is a matter of keeping things in context with each other and with people. In architecture we call this "scale," and by that we mean that buildings and their components are related harmoniously to each other and to human beings. In urban design we also use the term "scale," meaning that a city and its parts are interrelated and also related to people and their abilities to comprehend their surroundings—to feel "in place" in the environment. While architectural and urban scale, in this context, cannot be defined in specific linear measurement alone, we can refer to several particular dimensions which pervade the sense of scale.

In our period of architecture and urban design there has been one system of measurement which has united both scale and module. That is Le Corbusier's "Modulor," a remarkable system which made man the measure in a system of rhythmic harmony and elegant proportion. It could be applied to a city as well as a building.

The sizes of buildings and cities cannot be limited by human physical capabilities but must be tempered by human capacity for

70

comprehension. The largest buildings and cities can be made to feel appropriate if we instill human scale in their often immense forms. We can also employ the principles of scale to create different impressions of size and importance in a building or in a city scene, creating a sense of grandeur in a tiny plaza or a sense of intimacy in a large square. The range of scale effects extends from intimate scale to our world of normal human scale, and on to a world of monumental scale. Intimate scale is childlike and protective while monumental scale can create two effects: one, ennobling, lifting us above our normal selves to a world of spiritual feeling; the other, overpowering, oppressing, and overwhelming us with crushing grandeur.

Where, precisely, do these feelings stem from, and how, exactly, can we manipulate them? We can begin by understanding the sources of scale in ourselves.

Scale and Human Vision

Our two eyes have a general field of view and a detailed field of view: the former sees general shapes, the latter, details of objects. The general field of view has an irregular conical shape, measuring about 30° up, 45° down, and 65° to each side. The shape of our faces establishes these limits. Our detailed field of vision is a very narrow cone within this larger cone. It measures a very minute angle, approximately equal to a dime or thumbnail held at arm's length. Because our eyes have overlapping cones of view horizontally, we can "see around" verticals placed in our view. An important limitation of our vision is that we cannot see an object which is farther from us than about 3,500 times its size.

How does this determine urban scale? A person who stands 3 to 10 feet from us is in "close" relationship to us, 8 feet being normal conversation distance. In this range we can speak in normal voices and catch the subtleties of speech and facial gesture which constitute conversation. We can distinguish facial expression up to about 40 feet. A great actor, it has been said, can "project" himself through facial expression alone up to about 75 feet. Beyond this distance facial expression must be complemented by body gesture, as in grand opera. We can recognize a friend's face up to about 80 feet. We can discern body gesture up to about 450 feet. This is the maximum distance at which we can distinguish a man from a woman, or can tell whether someone is hailing a cab, selling newspapers, or catching a fly ball. It is also the maximum acceptable viewing distance in athletic stadiums. The dimensions of such places and many of the details of stadium sports are determined by this fact. Finally, we can see people up to 4,000 feet, beyond which they are too small to see at all.

What is the connection between these distances and urban design? It is this: The "intimate" spaces of a city are usually not much greater than 80 feet across; the "urbane" space, no greater than about 450 feet. In monumental vistas greater than 4,000 feet, human beings cease to play a part. Of course, there are instances where these rules are broken, but not without a purposeful design intention and the addition of key design elements that make these instances plausible, all with the aim of producing a unique effect.

Scale and Circulation

Urban scale is also determined by the means we employ for moving around in our cities as well as the way we move between them across the country. We are well described as a nation on

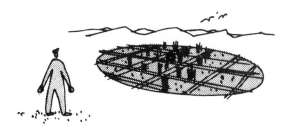

Scale in urban design is a quality that relates cities to our human abilities of comprehension and keeps the component parts in the same context.

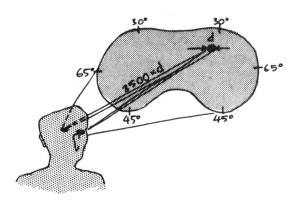

Our general and detailed fields of vision.

Maximum distance for seeing people. 4000'

Maximum distance for discerning action.  450'

Maximum distance for recognizing a face. 80'

 40'

Maximum distance for discerning facial expression.

10'

Range of conversational distance.

3'

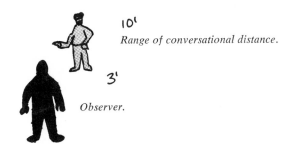

Observer.

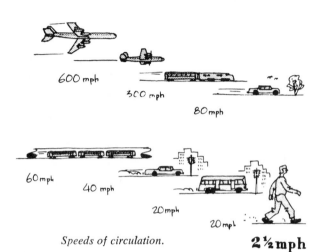

600 mph

300 mph

80 mph

60 mph

40 mph

20 mph

20 mph

2½ mph

Speeds of circulation.

Walking gives us the greatest freedom for intimate contact.

wheels, always on the go. No nation uses as many different kinds of machines for moving as we do. We can fly across the entire country now in four hours; soon we shall be able to go to the moon. Our zest for long-distance travel is more than matched by our need for intercity travel. We insist on maximum accessibility everywhere. Ironically, the more we perfect travel vehicles, and the more distances seem to melt before us, the more troublesome the short distances in the city become. Most of our cities cannot accommodate high-speed vehicles without considerable adjustments, often drastic.

We have been able to expand the scale of travel vastly where we are free, as in the air or in the open countryside, but only to a limited extent where we are bound, as in the city. Still, the scale of the city, as determined by accessibility, has expanded tremendously. At one time determined by horsecars, then by streetcars (which allowed us to have our first modern suburbs), the scale of accessibility in modern cities is now greater than ever before—and so is congestion. In our struggle with traffic congestion we have been considering every possible means of travel. We have contemplated helicopters, only to find that they are of limited use; we plan more subways (rail rapid transit as they are properly called) because they remain one of the best means of mass transit, but we are often unable to build them; we are fascinated by the idea of monorails, the old elevated railway in streamlined form; moving sidewalks have already lost their recent vogue—they were first used extensively in a world's fair before the turn of the century; and shuttle buses may prove to be useful for short trips in the central city—they are up-to-date jitney cabs.

All these modes of transportation help determine the movement or circulation scale of the city, that is, the extent of the city which is readily accessible to use. But there is one very basic and ancient mode of transport which is too often disregarded; it still remains one of the best systems and one of the essential determinants of urban scale—our own legs. As we walk around, we are completely free to stop, turn around, go faster or slower, go to the left or right, or change our pace—in short, to enjoy the greatest freedom of choice and degree of contact with the people and places we are passing by. Every mechanical device for moving has limitations on such contact. Foot travel has the least. Mechanical devices can extend the scale of accessibility, but the maximum contact with a place, so essential to every human settlement, is achieved by walking.

The major limitations on walking scale are distance and speed; most people in performing their routine tasks are willing to walk only about a half-mile, and walking speed averages only about 2½ miles an hour. This scale determines the size of major groupings or hubs in a city. The central shopping areas are only as extensive as this walking scale allows, although they may also function as linked centers. The Wall Street area of New York as well as its several shopping enclaves, Disneyland and Farmers' Market in Los Angeles, large airport terminals, and suburban shopping centers—all are subject to this basic fact of urban scale.

If travel radii of the different means of circulation are plotted, using downtown areas as centers, their effects are apparent. Even the largest metropolis is seen as a series of pedestrian enclaves—shopping centers, downtown hubs, and neighborhoods. Superimposed on the pedestrian enclaves, the public transportation radii and the automobile radii reveal much larger travel zones but they are closely linked to the pedestrian zones. Any mechanical means of transportation can link the pedestrian zones and make them more accessible to more and more people—but the pedestrian zone itself remains the basic enclave of urban design.

Mechanical transportation systems—cars, buses, subway, monorail, helicopter, etc.—can also obscure the distinctions between the pedestrian nodes and enclaves. Further, they can destroy the qualities that make the enclave amenable to the pedestrian. On the other hand, mechanical transportation systems can be designed to reinforce and even create pedestrian enclaves. A subway station can be located right in the center of a shopping area, thus supporting the center's function by bringing people to a people-oriented place. A car parking plan can carefully locate garages on the periphery of a central area, bringing a pedestrian flow between periphery and center. The roads leading to the parking garages, being traffic feeders, can be designed to define the center in its surroundings.

Scale in Neighboring Buildings and Spaces

Buildings and spaces not only have to be in scale with people, they have to be in scale with each other. A gigantic tower building in the midst of intimate row houses is out of scale. A huge plaza bordered by tiny buildings is out of scale. Generally we refer to the offender in such a situation as being "out of keeping." This applies to the design treatment of a facade as well as a building's materials, color, bulk, and siting.

This is not to say that differences are bad per se. If a change in urban pace occurs, it is an accent in the city's panorama. Such accents should be intentional and not haphazard, particularly where urban grain is fairly uniform. A small church amidst tall skyscrapers can give a needed element of scale. Scale is both a matter of compatibility and human measure.

Scale and Neighborhood Size

A basic unit of urban design is the neighborhood. There has been considerable debate as to the size of an ideal neighborhood, indeed ideal urban size. The English New Town planners have been pondering the question of size ever since Howard proposed the garden city. Recently the question was reexamined—in the design of an American town. In the planning of the new town of Columbia between Washington and Baltimore, several consultants were asked to advise on appropriate neighborhood size. These consultants represented the fields of education, sociology, psychology, health, housing, recreation, economics, etc. Their advice was meshed into a plan of neighborhoods, villages, and the whole town. A neighborhood would consist of 300 to 500 families (1,200 to 2,000 people). Five neighborhoods would form a village. The villages would consist of 3,000 to 5,000 families (12,000 to 20,000 people). The entire town, as proposed, would have an eventual population of 125,000.

The neighborhood is a convenient project size and can support a small neighborhood center—shopping, nursery, and possibly elementary school. A village can support a larger village shopping center, schools, churches, clubs, etc. Of course there are several variations possible in this general theme of design. But the point is that neighborhoods and villages can be taken as a module for urban design, not only in new towns and new communities but in old ones as well.

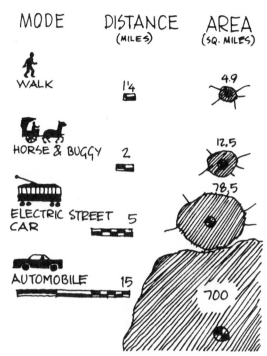

Thirty-minute travel distances and city area transversable.

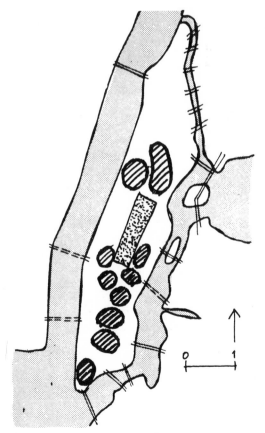

Many of the enclaves of Manhattan are within pedestrian scale.

Intimate scale.

Urban scale.

Monumental scale.

Familiar objects—poles, people, and cars—lend a sense of scale.

Scale and people's ages and habits.

Swollen masses of the city's residential areas can be given needed articulation as well as focus by delineating them as neighborhood, villages, communities, etc. Modern transportation would connect them all—where previously it has caused much of the present formlessness. The focal points could be the common neighborhood facilities, including places of work. The delineation could be park-like open spaces and urban freeways.

Similarly, the downtown enclaves of the city could be delineated by applying the principles of pedestrian scale to them, by determining their anchor points, and by a conscious policy of garage and arterial traffic street design together with a plan for public transportation.

Scale and Parameters

Another essential element of urban scale is the familiar objects whose size we have become accustomed to. A building or a monument which we know very well, cars, trees, people in the distance, light poles, windows, an archway, a bridge—all these are objects whose sizes we refer to when we judge the sizes of things near them. They may be conveniently termed "parameters," objects whose familiar size furnishes a scale of reference for the objects near them.

Scale: Time, Convenience, Age, and Habit

Our sense of urban scale varies according to our ages and habits. The world of a child is his home, yard, the houses and yards of his playmates, his school and, somewhere off in the world beyond, daddy's office and grandma's house. As a child grows, his world enlarges and the separate parts are linked together. In their years of young adulthood, people venture out to explore new things, new places, and new people, and thus the scale of their world enlarges. In the years of early parenthood, it very likely contracts to a world of home, work, friends, and recreation. In the years of fuller maturity, activities are tempered by more sophisticated choice.

Our sense of urban scale also varies according to what we are accustomed to. Chicago or Detroit are at first quite awesome for most people, but in time they become accustomed to them. People are quite adaptable, and urban scale is as much a matter of detailed treatment of the city as it is a matter of its overall size. Let us now see how these aspects of urban scale are applicable to the design of urban spaces, masses, activity areas, and circulation.

Urban Space

Urban spaces, like architectural spaces, may be self-contained islands, unrelated to neighboring spaces, or may be interconnected and best appreciated by moving from one to another. They may be purposefully designed to display their linkage, to highlight a special building in the space, or to suggest an important direction of movement.

Urban as well as architectural spaces may be conveniently pictured as rooms and corridors of space, or perhaps somewhat abstractly, as channels and reservoirs of space. Urban and architectural spaces form a hierarchy of spatial types, based on their size. In urban design this hierarchy ranges from the scale of small, intimate court spaces on to grand urban spaces and culminating in the vast space of nature in which the city is set.

74

The categories of urban space derive from the distance scale of human vision. Thus urban spaces up to 80 feet induce an intimate feeling. Within this distance we can still distinguish a human face. It is the scale of our fine old residential streets. Grand urban spaces cannot exceed 450 feet as a maximum without seeming to be too large—unless some intermediary elements are introduced to sustain the character of the place. Few grand avenues and great urban plazas exceed this distance. Of course, great spaces or vistas can function as foreground to a major monument. Beyond 4,000 feet, when people are no longer visible, the vista or monumental setting functions without visual reference to the human figure.

A fundamental requirement of urban space is actual physical enclosure or its strong articulation by urban forms. Enclosed urban space, like the space in a bowl or a tube, is formed by material surfaces. But just how much enclosure is necessary? In a plaza we must be sufficiently enclosed on all sides so that our attention focuses on the space as an entity. On an avenue the enclosure can exist on only two sides, but it must be sufficient to hold our attention to it as a channel of space.

As we move about in the city we move our heads and eyes this way or that, according to what attracts us. Nevertheless our normal frontal field of view, the view we see when we look straight ahead, furnishes us with a major impression of the space we are in. Our normal frontal field of view in a space determines the degree of enclosure—the sense of space—which we feel. The feeling of enclosure, whether channel or reservoir, is largely determined by the relation of viewing distance to building height as seen by our normal frontal field of view.

When a facade height equals the distance we stand from a building (a 1 to 1 relationship) the cornice is at a 45° angle from the line of our forward horizontal sight. Since the building is considerably higher than the upper limit of our field of forward view (30°), we feel well enclosed. When a facade height equals one-half the distance we stand from a building (1 to 2) it coincides with the 30° upper limit of our normal view. This is the threshold of distraction, the lower limit for creating a feeling of enclosure. When facade height equals one-third our distance from the building (1 to 3), we see the top at about an 18° angle. At this proportion we perceive the prominent objects beyond the space as much as we do the space itself. When the facade height is one-fourth our distance away from the building (1 to 4) we see the top at a 14° angle, and the space loses its containing quality and peripheral facades function more as edges. The sense of space is all but lost, and we are left instead with a sense of place.

Renaissance architects thus derived a simple rule of thumb for the length-to-width proportions of an urban plaza: where facade height is uniform, length-to-width proportions cannot exceed 1 to 3; if they do, the end walls are too low and the space "leaks out." Spatial enclosure is also a matter of continuity of wall surface: the role of building facades must be subservient to the spaces they form. Spatial enclosure is weakened by too many gaps in building walls, drastic variations among the facades, and abrupt changes in cornice line.

These principles must serve as starting points. Some urban spaces might well be designed to be only partially enclosed—an alcove along a busy street, for example. Rockefeller Center in New York City is a small space relative to the corporate giants which center on it. Its corners are open prisms of light and air, affording

A channel of urban space.

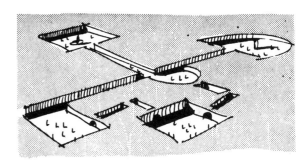

Connected urban space.

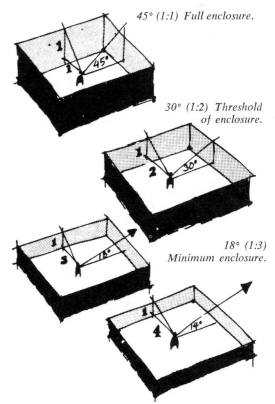

45° (1:1) Full enclosure.

30° (1:2) Threshold of enclosure.

18° (1:3) Minimum enclosure.

14° (1:4) Loss of enclosure.

75

Park or "open" space.

Universal space.

*Stonehenge and a New England village common—
a sense of space or* place?

*The components of urban mass—buildings,
trees, walls, statues, etc.*

Appearance depends largely on light conditions.

views to the city beyond. The gaps between the prisms, in this instance, relieve what would otherwise be an overpowering oppressiveness because of the buildings towering above.

Still, it is simplicity of form and detail which underlies the design of a successful urban space. Imagine, for example, an urban space seen under conditions of bright light; the details are more apparent than the space as a whole. In the evening or on a dull, cloudy day, when there is a dim light, we notice sharp features less and thus the space more.

The advantage of thinking in terms of urban space is that we can embrace a myriad of urban elements as an entity rendering these elements more distinctive and valuable than they are alone. Attention to urban space can be extended to the design of a pattern of spaces on a city-wide scale—to the formation of a network of channels and reservoirs which knit separate districts into a fabric intelligible to its users. In planning a spatial structure for a city we must be careful to plan intimate and grand spaces for the purposes they serve. Too many large squares and broad avenues may not be appropriate and can sever a district as easily as they can unify it. For most cities, one major public square suffices, if there are also many smaller ones to serve less lofty functions. Too many grand spaces dissipate the sense of occasion they attempt to proclaim.

Open space is another type of space, and one which we should be very careful to understand. Open space generally describes parklike areas of greenery in or near the city. It is often confused with urban space, which is a formal focus of urban activity. Open space is informal, natural, and parklike. It relieves the harshness of urban form while complementing it.

Urban spaces are the products of cities, specifically the juxtaposition of buildings. The larger spaces of nature in which cities sit cannot be enclosed by urban form, but can nonetheless be urban spaces in the sense that they are qualified by the urban presence. The city, as a whole form, accents this vast space.

Urban Mass

The ground surface, buildings, and objects in space constitute the second basic element of urban design: urban mass. We can arrange these elements to form urban space and to shape urban activity patterns, on both large and small scales.

Our eyes and light conditions govern the way we see masses. From a viewing distance which equals the height of a building or object (the 45° angle or 1 to 1 relationship) we tend to notice details more than the whole facade or object; at the 30° angle or 1 to 2 relationship, we tend to see the object as a whole composition, together with its details; at the 18° angle or 1 to 3 relationship, we tend to see the object in relation to surrounding objects; and at the 14° angle or the 1 to 4 relationship, we tend to see the object as a forward edge in an overall scene.

Under conditions of bright, clear sunlight the individual parts of objects stand out; as light diminishes, in the evening or on dull, cloudy days, the whole composition presents itself to our view. Vigorously sculptured objects are best seen in even light such as shadow light or northern light, their delicate outlines requiring less light contrast. Thus, southern facades may be vigorously articulated while northern facades may be more successful if delicately articulated.

Dark objects seen against light backgrounds recede, while light objects seen against dark backgrounds advance visually. Warm-hued buildings also advance while cool-hued buildings recede and seem less solid. Warm-hued buildings in cool light, and cool-hued buildings in warm light, will appear awkwardly discolored. Rough surfaces seem thick; smooth surfaces, thin. Reflections are darker and less colorful than the objects themselves. Our depth perception on clear, bright days comes largely from seeing the sizes of familiar objects in relation to each other. On dull, cloudy days depth is conveyed by varying degrees of haze which increase with distance.

Far and near scale in a building group.

The ground, or "floorscape," is the platform of the city. Ground surface can be textured to aid fast walking or induce slow walking. In a large, open plaza the surface can be designed to subdivide the floor into more intimate pieces; a small vertical edge with a slight lip so that it always casts a visible shadow will "scale down" the expanse.

Surface contour should also be treated as an important design element. In a plaza or on a long avenue a bowl-shaped surface is more visible than a flat surface, and so we feel greater familiarity with the place, simply because we can see more of it. Terracing on slopes can be useful for establishing different degrees of importance; however, for buildings which profess no lofty function a gradual incline of small steps is more appropriate. Usually, ascent is conducive to feelings of spiritual elation, and descent, to security or relaxation.

The surface of St. Peter's Square is bowl-shaped.

We furnish our cities with all sorts of objects which we must regard as the city's interior decoration. By recognizing them for their esthetic value as well as their practical value, they could assume a far richer role. Sculpture itself can highlight a plaza, giving it a focal point. A colonnade linking different kinds of buildings around the plaza or along a street can soften the differences between them and lend unity to the buildings. A row of regular trees can do the same for an avenue.

In contrast, a free disposition of trees can act as a pleasant foil to an overly rigid array of buildings, injecting an element of relaxation in an area of harsh regularity. A screen of columns can act as a fine transition device between two different kinds of spaces, or two large spaces requiring a division which does not sever them. A vista can be framed with flanking foreground objects such as pylons, or by an arch which centers the vista and acts as a strong foreground reference.

The surface of Red Square is humped.

Individual buildings themselves may play a very great role in the total visual cityscape. A tower or dome can be a fine vista termination, either at the end of a street or on the skyline. Objects of much smaller scale can also serve this purpose, for if their profile is unique and if they are located so as to be readily seen in silhouette, they can be effective at great distances.

A building projecting into a space.

Through the skillful design of building masses we can create successful urban spaces of almost any shape. The essentials of a successful urban space are its proportions, its floor and walls, and the activity which enlivens it. A long plaza can have prominent focal buildings at its ends, as well as a sculpture group in the center; a very large plaza can act as a setting for a major building; an L-shaped plaza can turn about a tower building at the corner. An overly broad street can be brought into scale by inserting small buildings in the center of the street, which subdivide the space without cutting it in two.

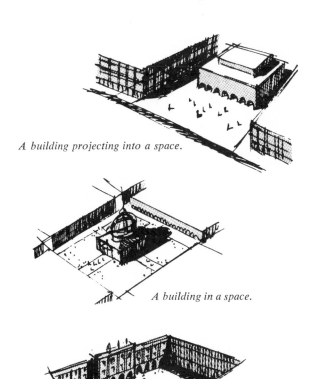

A building in a space.

A building on a space.

45° (1:1)
The distance relation for seeing facade details.

30° (1:2)
The distance relation for seeing the whole facade and its details simultaneously.

18° (1:3)
The threshold of distraction for distant vistas.

14° (1:4)
The facade functions as an edge to a distant view.

Colonial Richmond, Virginia. A harbor of diversity.

Washington, D.C. Diversity precluded.

Facade articulation can bring large buildings down to human scale, and give small ones an air of importance. A long facade can be subdivided periodically into more digestible elements. A very small facade can be more assertive by exaggerating the sizes of its component parts.

Groups of buildings are also seen as clusters, ensembles whose juxtaposed facades convey the excitement, flourish, and vitality of the city. Nearly every new building should be treated as a partner in the whole scene. We would do well to consider the appearance of each new building from the actual vantage points from which they will be seen.

In the less dense periphery of the city, buildings are seen more as individual objects than as facades. In a sense, they then become spatial parameters rather than formers of space. But where we have the opportunity to design several of them as a group, we can treat them primarily as a "mass cluster" to be seen from afar and then as a group forming a space, to be used close at hand.

Rockefeller Center and the Empire State Building, for example, are easily discerned from many parts of New York City. In Rockefeller Center we find buildings clustered about a relatively small space filled with people. We never lose contact with the whole group. The Empire State Building, however, a landmark from afar, disappears as we approach. Its base lacks the distinction necessary for close-by recognition, which could have been accomplished by even a "postage stamp" plaza in front of it.

A whole city can be regarded as a large form, which lends itself to design—the center, dense and close, is the harbor for enclosed urban spaces; the periphery, loose and scattered, is the setting for individual works articulating the land surface and the vast space of nature which envelops it.

Urban Activity and Circulation

Nothing is more disappointing in a work of civic improvement than to find that the results of our efforts are dull and lifeless, devoid of human presence and activity. No works are more deserving of criticism, for their lack of vitality stems from the fact that they discourage people from using them.

While it may seem presumptuous to think that patterns of urban life can be shaped, that is exactly what we are doing every time we make major changes in our cities. The arrangement of urban activities is a basic element of urban design. So important is it that we often recall a particular city we have visited largely by recalling the experiences we had there. The key to the design of patterns of activity in a city is intelligent disposition of major activies in relation to routes of movement, while trying to achieve maximum diversity in each area itself. The city is basically a place of exchange, and its capacity to effect exchange depends on the proximity of complementary elements, the separation of mutually harmful elements and, above all, the location of major functional groups in the most advantageous places from the point of view of transportation access.

Our early cities were good examples of this. The harbor was the center of the city and around it grew the houses of commerce and finance. Government buildings and public halls were sometimes built above market buildings, and hotels developed near the places of commerce. Outlying shorelines became the locale of shipbuilding and repair. Remote downwind sites near water were good for odoriferous tanneries. High grounds were best for residences, churches, and lookout towers.

As Henry Churchill observed, our colonial towns differed from medieval towns in that ours were generally not contained by fortifications. Still we found compelling reason to build our towns tightly, to put everything in convenient proximity. Our towns were small; they could easily be traversed on foot and nature was close at hand. The lesson to be learned from such towns is the natural and intelligent disposition of urban activities in complementary proximity, the grouping of interdependent portions, and separation of conflicting ones. In small towns this was relatively easy to accomplish. In our time this principle remains the same, but the complexity of our own problems of arranging city form is vastly greater. Still we can and must practice the art of arranging urban activities on a small, as well as an extensive, urban scale.

On a small scale, as in an urban plaza, we can seek to locate diverse types of buildings, so that the square is animated by people moving about in the plaza. We must remember that a large institutional or governmental office building has minimum inflow and outflow of personnel during the day, while a general-purpose rental office building has much more. Hence urban areas consisting solely of large single-use office buildings are often lifeless, while areas of multiple-use office buildings are usually the opposite. The principle of multiple use is well extended to squares. For besides functioning as daily crossroads and meeting places, they may also serve as constant reminders of traditional occasions or ceremonies—often, this alone justifies their existence. The paths of flow of people in a city are clear to most observers. They can be quantified by actual pedestrian counts. Pedestrian avenues and plazas can accommodate these flows. Paths of flow largely determine the kinds of little shops and conveniences that complement the larger and anchor-like functional nodes of the city. Of course the larger anchor nodes attract circulation and may cause the creation of circulation routes. Or the anchor itself may be located to take advantage of an existing but underused route.

The central city, once the harbor of a panorama of life even fuller than that of the colonial town, must be invigorated to the state of fuller urban function it once had. Too often do we see our central cities ringed with fields of parked cars, isolated by this encirclement of storage when they should be fortified by an encirclement of directly complementary live use. These central areas have come to depend on automobiles as a principal means of access to them. The more people they serve, the more auto access they must provide. That access is accompanied by increased demand for parking with the result that as such facilities grow, more in-town residences are squeezed out. An increased in-town residential population generates pressure for even more facilities in the center, and these residents enliven the centers by their presence.

San Francisco is blessed by a circumstance of topography which has encouraged close-in residences throughout the city's history. The hills of the city, too steep and inaccessible for commercial buildings, are well suited to residential use. Thus an in-town population has prevailed, and with it, central city vitality.

The activity patterns of large cities exist as a series of hubs, many of them determined in their geographical extent by our ability to walk from one part to another. Some of these hubs are of ancient origin and have individual characteristics of change. Financial centers in cities do not migrate. Other centers were the product

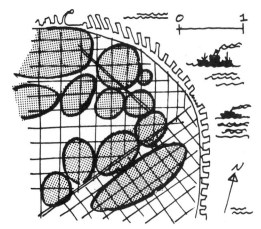

San Francisco's variety of enclaves enliven each other.

Society Hill, Philadelphia, designed by I. M. Pei. Diversity in building design and age.

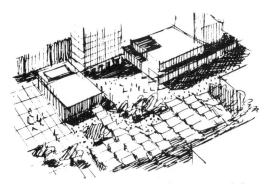

Student Center, University of California, Berkeley, designed by DeMars and Reay. Diversity with design.

Queen's Boulevard, New York City. Diversity in chaos.

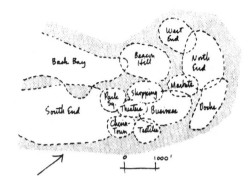

Variable boundaries of districts in central Boston, from a drawing of Kevin Lynch's Image of the City.

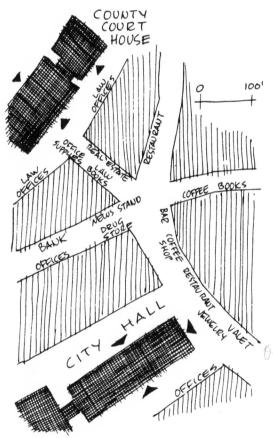

In Boston two magnets, the City Hall and County Court House, generated a myriad of complementary facilities. This is the site of the new Government Center.

of an original convenience that no longer exists, such as former dependence on ship or rail transport which was replaced by truck transport. Shopping areas do migrate, the "100% corner" usually moving in the direction of "uptown," the modern outgrowth of the old downtown. Residential areas can migrate, too, largely depending on their quality and adaptability to changing modes of living. Some changes in city activity can be opportunities for new growth. An obsolete wharf area can become an excellent in-town residential area or institutional campus.

The different areas of a city, whether new or old, require varying degrees of intermixture with complementary facilities in order to function well. Because there have been severe abuses in the juxtaposition of incompatible elements in the city, the term "mixed-use" developed, a term used to describe these abuses but which has led in some cases to the opposite extreme of wholesale functional segregation. Mixed-use, or better still, diversity and intensity of use, does not mean overcrowding of facilities, but their complementary proximity. It does not mean that there is no relief from the bustle of the city but, on the contrary, that near the center we can enjoy the relief of a restful park—simply another complementary use—in which there should be places for gathering.

Urban design on the small scale of a plaza or group of buildings consists in accommodating a variety of functions. As the scale of design increases, the complexity increases too, but the objective is the same. On the scale of the city the design of urban functions is a matter of allocating the major hubs of activity to the most desirable places functionally, intermixing them with other facilities that complete them, and finally linking all of these to each other.

The principles of design of urban scale, urban space, urban masses, urban activity areas, and urban circulation patterns form a basic palette for urban design—they are the primary colors of the urban design palette. Their application as an urban design *modus operandi* is supplemented by other principles and techniques—the intermediary colors of the urban design palette. The appropriate use of both the primary and intermediary "colors" becomes apparent when different urban design programs are examined, taking them in order of magnitude.

The Region and Subregion

Henry Churchill has commented in his book, *The City Is the People*, that most American towns would improve themselves given a healthy economy. He was reflecting Benton MacKaye's regional outlook in which each town, however small, depends for its well-being on the health of its region—geographic and economic. In the 1930s the National Resources Planning Board delineated such regions for the entire country and proceeded to study them along the lines that Henry Wright used in his classic study of New York State. Such regional outlooks relate rural to metropolitan areas and circulation networks to points of collection, distribution, and exchange. They relate natural resources to centers where these resources are transformed and distributed.

A revision of the NRPB regional plan would consider regional cities as well as regional areas—the megalopolis on the East Coast, the Seattle-Tacoma megalopolis in the Pacific Northwest, the San Diego–Los Angeles region in California. These totally urbanized regions are additional developments to the NRPB rural-urban regions, not a displacement of them. While they are best understood as results of our changing economy, increased industrial efficiency, and improved communications, they are also physical areas and should be so designed.

The basic urban design palette would be applied at a scale such as a regional spatial network, a regional transportation network, and a pattern of urbanized areas of different size. The uses of the area would be studied in relation to land uses and needs. Recreation areas would be plotted in relation to radii of accessibility around metropolitan areas and in relation to highway networks. Water resources and flows would be studied as part of the region's natural resources situation.

The RPA work of the twenties and the NRPB work of the thirties remain the classical examples of such regional studies. Specifically, they included the plan for the State of New York by Henry Wright, the water resources plan for Massachusetts by Benton MacKaye, TVA, the Columbia River development, and the Colorado River proposals. More recently the State of Wisconsin prepared a plan called *Recreation in Wisconsin* in which open space, circulation routes, and urbanized areas were examined together. Included in their study were suggestions as to methods for completing a visual survey of the state and for preliminary assessment of appropriate open space uses.

A state must be regarded as a political fact of life within a physical region, but it can be subdivided for practical study purposes into valley areas for design purposes and county areas for political and administrative purposes. In regional planning one must always work with physical facts as the prime regional determinants and with political subdivisions as administrative zones. The two are, obviously, not always well related.

The tools for realizing a regional plan are a regional open space network coupled with the regional transportation system—these being matters for regional control and decision. A regional zoning system could be developed as a means of effectuating a regional plan.

The Metropolis

The elements of urban design at the metropolitan scale are open space, built-up areas, a transportation network, and the various urban subdivisions.

The open spaces are a weave of parks, rivers, shorelines, bird sanctuaries, palisades, urban parks, etc.—all intertwined with the metropolitan urban fabric. The urban fabric itself, the built-up city, is a series of communities and community hubs needing definition and refinement so as to be distinct and recognizable parts of a whole.

Examples of this are the regional plans for the New York metropolitan area, the Pennsylvania–New Jersey–Delaware (Penjerdel) studies, and the regional plans for Chicago (Northeast Illinois Regional Planning Council). Such plans are metropolitan plans in a regional context.

A very good example of this type of planning in physical terms is the so-called finger or open space plan for Copenhagen. It is a study of the needs of that metropolis in the foreseeable future and the study of different land areas to ascertain their best possible uses. Further, there is an examination of the various types of circulation and a discussion of their implications on the central city and outlying communities. The result is a plan for all types of circulation systems, open space, and corridors of urban growth.

The major geographic regions of the U.S.

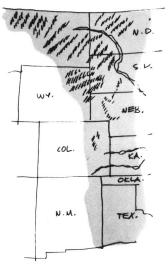

Rivers, mountains, plains, and state lines in the Great Plains Region.

The Copenhagen finger and open space plan will combine urban corridors with natural open space.

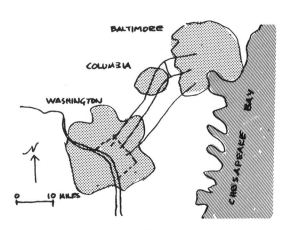

Concept. "Metrotowns" around Baltimore by Rogers, Taliaferro, Kostritsky, and Lamb.

Location of Columbia. A 15,200-acre site with 3,469 acres of permanent open space; 1,674 acres for industry and primary employment; 6,739 acres for residential; 345 acres for commercial use; 1,780 acres miscellaneous; 600 acres of water in five lakes. Total population will be 110,000.

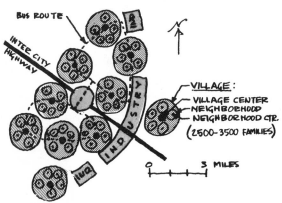

Columbia, Maryland. A satellite town between Washington, D.C., and Baltimore planned as neighborhood and village clusters by Community Research and Development Inc.

Metropolitan Sectors

The metropolis must be articulated into workable component parts with physical terminations and visible structure. Most metropolitan areas are composed politically of counties and a central city. Variations on this are the older cities which include townships which are still independent, or cities which consist of annexed townships and counties. These divisions are valid, in many cases, as the subdivisions of the metropolis. Physical planning, at this scale, is a matter of providing a substructure for this subdivision.

But the components themselves can be designed in various ways. Existing peripheral communities—former crossroad villages—are usually bisected at their very center by the old crossroads which eventually became major arteries. To work as real centers they must be reformed physically. Through traffic must be removed so that they can function as stopping places. A pedestrian and local circulation system must be inserted. These districts can be further subdivided as villages, their nuclei being local schools, churches, and shopping areas.

Here again the design palette is open space, urban mass, circulation and activity areas—directed toward the creation of viable form at a neighborhood scale.

Newly forming communities can be built as clustered villages adding up to larger neighborhoods—the villages focusing on their modest central facilities, the neighborhoods on their larger communal facilities. In such areas political and administrative jurisdictions must have plans for such developments in general outline terms; through their zoning ordinances or through more specific plans.

Where development potential warrants it, new towns can be built as satellites to existing urban centers. Nearly a hundred such efforts are underway throughout the country as of this writing. Their design components are the house cluster or village, the clusters or villages adding up to neighborhoods, and the neighborhoods adding up to the whole town. A central area and areas of specialized purpose complete the components. Form can be articulated by carefully placed verticals on the skyline. Pattern and layout are a matter of relating the components to an open space and circulation network.

Two good examples of this approach are at the outskirts of Baltimore—the proposed new town of Columbia and the plan for the Green Springs and Worthington Valleys. The Columbia plan is precisely the village-neighborhood-town concept. The "Valleys" plan proposes to preserve a handsome valley area while building house clusters on the wooded slopes and plateaus of its hills. Columbia will be a new town. The Valleys will be a series of residential villages less distinct than a whole town but rather a series of settlements in a large suburban context. It is noteworthy that the Valleys plan would accommodate even more houses than the area developed with typical tract subdivision. Of course the clustering of houses would mean fewer roads and shorter utility lines, not to mention the retention of the valley floors as scenic assets. In some cases the valley floors would remain in productive agricultural use.

A program for articulating neighborhoods in an existing urban area involves several additional techniques. Obviously it is more complicated because of problems in landownership, public and private rights, and, not the least, suspicion and unfamiliarity with

82

past experience. Essentially what is involved is a full-scale and clearly understood program for creating new neighborhoods out of old ones that exist in muddled form, coupled with a program for supplying more housing than is being razed under a slum clearance operation. From a design standpoint the program would seek to create new centers, define comprehensible neighborhoods, provide needed open spaces, and reshape the local traffic pattern.

In the early 1950s a plan for doing just this was prepared for Washington, D.C., by James Rouse and Nathaniel Keith. The plan was aptly called *No Slums in Ten Years*. A present-day revision might enlarge its recommendations to include the creation of satellite towns but its general approach is entirely valid. The approach was to transform the amorphous residential areas of the city into a well-related pattern of clearly defined neighborhoods. Slum clearance would be preceded by the creation of new housing. A most important part of the plan was a dollars-and-cents budget for the plan in operation. If adopted the city could have rid itself of its unhealthful areas, generated considerable economic activity, created a sense of confidence and investment security, and acted as a model for cities coast to coast.

Two important lessons are inherent in the "No Slums" plan. First, every modern city must adopt a policy of continual renewal as a normal and continuous civic function. No one stroke of action will correct any of our urban ills. A concerted and continuing program, soundly financed, can. Secondly our urban ills are not a result of lack of design know-how. They are a result of not using that know-how.

New Techniques

Since World War II urban planning has experienced a new wave of interest commensurate with an increased urgency for it. Many of the plans were of the classical land-use and circulation type with recommendations for zoning and policy as addenda. As design proposals these plans were quite sound but in too many cases the instrumentality to effect them was absent—no fault of the plans, to be sure. In many cases, had the plans been followed, our cities would not be suffering as they are. What was missing were means to effectuate even a portion of the recommendations.

In recognition of these unfortunate realities, some urban theorists have developed concepts for urban improvement that attempt to employ the more tenable tools of city building. They have singled out what they feel are the bare but essential bones of city form and city building and proposed that these be taken as programs for civic action. Viewed separately some of their ideas may seem to neglect aspects of urban form, scale, detail, or esthetics. Seen in the context of their conception, it is evident that these finer points are well implied in the bare-bones ideas. Indeed if the bare bones are really correct—and they have proven themselves in many cases—the finer aspects of urban form are a consequential outcome. This conceptual approach to our terribly complex urban situation was candidly expressed in a recent remark of a great composer of modern music, Igor Stravinsky.

At the age of eighty he was interviewed by the *London Observer* (June 17, 1962) in an article called "On Being Eighty" in which he remarked, "I was born to causality and determinism, and I have survived to probability theory and chance." In terms of urban design causality and determinism are for the most part the ap-

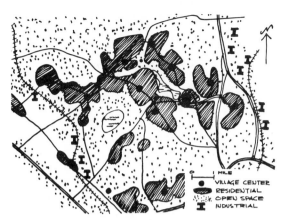

Plan for the Valleys, Baltimore, by Wallace-McHarg Associates. Houses on the hills; valleys as green open space.

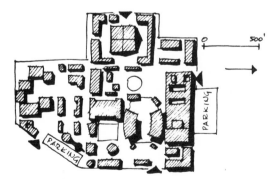

Project scale, the scale at which causality and determinism can be fully relied upon. The Seattle World's Fair.

83

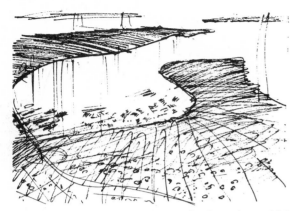

Metropolitan scale, the scale at which chance and probability must be reckoned with. Tacoma, Washington.

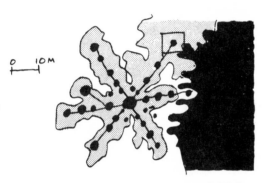

0 10M

The Year 2000 Plan *for Washington, D.C. Wedges of open space would separate urban corridors.*

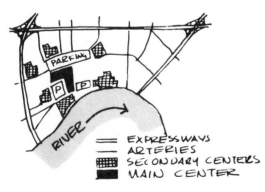

EXPRESSWAYS
ARTERIES
SECONDARY CENTERS
MAIN CENTER

Circulation concept for central New Orleans.

proach of the past, when decisions were in the hands of a few, when architectural vocabulary was rich but building technology limited, and, most of all, when tomorrow and tomorrow could be envisioned as the word's todays and yesterdays. This is not at all to say that that approach is irretrievably invalid—there are still techniques of the past that work today. But "probability theory and chance" is more in step with today's realities of town building.

In fact the two approaches go hand in hand. There are urban design projects today where rather complete control is possible; where causality and determinism can be relied upon. Generally these projects are small in scale and built in a relatively short interval, three or five years in all. It is at the larger scale of urban design that factors become indeterminant, many of them matters of unpredictable chance. This larger scale is a scale of time, physical extent, and uncertainty; when projects are built over long time spans, over large urban areas, and when all clients are not known. Here is where the ideas of the bare-bones theorists take their place.

The Open Space Technique

"The essential question of planning," wrote architect-planner S. B. Zisman recently, "is not where to build but where *not* to build." The essential question to the planner is where to create open space reserves. In an open space plan he would include every conceivable use and type of open space—open space for parks, watersheds, public transit lines, airports, community buildings, urban plazas, greenbelts, green wedges, avenues, sidewalks, etc. An open space structure would be the framework that would relate land development to transportation and which would allow a wide latitude of decisions. Corridors of open space radiating from a city's center could be used for expressways or rail rapid-transit rights-of-way. Open space reserves in developing suburbs would become community centers with schools, churches, and shopping. Large open spaces would be reserved for airports and airlane glide and take-off paths. In other words, open space itself would be recognized as the essential classification of public land use. Clear distinction would be made between open spaces for active uses and for more passive uses.

The Transportation System Technique

In the 1950s Louis Kahn, FAIA, made a plan of patterns of movement in central Philadelphia. His plan was unlike any that had previously been made for a city. Instead of showing fixed buildings and static urban spaces as a composition it showed motion: circulation. In many ways it resembled a drawing by Paul Klee, in which forces and ideas are represented rather than objects. About the same period Kahn wrote an article for the Number 2 issue of *Perspecta,* the 1953 publication of the Yale University School of Architecture. In this article he wrote about motion as design. He wrote at the head of the article:

Expressways are like *Rivers.*
These *Rivers* frame the area to be served.
Rivers have *Harbors.*
Harbors are the municipal parking towers.
From the *Harbors* branch a system of *Canals* that serve the interior.
The *Canals* are the *Go* streets.
From the *Canals* branch cul-de-sac *Docks.*
The *Docks* serve as entrance halls to the buildings.

84

A city's expressways would be tied to its network of slower-speed arterials. These in turn would tie into a still slower-speed network of stop-and-go streets. Related to these would be garages or "harbors." This concept can be varied in many ways to include a broader category of street types. Le Corbusier, for example, proposed it as a series of seven types of routes, from high-speed interurban connectors down progressively to pedestrian pathways.

Alvar Aalto uses it as a network which resembles in plan the branches of a tree. Through routes are progressively branched into even slower streets. The recent first-prize winner in a competition for enlarging Toulouse, France—the plan for Le Mirail—was also a branch circulation system.

The premise of this concept is that circulation can be controlled because it is the prime effort in public works projects, from urban to state to national scale. As such it is the chief determinant of urban form. Once a reasonable urban form is laid out, a circulation network can be planned to fit it, and the urban form itself, with all its parts, can be left to develop as an inevitable result.

The Capital Network Technique

A public transportation network is obviously not the only thing the public can determine. Any urban development of any consequence requires considerable coordination, not only between private parties but also public agencies. Further, the public itself builds civic centers, transport terminals, and public utility systems. When these controllable elements are added together the result is a functional framework of urban circulation, service lines, and urban centers or nodes. The circulation and utility lines are the lifeblood arteries of the city. The nodes are its vital organs. Having established these in plan, it remains to build them under a coordinated schedule.

Such scheduling can be in the form of the city's annual capital budget program. The construction of roads, new utility lines, site clearance, public expenditure for the public costs of a new project —all can be coordinated into a carefully planned program which adds up to a continuous effort for civic rebuilding or enlargement.

The prime example of this technique in action is the story of Philadelphia's renewal. A number of American cities have long used the capital budgeting technique to create a network of capital improvements. It is a principal tool for reshaping the city and for clarifying its form. In Philadelphia this technique consists of relating programs for urban circulation to urban renewal programs. The circulation programs involve all modes of transport from car to bus to subway to foot. The urban renewal projects are carefully related to the overall circulation network—Penn Center, Society Hill, the Waterfront.

An advantage of a capital program is its flexibility. With changing emphasis the program can be refocused. The renewal projects, for example, can vary between total clearance projects to conservation and rehabilitation. Or they may include both residential renewal and efforts to create civic centers or institutional campuses. The balance between public works programs and area renewal efforts can be readjusted each year. The programs under way in Boston in the last several years are of this nature.

The Public Policies Technique

In 1964 a report for planning central Chicago was published entitled *Basic Policies for the Comprehensive Plan of Chicago*. The

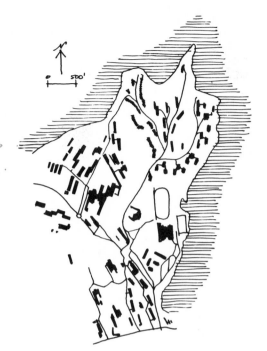

Alvar Aalto's master plan for the Technical University at Otaniemi, Finland. Conceptually, a branched circulation pattern.

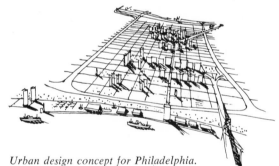

Urban design concept for Philadelphia. In the foreground the proposed waterfront redevelopment by Geddes, Brecher, Qualls, and Cunningham, Architects.

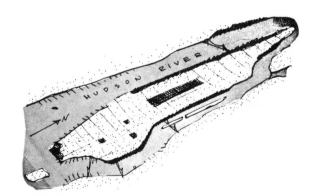

Manhattan. Policy led to a program for developing the river edges as park drives —the East and West Side drives and the Hudson River Palisades.

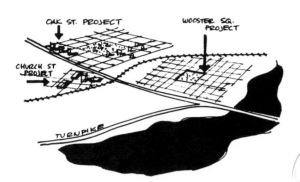

New Haven. Public policy led to three urban renewal projects and a highway program.

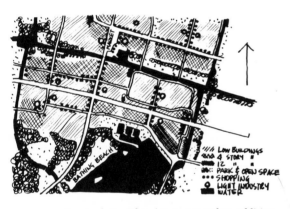

Amsterdam. Plan for a new urban addition. This is a control plan which allows breadth of interpretation with mixture of compatible land uses.

The design plan from which the Amsterdam land-control plan derived.

thesis of this plan was that the city operates as a net of interlocking systems. The "Policies Plan" proposed that public policies be based on the logic of these vital relationships.

A series of twelve diagrams showed how a rundown area would be subjected to a policy for improving its streets; improving its public transit lines; locating industry in relation to rail and arterial roads; density changes; public facilities; business location; recreation areas; and lakefront development. The policies were based on determining logical locations for related facilities. In a city as complex as Chicago it is more useful to have a clear-cut program of policies and responsibilities than a specific plan for each neighborhood in the more traditional plan form. The policies can effectively guide the city's many decision-making departments. The policies are in fact a plan, but a plan of action and responsibility geared realistically to a complex city's management to produce functional and amenable physical results.

The Physical Design Technique

About forty years ago H. P. Berlage, architect of the extension of Amsterdam, prepared plans for new housing areas which were to be designed and built in stages. Berlage's study included a physical design in which buildings were shown as blocks in relation to open spaces, transportation, and other building blocks representing schools, churches, and community facilities.

The physical design studies were an assurance that concentrations of people could be accommodated in the space shown. The designs were then translated into maps showing density, open space, community facilities, and transport lines. This was a legal statement of requirements to the developer and architect of the individual sectors. If they wished they could subscribe exactly to Berlage's design. Otherwise they could make their own design while fulfilling the requirements of the plan. There are, after all, several ways to slice a cake. Berlage's technique assured that the slices were reasonable. The use of space, mass, activity areas, etc., as a *modus operandi* is obvious here.

Not long after a more rigid technique was attempted in Sweden. The entire city was designed as blocks, and a model was prepared to show exactly how the city would be when fully developed. On one handsome avenue bordering Lake Mälaren, the Strandvägen, a row of seven or eight apartment units was built, each with exactly the same form but with different facades. The result was architecturally awkward.

In the postwar satellite town of Vällingby a design model again was made but this time more latitude was given. Sections were specified for house type, density, and population. Individual architects could interpret the specifications as they saw fit. In the center of town the model, which showed high-rise buildings strategically placed for reasons of overall visual composition, had to be more closely followed. In effect the physical design plan was specific where it had to be specific and relaxed wherever possible.

In the Government Center of Boston this system of form control was also used. The essence of the site plan was to create a main urban plaza as a setting for a key focal building, the city hall itself. The design problem—and it was an extremely difficult one—was to assure that this key building would always be the main feature. By giving it the prime location on this new plaza and by specifying that it be kept lower than the future buildings around the plaza, the city hall would always be the featured building. A plan was made to specify building heights and bulks as they related to the new plaza and the new city hall.

In fact this plan allowed for some degree of abuse—which it later suffered. The carefully plotted bulk height and space specifications could be stretched this way or that, but the main theme of a low principal building on a plaza, surrounded by higher buildings, prevailed. Here the elements of design were space, mass, circulation, and activity pattern.

Another application of this technique is to be found in Detroit, a horizontal city of great extent. Detroit has several clusters of high vertical buildings, the most prominent of which is at the city's center. Several lesser vertical clusters are to be found at outlying locations. These are mutually inter-visible, enjoying what Renaissance designers would term "reciprocity of view." Like Los Angeles, Detroit is an automobile-oriented city but its tower clusters act as prominent landmarks, indeed metropolitan landmarks, and are carefully related to the expressways. Charles A. Blessing, FAIA, author of this design, sees in this the conscious design of a comprehensible and functional metropolitan landscape. To direct its formation, renewal projects are chosen and developed with these visual principles in mind. Close coordination with developers is, of course, necessary for success; but the vital visual relationships inherent in such a design can be specified as part of the redevelopment regulations. Indeed, they can be drafted in a form similar to that used by Berlage in Holland. More directly, they can be specified as requirements to keep certain vistas open or framed by flanking buildings.

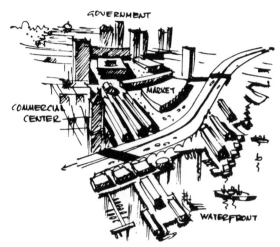

Quite the same technique as used in Holland was used for the Government Center of Boston, but on a smaller scale.

The Plug-in Technique

In a recent competition for a master plan for the University of Berlin the French architects Josic, Candilis, and Woods proposed a design that resembles a panel for electronic components. Evenly spaced and parallel corridors, perhaps a hundred or two hundred feet apart, act as circulation corridors and contain utility trunk lines. Between these parallel corridors can be inserted or "plugged in," a classroom block, auditorium, dormitory, laboratory, library, or whatever else might be needed as the university grows. Of course, the initial units would be built according to the university's needs, but later buildings could be added as needed, with a maximum of choice and convenience. Courts of varying sizes are formed between the inserted buildings.

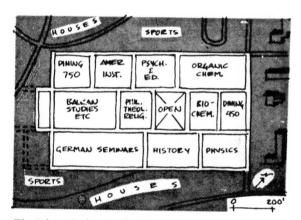

The "plug-in" plan for the University of Berlin by Josic, Candilis and Woods.

The Individual Building

Every building in an urban setting is an element of urban design. A tower building may accent a prominence. A curvilinear building may emphasize a terrain contour. A special building can act as a focus. Plain buildings can act as modest background architecture. A plain building can also be a visual link, filling a gap between a row of existing structures.

Any of the techniques of urban design discussed here have definite implications for individual buildings which require careful examination. Without such study an urban design plan could conceivably raise great difficulties for the design of later buildings.

Good architecture in urban design calls for good manners. A good work of architecture in urban design is one among many fellows, joined with them and not striving to outdo them. One or two works may stand out as special pieces, the others acting as background setting for them, but for most buildings architectural hu-

Good manners in architecture are a prerequisite to distinction in urban design—a New England colonial village.

87

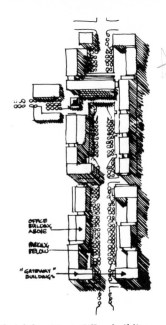

Plan for Philadelphia West. Office buildings are built above parking structures; a science conference center would straddle the street, acting as a visual and functional terminus; all building sizes controlled by a geometric module.

View looking towards the science conference center.

mility is the basis of urban design distinction.

Conclusion

There are variations on all of these techniques which might be classified separately. For example, another type of plug-in design, also applicable to a college campus, would make use of a central spine of space. This would be lined with buildings and could be enlarged by adding new buildings as branches to the main spine. Such a plan was recently proposed by the Texas architects Caudill, Rowlett, and Scott.

A variation of the technique used in Philadelphia is the design of the Philadelphia West area. It amounts to the design of an arterial street to allow buildings to be added as needed. The designers of this plan, architects Geddes, Brecher, Qualls, and Cunningham, propose that the essential elements of an automobile arterial street be constructed as a skeleton for future development. The skeletal elements are parking garages, carefully related to auto traffic, and the design of the street itself, which includes its profile, paving, lighting, and trees. By the logical dispositions of these elements and careful consideration of the visual results, this plan would assure a functional and visually cohesive development.

All of these techniques, new or old, and despite the names we find convenient to describe them, can be applied at any scale of design. Some of them, indeed, may not be so new after all. One wonders if there is not a similarity between modern Philadelphia's program with that of Renaissance Ferrara. If there is some similarity it is probably because the conditions of building then were comparable to those today. But that is beside the point. The point is that it is possible today to shape urban form. If our problems are complex, the techniques can be tailored to respond. Certainly the need for shaping the city is made ever more urgent simply because the city is more complex. Through the application of the principles and techniques of urban design, our energetic urban buildings can be made to result in wholesome and visually harmonious cities.

5

Examples and Scope

Some Contemporary Examples

Until relatively recent times it was common practice for architects to carry around a sketchbook for jotting down sketches and ideas. Alas, this habit has been on the wane. Spontaneous on-site sketching has been largely replaced by slide photography and note-taking for ideas by voluminous office files.

This change stems, of course, from the nature of the times. Photography is quick and office files are orderly. But current times require, far more than before, a clear conceptual grasp of whole situations, ideas, and designs—particularly when they are complex. This is especially true of urban design concepts, which are often more readily portrayed in a sketch than in a photograph or even a carefully drawn plan. A sketch can not only be a visualization of a design; it can also be a diagram of the essential elements of a design, as well as a diagram of the forces which lead to a particular design arrangement.

The *visualization type* of drawing is quite familiar. The *diagram type* of drawing is also familiar: the cutaway view, the diagram of machinery, electronic components, or structure. The *force type* of drawing is less familiar and possibly will occupy an increasingly important role. Examples of it range from economic charts to the drawings of Paul Klee.

With this in mind we offer this fifth chapter in sketchbook form. Appreciating the difficulty of including all worthwhile examples and, further, the limitations of any system of category, we present this chapter itself as an example of the kind of notebook you might start to create for yourself.

A NATIONAL AND REGIONAL OUTLOOK

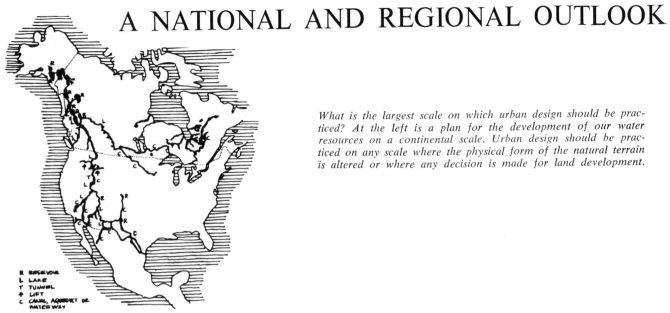

R RESERVOIR
L LAKE
T TUNNEL
↑ LIFT
C CANAL, AQUEDUCT OR
   WATERWAY

*Continental engineering. A proposal for a
North American water and power alliance.
Ralph M. Parsons Co., Engineers.*

*What is the largest scale on which urban design should be prac-
ticed? At the left is a plan for the development of our water
resources on a continental scale. Urban design should be practiced on any scale where the physical form of the natural terrain
is altered or where any decision is made for land development.*

*Already a third of our population lives in eighteen
metropolitan regions (black areas). Some of them
form linear urban configurations such as the
East Coast megalopolis or the New York to
Minneapolis–St. Paul industrial corridor.
We have crossed the threshold of economic
and industrial planning for these areas.
We must now cross the threshold of design
for these areas.*

*A sketch map of our national parklands (black)
reveals that our large wilderness and preservation
areas do not coincide with our population centers.
This scale of design should suggest
an acceleration of programs to acquire open spaces
on all scales.*

*The National Highway System is another example
of planning on a national scale. It follows a
tradition as old as our republic—
the stimulation of interstate commerce
by creating access. The physical design of this
system was long ago accepted as a premise
of its engineering.*

The Autobahn in Germany is an example of rural highway design.
It is aligned to accommodate itself to the form of the terrain it traverses.
It was also designed to afford the most handsome views of natural
features and existing towns. The principles of this design were developed
by American landscape architects around the turn of the century.
We have yet to fully extend parallel design principles
to the modern metropolis.

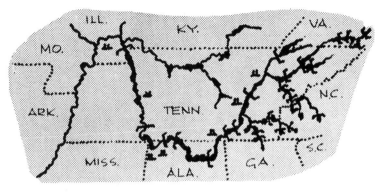

The Tennessee Valley Authority was set up to harness a 72-inch
annual rainfall, which formerly wreaked havoc in floodplain valleys.
Every detail of the TVA was designed, from approach vistas for the dams
to the handrails of the catwalks atop the generators.

Hiwassee Dam in the TVA.

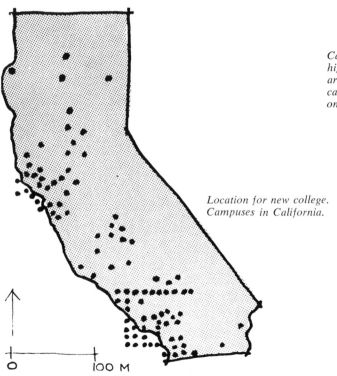

Location for new college.
Campuses in California.

California, now our leading state in population, has a plan for
higher education to match its needs. Sites for college campuses
are chosen on the basis of population served. The design of the
campuses themselves confronts the architectural profession with
one of its greatest opportunities.

Foothill College, designed by architect
Ernest Kump, establishes a level of
design excellence for all the campuses
of the California plan.

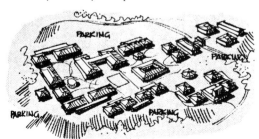

URBAN DESIGN ON A METROPOLITAN SCALE

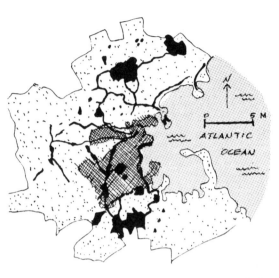

Land for development; now built up.

Proposed park space; mostly all created according to plan.

Central Boston.

THE BOSTON METROPOLITAN PARK SYSTEM, PROPOSED IN 1892.

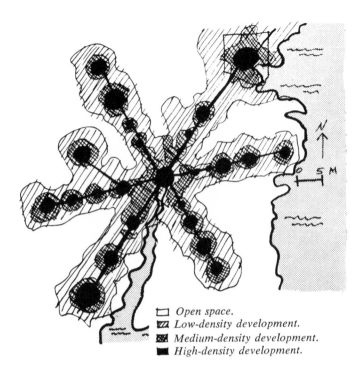

☐ Open space.

▨ Low-density development.

▩ Medium-density development.

■ High-density development.

THE YEAR 2000 PLAN FOR WASHINGTON, D.C.

On a large metropolitan scale we must think of the form of the entire physical setting. The farsighted plan for parks in Boston established a system of nearly continuous parklands for the city which would relieve the dense development that was to ensue. The Year 2000 Plan for Washington proposes intense corridors of settlement which will be supplemented by wedges of open space penetrating to the center of the city. The plan for satellite suburban centers for Baltimore would order more rationally the distribution of population of that city and also ensure the relieving presence of natural open space.

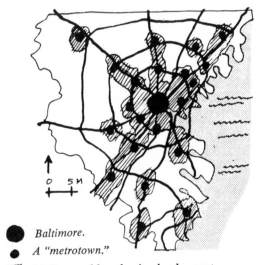

● Baltimore.

● A "metrotown."

▨ Medium and low-density development.

A PROPOSAL FOR "METROTOWNS" AROUND BALTIMORE.

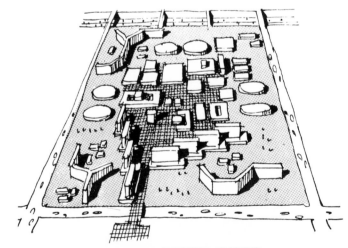

A "METROTOWN" CENTER.

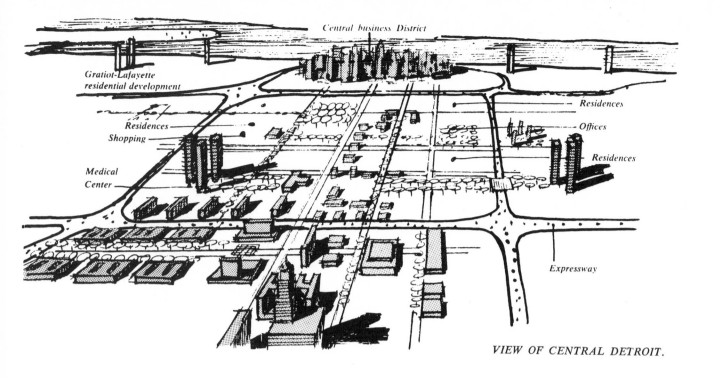

VIEW OF CENTRAL DETROIT.

A metropolitan area is a man-made landscape. In Detroit the topography is flat and one termination of the city is the edge of the lake. To this landscape is added a network of expressways connecting the parts of the city. This is accented by dominant clusters of key buildings. In Philadelphia two rivers and a rectangular inner-loop expressway determine the center of the metropolis wherein successive building projects are keyed to the whole ensemble. Many of these are vertical in form, assertive centers on the profile of the city.

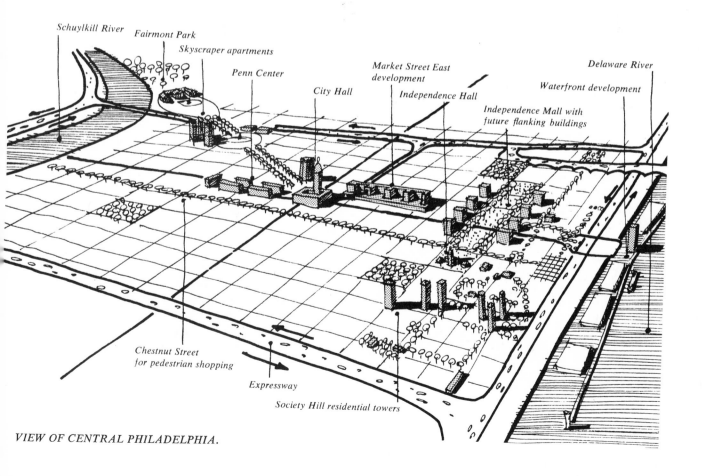

VIEW OF CENTRAL PHILADELPHIA.

URBAN DESIGN ON AN URBAN SCALE

Vällingby is a foremost example of a satellite town. Following the concept established by the English garden city movement, it intersperses many types of housing in generous open spaces. Some designers have questioned the density standards of Vällingby, feeling that higher densities would be more desirable. Vällingby was divided up into development sectors, each designed separately according to certain specifications of a master plan. A principal lesson of such new towns is that either they must be appendages of existing urban complexes, based on existing urban economy, or they must have a firm economic base of their own. Vällingby is an example of the former and is linked to Stockholm by road and rail.

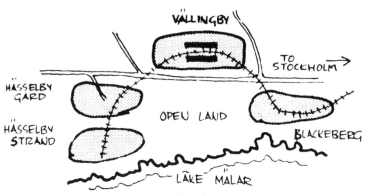

Vällingby is the largest of four residential communities which form a major satellite development near Stockholm.

Round houses are one of several innovations in housing in Vällingby.

Some areas of the town are developed with row houses flowing along the rolling landscape amidst rock and trees.

High towers mark out the center.

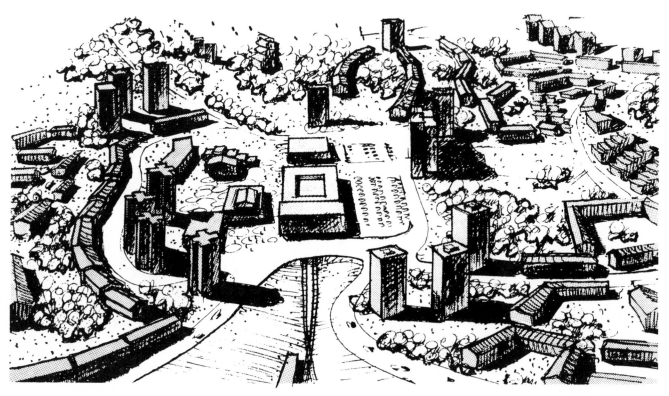

VIEW OF CENTRAL VALLINGBY.

A contract to the design concept of Vällingby was that of the proposed new town of Hook, England. Hook was designed by a team of architects and planners of the London County Council. Unlike Vällingby, Hook would have been concentrated in form. It would have been laid out along a linear spine with several levels, much like an ocean liner. The lower levels would have been for vehicles, the upper levels for pedestrians. Concentrated urban form would allow people to walk to the center and would keep open nature close at hand. Hook was not built, but the town of Cumbernauld in Scotland is being built according to these principles.

High-density housing in Hook interspersed with nature would recreate the atmosphere of a medieval town, urbane and humane.

Looking up from the vehicular level to the pedestrian level in Central Hook.

A cross section of Central Hook shows how vehicular circulation would pass below an upper pedestrian level.

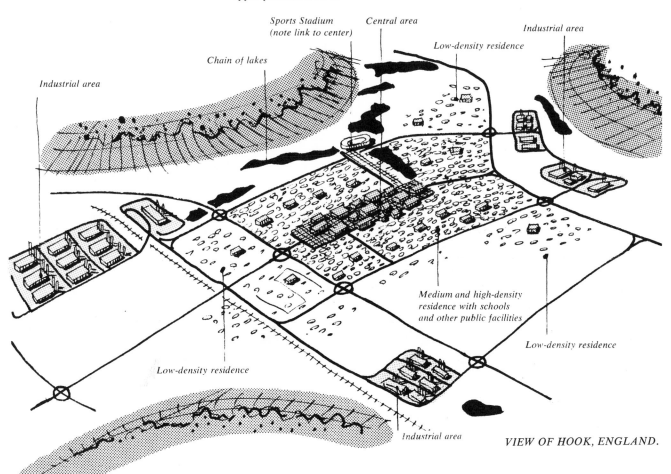

Industrial area

Chain of lakes

Sports Stadium (note link to center)

Central area

Low-density residence

Industrial area

Medium and high-density residence with schools and other public facilities

Low-density residence

Low-density residence

Industrial area

VIEW OF HOOK, ENGLAND.

SOME URBAN DESIGN PROJECTS

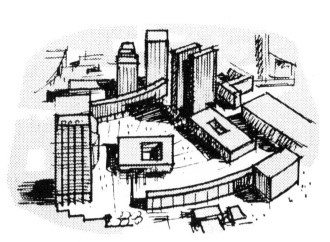

GOVERNMENT CENTERS: *The government center in Boston focuses on a plaza formed by new and existing buildings. The plaza is keynoted by the central City Hall.*

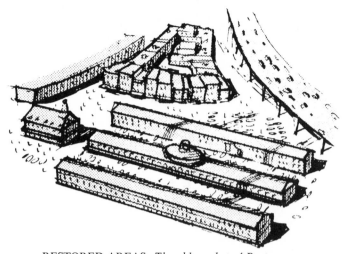

RESTORED AREAS: *The old market of Boston, a hub for tourists and intown residents. It adjoins the lower portion of the government center.*

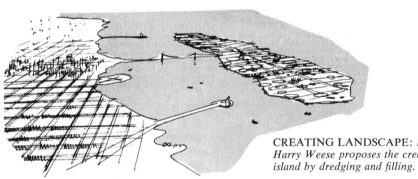

CREATING LANDSCAPE: *In Chicago, architect Harry Weese proposes the creation of an offshore island by dredging and filling.*

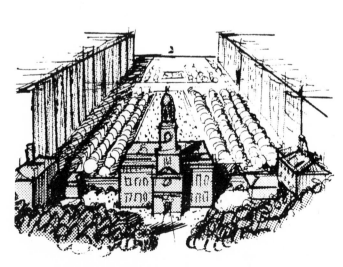

PRESTIGIOUS SPACE: *Independence Mall in Philadelphia forms a setting for historic Independence Hall and creates a prestigious location for future office buildings.*

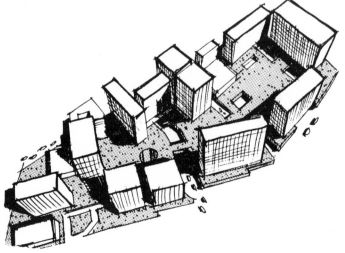

NEW SETTINGS: *Charles Center in Baltimore was conceived as a series of linked spaces affording settings for new buildings and continuity with the surrounding cityscape.*

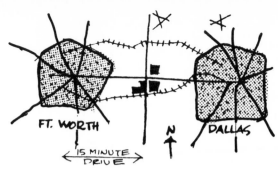

COMMUNITY ESTHETICS: *Aarhus University in Denmark is a composition of mostly rectangular buildings made of identical buff bricks and yellow roof tiles. This simple theme gives artistic unity to the whole campus.*

INDUSTRIAL PARKS: *The great southwest center midway between Dallas and Fort Worth, Texas, is convenient to both cities. It was planned as three separate communities.*

A NEW TOWN CENTER: *Alvar Aalto proposed a linkage of islands between the two parts of Oulu, Finland, as a center for government, culture, and leisure facilities.*

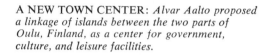

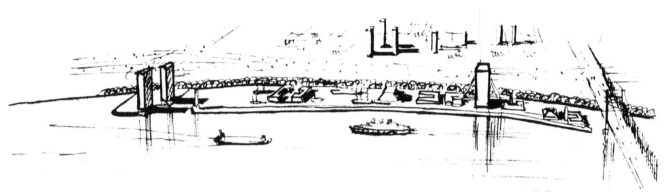

WATERFRONTS: *The proposed Philadelphia waterfront development highlights a key problem existing in most of our harbor and river cities. The neglected waterfront, often obsolete for its original use, is a splendid opportunity for urban redevelopment.*

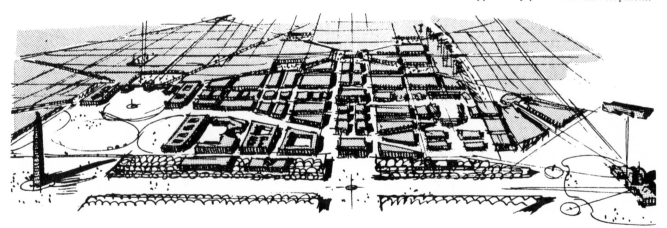

DOWNTOWN: *Many American downtowns, such as downtown Washington, D.C., are opportunities ripe for revitalization. Downtowns are in the unique position of being able to serve more people with a greater variety of facilities than any other location in a city.*

RESIDENTIAL ELEMENTS

In Philadelphia, the towers of Society Hill will act as orienting landmarks for the lower town-house residences and historic rehabilitations nearby.

Southwest Washington, D.C., is one of the largest urban renewals in the country. Basically a concept of medium-rise and low-rise residences, it was developed as a series of developer competitions, selected largely on the quality of design.

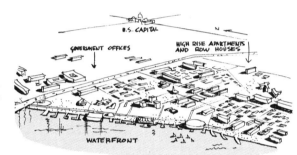

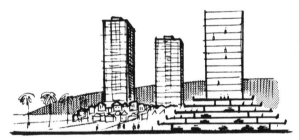

In this redevelopment concept for Santa Monica, Calif., architects DeMars and Reay proposed an important innovation in high-rise and low-rise buildings. Cars would be parked in pyramid-shaped garages in several stories at the base of the towers. The surfaces of the pyramids would be covered with small terrace houses reminiscent of a Mediterranean village.

The redevelopment of South Chicago is an example, in its ultimate form, of the concept of large block buildings set far apart in open landscape.

The town center of Färsta, Sweden, is marked by tower buildings and a commercial center.

The cul-de-sacs of Radburn, N.J., could well be copied in many subdivision layouts.

Baldwin Hills Village's cul-de-sacs are parking areas close to the houses. They form entrance courts for the houses. The absence of through roads for vehicles frees the interior of the block for a common green space.

The restoration of old houses, as in Georgetown in Washington, D.C., is a great resource for creating livable neighborhoods of intimate scale.

The "greenways" of Philadelphia, occasionally leading to small plazas, are a pedestrian thread in the weave of the city.

José Luis Sert's atrium house in Cambridge, Mass., could well be copied in a variety of forms to provide a maximum of living space in a minimum of urban land.

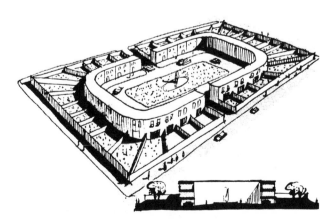

Architect Don Hisaka's concept for a residential block of row houses in Milwaukee gives each family a private court and a common entrance green. Cars are parked under the houses and are accessible from the green by a simple manipulation of grades.

LEISURE

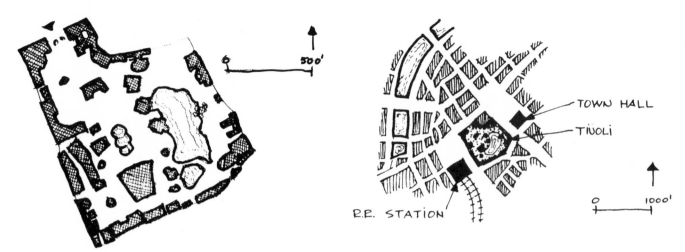

The form of Tivoli Gardens in Copenhagen evolved over a long period of time. Particularly important is the location of major traffic generators on the periphery. This prevents any area in Tivoli from becoming lifeless at any time of day or night. Tivoli Gardens is strategically located on a main street between the railroad station and Town Hall square.

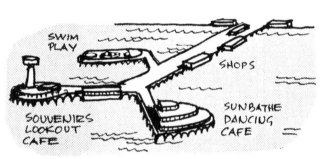

The recreation pier in Scheveningen, Holland, designed by architect Hugh Maaskant, projects out into the sea and branches into three pavilions which house a myriad of leisure facilities.

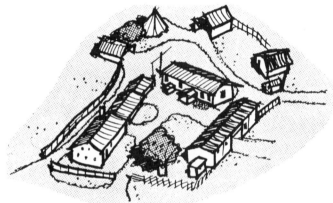

Skansen Gardens in Stockholm is a counterpart of Tivoli. Internally it is somewhat different, having also a park and a museum of Swedish folk architecture. The museum consists of reconstructed old buildings arranged as they were originally grouped.

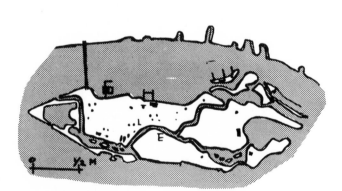

Belle Isle Park in Detroit is one of the largest and most beautiful city parks in the country. Originally a natural island, it has canals for boats, yacht clubs, a zoo, sports fields, bridle paths, restaurants, and a large lagoon for pageantry.

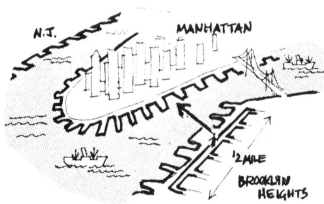

A half-mile promenade built above the docks in Brooklyn Heights, N.Y., presents a superb view of the skyscrapers of Lower Manhattan. It is a favorite strolling place for many nearby residents.

MALLS AND PLAZAS

The shoppers' mall in Knoxville, Tenn., is one of the most successful of such efforts in the country. It was largely the work of the local AIA chapter.

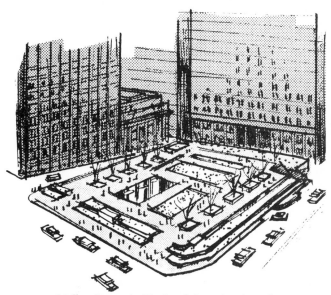

Mellon Square in Pittsburgh has a handsomely landscaped park above an underground parking garage.

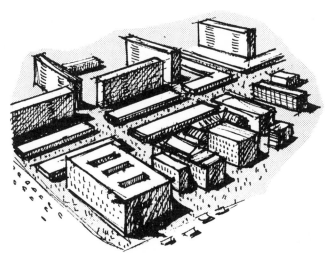

The Lijnbaan in Rotterdam was a key element in the reconstruction of Central Rotterdam after the war. It is a spine of shops along a pedestrian mall. Around it are large apartment buildings, offices, and department stores.

The Paul Revere Mall in Boston is a small plaza in the heart of the "North End," the city's long-time Italian area. Children and mothers use it during the day. In the evening it is filled with people of all ages.

Lincoln Center in New York will form a series of broad plazas which will act as forecourt settings for the buildings which will enclose them.

THE INDIVIDUAL BUILDING

A transportation terminal is a portal to a city.

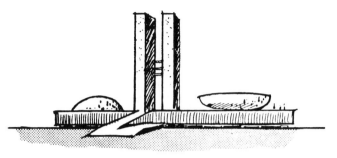

Architecture often functions as a piece of sculpture in the city.

Saarinen's original plan for Brandeis University would have grouped clusters of buildings around a central open space. Unity would have been achieved through consistent use of scale and materials.

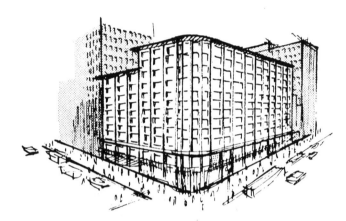

Architecture can be a hinge at a key spot in the city—a turning point at the meeting of two major paths.

A building may be a focus, filling a role that is functional, symbolic, and sculptural. Nearby architecture can further emphasize that special role.

Buildings may be subservient to other buildings nearby, although they may be far greater in size. A pair of buildings flanking an old landmark visually, although taller than the landmark itself, focuses attention on the smaller building.

Every piece of architecture in a city is an element of urban design. Two recent buildings demonstrate this forcefully: the Torre Velasco in Milan, designed by Rogers, Belgiojoso, and Peressutti, and the Enso-Gutzeit Building in Helsinki, designed by Alvar Aalto. The Torre Velasco is significant as architecture and urban design for three reasons: It was designed in the unique vernacular of Milanese architecture; it was designed particularly for its unique site; and its appearance and detailing were determined by the angles from which it would be commonly seen—across the skyline of Milan and from its base, looking up almost vertically. The unique character of Milanese architecture presents itself in the detailing (almost brutal in quality) and in the turret-like enlargement of the top stories. This building was designed for a particular site in a particular city. It is a modern skyscraper that evolved from a particular place. It could not be built anywhere else. How many modern skyscrapers have this quality?

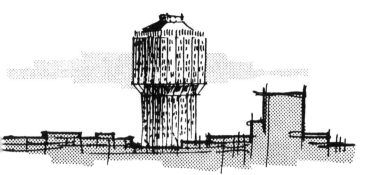

The Torre Velasco seen on the skyline of Milan.

The Torre Velasco seen looking almost straight up from its base.

The Enso-Gutzeit Building in Helsinki harbor, a recent work of Alvar Aalto, was also designed for its special site and for the unique viewing conditions under which it is seen. The existing buildings of Helsinki harbor are a series of classical prisms forming a facade on the water's edge, dominated by a stately domed building and terminated by a lofty church. Aalto's building continues the scale of the prismatic facades. It was designed to be seen from afar as one of the series of prisms, as a whole in itself as a plain but dignified grid, and from close up as an intricate play of windows framed in robust marble encasements.

The Enso-Gutzeit Building seen close up.

The Enso-Gutzeit Building seen as a whole facade.

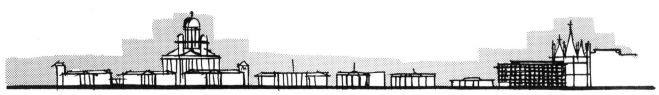

The Enso-Gutzeit Building seen in Helsinki harbor.

DETAILS

Urban design is also the exercise of artistry in every detail of city building—artistry in urban objects built for people who live in cities. The bridges and roads that bring us to the city, the benches we sit on, the places where we wait for buses, the places where children play, the places where we browse for books, where we have our shoes shined, the lights that illuminate our cities, and the signs that give us directions—all these are but a suggestion of the everyday urban objects which we should carefully design as the details of the city.

An automobile bridge in Stockholm.

A steel expressway designed by Pier Luigi Nervi for the Kaiser Steel Corporation.

A bird house and flower pots.

A two-way bench and a play sculpture.

A reversible bench.

A bus shelter.

A picnic shelter.

"Disappearing" book stalls along the Seine.

Lights in Vällingby, Sweden.

A poster column (a colonne Morris) in Paris.

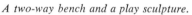

A shoeshine stand in Stockholm.

European traffic signs.

6

Urban Esthetics

Beauty in Cities

This chapter is about landscape painting—in reverse. It is about landscape, and cityscape, creation.

John Marin, the American painter, once remarked about one of his seascape paintings: "It is for the artist to paint a paint-wave a-splashing on a paint-shore." Marin painted natural landscape and the urban scene in somewhat abstract form, perhaps in "extract" form, since he chose the elements of nature which he could simulate in painter's terms on canvas. Marin was moved by the American landscape, and cityscape too. The American landscape has moved many artists to paint its beauties—more, alas, in past years than it does now. George Innes, for example, painted the landscape of the Delaware Valley. It is difficult to find the sights there today that Innes saw yesterday.

Where our American landscape used to move artists, it now more often moves cars. One of the purposes of urban design is to allow it to move both and, in addition, accommodate all our vast new constructions in a pleasing and harmonious manner. Where Marin and Innes extracted as artists, we must insert as urban designers.

The following eight sketches are by Charles A. Blessing.

Monument Valley.

Hong Kong.

San Francisco.

Constantine, Algeria.

Auckland, New Zealand.

Berne, Switzerland.

Sticks and stones, nails and glass make a house. If they are assembled with art, the same materials become architecture. Similarly, a city is an assemblage of buildings and streets, systems of communications and utilities, places of work, habitation, leisure, and meeting. The process of arranging these elements together, both functionally and beautifully, is the essence of urban design.

Because urban design is a matter of arranging material objects, it is a plastic art, concerned both with how things appear and with how they actually operate. A city is constantly changing, like the natural landscape. But nature will take care of the landscape; *we* must take care of the city. As long as men have dwelt on the earth they have found ways of making their habitations—tents or towns —harmonious objects in the landscape. The appearance of primitive towns, ancient or modern, usually is part of a balanced picture of man's constructions in nature, harmonious in its own parts, functional for its own purposes, well arranged for its inhabitants.

When we see a picturesque town we often feel as though a happy sequence of accidental forces had made it so. Accidents there may have been, and happy ones at that, but there is too much evidence to the contrary to conclude that it was all by chance; evidence that our ancestors thought very carefully indeed about the way their cities looked and functioned. Perhaps, too, our rationale of the happy accident and the picturesque serves as an excuse for our present shortcomings. In most of our cities we have not been able to approach the old village for simple planning sense and visual harmony. True, the village is smaller and less complex. But so were the means to overcome its problems. True, too, there was a general consciousness of the arrangement of the village. No experts or consultants were needed; no illustrated brochures were produced. The beauty and function of the old villages and towns we admire were the products of a general awareness and active concern.

Surely this concern is not new. What is new is the compartmentalization of all the many specializations concerned with the city. What is very old is the comprehensive view that refined city or town dwellers achieved, embracing all of this. Perhaps the great contribution of today's urban design concern will be to set the proper goal for all these efforts. Even if we do have the best sewers, the best telephones, the best roads, the best houses—what have we achieved if we have not also created beautiful cities?

Beauty in cities is not an afterthought. It is a necessity. Man cannot live long without beauty without becoming distorted as a human being. Order and beauty in man's surroundings are as much a prerequisite to human health as fresh air. Perhaps future generations of Americans will look back on the past, our present, with amazement—and, let us hope, sympathy. Perhaps they will be surprised at the way we polluted our air and streams. Perhaps they will react to that practice as we react to the practice in past centuries of throwing garbage into the street. Is throwing filth into the air any less offensive? Perhaps the typical city dweller of the future will look back in amazement at the ugliness tolerated by the present-day city dweller. Does not living in the midst of ugliness come at considerable cost to the human spirit?

Because this outlook toward cities is from the standpoint of "art," it stands on shaky ground. The concern for urban design, therefore, must be both practically and realistically broached. As J. B. Jackson observed in *Landscape,* "a city exists only by grace of the life which pulsates in its streets and squares. . . . Art can only adorn something which the spirit has created." Certainly we

106

are a people of spirit, but where is our art? It lies in our imaginations and will come forth through long, hard effort. We can see the possibilities for beauty in the form of cities by first understanding their nature.

Basically, a city is a place of exchange—first a place for exchanging goods, then services, then ideas. Ultimately, it is a place for exchanging everything, and it generates the further creation of the ideas and products which foster the advance of civilization. Where, then, do cities originate and develop? At places convenient for exchange, naturally enough—at the crossing of routes: land routes, the meeting of land routes with water routes, or the entrance to a fertile valley.

Our own cities and towns are relatively new and their own reasons for being are not unlike those of the cities of the past. The rapid changes they undergo, including decay, are but aspects of their continuing evolution. Understanding this evolution, from the time of the pioneer settler to the family farm era and down to the present period of vast consolidation of social efforts and national production, is prerequisite to realistic and effective urban design. We must always search for, and acknowledge, the ideas and opinions of men who have turned their energies to the creation of better cities and towns—better living for all of us. But we must also add our own dreams of a beautiful country and beautiful cities.

The late teacher Henry Vincent Hubbard defined beauty as the "perceived harmonious relationship of all the elements of a thing observed." This definition applies to the relation of a city to nature, for that is perceived. It also applies to the relationship of a city's parts, and to daily living in all its details, since the quality of life of a city's inhabitant is largely determined by the form of the city. A city which is in harmony with its natural environment and which harbors harmonious urban life creates further systems of harmony. Such cities derive creative power from their sites and their people and, in return, transmit a life-giving power to them. In this chapter we shall explore this harmony in some of the great cities of the world and, further, project images of what our own cities and towns can become.

Relationships between Site and City

Extracted Form

Beauty in architecture rests largely on the harmony between buildings and nature. Throughout history this relationship has been one of architecture's major goals.

In Taliesin West, Frank Lloyd Wright used an acute angle of about thirty degrees throughout the junctures and form of his design. This angle, he explained, was the basic angle of the hill and rock formations of the desert site. It was a dominant and pervasive fact of nature which he recalled and extended into his architecture, a key to the harmony between his buildings and their setting.

Alvar Aalto developed a different method for suiting his buildings to the unique Finnish landscape. That landscape is undulating, accented by rock outcroppings, and almost entirely covered by stands of straight, polelike trees. Aalto's facades proceed from the ground as stepped foundations, rising or falling according to the shape of the terrain. Most of his facades are long horizontal blocks which undulate in sensitive adjustment to both the building's interior function and the external landform. This horizontal emphasis is seen against the vertical subdivision afforded by the trees. In

Medieval hill town.

Detroit.

Taliesen West by Frank Lloyd Wright.

Säynatsälo Town Hall by Alvar Aalto.

107

La Tourette by Le Corbusier.

Roof of La Tourette.

Machu Picchu.

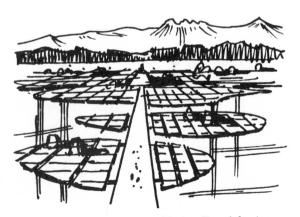

Mexico City of the Aztecs.

plan, we often see a free form whose shape mirrors that of a typical Finnish lake. In this fashion, Aalto extended the forms of nature into his buildings.

Deference

Wright and Aalto extracted characteristics of the site as bases for their design concepts. Le Corbusier also has shown that deference to the conditions of a site is the basis for harmony between building and site. In designing La Tourette, the Dominican monastery in Central France, Le Corbusier found himself confronted with a magnificent site; one which would ask something very great of architecture, including where, exactly, the monastery should be placed. La Tourette was sited facing westward just below the crest of a long ridge. Le Corbusier took careful note of the natural conditions of this spot; he noticed that the trees at the crest were quite mature and full, and that their tops were uniquely level, forming a great horizontal plane; he noticed the view to the west over the surrounding farmlands; and he noticed, too, that the sun's rays in the early morning lit the grassy slope with a beautiful sidelight.

Of course, the design reflected the inner function of the building, but added to that determining factor was the recognition of the facts of nature. La Tourette's roof is flat, like the treetops, but is, respectfully, about thirty feet below them. La Tourette stands on pilotis, the grass flowing uninterruptedly beneath the building. The early morning sunlight now lights the pilotis as well as the grass. And on the rooftop there is a promenade for contemplation and viewing the countryside below.

The buildings of these architects owe a large part of their success to their harmonious relation to nature. That basic harmony is not only a prerequisite to beauty in architecture, but is also essential to beauty in cities; and so cities can be examined from the same point of view.

Extension

Macchu Picchu, the pre-Columbian city of the Incas, is set in a wild mountainous area of Peru. There the mountaintops soar as high as 2,000 feet above the stream beds. With incredibly skillful stonework the Incas terraced hillsides, covering them with walls and buildings. The form of Macchu Picchu developed as a series of regular geometric shapes, contrasting with the irregularity of nature. The architecture of Macchu Picchu consisted of large rectangular courts, large and long rectilinear building masses, and assertive pyramidal structures. The landscape was a series of uniquely shaped hills forming valleys and ravines. Thus, the forms of the city repeated this theme, but in highly sophisticated geometric shapes. The regular buildings were counterparts to the irregular valleys. And the regular pyramids were counterparts to the unique form of the hills.

The Mexican city of the Aztecs, too, must have been a splendid sight of city form as a response and complement to nature. Originally it was a group of islands floating in a lake, which gradually affixed themselves to the lake bottom. Eventually the islands were stable enough to support heavy structures—pyramidal stone altars and buildings. At the height of its beauty it was a series of island pavilions mirrored in the lake, the background being a rim of mountain ranges. Here was another composition of city form as a response to land and lake form.

108

Geometric Contrast

The practice of compositional response to nature is found the world over in both sophisticated and primitive town building, as in the American Pueblo Indian village. Pueblo Indians built their villages in landscapes which had one main characteristic: great expanse. Their sites varied from flat plain to mesa top. The form and appearance of the villages were quite simple. Seen from afar the Pueblo villages were an array of cubic blocks on the horizon. Within the villages were narrow streets and at least one open ceremonial plaza. Their holy places were underground rooms called *kivas*, symbolizing the Indians' belief that they came from the ground. The ladder by which the *kiva* was entered had arms which projected far above ground level—and rooftop level—sweeping up into the sky as a graceful curve, perhaps symbolizing the flight of a bird. Thus, the Indian village presented itself in the landscape, its cubic houses in geometric contrast to the rocks and open plains, and its sweeping ladders accenting the village against the horizon.

Taos Pueblo with kiva *poles.*

A use of more advanced geometry is found in more sophisticated societies. Helsinki, Finland, is a good example. A striking contrast exists between the city, laid out in the orderly classic style of the early eighteenth century, and its topography. The geometry of that old plan could not contrast more sharply with the flowing forms of shoreline, lake, and landform, and yet, could not be more suited to it. Imagine approaching Helsinki from the sea, passing through the archipelago of islands strewn about as if by a careless child, and then arriving in Helsinki harbor, there to be confronted by the crisp classical facades, the city plan's extension in three dimensions.

Classical Helsinki.

There are neither magic rules for success, nor foolproof principles for design, in these examples. Rather there are only challenging problems which insist on superb effort in pursuit of beauty.

Accent

San Giminiano, Italy, is an example of a city whose appearance would seem to defy nature. Yet, in its defiance, it serves, by accentuation, to extend nature itself. San Giminiano is on a round hill amidst gently rolling countryside. The sight is striking, unlike that of any other city except, perhaps, Manhattan when approached from the sea. San Giminiano once had nearly sixty slender stone towers, the treasuries and strongholds of the city's wealthy citizens, as well as their ostentatious displays. Now it has less than thirty, but those few are enough to remind us of the city's former appearance. The towers rise from the cubelike array of two- and three-story houses, extending their geometry skyward. Here, natural form is emphasized by complementary urban forms.

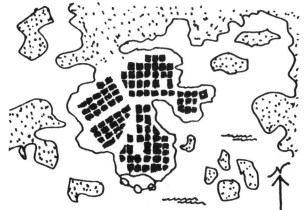

San Giminiano.

In almost direct opposition to this course of design is the modern city of Rio de Janeiro, Brazil. There, the immense mountains are more dominant than any architectural feature man could provide. One hill, Corcovado, or "hunchback," is topped with an enormous crucifix, the Christ the Redeemer. But for the most part Rio has a natural site which cannot be overwhelmed by even the most dominant structures one might devise. The city of Rio sits in the lap of nature. Its lesson is to let nature do the work, not to try to overwhelm or diminish its forms. In Rio that, of course, would be difficult; but in most other sites it would not.

Rio de Janeiro.

One can ponder so many of the cities in the world and find so

109

Assisi.

Chartres, far and near.

St. Flour.

Istanbul.

many different arrangements of city form in natural form. Where they achieve a harmonious poise which our deeper instincts respond to, where they arouse the sense of reason and poetry in us, there we find beauty.

Site Supremacy

Such is the case of Assisi, the hill town of St. Francis, which sits on a long ridgelike hill amidst farmland and terraced hillside. Assisi has a form found in few cities in the world. Most of the town is on the southern side of the hill, obviously for the sunlight's warmth. But the cathedral of Assisi and its related monastery group is built on an arched masonry terrace extending from one end of the hill. Here architecture dominates subtly while, at the same time, avoiding a heavy-handed suppression of the essence of the landscape. The church group is an extension of the key aspect of the hill, its length.

Assisi has another asset which is often overlooked when considering the aspect of cities. While the view of it from the surrounding land is superb, the view of landscape *from it* is equally striking. From unexpected niches and openings, set in some of its most dense quarters, one often has a beautifully framed and quite unexpected view of the green tapestry of terraced countryside.

Architects, working in even the most fortuitous periods, can seldom hope to design whole cities. More often they contribute a key accent to its form, one which may be as telling as the alchemist's touchstone. Two old French towns demonstrate this: Chartres and St. Flour.

Expression

The first view of the town of Chartres has a magic that challenges explanation. Is it the beauty of the flat farmland which surrounds Chartres? Is it the sense of expectancy that is the prelude to actually seeing one of the greatest works of Western art? Is it the sight of the two towers? Perhaps the Gothic towers are a partial clue. They do more than mark the facade of the church. They also mark a key spot in the town and accent the landscape in precisely the right way. They are delicate and lithe, spears pointing to heaven, their differences in treatment and height only emphasizing this symbolic role. For the plains around Chartres, for the huddled town itself, these towers are perfectly right.

St. Flour is in a different landscape. A fortified town on a hill, it was a sentinel among harsh valleys and hills which were difficult to traverse except through the valley St. Flour guarded. Its foreboding aspect is emphasized by the color of the native stone used in its buildings and its cathedral. That stone is a dull, leaden gray. The towers of St. Flour, earthbound and guardian, are as suitable to their valley setting as the towers of Chartres, graceful and lofty, are for its plain landscape.

Entrance

We can also find clues to the role of urban form by considering details in conjunction with each other; for example, accent and entrance approach.

Istanbul, approached by sea, is seen as a moundlike hive of buildings on a peninsula. Minarets and mosques accent its skyline. There are no grand landing places for ships. Ships coming to Istanbul pass around the city and enter the protective Golden Horn. The climax when arriving in Istanbul in the past was not at its entrances, but rather in the palaces of its rulers and at its religious and cultural focal points, the mosques. The mosques can be spotted from afar by their pencil-like minarets which mark out the space of the mosque. Indeed, the mosques do just that—they occupy a space, a space which makes a profound impact on the visitor who has traversed long, crowded streets to get to it.

In contrast to Istanbul, Venice presents a grand entrance to the visitor arriving by sea. Venice is reached by water through the Adriatic, and is entered through a channel through a long sandbar which encloses the Venetian lagoon. It is clearly seen from afar— the entrance being marked out aerially by the Campanile of the Piazza San Marco. Flanked by a pair of columns, the entrance Piazzetta affords a fine view of the Ducal Palace to the right, the Church of St. Mark beyond, to the left the tower and library. In an earlier day when Venice could only be approached by boat, all this said welcome to the visitor and drew him into the Piazza, the heart of the city. At this portal spot begins the main corridor of the city, the Grand Canal, which winds its way as a giant "S" through the whole island group.

Venice.

Color

Every decision on urban form and appearance must derive from the artist's awareness of the conditions of the place. Often the decision for action can take a very simple form. Such was the case in Renaissance Rome under the popes.

Rome is characterized by many orange-colored buildings which act as foreground and surroundings to the monumental churches and palaces. The orange color is not an accident; it was once a legal requirement imposed on all secular buildings by a Renaissance pope. His purpose was to ensure that church buildings and monuments would always be visually dominant. His choice of color indicates considerable esthetic sensibility.

Orange is an "advancing" color, that is, it seems to come forward. It also makes buildings seem more solid, as compared to blue, which is transparent. An orange building, seen against the prevailing blue Roman sky, looks solid and static. As foreground for a richly sculptured white church or palace facade, the orange buildings make these facades seem more distant and yet direct our eyes to their sculptural delicacy. The orange buildings are very appropriate foreground to the monumental architecture in Rome. This theme gave much beauty to Rome and was accomplished through the choice of a single color.

The use of colors is a significant aspect of beauty in cities. How correct is the vermilion bus of London seen against the somber gray facades. How correct the sky-blue streetcars in Zurich, and the yellow and orange stucco facades of Scandinavian buildings.

The Spanish Steps, Rome.

Light

Another visual factor is the particular quality of natural light. Some architects gave this great thought. The architects of ancient Egypt were confronted with the problem of how to make a monumental group of buildings assertive under conditions of blazing sunlight. They created great avenues lined by sphinxes. The avenues led to huge pylons which marked the entrances to the temple groups. The avenues of sphinxes proclaimed order in the desert; the pylons were gigantic placards which announced the sacred precinct. These pylons, seen in brilliant sunlight, were of the same light intensity as the sky and desert, for the bleaching sunlight

Egyptian pylons.

Egyptian temple interior.

Dutch landscape.

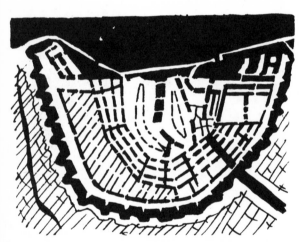

Plan of Amsterdam.

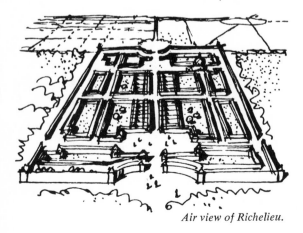

Air view of Richelieu.

muted differences in color and texture. To combat this, the Egyptian architects incised the pylons with large, brightly colored figures. Further, they outlined the corners of the pylons with a three-quarter-round molding and the top with a deep concave projection, thus creating a permanent shadow line which would always mark out the pylon forms against the sky.

Thus announced, the architecture of the temple group proceeded to employ sunlight in decreasing amounts. Entering the temple along its axis, a procession first came into a large open court, then passed between more pylons to a more fully enclosed court. As it advanced, the sunlight was progressively excluded until in the hypostyle hall it barely lit the forest of columns, making the number of columns seem infinite. Finally, at the central altar, a sacred place, a single beam of sunlight illuminated the statue in the inky darkness.

Featureless Landscape

Of the examples mentioned, the small cities are seen as entities in nature, whereas the large ones create new landscapes, or cityscapes. In some cases, where the features of nature which one might seek as clues to form are wanting, the cityscape must substitute for landscape. The city form is not unresponsive to nature; rather it employs the less demanding landform, more as a point of departure than as a condition to be extended, amplified, or contrasted. It goes further to create its own conditions. Amsterdam is an outstanding example of this theme.

The Dutch landscape is absolutely flat. Very prominent in the landscape are clumps of trees which are usually found around farmhouses. Water cannot be seen from afar, but only when one is standing on the edge of a canal or channel. Often, rows of trees mark out the line of a canal. One is constantly aware of the sky, since it is full of changing clouds and usually very dramatic. In contrast to this spacious landscape the Dutch towns are highly concentrated, generally because farmland was always precious. The streets are small and open on a central market square. Orientation is aided by views of church spires and other landmarks.

But Amsterdam, long one of the largest cities, was too extensive to depend entirely on the basic orienting device of landmarks. Its beginning as a small medieval cluster on the Amstel River became the nucleus of a concentric growth which has continued to this century. But what form could Amsterdam take? What could cityscape substitute for landscape? In Amsterdam the answer evolved in time as the city grew, particularly in the seventeenth century, Holland's golden years. At that time four concentric canals were constructed around the original medieval complex. Canals, houses, and bridges were designed and built simultaneously as whole design entities. This theme has prevailed. The result is a city of nearly a million people, quite compact, very low, and never waning in visual interest despite the very simple theme of form. One of the delights of the city is that the sense of orientation is never lost. The center is always indicated by the direction of curvature of the concentric streets and canals, which reoccurs as the radial streets are traversed.

Urbanity

The cities mentioned thus far share two qualities which underlie their beauty: their forms are artistic responses to the conditions of nature and the culture of their societies; and they possess a high

112

degree of urbanity—that quality of civility and good manners in architecture which allows buildings to stand close to each other, creating compositions which are greater as wholes than any part alone.

Richelieu, built as an adjunct to Cardinal Richelieu's castle south of the Loire Valley of France, is a prime example of the quality of urbanity in city form. The town is a tiny, walled rectangle measuring about five hundred by seven hundred yards. Its population was and still is a mere two thousand. Yet it has all the elements of city form which constitute the physical aspect of urbanity. It has clearly marked portals in the walls, making a distinction between town and country, a main street of handsome proportions, two main squares and several minor ones, an impressive church, and small town house gardens behind the row houses which form the walls of its streets. It could not be more different from the sprawling suburban clusters we build today.

Richelieu.

Uses of Geometry

An interesting counterpart to Richelieu is the core of the ancient Indian city of Fatehpur Sikri, whose population once numbered 50,000. At the core of the city was a court area called the Mahal-i-Khas. It served as the residence of the ruler. It was also his administration center where he sought the council of his ministers and held audiences with his subjects. It was a city within a city. Like Richelieu, the layout of Fatehpur Sikri is highly geometric, both cities being rectilinear, but there the similarity ends. In Richelieu the observer sees things along axial layouts; in Fatehpur Sikri his powers of observation are assumed to be more advanced. There, the entire complex can be viewed obliquely, as well as along its axes. In Richelieu one experiences a series of head-on or profile views; in Fatehpur Sikri one experiences profile views plus the more subtle, and sometimes more telling, three-quarter or oblique views. We may see a similarity to Frank Lloyd Wright's Taliesen as we walk through Fatehpur Sikri. So, perhaps, would contemporary interpretation have it. Aside from the validity or error of such conjecture, we have at least established the richness of possibility that can extend from one aspect of urban form—the various ways of employing geometry.

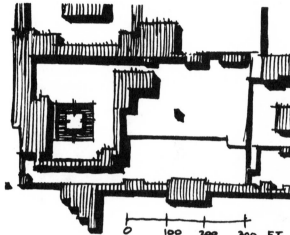

Plan of Fatehpur Sikri.

Concept

If there is one city that incorporates more of the qualities we have been mentioning to a greater degree than any other in the world, that city is Peking. Its form, its arrangement, its details, and its life create a superb example of a beautiful environment in which urban life can be conducted most graciously. Peking has had several forms, all more or less rectangular, and all occupying the same site—on a plain between the sea and the Mongolian hinterlands to the north. Peking's form is full of symbolism, but a practical symbolism, reflecting the beliefs which were derived from the experience and understanding of its people. It was walled to keep out invaders, just as the whole of China was walled. Its houses were oriented around courts which faced south, a symbolic and practical measure, since both cold winter winds and barbaric invaders came from the north. Indeed, the whole city is laid out as a giant house, the emperor being at the center, facing south on his own household—an arrangement followed in the individual households, modest or grand, throughout the city.

The landscape around Peking is flat, except for hills on the

Fatehpur Sikri.

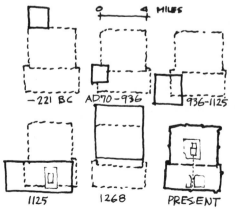

The evolution of Peking.

113

distant horizon. There was little in the way of natural form to extend, as in Amsterdam, and thus, lacking strong hints from nature, the Chinese had to invent their own urban forms. Kublai Khan, in the thirteenth century, called together his wisest men—philosophers, scholars, artists—and told of his ambitions to build the world's finest city—a veritable throne of heaven on earth. He urged his assemblage to advance far beyond what was then their sum of knowledge, and inspired them with one ringing thought: "To build a beautiful city," he said, "we must start with a beautiful concept." That concept was not simply a concept of form; it was a concept of living, for which form was but the physical extension.

The detailed results of Khan's thinkers are vast. Shopping, they decided, should take place in wooded groves—the hustle of shopping would be relieved by the calm of the grove. The infinite variety of activities, and the complex constructions which housed them, were cleverly ordered by broad major avenues dividing the town into regular rectangles; the disadvantages of close quarters and narrow streets being thus relieved by the orderly grand avenues. The rigidity of the rectilinear plan is complemented by the natural flow of stream and park which enters the city from the north and winds its way through to the center.

Perhaps the greatest value of observations such as these lies in gaining an attitude of optimism and deference toward the creation of beautiful cities. Our optimism can rest in the knowledge that beautiful cities have been created in all types of topographical situations and cultural conditions, including times of uncertainty and unrest, times like our own. Our deference must come from the attitude that a city is a guest in nature, and as such, must practice its best manners. The life and form of a city must defer to the customs of the place established by local climate, topography, light, and the past and present populace. Only then can we absorb graciously the abrupt changes and conditions which evolving life and developing technology present. And only then can we proceed to establish the harmonies and refinements which constitute beauty in cities.

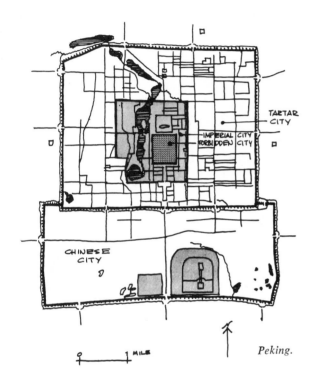

Peking.

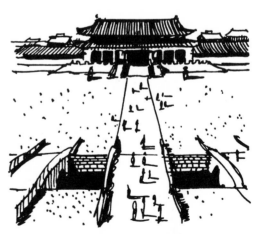

Palace in the Forbidden City of Peking.

A main street in Peking.

Possibilities for Reshaping American Cities

Consideration of the beauty of the cities of the past is a spur to the consideration of the future of our own cities. If we are to fulfill the promise of our cities, we will have to match and surpass the accomplishments of our predecessors of other times and places. We can begin by adopting the philosophy that *to create a beautiful city we must start with a beautiful concept* and the conviction that *every city can become its best self.*

Survey

This very large-scale work should begin with an equally extensive evaluation of the possibilities of the site. We should make surveys of sites to discern their design capacity—their potential to support additions and the character of those additions. We should examine sites which have been built upon almost as if they had not been touched, and ask what would be better there, considering the site and its most artful development potential.

This approach was vividly stated by Ian Nairn, the English architect-planner. Nairn pointed out the fallacy of using statistical analysis in making planning decisions which are matters of artistic judgment—matters of seeing the whole picture through a design survey with both the mind and the heart at work.

Design surveys can be made on any scale. Their physical boundaries can be delineated as areas which function interdependently, such as metropolitan or state regions. Henry Wright's and Clarence Stein's plan for the State's plan for the State of New York in 1926 is a landmark in this field. Benton MacKaye had an even broader perspective. More recently a survey of Connecticut was completed by the Connecticut Redevelopment Commission, and was published as a report entitled *The Appearance of Connecticut.* It assessed the appearance of the entire state and discussed the character and function of its parts, entities which were largely determined by distinguishing physical and visual characteristics.

Such surveys should be preludes and accompaniments to all planning actions. This would in no way replace any of the other analytical surveys necessary in planning programs. It is, however, a vital link to understanding what an area's physical and visual resources are, along with the other more conventional development surveys. Each state in our country should embark on such a survey program.

On a smaller scale, regional entities encompassing several interdependent cities and towns could be taken as the "field" area. Such an instance is the Cape Orlando-Daytona Beach area of Florida. A conference of planners of all outlooks was held to discuss the course to be taken for that area. Among their conclusions was that of Carl Feiss, FAIA, who recommended that a design survey for the area be initiated in order to suggest development sites and possibilities, as well as to give direction to the planning.

There are countless such situations in this country—groups of related cities or towns which are destined to grow. They need a large plan of physical development to set a beautiful direction and goal for their efforts. For most practicing architects a more likely scale would be design capacity studies of their own cities or towns, stated in general terms, pointing out how the more obvious errors of the past could be corrected, and giving new images of better communities.

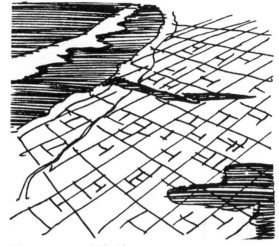

The east coast of Florida.

Topographical features of Connecticut.

115

View of Pittsburgh.

Hillside development in Pittsburgh.

A proposed building over a valley expressway for Pittsburgh.

Proposed point buildings for Pittsburgh.

(Sketches adapted from drawings by Richard Farley and Joe Johnson in "Pittsburgh Perceived.")

Relation to Nature and Topography

We would begin our proposals of urban form by considering our city's basic relationship to nature. We would then go on to examine its form as a satisfaction or an encumbrance to its function. We would then examine its forms and their relationships as satisfactions or insults to our human senses. We must always question the quality of the city's forms as a response or a repudiation of all these conditions. And we must discern in the disarray the elements which are the true bases of its forms. The recent study of Pittsburgh by Patrick Horsbrugh of the University of Texas is a landmark in this approach.

Few cities have as discouraging a reputation for ugliness as does Pittsburgh, the "Cinderella of American Cities," as Professor Horsbrugh described it. Curiously, it may be our ugliest cities which turn out to be the most amenable to civic redevelopment and beautifying. Professor Horsbrugh's study suggests how this can be done for Pittsburgh, basing the new forms on the prevailing conditions of the site, specifically its topography and its way of life. He designated various areas for housing, roadways, or factories, or simply for preservation in their natural state.

The great error which Horsbrugh pointed out was the lack of recognition of the outstanding natural beauty of the site as the design basis of its urban forms. He pointed out how both the character of the terrain and the many cultures of Pittsburgh's citizens, its industries and its unique position, should be used as the real basis for re-forming the city. Horsbrugh's report is a sensitive appraisal of delicate topography which has been abused. It is done, not with a statistician's measure, but with a heart and mind poised for seeking a more harmonious relation between nature and human settlement on this site. And he implies that every city has its own personality which its form should express—the basis for developing the city as "its best self."

Of course, few cities have as striking topography as Pittsburgh—San Francisco, Troy, Atlanta, Seattle, and some parts of Los Angeles and Portland are among the few—and all of these need and deserve the kind of penetrating study which Pittsburgh obtained.

Water

A more commonly found natural asset is the proximity to water. Many of our cities were developed on water for obvious practical reasons; for these same reasons we have neglected the potentials of the water edges in our haste to develop industry and commerce. This abused resource has begun to receive wide appreciation and in many cases, forward-looking redevelopment proposals. Boston harbor, for example, is a fertile field of urban design potential, considering for redevelopment not only the shoreline immediate to the city, but the entire bay with all its islands and water areas. Some of the islands could be residential, some institutional. Others could have satellite communities connected to the central city by water transport or perhaps, in the not too distant future, hovercraft vehicles. Many islands should, of course, be left alone.

116

Conjecture

Recently, members of the Northern California Chapter of the AIA submitted imaginative proposals for redeveloping Alcatraz Island in San Francisco Bay. Ellis Island in New York Harbor has also received design attention for redevelopment.

Greater Baltimore harbor, the whole of the Norfolk area in Virginia, much of New York and Long Island, the Tacoma–Seattle Bay area, the Detroit–Windsor water area—all are dormant worlds waiting to be awakened by the magic of urban design vision. Modern engineering has made possible the creation of artificial or man-made landscape—landscape sculpture on a vast scale. The precedent for this work has been established, and forward-looking urban design could give direction to our continuing urbanization.

The great land speculations in Florida of the twenties included many imaginative designs for artificial islands for hotels and housing. Much of the Florida coast was developed by infilling. In effect, what nature had begun, developers tried to refine. Some of the plans recalled the character of Venice. Indeed an airplane flight along much of our coastal shoreline reveals a considerable amount of marina housing development.

There is an opportunity for creative shorescape in many of our water-edge cities which are flat and otherwise topographically featureless, except for the meeting of land and water. Meager rivers could be dammed to created large inland lakes. For example, the Trinity River in Dallas, Texas, already has flood dikes along its shores. The river itself is a narrow stream most of the year. If it were dammed up some miles below the city, one of the world's largest inland lakes could be formed. Artificial islands could be built in the lake and the cost of the whole undertaking could be paid in tax revenues. Its value as a recreational resource would be immeasurable.

Water can be brought into the city in the form of canals and reservoirs. The value and attractiveness of these sites would be increased by the proximity of water. Waterways could be active as well as passive: some could have marinas, others could be used for rowboating, fishing, sailing, and swimming. The engineering potential is in our hands. The real estate and speculative inducements could be strong, but the urban design vision must first be tapped.

The treatment of a hillside, whether a palisade or a slope, overlooking an urban view is a perplexing design problem. Should the hill be left intact as much as possible, and accented with contrasting architecture, or should it be terraced? Our engineering skill has made terracing more and more feasible, and the shortage of good urban sites undoubtedly will increase the practice. Artistic judgment must be applied to these situations. Los Angeles is fast becoming a casebook of both good practice and serious failure from a design standpoint. Some of the hillsides have been used as homesites whose design artfully recognizes the hill form. Some of these homes have been built on stilts or masts. The other extreme is the wholesale terracing of the hillside into suburban 1-acre lots, an attempt to make a hillside into a flat area, which it cannot be.

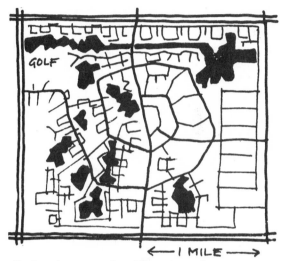

Design of a community with waterways in Florida by Lester Collins, FASLA.

An air-approach view of Miami.

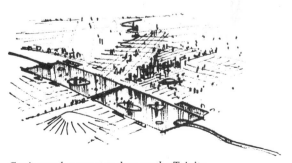

Conjectural concept to dam up the Trinity River in Dallas, creating a huge lake for recreation and island developments.

117

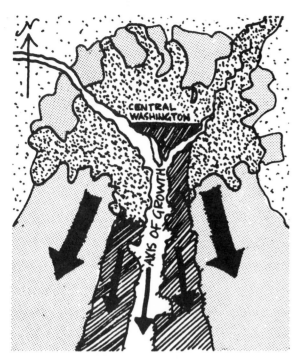

Constantine Doxiadis' concept for the southward growth of Washington—from "Dynopolis."

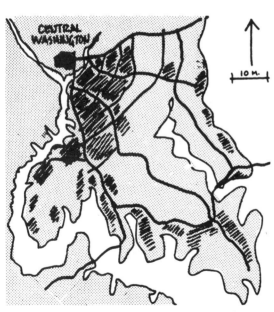

Development study from a class project by the students of Kevin Lynch of one of the sectors suggested by the Year 2000 Plan *for Washington.*

Growth and Form

Hillside treatment, palisade accentuation and artificial hills, waterways and islands—all these are but preludes in the developing palette of urban design. Urban design, insofar as it recognizes natural terrain characteristics, must respond to every situation, from the dramatic landscape to the nearly featureless flat plain. Of course, the day-to-day life and culture of a city can never be neglected, but the direction and forms of a city's growth are largely determined by the land. Two design proposals for a sector of Washington, D.C., illustrate this.

From its original core, Washington grew out along routes of transportation which connected it to neighboring cities. Bridges were built across the Potomac to effect communication with the South. The route north to Baltimore was overland and presented no obstacles. The northwest sector of Washington was not developed until recent times when the pressure of real estate development and the need for communication with towns in that direction urged the spanning of Rock Creek Park, a deep natural gully. This opened that entire area for building. Today another sector has begun to develop—the area of the city stretching southward along the Potomac.

The two design proposals which recognized the possibilities of the south sector were based on two very different design theories. Constantinos Doxiadis, during a visit to Washington, pointed out how the center of Washington could move gradually southward. That direction, he felt, would best serve his concept of "Dynopolis," a city whose center moves according to plan to perform an ever-larger service that the preceding center is ill-equipped to provide. This movement, according to the doctrines of Dynopolis, is a characteristic of modern cities. In the case of the southern sector of Washington one major obstacle to growth is the Anacostia River. Doxiadis proposed a substitution in transport to overcome this difficulty—waterborne traffic.

The second design proposal was published in a study made by Kevin Lynch and a group of graduate students. This study applies to a real situation the findings of Professor Lynch's research on the form of a city. The design of the sector proceeded with the standard planning considerations, aided by the methodical application of considerations of form which would lead to better decisions in land use, roadway placement, vertical or horizontal development—in short, a full plan which also considered form as a major aspect of design.

The point of these proposals was that they were based on the realities of topography. An interesting study could be made of most cities along these lines—the recognition of dormant sectors for development, possibly applying a theory of growth.

Further Possibilities

In some cases an urban sector might be entirely uninhabitable, like the marsh areas of San Francisco Bay. Here is a piece of geography ripe for development and the ultimate in land and water sculpture. At this scale the appreciation of movement through landscape is essential. In some cases it has been recognized. The air approach to Miami, for example, is carefully plotted to give arriving vacationers a view of the ocean-front development.

As long ago as 1930 Elbert Peets proposed that cities be de-

118

signed to be seen from the air as well as from the ground. This consideration could involve the skyline of a city, something we might call vertical texture. Studies of a town or city could determine where on the skyline assertive verticals should be placed, perhaps as cluster groups. In prairie cities the grain silo has often been both an accent and a symbol on the skyline. The Price Tower in Oklahoma by Frank Lloyd Wright suggests an amplification of the role of the vertical in a small town. Some towns could be ringed with slender towers, marking them out on the flat plains as the minarets of ancient Istanbul did for its mosques. Pairs or clusters of towers can often serve an old city as a portal accent, marking a significant point of entry.

Wright's Price Tower in Oklahoma.

The possibilities are limitless, and can derive from every outlook. For example, one might recall a town's history by reviving an old element. Such is the case in a proposal a few years ago in San Antonio, Texas, to revive the old Mission Trail. The Mission Trail is now somewhat indistinct; it once connected the original Spanish missions. The route roughly follows the San Antonio River, which was used to irrigate the farm fields of the missions. Some parts of the fields are now used as parks. The Mission Trail would revive the stretch of agricultural land as a grand greenway, reaching nearly to the heart of the city. Its land uses would be both active and passive, but wholly varied.

We may find that some legal actions have significant urban design effect. The relaxation of laws which hamper leisure pursuits might give tremendous impetus to a more wholesome and adult use of the city. An example of this was the alteration of laws in Washington, D.C., first to allow sidewalk cafés and later to allow alcoholic drinks to be served.

The Mission Trail which became San Antonio. The Alamo is at the present center of the city. Irrigation channels and dams watered the fields of each mission.

A Human Approach

Although we have concentrated in this chapter on the physical aspects of urban design, we do not mean to deny the social and cultural bases of it. The latter factors are implicit—as implicit as in architecture. We have dwelt on the aspects of form because that is the medium through which we, as architects, make our contributions. In conclusion, let us recall the advice of two great masters of our arts, Alvar Aalto and Eliel Saarinen.

Aalto once told a group of students how he designed the tuberculosis sanitarium in Paimio, Finland. He considered how each inhabitant would use it and feel in it, from director to patient to janitor. He imagined himself the director, arriving, parking his car, entering "his" hospital, feeling proud of his role at every moment. He then imagined himself in the role of every member of the hospital's staff, and checked his design to insure that everyone who used it, who worked in it, could feel the importance of his own part in the hospital's operation. The janitor, for example, had to have his own small closet for his work clothes rather than an impersonal hook in a locker room.

Aalto also imagined himself a patient, arriving at the hospital, depressed at having to leave his family, and faced with a long period of convalescence. He pictured himself in every moment of a patient's experience, traveling through the wooded landscape in which the hospital is set, arriving and seeing for the first time the large white building with its outstretched welcoming arms, entering and being cheered by the warm colors and the warm, textured woodwork. Aalto designed the patients' rooms thinking of the

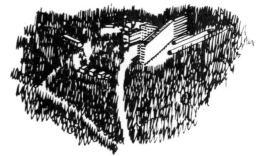

Air view of the tuberculosis sanitarium in Paimio, Finland, by Alvar Aalto.

119

The Church of Christ in Columbus, Indiana, by Eliel Saarinen.

angle at which patients would be looking at them—horizontally, from a bed. In this, Aalto went beyond function, utility, economy, and proportion; he entered the area of real experience.

Eliel Saarinen related how, when designing the Church of Christ in Columbus, Indiana, he visited that town and proceeded to imagine the future church. He conceived the whole plan, the appearance of the church, the experience of its congregation living in the town and attending the church—all from the point of view of the people who would be using it. Before making a single drawing he checked and rechecked his design, altering it to satisfy all the conditions and requirements the church would have to meet and the spiritual effects it would create. Then he was ready to draw up his design.

This procedure of conceiving the physical environment in such real terms, with beauty as the ultimate goal, must now be extended to the design and re-creation of all our towns and cities—a task which we must never be reluctant to approach with a sense of poetry.

Designing the Parts
of the City

Suppose that the city were not a creation of man but of nature. Suppose that it were an animal. In some ways it functions very much like one, considering that each of its parts is comparable to the vital organs of an animal body.

The Arab cities of North Africa illustrate this idea. In the center stands a mosque, the spiritual and intellectual center of the city—its brain and heart. Nearby is the palace of the ruler, and so the center is a place of decision as well. Then, near the mosque, one finds candle and perfume makers who supply the mosque with some of its ceremonial requisites. As a center of learning the mosque is bordered by the university which includes an ample library. Merchants of fine leathers, papers, and cloths supply the materials for binding the books. This center of finery supplies goods for clothing as well as for the mosque and its library, and the cloth merchants require a sheltered enclosure, a roofed hall, which can be locked. Consequently, the quarter for carpenters, locksmiths, and metalsmiths lies alongside. Taking a few more steps we are at the city gates, where we find saddle-makers and hostels for travelers. Thus the component parts of the organized Arab city are located as logically as the organs of the human body. Their dimensions and distances are also largely determined by the mathematics of pedestrian circulation.

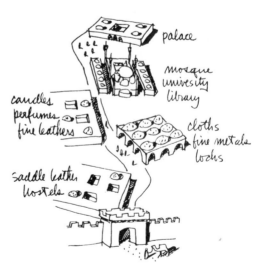

The structure of an Arabic town.

121

Considering the city in this light we see that there are vital relationships between a city's parts, vital links which can determine their size, position, and form. We also see that some parts are healthier than others, that some maintain themselves, that some need constant housekeeping, that some in disrepair need emergency treatment, that some need plastic surgery, and that still others should be amputated. When these relationships are changed, the whole system can be thrown off balance. One quarter may then suffer. New quarters may come into being. Such a change may come with a change in circulation habits—switching from foot to camel or from bus to car. In a period of change the whole system is constantly seeking a functional balance of parts.

In this chapter we shall approach our own cities in somewhat the same fashion, recognizing that the parts of our cities, unlike the relatively static Arab cities, exist in a state of nearly violent physical change. We shall try to understand the parts of our cities and foresee what forms they are seeking to attain in the face of our dynamic times.

Centers in the Metropolis

Downtown is the center of the American city and heavy is its responsibility. Louis Kahn has written that "the center is the cathedral of the city." It is its soul and brain. To fulfill this role the center must also be the acropolis of the city, the physical evidence and embodiment of all that is best.

Downtown developed at the most strategic point in our cities, usually on a preordained street grid. At its best, downtown contained the highest concentration of services for the whole community. Now we see this function diminishing and many virtues of our downtown lessening. This is very much a concern of urban designers, for through the application of their techniques much can be done to retain the valuable facilities of downtown while the areas around take on new forms.

Change and development is the key to understanding the downtown's role, for no downtown ever remained static in form or function, but grew as the surrounding communities grew, as long as the means of access between the two were ample. Close around the downtown were complementary parts of the city—the early downtown was bordered by close-in residential areas, by manufacturing areas, and by a harborfront or railyard. Thus access was to a large degree by foot as well as horse and wagon. As cities grew, the downtown thus found itself constrained and its possible directions for growth limited. Consequently, the growth of the center was usually somewhat linear, in the direction of the city's general growth away from harborfront or riverside. As fashionable areas of the city grew, "uptown" developed as both a complement and a competitor to downtown, the original center. As the city grew further and its needs increased, an offshoot of both uptown and downtown developed—"midtown," a third form of the center.

At this stage of development, the degree of access required taxed heavily the form and appearance of the center. In order for this complex to operate it had to support an inordinate amount of movement. The center's physique broke down and failed, unless a remedy could be found in a new and more efficient means of circulation.

The early public transportation systems were such remedies.

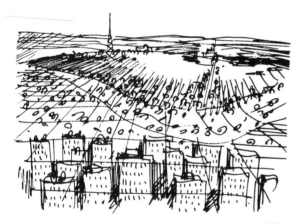

Schematic sketch of downtown Cincinnati, Ohio. In the foreground, downtown skyscrapers. Beyond is a residential-commercial fringe culminating in hills, upon which are located hospitals, fine houses, and schools.

In fact, they were built when people could not live without close and direct access to the center. For the population depended on the center, if not for its livelihood, then for its services. Public transportation systems prior to the automobile—trolleys and subways—allowed cities to take their first giant steps. The subway systems were rather drastic remedies in this situation, but they had a major saving grace: they could be built underground out of sight. They imposed little on the physiognomy of the city. The opposite practice of raising the tracks above ground as elevated railroads was as destructive of a street's amenities as it was a boon to its commerce. Circulation systems can have a constructive as well as a destructive effect on a street or on an entire quarter of a city. It depends on how intelligently they are designed, starting with these overall concepts and continuing down to such details as the design of passenger seating.

However, even with the best circulation and access systems, there seems to be a limit to how big and all-encompassing an urban center can be. The change in the traditional form of our downtowns is not an American phenomenon alone. It is seen in all the large administrative cities of the world's more advanced nations. As the size and age of a city increases, the center becomes a series of centers. The central functions become nucleated and widespread. New York, for example, has several centers rather than a distinct downtown. So does Chicago, Los Angeles, Detroit, and St. Louis—all in varying degrees. Paris has a series of hubs connected by spokes of central city services. London has its quarter for law, its street for doctors, its section for the theater, its area for clothing, but overall it is a rough tweedy fabric of facilities rather than a clear-cut focus of them in the center.

In a word, the services and functions of cities are spreading increasingly over the ever-widening metropolitan area, through our use of the automobile together with other modes of modern transit. Altogether the vehicles of modern transportation have brought a compelling new geometry to urban patterns and to the disposition and size of urban nuclei. To recognize the powerful effects of a new transit system and to use them at all, is one thing, but to use them wisely, is another. If all modern means of circulation were brought into use in all of our large and congested cities, the major effect could be one of spread and nucleation—enlargement and a new pattern of "centers." But it would be a real question as to how desirable that would actually be if carried to the ultimate limit. Accessibility to all of the nuclei and the infilling urban areas would be very high, and there could not possibly be any need for it. The much maligned form of Los Angeles is a rough model of this possibility. Access is very high, comparatively, and it will be increased further by more freeways. These will, as they are built, increase access and so spawn ever more urbanization and urban centers. The question is not one of the level of access, as much as it is the desirability of making such a high urban agglomeration in the first place. In actuality the most desirable parts of Los Angeles are precisely those that are physically limited and distinct—Santa Monica, Pacific Palisades, Beverly Hills, etc.

A discussion of the newly forming pattern of the dispersed metropolis was a major theme of the book *The Future Metropolis.* In that book Kevin Lynch posed the implications of several form possibilities, ranging from a totally dispersed pattern of living, working, servicing, and leisure, wherein there would be

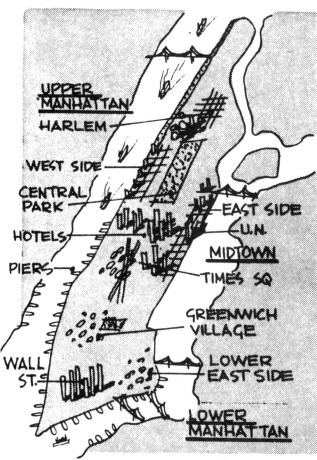

The various parts of Manhattan emerged as the city matured.

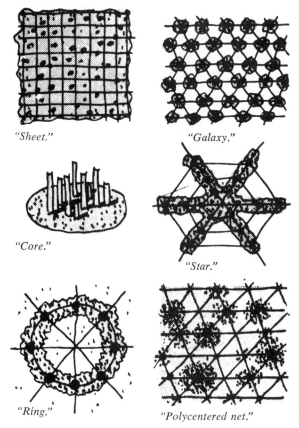

"Sheet."   *"Galaxy."*

"Core."

"Star."

"Ring."   *"Polycentered net."*

Various metropolitan forms and the arrangement of their parts. (Adapted from Lynch.)

123

Development of the parts of a river city.

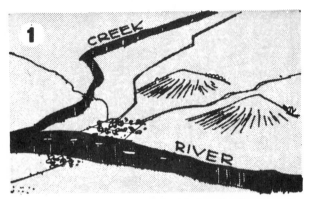

Original agricultural and trade center.

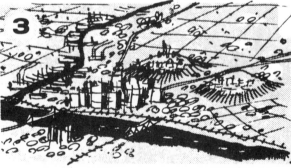

Later development as an industrial center as well.

Present-day confusion of form.

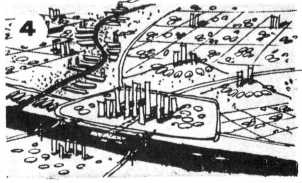

Tomorrow's refinement of form.

minimum physical or functional differentiation (Wright's Broadacres is an example of this as a design), to a highly concentrated center with spokes of peripheral use interspersed with spokes of open space (_The Year 2000 Plan_ for Washington, D.C.). One of Lynch's illustrative form arrangements was a blend of both, a pattern in which there were a number of foci which accented the general pattern of close-knit intermingled uses. The foci were functional and physical. Thus there might be a center of offices demarked and visible from afar as a cluster of skyscrapers, or a focus might be a medical group or a university-law-government complex.

This seems to be the pattern we are developing most frequently. How well we attain it, for large cities as well as small ones, depends on our ability to recognize the urban groupings we have at present as valuable resources, and to see in the currents of change and development, phenomena which we can use to refine the form and arrangement of these groupings.

In _The Future Metropolis_ we are told that the center itself is likely to become more of an administration center than a center of various services—that the breadth of its function is narrowing. Thus, shopping in the center may increase in absolute terms only slightly while the increase in shopping in a metropolitan-wide area will increase both absolutely and proportionately. This simply means that shopping and many auxiliary services once found only in the central city will follow population, leaving behind a central city of a new sort, with new and different possibilities.

We are also finding that there are new possibilities for mixture and relationship in land uses and urban activities. For example, many modern industrial plants can be appropriately located in, or quite near, residential neighborhoods. A small plant which produces neither smoke nor noise, and which does not generate large amounts of traffic, can be nicely landscaped and constitute a good neighbor. Good design in architecture and landscaping is largely responsible for making this possible.

Further, it may be wise to encourage policies that induce the creation of new in-town residential areas. Many downtown fringe areas are quite appropriate for new residential groups. In fact, many of them have little potential for other uses.

Policy and Design

The possibilities for reforming a center depend on many factors. The commonly accepted role of urban design is that of arranging the building blocks of a city to form a street or square or a new quarter. Or the role of design may be to reform some of these parts with a few choice building blocks here and there. The building blocks themselves constitute the whole gamut of our urban technology. A new or hitherto unused mode of urban transport is an urban design "building block," for it can be employed as a prime reshaping device. Several related building blocks may have such inherent importance as to constitute together an actual technique of design, as we discussed in the chapter on urban design principles.

Regarded in this way, the art of urban design is a method for arranging a part of a city or a whole city. It is also a method for implementing in urban terms a large social and economic fact. But urban design has a larger role, still; that is, to help shape those larger regional and social facts which make one city a highly desirable place to live or, on the other hand, stagnate the economy and society of another.

Perhaps it is incorrect to think of such large courses of action as urban design. Perhaps "policy" is a more acceptable term; policy which shapes a region's transportation, its resources, its national role, and its social composition.

Heretofore the role of policy has been largely assumed by the events of happenstance and the pressures of one group or another. The result has been, and is, the state of our cities. The benefits, such as they are, have been proclaimed as virtues, and the shortcomings, such as they are, have often been answered by narrowly framed corrective efforts.

If urban design is seen only as a fix-up of a city in disrepair, it will be a narrowly framed corrective effort. If it is seen first as a larger effort to direct the forces that are at the root of city shaping—call that policy—then the repair actions are firmly and correctly based.

Actually there is a scale of urban design actions that is appropriate to different problems. If a street is in bad shape, it can be repaired according to a street design. If a downtown is in decline, it can be revitalized by a sound and efficient urban transportation network which brings great numbers of people to the center without congesting it and without demolishing its supporting institutions. But none of these urban design actions make much sense without the ultimate role of urban design—regional policy or regional planning.

In addressing the problems of designing the city's parts, it is vital to recognize the various levels at which urban design must operate. It is also important to recognize that all of them must be in operation together. A man's job and happiness derive from the vitality of his region, whether that be an industrial area of the country or a part of its farm belt. That same man needs a pleasant place for his children to go to school. Altogether our urban population needs centers of various sorts to pursue its broad interests. To Louis Kahn's remark that "the center is the cathedral of the city" we can add: "the subcenters are the parish churches." The centers of the city are among the prime parts in need of design.

Designing with a Grid Layout: Streets and Blocks

The physique of most American cities is dominated by our predominant use of gridiron layouts. As useful as this was in apportioning land in the early days, the grid is a mixed blessing for urban design. Our extensive use of the grid places certain limits on the variations possible in urban design. But these limits are the facts of life with which many of us must reckon and, in fact, with which we can work with ample latitude. The grid is a geometry of street and square.

We can approach the problems of designing the parts of cities by considering the street. The street, perhaps more than any other single element of urban design, has two powerful effects: it can unite central enclaves or it can support or undermine the function of a particular enclave—it can be helpful or inimical to the area it serves. The street is one of the most vital factors of urban form. It is to the city what the wheel is to machinery. One of the first tasks of urban design in the central city, regardless of the degree of transformation it encounters, is to assure that the form of the street is appropriate. Consider the shopping street in the center of the cities.

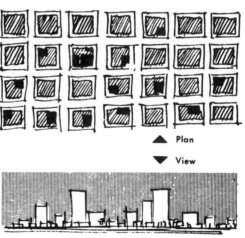

Geometric pattern in plan is a guarantee neither of orderly arrangement nor of visual clarity.

125

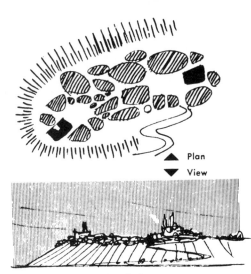

Plan ▲
View ▼

A seemingly disordered plan may possess more orderly arrangement and visual clarity than pure plan geometry. Coherent variety is a product of plan, not elevation.

Sitting places on upper Broadway, N.Y.C.

"Chinatown" in the evening.

A shopping street which is too wide precludes vital visual and physical contact with both sides of the street simultaneously; it is inimical to shoppers because they cannot maintain full contact with the shops on both sides of the street. Imagine having a 50-foot aisle in a department store—or even a 15-foot aisle. Conversely, if shopping diminishes in the city, this may have its advantages. The prophecy for central cities is that there will be an increase in administrative offices. This suggests that the shopping which will prevail will be largely for office workers, a white-collar class whose tastes run high. Along with the shops they will require restaurants, cocktail lounges, and the many nooks these people use during their working day.

The point for design is that an increase in administrative offices means an increased need for prestigious office buildings. The "wide" American downtown street may be an ideally urban size, an attractive and altogether appropriate setting for fine office buildings. With streets of such size, however, will remain a need for its counterpart, the narrow and more intimate scale of a "nook" street. Without that, the pristine glamour of the grand office street may be too overbearing.

Thus urban design for the central city could start with an evaluation of streets according to their widths and positions, and from that an idea could be gained of where different center city developments might take place appropriate to the physical dimensions of the streets. The recent plan for improving downtown San Francisco recognizes the physical characteristics of streets and their effects on shopping. That plan proposes a number of corrections to the form of streets, where the forms now are inappropriate to the uses the streets support, as well as improvements for better interrelations between streets and functional enclaves.

A key issue in regard to a street is the sidewalk and its treatment. A sidewalk, like a street, can be too narrow as well as too wide. It can be too open as well as too closed. It can be well landscaped or poorly landscaped. Too wide a sidewalk can be difficult to maintain and difficult to shade. It has more potential, however, than one which is too narrow, for that precludes the possibilities for shading by tree or canopy, or the development of sidewalk displays, cafés, kiosks, or simply a place to sit down. One good tree in an urban scene can be more effective visually than several sickly trees. Small potted trees seen against the virile facades of great corporation buildings or banks may seem puny and pointless.

Orientation is another key consideration of the street. A north-south street receives greater variety of light and shadow effects during a sunny day than an east-west street. The sunny side of an east-west street can be overbearingly hot during the summer, and attempts to shade a city street, particularly a busy shopping street, are not easy. Nor are the chilling effects of the blasts of winter wind easy to alleviate. A possible area of research and experimentation is the study of devices which could block chilling winter winds on city streets, and other devices—perhaps building shape and arrangement—which could induce and magnify cooling summer breezes.

One of the major contributions to urban design might be the development of a department of the city which will tend to the city's streets as well as our park departments tend to our urban greenery. We need a clearer understanding of all our cities' open spaces, ranging from the traditional park down to the sidewalk.

Perhaps such a program could result from an active liaison between the design section of a city planning staff and the local park or street department, in frequent consultation with local architects. The sidewalk is an urban space which complements the uses of bordering private land. The sidewalk is the free space for people as the roadway is the free space for cars. The sidewalk is the corridor for people. It is the resting place, the moving place, the shady place, the first contrasting relief from the office or shop as one steps out of a building.

If we reflected on the many sensations we experience in walking along a street, as we do on the sensations of driving, we might have the solid beginnings of a viable urban street design program. It is significant that the design of street lighting in the past forty years has been dominated by street lighting for the automobile. Few, if any, manufacturers' catalogs of street lighting contain designs for sidewalk lighting for pedestrians. If only 10 per cent of the standard fixtures were designed for pedestrians at walking scale, the problem could be solved. We criticize not the attention to good street lighting for cars; we criticize an oversight in the provision for the walker. It is no accident, then, that the old gaslight, either electrified or with its original wick system, is enjoying a fresh vogue. It is scaled for the pedestrian.

A key issue, too, is the length of a block as it relates to street dimensions. A city block can be too long or too short—too long to provide rhythmic relief and lateral access, and too short to allow substantial development. It is worth noting here the practice of urbanized Europeans in referring to the "street" or the "avenue" ("go down the street and turn left at the first avenue") while Americans refer to the "block" ("go down the block and turn left at the corner"). We have yet to capture the full potential of our streets.

The block is a basic module of urban pattern. Its geometry is a basic determinant of urban form. While it does have inherent flexibility of arrangement and use, it is also the source of great difficulty where urban accent is needed. An endless array of blocks is difficult to accent unless a block can be left unbuilt as an urban park or plaza. Even then it has limitations.

A small open block surrounded by broad streets is a weak focus, although it may be a welcome change of pace. A large open block, landscaped as an urban park, may be difficult to unify through the coordinated design of bordering facades. Indeed, it is quite unlikely that bordering facades can be coordinated at all. Almost always an urban park block is cut off from its bordering buildings by a roadway. Block patterns are a stretch of rectilinear islands, and their sizes and particular shapes impose definite limitations on the design of buildings.

However, it is possible to overcome these limitations to a large extent when several blocks can be treated simultaneously or when one block can be treated as a whole.

A group of blocks can be designed so as to form a composition of building masses, open spaces, parking, and pedestrian circulation. A single large block can also be treated this way. With a group of blocks, streets can be closed. Long blocks can be punctured with pedestrian walkways. Large blocks may offer possibilities for interior development, for plazas, parking, or pedestrian movement. Block interiors can also be transformed into places for intimate shops as complements to the more frequent and impersonal scale of large avenues and buildings. When a group

Maiden Lane, San Francisco.

Commonwealth Avenue, Boston.

Connecticut Avenue, Washington, D.C.

Michigan Avenue, Chicago.

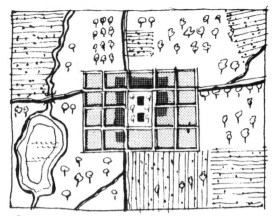

1 *Early settlement.*

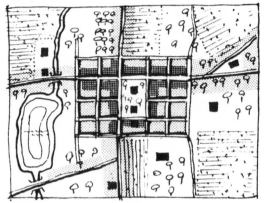

2 *Ensuing expansion.*

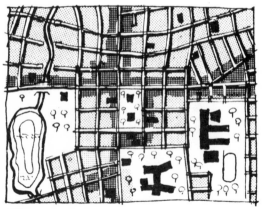

3 *Present development.*

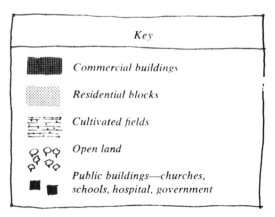

Key	
■	*Commercial buildings*
▦	*Residential blocks*
≡	*Cultivated fields*
♀♀	*Open land*
■ ■	*Public buildings—churches, schools, hospital, government*

Development of the central parts of a town.

of blocks is treated as a whole, streets can be bridged with buildings which link neighboring blocks, afford easy pedestrian passage, and give closure to the open street vista.

A comprehensive study of an area's circulation may reveal possibilities for closing a street for traffic entirely or for restricting its use to local service circulation alone. In such cases small plazas can be developed in the street itself, perhaps demarked by a dense closure of trees and shrubs. Such a possibility would do much to give needed focus to a church, post office, school, or community center.

The traffic patterns around outlying urban centers may offer several possibilities for rerouting through traffic. The shopping center can then function more as a stopping place for traffic. Where a shopping center covers several blocks, the interior streets can act as feeders to many small parking lots alongside the shops. Such an arrangement, though seemingly chaotic, may in fact be more functional than the rigid arrangement of ringing a shopping center with a broad belt of parking. The intermixing layout is more flexible and the whole center more intimate in character. Ideally, the parking should be handled as pockets—some around the periphery and some penetrating closer to the center. A network of pedestrian pathways could serve the whole complex.

The standard block pattern can be articulated by developing visibly evident and functional enclaves within it. These enclaves need carefully coordinated circulation patterns which exclude through traffic, but which receive and store incoming traffic. The enclaves must be designed to work for the pedestrian and must enable him to move about readily.

Enclaves can be joined to each other by pedestrian pathways. Enclaves should be linked and even blended with other complementary enclaves. For example, housing can border a shopping area. A light manufacturing area or an entertainment area can be blended into a commercial area. Enclaves, so blended, add up to the districts of a city. Periodically, however, these districts must come to a physical conclusion. They must end at a natural boundary such as a hill or stream. Where no prominent physical boundary exists, one can be created "artificially" as a reserve of parkland. No standards of design can be written to ascertain where boundaries should occur, except for one rule of thumb that comes from observation. One should be able to reach the edge of his district in a reasonable walk.

Amsterdam, Stockholm, and Venice possess this attribute. So do most parts of Manhattan, San Francisco, and Seattle. There are few such possibilities in the Bronx, in Los Angeles, or Houston. The problem is largely a matter of scale, conditioned by a rectangular pattern which needs accent, relief, and, ultimately, its own termination.

The Center's Clusters of Activity

Programs for revitalizing downtown must address it as a whole, although action may concentrate on a key section. Downtowns are really organized as a series of activity clusters linked to each other. These clusters can take a variety of forms in the existing downtown proper.

Because most downtown "projects" are built to replace worn-out sections of blocks of buildings, they are generally peripheral to the downtown's actual core. Even so they alter the core con-

128

siderably. One form which a downtown project can assume is that of an anchor, actually more of a function than a form. Two major projects in Boston are anchors. The Government Center, itself a key hub of the city, will form a nucleus of activity which will arrest the general movement away from Boston's old center. The Prudential Center, a mile or two away, will mark the culmination of Boston's center, a boomerang-shaped swath bending about the central Common and Public Gardens.

Another equally valid form is the project which extends the city's center. Such an example is Hartford's Constitution Plaza, lying off the main shopping street toward the Connecticut River. Philadelphia's Penn Center is also an extension of the city's center. Still another form is the center city project as a linkage. The project can bridge a void in the central city between clusters. Such is the function of Baltimore's Charles Center. It stands between Baltimore's shopping area and its office area.

These projects, in their various stages of completion, have already begun to pose such interesting questions of design that they have become required visiting. One major question is the form of the pedestrian areas in these projects. In some projects the street, in its traditional form as a corridor, does not exist. Instead the whole project is treated as a block whose interior is a large plaza of pedestrian movement. With such an arrangement it is particularly important to effect a strong connection to neighboring pedestrian streets. This arrangement gives rise to the serious question of liveliness in an area where autos are excluded entirely. It may be better to have auto streets visible, if not actually penetrating the central open spaces of a project, rather than to exclude them entirely. Autos and people in the city can exist side-by-side in harmony when they do not conflict with each other's movements.

A particularly vexing problem may be the edge of such a multiblock project, the difficulty being that an apparent edge is all too much an interruption between project and bordering area. A strong edge may be desirable since it marks out the new project and gives an opportunity for emphasis. Still, the interruption of the rhythm in the urban fabric can be too harsh. A remedy may lie in a simple expedient—drawing the project boundaries not through streets but through bordering blocks. This, in fact, is what the project does in its interior, if it is of any size: it bridges streets and transforms their demarcating quality into a conjoining quality. The same can be done across streets which demark old from new, by simply including a substantial portion of the area across the street.

A further problem lies in the visible vitality of the project. Who can say that Penn Center or Constitution Plaza are not intense, confronted with the facts of their worker populations? Yet how apparent is this during the course of the day? Perhaps we have to find a way to achieve an even greater diversity of use in our projects, perhaps including some shops of less polished mien: a delicatessen, a movie theater, perhaps a five-and-ten.

The clusters of the changing central city have varying degrees of strength and permanence. Perhaps the most solid are the financial districts. Seldom do they move. The reasons for this include the solidity of the construction of bank and financial buildings and the prestige and enduring importance which results from an early established locale of quality. Wall Street developed as the natural business center of the original port of New York. So with

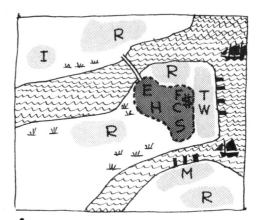

1 *Early settlement.*

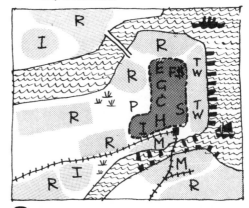

2 *Ensuing expansion.*

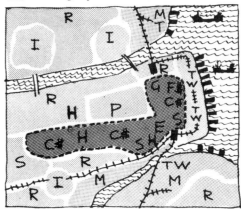

3 *Present development.*

Key			
⬤	Core	░	Core Adjuncts
F ⚏	Financial	R	Residential
C ⚏	Commercial	I	Institutional
S	Service	P	Park
E	Entertainment	M	Manufacturing
G	Government	TW	Transportation & warehousing
H	Hotel		

Development of the central parts of a city.

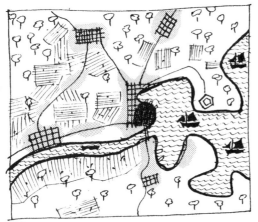

1 *Early settlement.*

2 *Ensuing expansion.*

3 *Present development.*

Key	
ᵠᵠᵠᵠ	Open land
▥▥▥	Cultivated land
░░░	Low density development
▦▦▦	Medium density development
▓▓▓	High density development

Development of the central parts of a metropolitan region.

the financial area of San Francisco, New Orleans, and Boston. Such permanent hubs are important anchors in a center. This identification is a major aspect of an urban design survey. Financial areas are generally masculine in character, which brings up another aspect of the various parts of cities—their gender.

Fine shopping areas are generally feminine in character, as witnessed by the theme of window displays. As shopping areas lose their fine quality, they lose, too, these feminine touches. It may not be too absurd to think of more delicate and graceful forms when we undertake designs for the improvement of worn-out downtown areas—forms and details more comfortable and pleasing to women. Similarly, there are areas of the city that are masculine in tone, such as financial and government areas, whose haberdasheries, barber shops, and bars are keyed to men.

The various clusters of the central city may not only have their own gender, they can induce gender in their surroundings, particularly in the channels of linkage which connect them to other clusters of hubs. In Boston, for example, there is a stretch of land between the State Street financial area and North Station, a major commuter rail terminal. Many of the men who work in State Street come from Boston's North Shore, and they come as commuters. The distance between North Station and State Street is a brisk fifteen-minute walk, a walk which attracts men but discourages women. The result is that the path between the station and the financial area is masculine in tone. Along it are found hardware stores, men's bars and cocktail lounges, oyster restaurants, used-book stores—all elements in a man's urban world.

It may not be a useless exercise of design imagination to think of the generator-feeder relationship of shopping areas in similar terms, but slanted toward women. The experience of the woman shopper who braves a car trip downtown, parks, and heads for the shopping streets may be formidable. Often it is enough to discourage her entirely. Here is an area of *generic* urban design: the design and treatment of all the things she sees and experiences so that she is put at ease, so that she feels assured and not threatened in driving, so that her heels will not be lodged in gratings, so that she does not have to encounter the gray fringe so common to our downtowns. It is a matter of designing the expressway-artery-parking-walking-shopping sequence for her.

The objectives of urban design in the central city can be simply stated: it must be made easy to get to by all means of transportation; it must be made so attractive and must have so many delights that it is worth going to; and it must be arranged so as to be continuously alive with humming vitality. In the central city these objectives are complicated by the remains of places which are not so palatable visually and are difficult to remove. Peripheral hubs may thrive amidst sprawling chaos. Both kinds of hubs can be remedied.

The central city contains many institutional clusters, particularly hospital and university groups. Two courses of design action can be taken for them, one having to do with their needs for growth and expansion, one having to do with their relation to the center city proper. Most of these institutions need more space for the growth of their plant, for parking and for nearby residences. The prevalent decay around institutions is providing more and more fresh ground for their expansion and, if wisely planned, can effect new continuities with nearby hubs. The American college campus, for example, furnishes us with a design device that wants extension—the series of linked spaces. This same device can be a basis for the sound design planning for hospital groups.

Another major type of cluster in the central city is the residential group, which we shall discuss in the next chapter, but which must be mentioned here. Suffice it to say that the main element of liveliness in the central city is people moving about, and the more people who live close by, the more vital and alive the central city is. The amount of new residential construction in very close proximity to our city cores should induce us to prepare land for it close around our central cities.

Certainly there is a case for preserving and stabilizing the amount of old housing in the city. At the very least we must prevent its further decay, for this kind of housing serves well the needs of low-income people, many of whom work in the central city. If modestly remodeled, this housing can serve the young people who come to the city to live and work. This is no small segment of the population. It may be that we can accomplish this by an indirect approach, namely, the removal of unrelated through traffic which deteriorates old neighborhoods near the central city.

Discussion of the various clusters of the central city must include the government center. Almost every city has some sort of governmental area, if only the modest but stately courthouse square. Government centers at any scale have two requirements: their forms must register as symbols of government function; they must be located and arranged so as to be part of their environs. The first of these requirements is easier to fulfill than the second.

By rather elementary arrangement, a space can first be created by the buildings themselves or, in the case of the courthouse square, a space provided for a single building in the center, to be seen as a showpiece. Physical continuity with the city can be achieved through an extension of the central space as a series of outreaching links and through careful blending of the form and character of the new buildings with the texture of the old.

Functional continuity with nearby parts can be achieved by introducing uses other than governmental into the government cluster. Law firms, real estate offices, a theater, perhaps a public library—any use which complements the function of government or is related both to government and business—can enliven the cluster.

In detail design, the arrangement and location of particular uses, the very location of building entrances, can spell success for the design of a government center. For example, the courthouse entrances can be located so that the daily parade of guarded juries across the square to a restaurant can be a subtle symbol. The continued arrival and departure of official cars, the path of lawyers and officials between their offices, the corners where the hangers-on congregate—all will take their positions from the design and treatment of the main elements of the government cluster.

Gray Areas

Thus far we have discussed the parts of the city which can be rebuilt in whole or in part, but extensively enough to give them an almost entirely new visage. We have also concentrated on the central area of the city. Before we go out to the city's new edges, its suburbs, let us imagine that all of the rebuildable parts were rebuilt. Let us imagine we had reconstructed our downtown, our

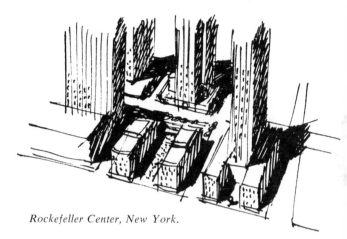

Rockefeller Center, New York.

Penn Center, Philadelphia.

Gray areas are functional and physical adjuncts to the center of the city.

We can diminish their visual effects by shielding our approach views. At the same time, we can relieve the gray areas with open space.

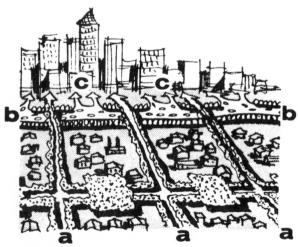

Better still, we can link them to the center city with their own system of paths (a), our expressways can bypass the gray areas (b), and both systems can enter the central city together (c).

center-city colleges and hospitals, our government centers, our new in-town apartments. If we were to go aloft in a helicopter and survey the results, we might experience some dismay. For we would see that a large portion of the center city was largely unchanged.

We would see that the entire city cannot be rebuilt in a decade; we have a limited capacity to rebuild which can affect only a portion of the city during each stage of its life. We would see, in short, that the gray areas of the city are extensive. These gray areas are also areas of concern for urban design, although they cannot be transformed as dramatically as some other of the clusters in the city. The possibilities of the gray areas are more elusive and more latent.

The gray areas of the city are its older parts, the places where you go to have a rubber stamp made, where printers locate, where office supplies and furniture are sold, where wholesale distributors do business, where cars are repaired, old sewing machines rebuilt, pictures framed, where city-bound hillbillies find their first urban dwellings, where rugs are cleaned, where restaurant linen is washed, where mufflers are replaced, and office equipment is repaired. The gray areas are not quite slums—they are the service quarters of the city, the place where small businesses may begin and, often, where major ones thrive. They are not glamorous areas, but they may be very much alive, if not with color then at least with people living and working. The gray areas of the city are a necessity.

For urban design, this fact of urban life should not come as a disappointment but as a realization to be reckoned with. What can urban design do for the gray areas?

For one thing we must start by seeing how well they actually operate. It may be that a gray area is definitely going downhill. In that case we should regard its land as a new resource for the near future. More likely it is threatened by problems of circulation. In that case we should attend to our traffic planning. It may be that there are pockets of leftover housing in a gray area which are unhealthy and whose occupants should really be relocated.

Perhaps the real defect of the gray zone is that we see too much of it. We pass by large extents of it on our new elevated auto expressways as we soar above the streets toward the center city. We pass through much of it as we proceed along our center city's major arteries. We see it as we approach the center in the morning on the way to work and in the evening on our way home. Its too frequent sight taxes our patience. The answer may lie in application of theatrics to the urban scene. If the gray area is too frequently visible, too depressing because it is too much in our presence, perhaps we can arrange our major routes to avoid it, to bypass it, to give us views of the parts of the city we hold in higher esteem. In the Renaissance, architects were able to recast the service elements of buildings into what appeared to be blank walls which could form entrance courts or the walls bordering a long passage. Could we not do this on the larger scale of the city? Could we not conceal, or at least play down, that which distorts the image of our central city's better self?

The Preservation of Some Old City Parts

The outstanding quality of our cities is the rapidity with which they change. How different they are from ten years ago, twenty years ago, fifty years ago. The history of our cities spans, and will continue to span, the most pronounced changes in the modes of human habitation that the world has ever seen. Such is the condition in which our cities exist. Some feel in the rapidity of this change an exalting excitement, a good fortune to be living in so dynamic a period. Yet change is not always good. With change comes new problems. With change comes the destruction of the better institutions of the city. Change is accompanied by the destruction of many of the landmarks of progress which we have created along the journey through time. On this problem rests the case for historic preservation.

If we can accomplish only a limited amount in the re-creation of our cities, then it especially behooves us to replace only those parts of the city which are entirely worn out and, particularly, to try to preserve the remnants of the past which are of special merit—high-water marks in the efforts of the past. This applies not only to individual buildings but to whole sectors of the city which come from a period of exceptional quality.

Patrick Horsbrugh, in *Pittsburgh Perceived,* stated the case most vividly. Horsbrugh points out that there is a "trough of disregard" for the works of the past, an interval of time in the life of a building or city area in which its existence is under greatest threat. Generally this period extends from thirty years to a hundred years after a building or sector is erected. It is in this period that the economic value of a building may warrant its replacement and in which our tastes may disdain the forms of the recently passed period. Perhaps the interval of the "trough of disregard" is shortening. With a more mature understanding of ourselves comes a more thoughtful appreciation of our yesterdays.

The preservation of historic buildings is but one example of the attention we must give to the form of our cities as collections of bits of historical development. Through programs for recognizing outstanding historical buildings we can begin to detect what is good. Somewhat more challenging is the task of acknowledging buildings and whole areas which, while not masterpieces, are respectable guideposts from our recent journey.

Our cities are a rather heterogeneous fabric, even the newer cities have built rashly. Our urban fabric is quite a crazy-quilt, a kind of nonobjective painting on an urban scale. That is really an advantage, simply because it expresses us so candidly. From a very practical standpoint, the recognition of what we take as the ordinary may open many doors of possibility for us in the improvement of our cities. It is one thing to know the outstanding works of the past, the masterpieces of past eras. It is another thing to recognize the various examples of "pop architecture" on an area-wide scale which line the flow of urban life from past times through to the present.

It is significant that we increasingly find in the renderings accompanying urban design proposals and plans, the careful inclusion of a Grecian bank, a Romanesque house, a Victorian Gothic church. Such buildings possess a wealth of sculptural detail and embellishment that is nearly impossible to obtain today. Such richness in buildings, where found, is sure to increase in visual value and in our esteem as we multiply the number of our more bland contemporary structures.

There are several positive approaches to preservation. We have the National Trust for Historic Preservation. A major interest of the AIA focuses on preservation through the Committee on His-

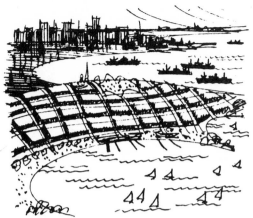

South Boston, Mass. A residential community originally established for clipper-ship builders.

A mixture of scales between new apartment towers and old row houses in Foggy Bottom, Washington.

Bay windows, cubic houses, and long vistas in San Francisco.

Dickeyville, a restored Colonial community near Baltimore, Md.

Fine old buildings are grandparents in the urban scene. Arcaded streets in Santa Fe, N.M.

A house in "Sauerkraut Bend" in San Antonio, Tex., an area settled by German immigrants.

Row houses with white marble steps in Baltimore, Md.

Old Mystic Seaport in Mystic, Conn., an assemblage of old buildings and famous sailing ships.

toric Buildings. There are numerous local societies that tend well their own historic riches. Necessarily a full discussion of these programs cannot be included here. Yet there is a guiding principle which is quite helpful.

In general, we should avoid compromises (or proposals) which satisfy neither requirements for modern living nor for historic authenticity. This means that we must find valid modern uses for old buildings and areas, and that we should restore them in ways that express the best of their two worlds—the past and the present. At least we can do this for the nonmasterpieces, the masterpieces can exist in their own right often solely as museum pieces. Even in those the touch of life through contemporary use and habitation underlines the merits which we desire to preserve.

Georgetown in Washington, D.C., or Beacon Hill in Boston would be destroyed if they were not lived in as areas of fine town houses. Old Mystic Seaport in Connecticut would be less convincing if modern yachts could not dock at its wharves. Indeed, it is when the touches of excessive preciousness dominate that old historic quarters begin to lose their meaning to us.

Thus it is that the old historic buildings around Independence Hall in Philadelphia, now cleaned and repaired, seem somewhat lifeless since they have been "freed" of their surrounding squalor. No one would expect that their surroundings should have remained slums, but we well may ask if a new living neighborhood of buildings of sympathetic scale and feeling should not have been built to replace the one destroyed. Fortunately, time is with us here. Some future generations may be able to do that and perhaps we should leave the task to the future, when our skills and understanding of these matters and our ease in dealing with them have ripened.

Our brief discussion of historic preservation must touch on one other area: the old market sections of the older cities. Boston, Philadelphia, Chicago, New Orleans, and many smaller cities have such old urban kitchens. Many have long outgrown their locations. The possibility of maintaining their former role as provisioners for the *whole* city is out of the question. Yet these old areas have real fascination and color—and perhaps a new role. Most of their operations have moved away to modern new terminals, conveniently located at the outskirts of the cities along expressway and railroad lines. Many of the provisioners remain and thrive—where they still serve a purpose. They supply in-town residents in those cities which have been able to maintain a continuous in-town population and which have a large number of in-town institutions and restaurants to provide for. Such is the case of Boston's old market area. Around these old markets we frequently find some of the best restaurants, often "holes in the wall."

The remedy for their preservation is real use—not artificial or quaint imitation of function. They must have an appreciative population to serve, a clientele nurtured through the years who insist on the quality of genuineness. Tourists who delight in visiting these old markets are an asset, but not without harm. For old restaurants and market areas that come to depend on tourists may relax their quality. The basis of the old town house's or market's survival is the same—authenticity of use.

134

Up to now we have been discussing the possibilities for the older parts of our central cities, which range from preservation to rehabilitation to transformation into a new cluster of function. Yet looking at the city as a whole, it is obvious that its growth is occurring in new sectors outside the old center, indeed along and outside the city's old physical limits. Many of these new parts are, in reality, emigrants in new forms from the old center. What are the implications of urban design for them?

With some dismay we see that the functions formerly taking place as cluster activities in the old center city may not find it appropriate to regroup as they migrate. Thus the old newspaper row disperses into a series of unrelated modern plants, forming no new "community" along their expressway locations. Headquarters offices, once conjoined in recognizable quarters of the city, seek rural pastures and become individual estates in the suburban landscape. Warehouses, once located alongside rail freight lines, join in the outgoing procession.

One major form which has resulted is the industrial park. Both the buildings which seek isolated sites or those that seek community in industrial parks follow a very old pattern: they line expressways as individual pieces or as groups in a new giant scale or geometry. Now they are seen as we speed by them at sixty or more miles an hour, where in former days we walked by them. Often, however, they are designed as if we were walking by them. Front entrances facing a highway, designed as if for pedestrians, emphasize the shortcoming of their design in failing to recognize a new scale of moving and seeing.

The choice of sites for these new buildings is little subject to the will of urban design, yet the decisions of architectural form for these sites is controllable. Architects have the full responsibility of designing new plants as appropriate components of the new view, both where the buildings are conceived as lone entities and where they can be clustered, as in an industrial park. Perhaps we have been overly hesitant in suggesting more verticality in their forms. We may be too much the captive of horizontal function; some vertical function could be equally if not more functionally appropriate, and give greater visual richness to the highway.

A typical plant requires a large amount of horizontal space for its machinery and production flow lines, but it also requires "front office" area for executive and clerical operations. These elements could be housed in a tower form, and in an industrial park several towers could be clustered in a clear and powerful design relationship. In short, the industrial park and the individual plant could more clearly state their presence in the landscape and so add more dramatic accent to it.

Radial Routes—The Automobile Shopping Street

Outstanding characteristics of every growing city are the ugly traffic arteries which reach out from the center and extend far into the suburbs. Often lined with marginal businesses, they are the predominant scenery of the developing American urban motorway landscape, for these routes are usually the main routes of auto access into and out of our cities. Zoning once sought to control these arterial land uses, but the pressure to strip-zone

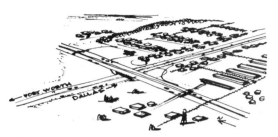

The Great Southwest Corporation development midway between Dallas and Fort Worth, Tex.

Articulation of industrial parks in the rural landscape.

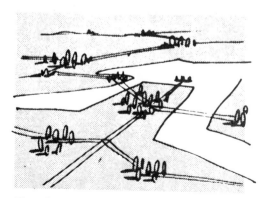

The enlarging scale of parts of the town and the city—and our kaleidoscopic movements through them—requires an enlarged sense of urban design.

135

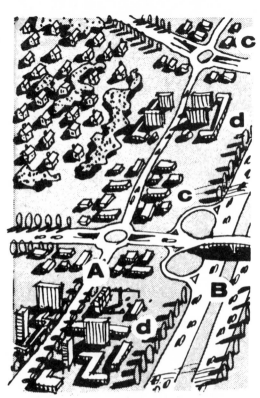

The future of the old automobile shopping street.
(a) *the former automobile-oriented shopping street;*
(b) *new expressway;* (c) *clustered auto-oriented shopping facilities;* (d) *new developments as clusters on the old auto-street.*

New towns in the metropolitan landscape.

them (zone the sides for commercial use) has been irresistible. The traffic hazard they present has been inadequate to arrest them. In these arteries lie the sources of the deepest woes for those seeking to improve the forms of our cities.

The future may hold the keys to a solution. The traffic function of many of these ugly main arteries is being replaced by the new superhighways. Here we have the chance for at least a choice: we can avoid these places by using alternate routes.

The strip road, however, does serve a purpose. It is, like the downtown gray areas, a kind of second-rate marketplace, but oriented to the auto customer. We should, however, try to reroute through traffic so that it does not have to pass through such honky-tonk roads. We might even rearrange traffic patterns so that these roads are not through arteries, leaving them as linear "free markets," wild with their arrays of signs and structures.

It may be, too, that some of these strip roads, when replaced by paralleling superhighways, will become ghost roads, just as we have had ghost towns. What then for the future use of this land? What then for the future of the businesses now there?

Perhaps we need some visionary planning for various free-market clusters, something less polished than our new shopping centers yet understood as an adjunct to the whole community.

New Hubs

Clearly, the major challenge for urban design in our growing metropolises, cities, and towns lies in their new parts and in the new forms which have been developing.

The regional shopping center has achieved a form that would seem almost to preclude its further development. So successful is it as an arrangement that it has been introduced right into the city. While its form and interior planning may have reached a high point, its relationship to its surroundings has not. No design has yet resolved the problem of the unsightly sea of cars surrounding the large shopping center. Almost in no instance do we find its central malls extending into a nearby old community.

Perhaps some advances can be made by diversifying the purpose of the shopping center. It could become a community focus as well as a commercial highway focus. The inclusion of high-rise apartments and office towers is an obvious first step. Why not connect it with a "second-rate" shopping cluster? Most polished shopping centers are set amidst such a fringe. Why not recognize this fact and plan a continuous linkage?

Perhaps we can find ways of including a YMCA, a neighborhood athletic club, schools, churches, a zoo, and small factories as adjuncts or parts of it? This is a challenge to urban design (not to mention our society's outlook)—the realization that the basic linear form of shopping cannot be interrupted, but it can be supplemented with many other facilities linked to it laterally.

The fact that the new shopping center is an emerging urban center is evidenced by the attraction it has as a strolling place on Sundays when its stores are closed. Less recognized as a new suburban focus are the many new school buildings we have built around our cities and towns. Their potential role in the community has hardly been tapped, let alone expressed in design terms. The community school plant serves far more than children. In the evenings it is the setting of adult education, adult amateur theater companies, and adult physical exercise. In the summer it

136

might house higher education programs. School buildings are the major community facilities for many of our smaller cities and for most of our suburbs. What of the development of its form and arrangement as a more related community component?

Land bordering the large school could be occupied by buildings other than houses. We might have some businesses around it, perhaps small factories of an inoffensive nature. School courts could open into the neighborhood as part of the weave of a system of linked open spaces. The Conte School in New Haven's Worcester Square Redevelopment area demonstrates these possibilities and suggests even more.

Large schools are being designed as a series of parts—a wing of classrooms, a block of gymnasium, auditorium, and library buildings which are not so much separate entities as they are, in fact, a series of component buildings in a community. In smaller towns we could introduce the elements of the school plant into a community design right in the heart of the town. School buildings could be strategically placed around the town green, as part of the real fabric of the town's heart.

The more we ponder the new formations in and around our cities, the more we see new questions arising. These raw questions are directed at forms that are yet embryonic and forms that often seem on the surface to have found their balance. We have been able above to discuss only briefly some of the questions and some of the possibilities. We can suggest some other parts of the newly forming urban fabric for conjecture. The marina residential developments could bear some thought. The mobile-home community (trailer camps) could be an entirely new kind of community which could be a more positive urban element. Perhaps the sites for such communities could be selected so that they had fine vistas out over the nearby towns, to give their inhabitants some degree of belonging. We could at least find some modest landscape techniques to soften their harsh metallic appearance.

Perhaps we should contemplate the possibilities for *rural* governmental centers. Frank Lloyd Wright's Marin County government building give us a clue to the possibilities of that. Wright's building should be studied in relation to the whole site plan, which is a slice of Wright's old Broadacres proposal. Its lesson is that even in the countryside so major a building as a government edifice is one component in a series of central community facilities. We might do well to ponder the changing use of our urban parks. We use parks quite differently from our Victorian predecessors, although many of our parks are inheritances from them. Are we making a mistake in the siting of large new convention halls and sports arenas in our central cities? Should their behemoth bulks be so openly displayed, or could their bulks be buried in the mass of the city, revealing only the entrances? Could their now-bland peripheries become shops, offices and hotels rather than remain large extents of unusable wall?

In trying to develop large spaces of natural greenery around the cities, we might consider the validity of the small operating farm as a provisioner of fresh vegetables to the city. Could there be some thought as to the economics of this and to the steps necessary to encourage the small farmer to continue his way of life near the cities? The sight of genuine operating farms near the cities may be more desirable than the sight of unused natural land. Of course, we would need a mixture of both the real farm and the real green open field, left free.

An arena contained in a building whose edge uses are continuous with surrounding urban functions.

A high school (foreground) set alongside a small town's central square with town hall and shops forming a true town center.

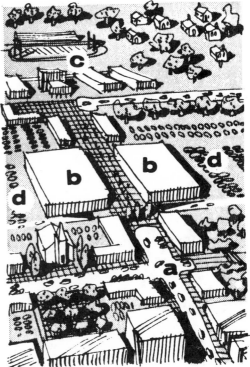

The integration of a shopping center with a town's central facilities:
(a) *original town center*
(b,b) *new shopping center*
(c) *school facilities*
(d,d) *parking to serve all the town's central parts.*

137

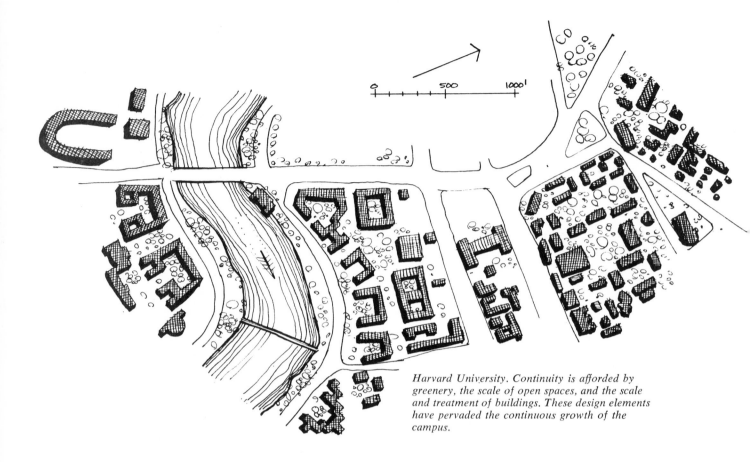

Harvard University. Continuity is afforded by greenery, the scale of open spaces, and the scale and treatment of buildings. These design elements have pervaded the continuous growth of the campus.

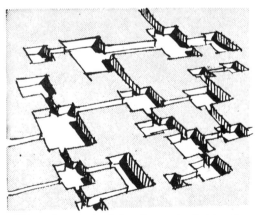

The various parts of the city can be tied together by spatial linkages . . .

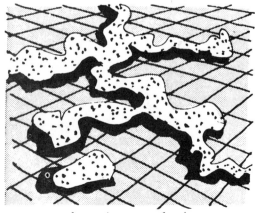

. . . by continuous swaths of greenery . . .

Putting the Pieces Together

The overriding question that emerges from a discussion of the city's parts is just how do we go about putting all the pieces together? Indeed, just how distinct should the pieces be? The discussion of the city as a series of organs connotes its division into a series of separated functions. This is the hidden danger of such a discussion. The question is one involving a decision to blend or not to blend certain parts with each other, of the degree of mixture that a part can sustain. It is, as well, a decision for the degree of visible articulation of a part. Some present developments give us a glimpse of the range of possible answers.

Topography is usually the basis for the physical termination of a part of the city as an edge. Where topography imposes no edge, and where functional continuity is desirable, blending may be desirable. One of the best examples of this is in the center of Philadelphia, where the fine town houses around Rittenhouse Square, punctuated with the buildings of some of Philadelphia's best clubs and institutions, give way to tower apartments, then blend into fine shops, then culminate in the office towers of the central city. The change is so subtle as to be almost unnoticed. In this case interruption by articulation of this subtle progression would be harmful. The lesson in such areas is to design individual buildings not to counter this blend, but, rather, to reinforce it. Conceivably that could mean that an extremely large building for such an area would best be arranged as a series of parts rather than a large monolithic form, in this way to join with big and small buildings together.

Thus separation and blend can have definite social implications. It may be convenient to think of the parts of the city when programming its needs or evaluating certain problems, but the fact is that people do not live in neat planning units. They live in cities and they use whatever parts of the city they choose to use. The purpose of blending or separating parts of the city is not to restrict one part from another. It is to make the whole more intelligible. In present-day life, this means that we have to see clearly the parts of the city to recognize where we are and where we are going. In present-day terms of circulation, this means that much of our seeing is done from fast-moving cars along ribbon expressways. Thus the design and placement of visual landmarks and expressways must be joined on the urban design palette.

If an edge is developed on a fall line, the edge becomes a visual guide. Separation of a residential area from a factory zone is, of course, desirable. That is the kind of result we get from good planning. But if we set up artificial barriers between certain residential and commercial zones, we may be doing real harm. The point is that we do not have to clarify the form of the city and the position of the various parts by creating physical barriers between them. There is another method we can employ. It is well illustrated by developments now occurring along the Charles River in Boston.

The Charles River is one of the most pleasantly developed rivers in an American city. Once a swamp, it was filled and its banks landscaped. The City Beautiful Era endowed it with a handsome embankment on the Boston side. For many years it has had a fine river drive on both sides. Even a rash modern highway along the Boston shore failed to destroy its charm.

This river wets the feet of three major universities—Harvard, Boston University, and the Massachusetts Institute of Technology (M.I.T.). Of these three, Boston University never had a real campus. Harvard has its yards and M.I.T. has its great court. All have the lovely river. Not long ago these universities had only slight emphasis on the skyline. M.I.T. had its dome, Boston University had a little tower, and Harvard had a profile of Georgian chimney pots. That emphasis was rather elegant.

The old skylines are a thing of the past. To one who has known the old skyline the first impact of the change is shocking. For now, all three schools have major tower buildings. It may require considerable thought to comprehend the latent merits of the transformation. Harvard leads in the development with a pair of dormitory towers and a tri-cluster of towers for married students. Boston University follows with a central vertical block. The central block emphasizes Boston University's lack of a real campus when considered in contrast to M.I.T.'s two towers, which mark out the ends of M.I.T.'s linear campus. M.I.T.'s two towers will probably be supplemented by more towers in the future.

These towers serve to locate and present the three universities on the river to us in a new way. They aid the intelligibility and clarity of the enlarging city form. They tell us with varying skill of the forms of the campuses they articulate. What is more, these towers do not interrupt the flow of form from university to surroundings, from "gown to town." It is all part of the same fabric. The appearance of these towers must be judged while driving along the river. There is no question as to the message they convey. Yet there is a further aspect of their appearance. They are by no means the only sets of cluster towers seen on the Boston skyline.

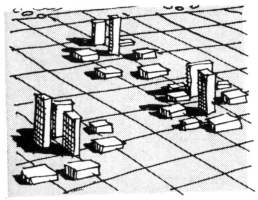

. . . by vertical articulation . . .

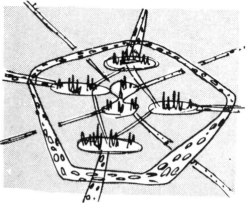

. . . and by clarity of the connecting pathways.

The original form of Boston's Beacon Hill —a three-peaked hill on a flat horizon.

The hill, refined by grading into a round form and topped with a golden dome, climaxes the panorama of the city skyline.

139

Twentieth-century tower construction blurred the earlier image.

Some other towers are seen encamped about the golden dome of the State Capitol on Beacon Hill. Others of doubtful profile mark various parts of the city.

One tower in Boston serves as the flagpole for the whole system —the slender new Prudential Tower which is higher than any of the others. This will be the ultimate visual rallying point of Boston—the visual center of gravity of the city. This entire visual system is really very old but on a major new urban scale—quite likely surprising at first but a scale which we are quickly comprehending. Before these towers were erected, Boston's profile was low, accented by lithe church steeples and culminated by the State House's gold dome. Many may mourn the passing of the more intimate old system. The new scale of the towers is but a new product of our ever-changing way of urban life and ever-developing urban centers.

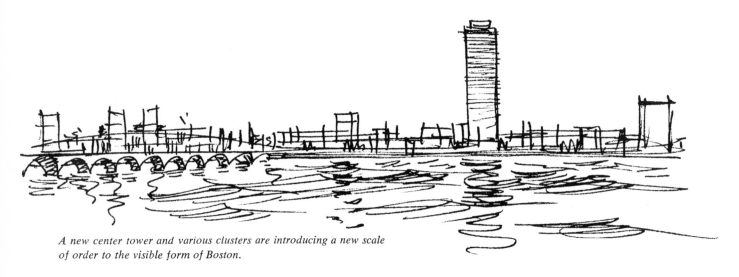

A new center tower and various clusters are introducing a new scale of order to the visible form of Boston.

8
Residential Areas

The extensive literature of city development deals mainly with residence, the consideration of the dwelling place, and the residential community. This concern accurately reflects the importance of the dwelling place in our lives, of the family as our basic social institution, and the fact that the majority of our buildings are dwelling places. Thus, a discussion of homes and residential communities is confronted at the outset with a profusion of ideas already offered. Although this vast source material can be acknowledged, it would be difficult to enumerate it even briefly. However, this dilemma suggests its own solution. We can consider our whole knowledge of the dwelling house and the residential community in the most basic terms and, in so doing, refresh our perspective.

We can approach the problem of residential communities from the point of view of the people who live in them, applying the method of Eliel Saarinen who, during his design process, created in his own mind every sensation which would be experienced by the people who would use his buildings. We can further humanize our approach by remembering Frank Lloyd Wright's disdain for the word "housing" as being too suggestive of "stabling." We can concentrate on the essence of the design problem by recalling Louis Sullivan's advice "to think in simples."

In this chapter we offer fundamental considerations for the

design of the residential community as part of the general urban fabric in which we all live and grow.

Formulating Objectives

The basis for judging an urban design proposal is how well it accommodates the lives of its inhabitants. In the design of residential communities *accommodation* amounts to *livability*. Where urban design is the design of a community and its facilities, urban design for the residential portions of a community is architecture for every one of us who goes home at night to the center of his family life, the focus of his life in society. How well do we understand the lives of different people in their various neighborhoods, and how well do our existing neighborhoods answer our requirements? Indeed, just how varied are our neighborhoods? We can answer this question adequately in rather general terms.

The kinds and variety of residential communities range from low-density to high-density . . .

Margaret Mead has written a penetrating sentence concerning the needs of children in their communities, and it is here that we can begin to formulate design objectives for residential communities. Dr. Mead wrote: "The infant and the growing child must be surrounded by a community of persons of both sexes and all ages, of sufficient homogeneity so that the child acquires his primary cultural characteristics and depth, through all five senses, and with trust in the reliability of the culture he has learned, and with sufficient experience of the strange and the stranger, the not-known and the later-to-be-known, so that he can move with assurance, transforming his primary learning . . . into other, wider, cultural forms."

As we ponder Dr. Mead's statement we see, first of all, that a residential community must be far more than a dormitory for assuring health and safety. Stimulating exposure, exposure that makes children grow into balanced and well-adjusted adults, is a main objective of residential community design. If we examine typical residential communities, we see that this objective is not always achieved, let alone recognized. We are too much prey to the attitude that a residential community is a place of insulation from the realities of life rather than a place for their presentation. We feel, too often, that children should be "protected" rather than stimulated. Of course, the confrontation of new and often perplexing experiences requires a base of operations for its absorption—the hustle of the day with one's fellows requires the repose of the evening in one's home. But hustle often seems to be regarded as a danger rather than as a normal part of the day's events.

. . . from urban to rural . . .

The community in which a child grows and develops is very simply a miniature of the world he lives in. To the extent that a child's community reflects the scope of life in the world at large, to that extent will the child grow soundly, as Dr. Mead has learned through her research. The scale of this community must be in scale with the child. He must be able to traverse a broad range of its parts on foot or on a bicycle. His daily experiences should include firsthand contact with the many people, places, and activities which constitute a cross section of modern life.

In this attitude, starting with children, lies the beginning of the formulation of rather clear and basic objectives for the design of a residential community. If, upon the commencement of the design process, we would take the time to imagine the daily life of a child, we could draw up a fair list of the facilities we should be designing or, in some cases, relating to our design. That list

. . . from new to old . . .

would be a basic checklist for evaluating the merits of our design concepts as they develop. We could proceed, as Eliel Saarinen demonstrated in his work, to ensure that final results of our designs would have overlooked little and that they would be appropriate to their inhabitants.

The formulation of a checklist based on children's lives alone would be, of course, incomplete. Yet it would tell us much. An oft-heard criticism of many of our new suburbs is precisely that they are too much of a child-centered world. A somewhat more accurate statement of that shortcoming is that it is too narrow a world of experience, for both children and adults alike. The obvious next step is reflection on the lives of all the many types of people in our society who constitute neighborhoods and communities.

What are the needs of teen-agers who live between an extended world of childhood and the world of adults? What checklist would we draw up for college students, or for young adults on their own in the city? What checklist could we draft for young married couples, for young couples with children, for families in middle life, for grandparents, and for elderly people who find themselves alone? What checklist could we draft for the unattached people who wander from place to place, or for those families who migrate in search of work and better opportunity?

These questions have long been chief concerns of many of our colleagues and answers have been forthcoming according to the urgency of the problems represented. In large-scale undertakings the need to present these answers in more workable form has led to the formulation of standards, usually mathematical ratios which quantify the facilities of a neighborhood. These large-scale undertakings include the private development of large tracts, the programs of local and Federal government in community development, and the interests of mortgage banks in assuring that developments are sound.

We shall be referring to such standards as we proceed with our discussion. We hesitate to offer them even in capsule form. Out of context or summarized they can be misleading. But here again the profusion of standards and the complexities of their application suggest a course: "to think in simples," as Louis Sullivan long ago advised, to think of problems in their very basic terms. In that way standards fall readily into their proper places, as aids to design and as part of the check system in the concept-development process.

Standards are generally expressed quantitatively, that is, in mathematical terms as, for example, so many square feet of area for a particular purpose per dwelling unit or per family. But standards can also be expressed in qualitative terms, as objectives of design in a community—for example, the preservation of mature trees or the maintenance of a fine open vista.

We can demonstrate the use of quantitative and qualitative standards together by now embarking on an examination of the residential community, keeping uppermost in our minds the point of view of the inhabitants of the places we examine. We shall first consider residential community *size* and *density*.

Size and Density

Aristotle noted that 10 people are too few to form a city, while 100,000 are too many. So, in ancient times, without radio, tele-

. . . from elegant to plain.

All can be satisfactory and enduring . . .

. . . places to live and grow . . .

. . . if well designed in the urban fabric.

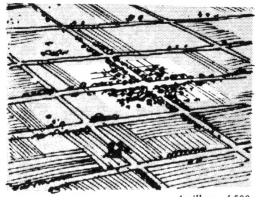

A village of 500.

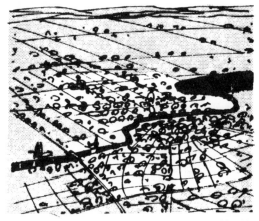

A town of 5,000.

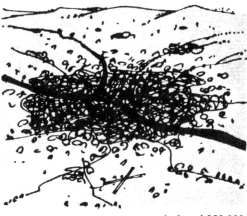

A city of 250,000.

A metropolis of 2 million.

phone, and speedy transportation, the upper limit was small (by our standards) yet the range of possible sizes was great. The size of an ancient colonial city, approximately 5,000, is thought to be about correct for a modern neighborhood. Cities or communities of 70,000 people can be self-sufficient but the optimum size for a modern city with the desirable cultural facilities and social institutions is held to be about 350,000—the size of Renaissance Florence.

The upper limit of a city's size seems now to be without bounds. The term "megalopolis" is part of our vocabulary. In using it we recognize that even our giant cities are part of a larger city still— the interdependent chain of large cities and small towns, all enveloped in a vast physical development. Only recently have architects begun to grasp this vast agglomeration as the field for design speculation. Architect Kenzo Tange, for example, has analyzed the major cities of the world's industrialized countries and found that characteristically they comprise 15 per cent of a country's population. Tange's recognition of this phenomenon was the beginning of his creative designs for a rebuilt Tokyo of 15 million people.

If we seem to be going astray from our consideration of the size of residential communities, it is only because the sizes of cities themselves are becoming so vast that their residential components reflect this growth, and thus speculation on optimum sizes is somewhat difficult. The best statement on the optimum size of a residential community, however, was the "neighborhood unit," a concept described by Clarence A. Perry in 1939. Perry wrote of the neighborhood unit thus: "It should cover both dwellings and their environment, the extent of the latter being—for city planning purposes—that area which embraces all the public facilities and conditions required by the average family for its comfort and proper development within the vicinity of its dwellings . . . the facilities it should contain are apparent after a moment's reflection. They include at least (1) an elementary school, (2) retail stores, and (3) public recreation facilities."

Perry's statement was the basis of much residential community planning, real and theoretical, some of it, alas, somewhat too literal. One outcome of his concept was, for example, the determination of how far elementary school children can walk to school, followed by calculation of how many families are needed to furnish enough children for the elementary school. Concurrently an ideal size for the elementary school and appropriate density were calculated. Thus the size of "communities" was determined, based on this number of families, circumscribed by greenery or something other than the continuation of the neighborhood.

Carried to its ultimate form, it was thought that residential communities could be a series of physical islands. The concept of a neighborhood was overstressed as a physical idea and somewhat exaggerated as a social fact. This was an unfortunate error, for people, no matter how satisfying a residential environment they enjoy, all have their own personal worlds—an individual network of personal places and paths in their cities which extends far beyond their physical "neighborhood."

Perry's concept is valid insofar as it gives insight into how a community operates within itself. Its proper application lies in planning elementary schools, shopping facilities, churches, or social halls within reasonable distance of a large number of people and with some sense of physical cohesion. And, of course, the

144

physical delineation of the several parts of the city remains an objective for residential as well as nonresidential areas—but not the sole means of applying the neighborhood concept.

The neighborhood unit concept has been interpreted in many ways in many designs. The English New Towns have various neighborhood arrangements, as do the new towns of Holland and Scandinavia. Prime examples of neighborhood groupings in the United States are Sunnyside Gardens, Long Island; Radburn, New Jersey; Baldwin Hills Village, California; the garden suburbs of fifty or more years ago such as Roland Park in Baltimore, Maryland; the privately built suburbs of the twenties, such as Mariemont, Ohio; and the well-known greenbelt towns of the thirties. In very recent years the layout of Chandigarh, India—Le Corbusier's magnum opus in city planning—is based on neighborhood groupings. Le Corbusier's Unité d'Habitation is a neighborhood in one building. Lucia Costa's design for Brasilia makes use of a neighborhood concept of another sort.

It is difficult to prescribe an ideal size for a residential community for several reasons. Most neighborhoods are built as large or small development tracts at one time or another. They are completed in whole or in part over a period of time. They come to enjoy the feeling of a "neighborhood" when they possess everyday facilities at convenient locations, when the larger community facilities are accessible to them, and when they possess a somewhat elusive quality called identity. The degree of identity is often well indicated by the name of the neighborhood and the degree of registration of this name in the minds of a city's whole population. Identity should never mean isolation, but it should mean clarification. It is a matter of developing identifiable character in neighborhoods and making the whole comprehensible.

Albert Mayer, FAIA, once remarked that housing developments should blend in with the neighboring city to produce a change of character but not a shock. He proposed, in effect, differentiation without division. Other architects, in commenting on public housing design, have gone so far as to suggest that "projects" should be abolished as such, that individual buildings should be deployed carefully within the city's fabric.

Studies of a community's size are important because they can tell us the amount and kinds of common facilities which are required for such communities. But size alone does little to tell us how to arrange these facilities. More helpful than considerations of a community's *size* are considerations of its *density*. Here, too, range is broad.

In rural areas small single houses on acre lots or larger have densities of about 2 persons per acre. Low-density American suburbs, with houses on generous lots, contain about 6 persons per acre. (Incidentally, 60 per cent of our population prefers this mode of life.) Group housing—two-family houses, row houses, the earlier English New Towns—have densities of 16 persons to the acre. Crowded city walk-ups of three to four stories have densities of 55 persons to the acre. Proper design at this density requires six- or nine-story elevator apartments in order to have sufficient open ground space. This density is the threshold of congestion. Slum densities average 160 persons to the acre, but can vary considerably since slums are a combination of physical condition and crowding.

By way of illustrating density in relation to architectural concepts, Frank Lloyd Wright's Broadacres proposed one acre or

Unité d'Habitation, Marseilles. 337 dwelling units (du) on 10 acres.

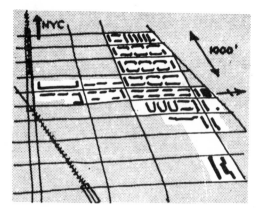

Sunnyside Gardens, Queens, L.I. 1,202 du on 56 acres.

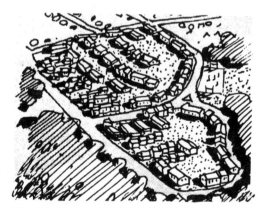

Chatham Village, Pittsburgh. 197 du on 45 acres.

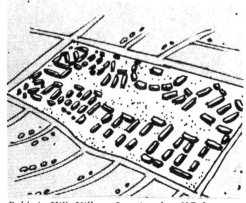

Baldwin Hills Village, Los Angeles. 627 du on 80 acres.

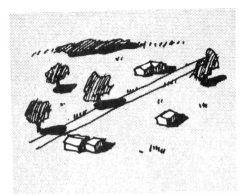

2 persons per acre (ppa).

6 ppa.

16 ppa.

40 ppa.

more of land per family, or about 4 persons to the acre. Typical American suburbs average densities of about 25 people to the acre. Chandigarh was planned for 56 people per acre. The Golden Gateway redevelopment of San Francisco will have about 90 people to the acre. The proposed town of Hook, England, a landmark in design, would have had 100 people to the acre in the center, a bordering area with 70 persons to the acre, and another area with 40 persons to the acre. Recent developments in high-density residential design would make these densities possible. Ping Yuen, in San Francisco's Chinatown, has 365 persons per acre. At the far end of the scale Le Corbusier proposed, in his vision of future cities as he foresaw them in the twenties, densities ranging from 120 to 1,200 persons to the acre.

Closer to local everyday practice, the Federal Housing Administration has undertaken studies of density and has emphasized the importance of considering basic amenity in relation to density. This is called "land-use intensity" and is indicated by mathematical ratios between right-of-way area for cars, car parking space, recreation and play space, and planting space, these being the components of open space in a residential area. Land-use intensity thus means, in FHA language, the overall structural mass and open space relationship in a developed property. This interpretation covers a broader field of planning factors than a concept of density used without qualification. FHA prefers to speak of density not as persons per acre but rather as dwelling units per acre.

Assuming that a dwelling unit comprises a family of four, FHA standards operate within a range of from 12 persons per acre in small single houses to 850 persons to the acre in twenty-four story high-rise apartments (the maximum density for prime land in large cities, tolerable to a very few people and ill-suited to children). The FHA has recently developed a formula for aiding in the determination of proper densities for various parts of different size cities. This formula tries to adjust density proposals (or rather the intensity of a development proposal—building bulk to open space) to the most suitable character of an urban area. This proposal should be carefully reviewed by all architects concerned with residential design.

If considerations of residential community size, density, and intensity are confusing to us mortals, there is a man who, a few years ago, clarified the whole picture. Hans Blumenfeld, one of our most illuminating colleagues, now a resident of Toronto, Canada, delivered a brief address at the 1957 meeting of the American Society of Planning Officials (ASPO), called "Residential Densities." Basing his remarks on observed density phenomena he described the *implications* of various densities. He prefaced his remarks by posing the question: "Does anybody know what the 'right' density is?" He answered his own question immediately by replying: "I do—it is 12,000 to 60,000 persons per square mile of residential area." (Twenty to one hundred persons per acre.)

In other words, the range is broad, broad enough to accommodate a great variety of consumer preferences. Yet in giving this range Blumenfeld established that there is *both* a lower and an upper limit of acceptable density.

The lower density is a matter of practicality and prevailing community form. Very low-intensity suburban development, 4½ houses to the acre (say 16 persons to the acre), means large investment for roads and utilities, long travel distances to commercial and civic centers and to work, the latter almost entirely by car. Since people are willing to walk a maximum of a quarter of a mile (an eight- or ten-minute walk), a circular area with that radius would contain, at the low 4½ family per acre density, no more than 500 to 600 families. If these families are of typical composition—some young, some old, some with children, some without—we find that this grouping can support only a below-optimum-size elementary school, that bus service is minimal, that a local shopping center is uneconomical, and that church and community facilities are insupportable. The accents and community focal points which would give identity to the grouping are missing. Social contact is frustrated and the sense of contact with nature that some would prefer in its place is marginal, if not illusory. There is too loose a relationship between building forms and open spaces. At the same time the open spaces are not sufficient for the countryside to stand unimpaired. Of course such an area can have its buildings clustered, but, again, there is an insufficient base of support for the communal buildings.

A further consequence of low density is the low availability of industrial workers. Very low density means long travel distances for workers, hence limited availability of staff, hence an undermining of local industries, and so the possible undermining of a community's economic base. The upper limit of density is set by the problems of congestion resulting in central city areas where transportation means are limited. Zoning regulations often set this upper limit. The lower limit (of the suburbs) is set by municipalities which sometimes desire to attract the wealthy and exclude the poor. The dilemma is obvious.

Very high densities in cities increase congestion and favor high-rise construction. This, too, tends to exclude the poor unless, of course, their housing is subsidized. A barrier thus exists at some line around the city beyond which the poor are excluded and within which their areas of possible dwelling continually diminish.

Blumenfeld advised two things: policies which would encourage the building, in suitable suburban locations, of row, apartment, and other modest types of houses less wasteful of land than the detached house on a 60- to 80-foot lot; and the removal of subdivision restrictions which now prevent such development. In this way we would both enrich our residential communities by combining a greater diversity of people in them and broaden opportunities for development. The essence of the proposal is a liberalization of a practice which has heretofore been restrictive.

The practical features of this concept are several: public transportation could obviously be more supportable; industries located in the suburbs would have a greater availability of workers; shopping and community facilities would have a broader clientele; and certain circulation problems would be diminished, particularly the radial inflow and outflow during peak traffic hours. Most important, if we could design with a broader range of density on an intimate scale, that is, if we could have a few lots of one density with a few of another, and nearby another still, and then even other mixtures, we would have more stable residential communities. Experience has shown conclusively that the one-class communities are the most susceptible to obsolescence, largely because they are least adaptable to change.

No better illustration of the wisdom of varied density in intimate mixture exists than the aforementioned town of Mariemont, Ohio, designed by John Nolen and started in 1922. There one finds small pensioners' cottages, row houses, and one-family houses of a great

60 ppa.

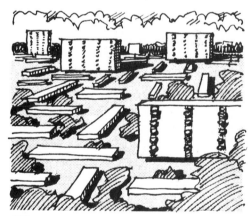

80 ppa.

100 ppa.

300 ppa.

147

A town center in Mariemont, Ohio.

A row-house street in Mariemont.

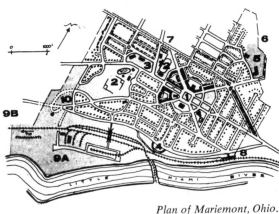

*Plan of Mariemont, Ohio.
(1) center; (2) playfields; (3) schools;
(4) overlook; (5) hospital; (6) hill with large houses;
(7) original trolley line; (8) planned commuter
RR station; (9a) planned factory site, later
located at (9b); (10) uncompleted road system.
The town is on a plateau high above the river.
Gray areas indicate public open space, parkland,
and woodland. The range of house types is
very broad.*

variety of sizes, to name but a few types. It is most significant that a hillside bordering this planned community later became the desirable locale of several-acre lots for the houses of the very wealthy. Of course, the high hillside on which those houses developed was attractive in itself, but in the case of Mariemont it is obvious that the planned community was a strong attraction.

Architect Vernon DeMars, FAIA, suggested a very simple test for judging the intimacy of mixture in a residential community. This amounts to imagining yourself standing in your proposed community and considering how much of the community's variety and mixture—its texture—you would want to see and how much you would actually see. An addendum to this "test" is to check on the proximity of school, shopping, public transit, open space, etc.

Thus the implications of density considerations in urban design are obvious: What is called for are more thorough and realistic community plans, perhaps, as FHA suggests, based on intensity of land development and, let us not forget, the artful design and poetic fulfillment of our landscape. Politically this may seem to be a matter of the degree of "government interference" in private land development matters, but this is far from the case. It may prove to be the wise community which can team up with its private interests in preparing for new developments, and such a community may well find itself with both sounder and more active development than one which abandons itself to the chances of ill-conceived speculation for its immediate rewards alone. The most obvious point of all in considerations of size and density is that standards alone cannot create community architecture. That will always be the product of creative design talent.

But we are getting somewhat ahead of our story. We have, up to now, considered livability from the point of view of the individual. We have put ourselves in our clients' shoes. Let us hope that we have seen more of the problem through this personal perspective. But let us now consider the shoes—the parts of a neighborhood which constitute the palette of the architect engaged in urban design.

Some Basic Neighborhood Design Elements

Let us draw up a simple list of the objects and elements we design in a neighborhood. Basically these elements are the pattern of street layout, land division, and planned open spaces.

As we stressed in previous chapters, patterns of land use and division must derive from overall topographical conditions. If the landform is hilly, it may suggest curvilinear streets in combination with certain straight roads, in which case the curvilinear streets would have a sense of containment and thus be suitable for intimate groupings of houses. The straight streets might then be suitable as major connectors and feeders to the more intimate curved streets. The pattern can be arranged so that the major feeder streets focus on an intersection of community buildings, or on a topographical feature, or are directed toward a salient natural vista or to an intentionally placed steeple, tower, or high-rise building.

Site-planning handbooks generally recognize a classification of street types: arterial streets or highways; collector streets which feed the highways; minor streets which feed the collectors; marginal access streets which parallel the highways; and alleys. Unfortunately, handbooks usually fail to point out the social implications of these basic types—but that may best be left to the designer.

In the layout of land-division patterns we may be overlooking the most basic configuration—the simple rectilinear grid. Perhaps we disdain it for its too frequent use in the past, or to be more accurate, for its often too artless use in the past. Both a rectilinear grid or a curvilinear pattern must be designed on the basis of appropriateness and artistry. The curvilinear pattern on flat land, without meaningful focus, accent, sequence of revelation, relief, or surprise, is as trite and, in the long run, as tiring as the rectilinear grid without complementary relief in form.

Rectilinear grids are basically suited to flat land and particularly appropriate if prominent vertical features, such as ranges of mountains or hills, can be seen from them. Where nature fails, art must substitute, and so it may be wise to introduce into the geometry of the grid a completely nongeometric sweep of green space, possibly a stream bed diverted or an artificial water channel created. A curvilinear pattern, it goes without saying, should be based on topographical roll or the presentation of major verticals to be supplied, such as tall building forms. Where curvilinear pattern is suggested, if not demanded, by topography, certain areas might appropriately be laid out with geometric regularity such as a community center in the form of a formal mall. There should be a logic to the design of these forms, arrived at through artistic effort with the mind's eye carefully tuned to experiencing the finished result.

There is an imaginative array of street designs which we can draw upon in the layout of overall street patterns. At the fore is the cul-de-sac, introduced and made popular through the example of Radburn, New Jersey. The most modest grid layout can well benefit from the introduction of this configuration in a variety of ways. Sections of grid streets can be treated as sectors, cutting off through streets to develop a pattern of major and minor streets and a series of dead-end cul-de-sac streets. Straight streets can be offset at certain intervals to create visual closure, or to put an important public building on a sight-line. Minor streets can be arranged to form "swastika" intersections, the small inner space serving as a postage-stamp-size park. If the space thus formed is larger, it can serve as the site of a playfield, a school, allotment or formal gardens, or local shopping.

The spaces of the street alone can be varied to provide parking bays for groups of four or five cars. Certain streets could have wide grass malls down the center, with the malls culminating at a local community focal point, a church, school, or group of stores. The location and form of such a mall must be judiciously chosen, to preclude the possibility of its later misuse as a traffic thoroughfare or for parking. To prevent it from being used as a thoroughfare it should not be too long or continuous and should dead-end at a point where no through traffic connections could be made. Commonwealth Avenue in Boston has resisted such pressure for just these reasons.

Another vital aspect of lot size and configuration is that lot subdivision constitutes a *module* of community design. Actual lot size is one of the keys to success in the conception of this module —in conjunction with building setback, street width, planting, and open spaces. Lots which are large in relation to their building masses result in dentelated or overly interrupted street facades, an effect which can, if too severe, cause a residential street to seem too loose as a composition. Large stately houses are suited to

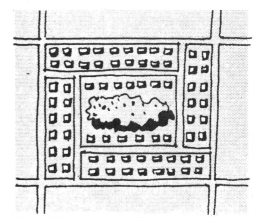

"Swastika" variation in a block.

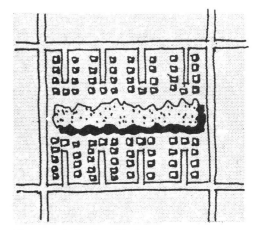

Finger variation in a block.

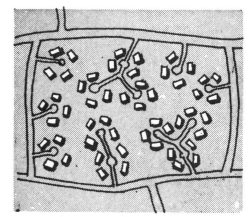

Cluster variation in a block.

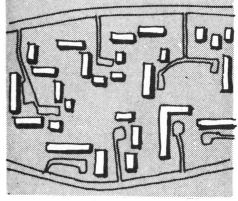

Mixed clusters in a block.

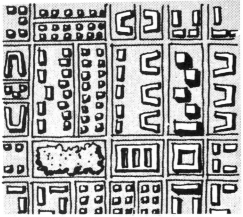

Grid variations for mixture of house types.

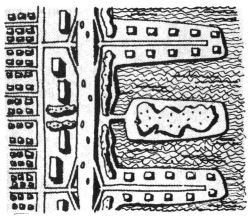

Grid arrangement along a shoreline.

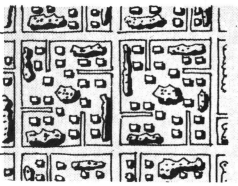

Fingers and clusters in a grid.

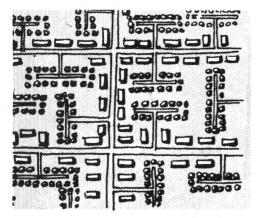

Variations with single and row houses.

generous spacing, for the houses are each objects of individual attention, but more modest houses seem only clumsy and pretentious in trying to ape the grander effect. Lots too small can obviously result in awkward spaces between houses. If the lot is very narrow, it may be better to eliminate side yards and build row houses with front and rear yards, or rear yards alone.

Quite often a street pattern is laid out before the actual houses are planned. In such cases it is important to ascertain that a reasonable variety of house types is possible. A useful test is to consider the relationship between house shape and lot shape in accordance with their sizes. Simply, that amounts to sketching the probable development of houses along a proposed street in order to study the reasonableness of the lot shape and size. Side yards, for example, may be perfectly adequate as long as we can look from a side room and see something other than the sidewall of a neighbor's house. The spacing between houses might be checked to see if a series of houses could be seen as a group of six or eight or more simultaneously. Six or eight or more houses of different facade designs and materials seem less awkward than two or three with the same appearance—like books on a shelf. Distinguished residential communities, we must remember, depend on well-designed streets for their distinction and well-designed streets are a matter of lot size, street width, greenery, and mass relation between buildings. Where these factors are present the street can even tolerate a considerable number of plain buildings. A reverse of these conditions—fine architecture without good street design—is a major if not absolute detriment to the best-designed houses and, consequently, to the sense of neighborhood and environmental architectural harmony.

Equally as important as lot size and house form (our basic module) is still another module: the block—that is, the grouping of houses which constitutes a block, and the size and relationship between blocks. This design problem may be taken as part of a larger and more fundamental problem still—the occurrence of interruptions or accents in the general continuity of a neighborhood.

Where the sequence of houses is uniform and continuous for some distance—say as far as one can see—there is a need for interrupting accents which relieve the continuity in order to avoid oppressive monotony. This problem occurs when we unthinkingly apply the methods of mass house construction over large tracts. On the other hand, where there is a lack of continuity and where building forms are mixed and varied in shape, size, and appearance, we need some elements of continuity or stability to tie the whole together. Accents—a focal point of stores, a church or tower, or a vista—are points of visual reference as much as visual relief.

Basic to the block module is its actual size. This problem is well approached by considering how far a corner of focal intersection should be from any one house. Could that distance be based on the distance a small child on a tricycle might ride, or on maximum walking distance to a mail box or a bus stop? Could it be determined by viewing distance—that is, might street intersections be made mutually visible, one from another? It is basically a question involving scale in urban design at a neighborhood level.

A further consideration of block design concerns orientation, grouping, and the building type. Single houses on ample land can forego immediate neighborhood common space. However, the frequent arrangement for the higher density of three-story walk-ups or row houses is a rather different matter, for there the open spaces for recreation, leisure, gardening, laundry, garbage, and car parking is shared. The street as a focal spine of space is paralleled in importance by the spaces behind the row houses. These spaces have received too little attention. They deserve and need much more. The private open spaces of individual houses, left to their owners, eventually find their proper arrangements of use, based on the entrances to the house, location of the car space, the sun, wind, and trees. It is not essential to know exactly what the uses will be for a small-house lot, although a good architect, of course, does know them and will plan them. In the block development of group houses, however, it is essential to know them and to be able to predict accurately how the various spaces will be used. As in the small house, it is a matter of entrance location, service areas, parking, sun angle, wind, and trees.

Basically there are active and passive open spaces, or prime and service open spaces—just as there are prime and service spaces in a building. There are a number of examples of Scandinavian row-house designs wherein the buildings are arranged as a series of U-shaped courts, alternately facing the street and an interior court. The courts facing streets are active, usually used for car parking and delivery. The courts facing away from the streets are passive, usually facing a green area. The inhabitants of these houses enjoy access to both courts.

Architects are familiar with the practice of checking their building designs in the plan stage, imagining how all the spaces will be used. This same exercise must be applied to the block in residential urban design. At this scale of design there is no excuse for neglecting it, even in those frequent cases where the budget is so limited that the spaces cannot be properly furnished at the outset. A space whose purpose is well conceived will, in time, become what it was intended to become, but its designers must give it that chance in the plans. This design phenomenon is best phrased by an expression of architect Morton Hoppenfeld, who speaks of the "seeds of fulfillment" in a design. The architect must arrange the essentials of a site at the outset so that it will, in actual use, function appropriately.

If the case for achievement of good urban design through lot size and block size seems crude as a technique, it is only because it is so fundamental. The evidence of the validity of this approach lies within the city around you. Examine the sizes of lots and blocks in your own town. A half-day's tour should be enough to gather some valuable design data. It must be done, however, with a very open mind because many of the good examples of neighborhoods are modest, and, like modest good men, they may never have stood in the spotlight of renown.

As fundamental as lot size and block size—the two modules of residential community design—is the pattern of a community's open space. Were we to plan the major open spaces of a community and their accesses alone, we could go far toward a major improvement in our community designs. S. B. Zisman's proposed open space design technique can be applied to a neighborhood as well as an entire city. It would even be possible to forego land-use specifications around the edges of the spaces. Developers would build and rebuild as the market and times allowed. Indeed, if we ponder this idea further, we see that the design of the open space itself can strongly influence, if not determine, the land uses border-

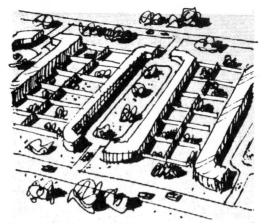

Row houses forming a "close."

Atrium houses with gardens.

Courtyard apartment clusters.

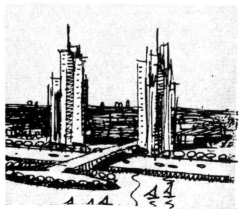

Twin towers.

151

A walk through Chatham Village in Pittsburgh . . .

. . . reveals an infinite variety of minute views . . .

. . . very suitable for a residential neighborhood . . .

. . . with simple pervading architectural character.

ing it. The open spaces would include all the urban spaces we employ in a community—the street, the postage-stamp park or plaza, the large and more urbane plaza, the boulevard, the play lot, the playground, and the park, large or small.

The value of open spaces in our communities is illustrated by an interesting phenomenon in the Don Mills community of Toronto. Don Mills is a carefully planned mixture of residences, shopping, and light-industrial plants. The quality of the architecture of the industrial plants is generally quite high, and they are very well landscaped. It has been found that the resale value of the houses facing the plants is higher than those houses facing each other—an interesting outcome of a well-planned community mixture.

The open space approach to community design could be coupled with the planning of community utility systems, to establish a nearly foolproof community layout. In essence the structure of a community would be firmly established and the pattern of open spaces would relieve whatever indiscretions might follow. In actual fact developers and municipalities often do just this, but in a crude manner, unaware of the system being established. It has been suggested that a community should decide in advance what actual development should be like, and that it can order this development by deciding on, if not actually building, the utility system before the developer arrives. "Developers will follow the sewers," notes Charles Abrams, in a terse but telling statement.

Architect David Crane, in his proposed design for the Eastwick redevelopment of Philadelphia, conceived a design wherein the "basic capital bones structure" would be first established, these being the utilities, main focal points, and interconnections which could be filled out by houses. We could improve the design of our residential communities considerably were we to use this method. We could design a desirable whole community, complete with a great variety of streets and lot sizes and a variety of open spaces linked and accessible. We could then extract from this design concept the structure—streets, lot sizes, utilities, and open spaces—which would be most likely to bring the optimum design about, at the same time affording a variety of developer opportunities.

In sum, the techniques of urban design which we discussed earlier in application to an entire city or sector would be applied to the design of the residential neighborhood, even at block scale.

Detailed Site Design

In the detailed design of a residential area we must consider the size and placement of building masses. This involves such factors as function, vista, sunlight, appearance, open space, circulation, climate, scale, climate control, and topography.

By now the study of sun angles in relation to building massing and placement is common knowledge, but, alas, still too seldom applied. The rules are simple and the application of sunlight angles to design decisions is rather basic. Briefly, it is desirable to cut off or shield direct sunlight during the later hours of the day and to assure, for cold winter days, some amount of direct sunlight, particularly for psychological uplift. This practice, like many others in architectural design, was once taken too literally and became almost the sole basis of building-mass placement. It is bad practice to base a design on only one factor and neglect other requirements.

152

In checking a group design for winter sunlight, for example, we may find that some ground-floor rooms receive no midday sunlight. Our group design may satisfy many other objectives and so be desirable to retain even with this disadvantage. Our check, however, might reveal several things. One might be that although no direct midday winter sunlight reaches some ground-floor locations, there are views of generous sunlit areas from them, adequate to render ground-floor apartments livable. We might then add a few projecting bay windows from which these views are more apparent and so more enjoyable. Reflections from light-colored walls, terracing, or nearby pools can also boost light levels in interiors. We might also have developed an apartment type with two or more stories, stacked units rather than horizontal ones, so that the upper stories receive sunlight. Thus there are several expedients which we can employ to relieve the lack of sunlight.

Sunlight can conveniently be studied with the aid of a simple block model together with a sun-angle device that can be made readily from easily obtained information. While studying sun angles it is well to consider which facades receive more or less sunlight and the angle of the sunlight as it plays on facades. In residential groups a certain richness of texture and sculptural effect is much to be desired, since it gives a sense of decorative warmth to what might otherwise be an overly austere character. It is only a slight additional exercise to determine the points on the horizon where the sun sets, possibly to retain open vistas of this most poetic daily event.

Fundamental, too, and almost as important as the sun-angle study is the consideration of prevailing breezes. This information is generally known locally and easily obtained from the U.S. Weather Bureau summaries. It is a simple matter to determine building entrances, balcony locations, even the opening swing of ventilating windows to take advantage of cooling summer breezes while blocking chilling winter blasts. It is also a help in locating incinerator and heater chimneys.

The use of simple models, supplemented by simple sketches and a few diagrams, can summarize both prevailing conditions and design intentions. It can help greatly during the normal and inevitable revisions, to make certain that our fundamental objectives are retained and not, as frequently happens, discarded in a plan revision. A study model is best regarded as a three-dimensional sketch. Too often we restrict its use to presentation. Study models can be used with a fan and some fine sand to determine if entrances will block up or remain free in snowy localities.

A perpetual question is that of view and vista from a dwelling place. Ideally, we would all like to have a grand view out over a great expanse of city or landscape, but of course this is impossible for all sites and all dwelling units. Even a great vista, however fine, is in a raw state when we first confront it with the addition of an architectural foreground to frame it.

Le Corbusier once made a now-famous series of sketches of the harbor view of Rio de Janeiro as it might be seen from the window of a new building. He showed first the raw view, then its enframement within an architectural opening, then its embellishment with some carefully chosen and carefully placed architectural details. The view was rendered far more poignant with these additions than it previously had been. The view was part of the architecture, and seen through a window, its changing moods would give continuous animation to a room.

Siedlung Halen housing group near Berne, Switzerland; Atelier 5, Architects.

Roehampton Lane, London; London County Council, Sir Robert Matthew, Sir Leslie Martin, Hubert Bennett, Architects.

Easter Hill, Richmond, California; Vernon DeMars, Architect.

Lakeview Terrace, Cleveland; J. L. Weinberg, Conrad & Teare, Architects.

153

Frenchtown, Mount Clemens, Michigan; Meathe, Kessler & Associates, Architects.

Mill Creek apartments, Philadelphia; Louis Kahn, Day & McAllister, Architects.

Group houses near Helsinki, Finland; Viljo Rewell & Keijo Petäjä, Architects.

Row houses in Rekingen, Switzerland; Cramer, Jaray & Paillard, Architects.

Some of the most artful enframements of a vista from a room are found in examples of Japanese architecture, and study of their practices proves very rewarding. In some instances a low window lintel obscures an exterior view until the entering inhabitant lowers his head as he takes a sitting position. In another instance still—at a corner sitting room of the Katsura Imperial Palace—one screened wall of the room looks out onto a formalistic garden while the adjacent screened wall looks out onto a naturalistic garden. By closing one side and opening the other, the entire character of that small room is transformed.

In our own residential design we could incorporate this level of design thinking to do much for even our most modest developments. In some instances we have done so. In the very early Lakeview Terrace in Cleveland, a public housing project of the thirties, the entrance courts between groups of dwelling blocks had long views out to the lake and the lake's foreground edge of industrial plants.

Perhaps the norm for vistas from individual dwellings in a group development should be that where buildings are close, there should be some means within the apartment for obtaining a long view, as perhaps from a balcony, but that the unavoidable absence of a view from some apartments should be compensated for by site landscaping or, if possible, vistas from the site proper. It is a matter of exploiting the natural advantages of a site to their utmost.

Somewhat less common a consideration is the view into the windows of a dwelling place. In the intimately scaled village of former times low windows were the rule, and people decorated their windows with fine curtains and small objects of pride to catch and delight the eye of the passerby. The window made a contribution to the exterior. Alvar Aalto once commented that architects should design windows as if their girl friends were sitting in them. The point is that facades and their details have architectural obligations to the street, even when those details exist for purposes basically interior to the house.

Obviously we should check the sight lines from the exteriors to ensure privacy in those parts of residences which require it, and probably provide means for blocking off exterior views altogether when desired. The design of views out of, as well as the exclusion of views into, a residence can readily be checked by an analysis of a design in plan and section.

In residential communities for multifamily housing a key consideration is the use of ground. In general it is desirable to provide each family with some amount of ground space or, as a substitute, an open balcony which need not be large if it is well designed. Even in cold climates where a balcony cannot be used actively for several winter months, it serves the purpose of affording a sense of openness for an apartment and canceling the feeling of constraint which an apartment usually has.

A final consideration in the siting and design of residential groups of medium or high density is the size of building masses themselves—a question of scale. In a previous chapter we discussed the basic mechanics of the eye and its abilities to discern distance and size. These basic facts of human vision were seen to underlie our sense of intimacy or "bigness" in urban spaces and in building masses. The cornice height of buildings together with the sizes of the spaces between them and the detailed treatment of facades were discussed. The application of these principles is intrinsic to the proper design of residential groupings, particularly to achieving a general sense of intimacy in our environmental architecture.

In general, this means that building masses should be kept small and generally low—digestible to the eye and to our comprehension as a series of intimate pieces. In the lower ranges of density this can be accomplished rather directly. In the higher ranges of density we must turn to more artful techniques.

If, for reasons of high density, economics, and other factors of site design, we find that our buildings must be very long, we can step a facade back and forth, breaking it down into smaller sections visually. We can also puncture it periodically at key points to form entrances and egress passageways from one space to another. The detailed architectural treatment of the facade can be designed to arrest the eye in a series of nonrhythmic articulations, which would avoid an overly long sweep. Thick foliage can screen a facade that is overly severe because of building economy.

Where tall buildings are required, they can be brought into the range of intimate visual scale appropriate to residences by introducing small foreground elements to act as foil to the large-scale masses. Groups of low buildings interwoven with the high, and seen in front of the high buildings, establish an intimate foreground scale which does much to obscure the scale of the giants. Indeed we would do well to design the entire group from the sequence of the experiences we encounter as we enter the area, proceed through it, and arrive finally in one of the apartments in a large tower or slab. It should be designed as a sequence of architectural experiences of changing scale, gradually unfolding to our comprehension —the principle of processional experiences of a cathedral transposed and adjusted as a method of design for residential groups. Architect Eliel Saarinen did this in the site design of his buildings at Cranbrook, for residential as well as for school buildings. As a matter of fact he did it so well that both place of work and place of residence blend almost imperceptibly. In pursuing this method we should recognize that just as there are design relationships between low-rise and high-rise buildings, there are design relationships between high-rise and high-rise, as Charles A. Blessing, FAIA, demonstrates in Detroit. We should also recognize the importance of paths of approach and inner circulation, spaces, vistas out and views in, landscaping as a screen and as a foil, and ground surface treatment.

Conclusion

We have been proposing here an approach to design based on objectives and undertaken through common-sense method. We have emphasized the role of standards as secondary to basic and thoughtful reflection on the objectives we are trying to achieve. Standards can be taken too literally. They can be taken for granted and so preclude the thorough design exercise which is essential to every design success. Standards can block innovation and can lull one into a false sense of design adequacy. They can be useful as part of a check procedure and, in some cases, to obtain a minimum of amenity, but even then they should be used with caution. We must remember that even our best engineering standards or specifications do not produce good engineering design. They help only when they are creatively used.

In the face of the vast literature and store of ideas on residential community design we propose a return to a basic method of design —an approach to design taken from the ground up by contem-

Baldwin Hills Village, Los Angeles; Reginald Johnson, Wilson, Merrill & Alexander, Clarence Stein, Architects.

A court in Sunnyside Gardens, Long Island; Clarence Stein, Henry Wright, Frederick Ackerman, Planners-Architects.

Soholm housing near Copenhagen; Arne Jacobsen, Architect.

Houseboats along an Amsterdam canal.

155

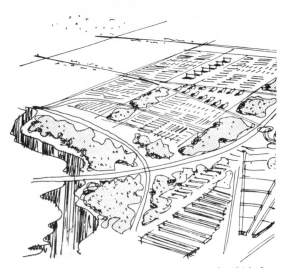

View of Amsterdam South, 1934 plan.

plating the real life which our designs would foster or, if poorly conceived, restrict. In this we recognize a practice of great craftsmen and artists, who in undertaking a new work, start at the beginning to repeat, step by step, a procedure which is derived from long experience and patient practice. It is almost as if every work were one's first—at least in this step-by-step approach. Almost always some failure is the result of a consideration omitted —something which a too hasty craftsman left to "skill" rather than conscious effort.

We have also been implying that too many design decisions are made on the basis of factors which are irrelevant to the objectives of the design. Building masses, placement, grouping, lot size, and block size—these may be thoughtlessly drafted in the guise of expedience when it takes but a few more steps to ensure both feasibility and good design together, and, very likely, also gain a real economic saving in both the short and the long run.

9
Circulation

Few urban problems arouse the interest of the general public as much as circulation. Conversations about where to live, about going downtown, about the city's appearance, about relocation problems—all lead quickly to discussions of circulation.

Few elements of city life have had more influence on the growth and form of modern cities than circulation. The development of trade centers, of residential areas, of industrial areas—all are intermeshed with circulation between and within cities. Few means of improving our cities have greater potential than circulation. The building of new factories and new housing, the rebuilding of worn-out urban sectors, the creation of open space, ultimately the clarification of the total form of the metropolis—all depend upon our wisdom in designing our circulation network.

The architect's interest in circulation stems from the fact that architecture, in its broadest sense, is the art of building for full human life. Since circulation is the backbone of urban form it deeply affects the well-being or malaise of a city and its people. The architect's interest in circulation cannot be limited to superficial aspects such as appearance. Of course, appearance is very important, but it is always the outcome of basic design decisions that must be right to start with. Otherwise attention to appearance results in nothing more than a thin disguise. The architect's par-

A six-lane sunken *expressway in Detroit.*

A six-lane elevated *expressway in Boston.*

157

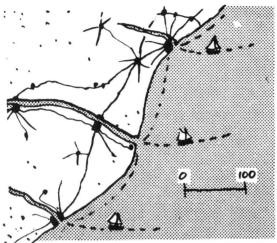

Individual settlements developed as small centers for their local areas.

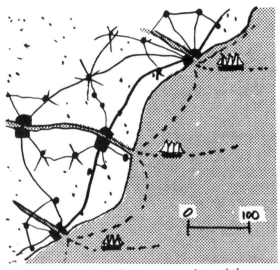

Topography and major routes favored the emergence of advantage settlements as regional centers.

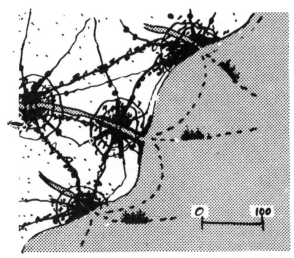

Depending on their own energies and resources, these centers became major cities and the routes were then made to accommodate them.

ticipation must begin with the thought of a circulation system as a total urban concept. The magnitude of the task now confronting our cities calls for this examination and participation.

Transportation and the Formation of the Modern City

The story of the modern city and its complex circulation network begins two hundred years ago with the industrial revolution. The main effect of the industrial revolution was to accelerate production and bring it from its traditional seat in the country into the city. In this change circulation played the first of its many roles. The cities that grew most rapidly were those most favored by long-distance routes of trade, distribution, or the collection of raw materials. These long-distance routes were over land and over water. Usually, they were gifts of nature. Occasionally, they were created by men.

By the middle of the nineteenth century effective means of long-distance travel between cities were developed: the steamboat, the canal, and the railroad. The telegraph served for long-distance communication. The scientific methods of the industrial revolution accelerated production and caused the division and specialization of labor. Dependence on the exchange of goods and services caused the dense clustering of people in the central urban cores.

Originally, the long-distance routes facilitated movement from city to surrounding countryside. Specialization prompted the connections from city to city so that trade could flourish. The overland routes were usually in existence long before they were adapted to the transportation requirements of the new industrial cities. The present-day New York Thruway, for example, was originally an Indian trail along the Mohawk River, then a settler's route, then a canal route, and later a rail route. Now an air route follows it also. Thus the transportation routes developed according to the purpose they served.

Efforts to improve circulation routes *between* cities preceded efforts to improve routes *within* cities. Cross-country routes brought increased traffic to the city and forced improvements in circulation. In time this external pressure compelled the creation of all means of internal circulation. The lag between external and internal circulation was and still is one of the outstanding characteristics of the modern city. Redevelopment expert Knox Banner once remarked that we will probably have earth-to-moon transportation before we solve our inner-city transportation problems.

By the end of the nineteenth century, however, means were developed to facilitate movement *within* cities, just as a half-century before means were developed to circulate *between* them. The inner-city vehicles were the horsecar, the street railway, and the early trucks and cars. Thus, transportation technology eventually extended to passenger movement inside the city. Inner-city communication was handled by telephone.

Prior to these innovations the new industrial city was very compact. It had to be, for the movement of its working masses was by foot and horsecar. This limited the size of the early industrial city to a 3- or 4-mile radius. The conditions of crowding which this produced are only too well known. They also planted the original seeds of a second major movement in the formation of the industrial city—the outflowing movement which we are still witnessing. The reasons for this outflowing movement were both practical and emotional. Certain industries could not operate efficiently in the center and sought to move out, and the city was becoming less desirable as a place for family life. But further developments in circulation technology were required before outflow could occur on a large scale.

The new modern city was unlike any city before it in function and form. It was both the seat of production and the seat of decision, and it offered a variety of employment opportunities. The internal makeup of the city evolved quickly. The port was the original center of exchange around which warehouses and factories grew. Clustered around them were the houses of banking and commerce. The very poor lived in shacks and hovels as close to the places of work as possible, in order to be near a wide choice of jobs. The poor lived on land not suitable for anything else, or else in enormously overcrowded tenements. The value of usable land soared in the city centers. In some cities marshy land was filled in to create "real estate." The wealthy established their own residential areas, insulated from the general ugliness of the surrounding city. The skilled and semiskilled middle class could afford decent dwelling only at the edges. So began their long history as commuters.

As the various urban functions found their most suitable locations, they set up movement patterns from one to another. The rights-of-way for public movement began to emerge. The "planned" cities, usually gridirons like Manhattan, had a clear geometric pattern to follow. The "unplanned" ones, like Boston, evolved a spider-web pattern. Certain areas in the city became dominant for one use or another. Many planned cities grew beyond their planned grids to add surrounding spider webs. As congestion increased, problems of sewage disposal, water distribution, and the dangers of fire necessitated sewer and water lines and rudimentary fireproof construction. These improvements were made along the principal circulation routes. Distinction between the public way and the private lot became clear—indeed, a matter of law. Thus the early circulation arteries hardened.

By the time the railroad came to the city, the central core was so ossified that the railroad could not penetrate it. It had to terminate at the edge of the core. Larger cities built peripheral rail terminals at their edges. In the prerailroad era canals were brought right through the city to act as linear distributors. In some cities, Washington, D.C., for example, it was also possible to do this with the railroad, since industry had not hardened the city's form. But in most cases the railroads ended at terminals which became new nuclei. Around these nuclei grew factories, warehouses, and hotels. Wholesaling companies located there, as did manufacturers of furniture and clothing who could display their wares to incoming buyers. The central core thus expanded, and traffic between the new terminals increased.

The railroad also made possible the first moves toward decentralization. Certain factories could be located in the country or along the radial railway spokes. Generally, they were of a noxious nature and required amounts of land not available in the central city—steel mills and abattoirs, for example, moved out. Their workers lived in settlements around them. The upper and middle classes began to use the railroads for commuting to work. But the central city remained the preferred location for almost all activities.

A map of a typical industrial city at the end of the nineteenth century shows a pattern of radial spoke routes emanating from the city's center and projecting far out into the countryside. The

INTERNAL ROUTES AND CITY FORMATION:

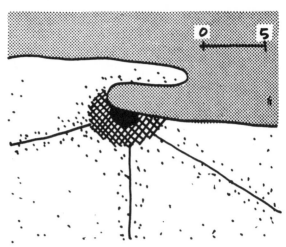

The city as a central hub was dependent on foot and horsecar transportation.

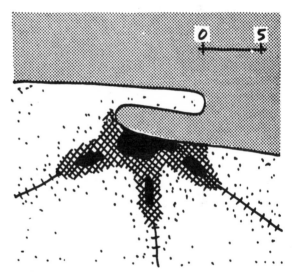

Subsequent growth due to the railroad created a spider-web form and new outlying hubs.

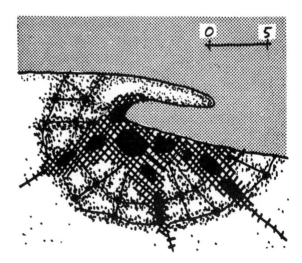

Pre-automobile growth due to the electric streetcar and subway created a spider-web form.

159

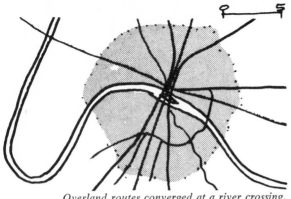

Overland routes converged at a river crossing. Paris was a walled medieval city with a dense maze of streets.

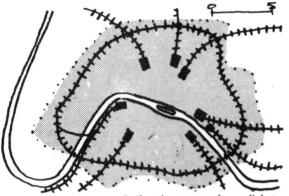

Railroads penetrated as radials to the edge of the central core; a railroad loop connected the radials; the city expanded.

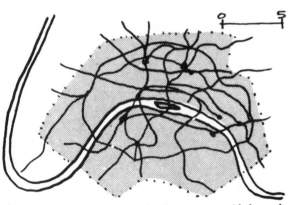

The underground subway net provided speedy internal circulation, connecting major hubs.

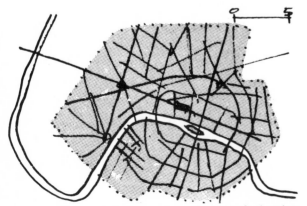

Haussmann's avenues formed a network of surface arteries.

radial spokes were a combination of vehicular and railway routes. Within the city a maze of roads developed a spider web. Streetcars ran on the main streets. Often they had "created" these streets. Later, rail rapid transit amplified the streetcar routes, first as elevated railways and later as subways. Horse-drawn wagons along with early trucks and streetcars created incredible congestion.

Two European cities, Paris and London, reveal the formalistic aspects of these developments very clearly. In Paris, Baron Haussmann had cut wide avenues through the city fabric, connecting the peripheral railway terminals to his new avenue pattern. Throughout the history of Paris, growth had been constrained by a series of enclosing city walls. Paris was thus a dense city with a spider web of surface streets connected to a number of peripheral rail terminals. Underground, a subway system created another spider-web circulation pattern, also related to the peripheral terminals. A peripheral rail loop connected the rail terminals.

London, in contrast, was subject to similar forces of urban growth, but it differed from Paris in two ways. It was not constrained and it never had a grand pattern of monumental streets imposed upon it. Thus, it spread far out into the countryside as a huge star pattern while its center became exceedingly congested.

The key points of both systems were: railroad terminals abutting the central core; an outer rail loop connecting these terminals; and an inner loop subway which connected the rail terminals for passenger movement and which, of course, served the core. The first subway lines thus formed inner loops and crosstown connections. The patterns of London and Paris represent whole systems which are clear in form and so constitute easily understood models.

Thus, the early subways were related to existing urban hubs—sometimes well, sometimes poorly, to be sure—but they were related. They were woven into the urban fabric. In addition, it was a matter of time before it was realized that circulation innovations were as much *creators of urban form* as they were servants. They created land use and land values.

In the United States the principles of development were the same—first movement between cities, then within cities, the innovations of technology being applied from the outside in. While we did not always produce a clear geometry in the layout of our systems, we followed the rules of location and connection. Obviously we tried to connect what needed connecting and, in so doing, created location by creating accessibility.

We also added a most significant twist of our own. The early developers of our trolley lines recognized the value of extending the lines into the countryside. Vast amounts of land were thus opened up for speculative development. Significantly, it was an

◀ *DEVELOPMENT OF CIRCULATION IN THE 19TH CENTURY CITY: PARIS*

American who persuaded the builders of the London subway to extend their lines into the surrounding countryside. These ideas had already made him a millionaire in the United States. We were quick to develop our streetcar suburbs in America because our middle class gained sooner from our industrial development than the middle class of Europe, and could afford it before they could.

To attract potential trolley suburbanites to the suburbs, amusement parks were often built at the ends of the lines out in the country. Sunday excursions on a trolley whetted the appetites of the city folks for country living, just as Sunday auto excursions were to do a generation or two later.

The streetcar lines produced a limited star-shaped city with a spider-web center. The center was further intensified by the addition of the peripheral rail terminals. With the development of commuter railroads the overall form became a giant star with a central spider web of movement. The outreaching radials often incorporated an outlying village or major route crossing. Such places were destined to become the later suburban centers.

Still another interesting contrast between our own cities and Paris or London is that the centers of our cities decay while the outer peripheries flourish. In Paris and London the situation is quite the reverse. Perhaps the forced attention to the center of Paris over the centuries established institutions there which became so well established that they ensured the center's permanence. Certainly in both Paris and London, the pattern of established and highly workable circulation routes had an important effect. Perhaps, too, the automobile is a force that challenges the best of other transportation means to the limit.

Before we turn to the automobile we must pay homage to the great era before it. The whole history of preauto transportation is full of invention. Its leaders were bursting with imagination. Very early, during the canal era, George Washington envisioned our capital city as the trade emporium to the West, but Baltimore was to eclipse Washington when it developed its port and western railroad. During Jefferson's presidency a public works plan was drawn up for the whole of what was then the United States: a plan for major canals and roads to connect the states.

The developers of our streetcar systems had more than simply a transportation system in mind. They were aware of the development opportunities they were creating and took full advantage of them, usually by speculating on suburban land. We can criticize their sometimes haphazard building, but not their lack of imagination. We can learn from these past developments as we look to the future, and as we take a close look at the automobile to see just what it is doing.

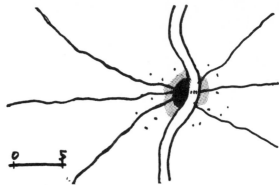

Overland routes converged at a river crossing. The original settlement was a trading center.

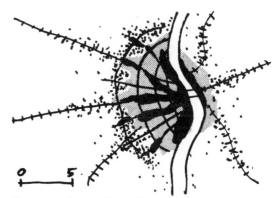

Railroads converged and a transcontinental route passed through; a spider-web form developed.

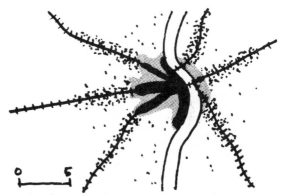

Streetcars allowed dispersal and the formation of a spider-web pattern.

DEVELOPMENT OF CIRCULATION FROM THE 19TH TO 20TH CENTURY: ST. LOUIS ▶

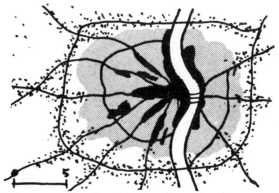

The automobile allowed further dispersal and infilling between radial corridors; the core created the radials; the circumferentials will relieve the radial movement.

The automobile forces its way through the city . . .
. . . requiring clear paths of flow.

The automobile raises problems of parking . . .
. . . requiring new forms of storage.

The automobile creates problems of intersection . . .
. . . which require new systems of movement.

The automobile has problems of interchange . . .
. . . which require new systems of transfer.

The Effects of the Automobile

The automobile is often regarded as the chief villain responsible for our current urban circulation plight. It should be obvious by now that it is but one of many agents developed to perform a job set up by the needs of the modern city. True, the automobile is the most apparent cause of central-city congestion and peripheral dispersal, but equally accountable is our attitude toward the use of land together with the rocky history of public transportation.

The trolley, subway, and commuter railroad produced the star and spider-web forms of the metropolis. The automobile allowed the infilling of the space between the outreaching star radials at a low-development density. The automobile started as a novelty, but quickly took hold as a very useful means of transport. It furnished the answer to a desire for low-density living and high freedom of access, to which we were barely awakened. We must remember that we have been a nation of prodigious inventors. Most of the possible forms of the airplane, for example, were patented before 1920. We call upon our inventions as we need them and then develop them. So it was with the automobile.

Public transportation, on the other hand, started as a necessity, flourished as a profit-making enterprise, and became victim to a host of intertwining circumstances. Operating under public franchise, streetcars and rail rapid-transit lines were built and developed as a profitable undertaking (the straphangers paid the dividends), and there was profit in the development of peripheral residential land. The public franchise to operate was eventually accompanied by public regulation of fares. In time, the companies were assessed for street maintenance and improvement. In many cases they had to carry schoolchildren at reduced fares. Equipment had to be replaced. Maintenance and operating costs went up. Fares remained the same or increased very little. The companies went into the red.

Meanwhile, the automobile habit was taking hold and spreading. After World War II, when production turned from defense to private consumption, the full effect was seen. Fare restrictions were lifted and fares went up. Many people turned to their cars for their journeys to work. Their choice of private car versus public transit was based on convenience and cost—but mostly on convenience. The private car, considered from all points of view, is by far preferred—although still the more expensive. Many studies have been made of the cost of getting to work by car as opposed to bus or subway, considering a host of factors. Such studies are the results of surveys which should be appraised with caution. It is impossible for a commuter to decide fairly between his own auto and a public transit system, for the latter usually appears more convenient on the questionnaire than it is in reality. The private auto is used largely because the present alternative, unimproved, is hardly worth considering.

Automobile usage hurt public transportation. It deprived it of passengers, it congested surface streets so as to slow down public surface conveyances, and it helped create a low-density residential pattern which was difficult to serve by public transit.

The result, in terms of city form, was the infilling between the legs of the star form of the metropolis. Where trolley and rail allowed people and jobs to go to the city's periphery—along the radial routes—the auto allowed them to fill in the areas between the radials. Thus the outlying lands were developed into what many critics feel has been one of the most socially and physically unimaginative land developments in history, but which also represents the crude beginning of a new city form.

Today, the metropolis has a commuting radius of from 30 to 40 miles. That is the area within which people can travel to work and conduct their urban affairs. In the early industrial city the commuting radius was 3 or 4 miles. The effective area of the modern city has increased a hundredfold. How has this affected the function of the original center and its surrounding periphery? What changes have occurred in their roles?

We find that the central areas of our cities have not gained very much in employment. Although white collar workers have increased in number, less of the city's blue collar jobs are in the center. Rush-hour inflow and outflow in the center have increased very little. For example, the number of people who enter Manhattan to work every day is about the same as it was in 1930. Rush-hour congestion has increased because more people drive to work than take a bus or subway, and the routes are overloaded. While central-city population increased 10 per cent in the last decade suburban population increase has been about 50 per cent. By 1980 the centers of our cities will hold less than half of the population of the large metropolitan areas. Jobs in the centers of the city will also decrease to about half the total jobs in the metropolis.

The role and function of the center has been in a rapid stage of evolution due to automobile use and metropolitan growth. Once the preferred locale for all communal activities, including manufacturing, its prime role is now limited to administration and certain services. Consumer services—shopping—have dwindled. Manufacturing, storage, and goods distribution have also fled the central city with some exceptions, such as garment manufacture which requires a high degree of communication and interchange. One of the unchanging characteristics of the metropolitan center is its volume of circulation during the working day. In many cities this results from inadequate bypass roads around the center but a large amount of the traffic is due to short-distance trips. Decision makers must move about in the center in pursuit of their daily tasks. Face-to-face meeting of executives is a prime function of the center. Japanese architect Kenzo Tange recognized this as a main design requirement in his visionary plan for Tokyo. He came to this conclusion as a result of studying the major administrative cities of the world. Tange believes that an individually operated vehicle is a must for such cities since no public transit system can handle the complex pattern of individual trips. This does not rule out public transit for many cities, however. Tange's design is premised on automobile usage. It is certainly conceivable that some untried mode of public transit could do the job that Tange identifies. That the public transit systems in their present form are inadequate is seen in statistics of the last decade or two in American cities.

The statistics on the switch from public to private transportation show that public transportation patronage has declined two-thirds overall in the decade following World War II. From 1945 to 1959 transit riders decreased 60 per cent in big cities and 70 per cent in cities of 100,000 or less population. Statistics on other modes of public transport show similar drops.

We have also made changes in the way we move goods. This has largely been a switch from rail to truck. Where railroads are limited to their trade routes and terminals, trucks are free to go

The automobile can corrode a city . . .
. . . or stimulate new building forms.

The automobile can destroy old architecture . . .
. . . or can be made subservient to it.

The automobile requires many directional devices . . .
. . . which require simplified design.

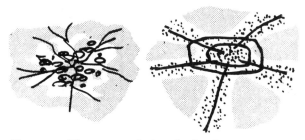

The automobile causes confusion of urban form . . .
. . . but can create a whole new order of form.

The medieval city was designed to be seen and comprehended at the scale of pedestrian movement. Camillo Sitte described this scale of design in detail.

The Renaissance and late baroque city was designed to be seen and comprehended on foot and in motion, at the speed of the pedestrian and the carriage. Wheeled movement did not cancel design based on foot movements; it added to it.

wherever there is a paved street. One out of every six vehicles in the United States is a truck, totaling 11 million trucks today. Half a million of them are long-distance vans. Trucks carry half the ton-miles of freight in our country. Trucking more than eclipses railroading in dollar-volume of business, carries all inner-city freight, and one-fifth of all freight between cities.

The facts of our land-use practices are also revealing. In general, we have been increasing the amount of new land we stake out for any particular use. New factories occupy much more land than they would have ten or twenty years ago, because of horizontal factories and the practice of holding land in reserve. Schools are now almost always horizontal in layout, requiring much larger sites. Our urban population density decreased from about 5,500 persons per square mile to about 3,800 persons per square mile between 1950 and 1960. This lowering of density operates hand-in-hand with the increasing use of automobiles and truck transport. By way of example, metropolitan New York grew 70 square miles for every million people it gained between 1900 and 1940. By 1985 it is expected to grow by 700 square miles for another 3.8 million people. Thus the radiocentric growth of our cities occurs in a gradual progression of rings of lower and lower density.

The overall effects of these developments are the increasing role of the periphery and the changing role of the old core—we have already noted the further adjustment of city form and function which spans the growth of the city into a metropolis. Where the central core started as an all-purpose center, where later it flowed out into the countryside, where later still there was an exodus of many of the functions of the center—we now find that many of the peripheral functions are taking a position of dominance, functioning as a low-density but high-activity peripheral ring. Statistics clearly reveal this. Radial highway movements in and out of our major cities will increase only about 10 per cent on the average in the next thirty years, while circumferential highway movements will increase from 60 to 135 per cent.

Wider recognition of this fact is essential lest we overlook the possibilities for designing our peripheral area development. The problems of rush-hour traffic in and out of the center occupy our minds to an inordinate degree. All of us have been caught in such jams, and they are easily captured on film, in cartoons, or in a text on urban problems. It is true that they are severe, but for many cities they will be largely corrected by a combination of improved radials, inner-ring bypass roads, and public transportation. Because radials develop before ring bypasses, much of the traffic in the central cores is through traffic. Three-fourths of the traffic in the central city is unnecessary traffic—it has neither origin nor destination in the central core. It passes through because no bypass exists. But the inner loops will act as traffic bypasses. In cities where inner loops are partially in operation, local surface traffic has been measurably reduced. The outer rings are quicker to be built since there are fewer obstacles in their paths. These conveyors of circumferential traffic are often jammed at rush times, but the jams seem tolerable in comparison to those on the old radials. The history of radial and loop routes seems to have repeated itself, from the railroad era to the highway era—first the radials, then the circumferentials.

The trends cited here indicate that the automobile is now the predominant means of passenger transportation. Although it is dominant, it cannot possibly handle all of our circulation problems. The evidence for this goes beyond the compilation of circulation facts. It forces us to consider all means of transportation together and, what is more, our social values.

The changing role of the central core is not a decline but a readjustment. Many people show no interest in it, but the fact is that it contains many vital institutions of our society which everyone depends upon, directly or indirectly. It remains the best place for the exchange of ideas, for night schools, for the meetings of the principal decision makers, for the best theaters. Major hotels and office buildings are still being built there. It is a mistake not to recognize the vital importance of the central core in the whole metropolis. Likewise it is also a mistake to overlook the rest of the expanding metropolis when considering the core. All must be examined together.

We must face this problem because there is a pressing question as to just how central-area circulation will be achieved. If one were to make a careful study of a typical downtown, serving its fullest possible role, one would have to delve into the changing uses and types of its buildings. Assuming that some kind of public transportation system were in operation, workers would come to the center by a combination of public transit and private cars. Basing the study on the economy, role, and nature of a particular city, one could estimate the number of new buildings to be built, existing buildings to remain in use, old buildings to be demolished or remodeled and—of key importance—the volume of parking structures. The volume of garages necessary, as sheer bulk, could prove to be disconcerting. Assuming that local streets could handle the inrush and outrush of all of these cars, the question of their occupying so much space horizontally and vertically is formidable.

Conceivably large parking structures could ring the city, as Louis Kahn has proposed, picturing them as great storage turrets. Or they could be buried visually—surrounded on the exterior with some active function, such as offices. In actuality we know that the central part of a city is not easily changed, and that alterations in the core necessarily emerge as patchwork, a less than neat cut-and-fill in the urban fabric.

The point is that we have raised a question of social values—one that begins to supersede the hard facts of circulation. Our approach must be to understand our tools while formulating a spectrum of social ideas. The tools lie in the understanding of movement: the facts of density, the different means of circulation for different densities, and the knowledge of which of the various modes of transportation work best in different parts of the city. Let us now consider them.

The automobile opens up a vast world of motion which overshadows the designs and scales of previous eras. We are just beginning to learn how to add this new scale to the old.

The ultimate world of scale which our new means of motion create extends far beyond an individual city. It links city to city and city to countryside. Travel is measured in time rather than distance. This scale, too, must be added to our older established scales of motion.

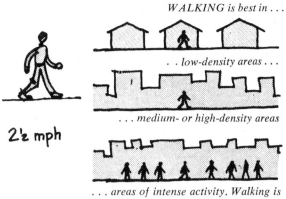

WALKING is best in . . .

. . low-density areas . . .

. . . medium- or high-density areas

2½ mph

. . . areas of intense activity. Walking is limited by practical walking distance, a quarter to a half mile.

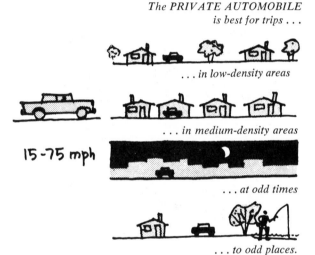

The PRIVATE AUTOMOBILE is best for trips . . .

. . . in low-density areas

. . . in medium-density areas

15-75 mph

. . . at odd times

. . . to odd places.

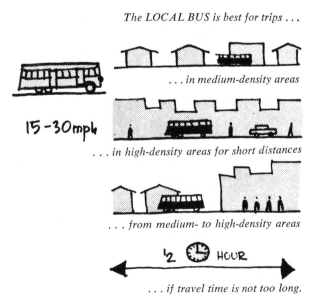

The LOCAL BUS is best for trips . . .

. . . in medium-density areas

15-30mph

. . . in high-density areas for short distances

. . . from medium- to high-density areas

½ HOUR

. . . if travel time is not too long.

The Characteristics of Modern Circulation

The characteristics of circulation are as important as the forms and patterns it takes. The characteristics are the "why" and "how" of circulation.

Statistics reveal that the core of the city draws less traffic to itself than the city as a whole. A city of a million people typically draws about 30 per cent of all traffic to its center. This traffic brings people to the center for work, meetings, or recreation. It has a purpose in going to the center. Much of the general traffic of the city has to pass through the center, however, because bypass routes are inadequate. This amounts to about three-quarters of the total traffic in the center, as we mentioned earlier. Thus, the most severe jams on the radials occur during rush hours, when through and local traffic mix. In the core itself random movements and through traffic cause jams at midday. The smaller a city, the more important its core.

Most urban trips originate from the home. Nearly half of these trips are to and from work. Other trips from the home during the work week, in descending order of frequency, are for recreation, shopping, business transactions, school, and medical appointments. On weekends most trips are for recreation and shopping.

Statistics of this type disclose the sources of traffic generation. Examination reveals that different types of land use occasion different types of trips. An acre of residential suburban land, for example, generates about thirty trips a day, whereas an acre of suburban commercial land generates about three hundred trips. The position of an acre of land in relation to the city center has an important effect too. An acre in the core of a large metropolis, for example, generates about fifteen hundred trips a day. Its immediate periphery generates about two hundred or more trips a day per acre; the 3-mile zone, about one hundred; and the 12-mile zone, about twenty.

Figures of this kind must always be derived by careful survey of a particular community. They furnish knowledge about how much traffic can be expected, where it comes from, and why. Once known, the next question is how are all these trips made?

The private car, first of all, is the best means of making trips in low-density areas. The auto also works best in medium-density areas (7,000 to 25,000 persons per square mile), at unusual times or for unusual directions such as weekend travel, which is very high, or for an evening out. To a certain extent it also works well for unusual trips at odd times in the high-density core. The car is the most natural substitute for poor public transportation.

Public surface transportation (bus or streetcar) works well within medium-density areas where many people are going to the same place—to work, for example. It also works well for feeder operations to a subway or rail terminal. It works well for short trips from a medium- to high-density area and for short trips within a high-density core, such as the center of the city.

Rapid transit (express bus) works well for long and medium trips in medium-density areas and for making trips from medium- and low-density areas to downtown and within downtown. Stops must be limited and the buses must operate on their own roadway.

Rail rapid transit (in a subway, elevated, or on the surface in its own right-of-way) is best for long trips from low- and medium-density areas to the central core, providing access to stations is good.

166

A commuter rail line can extend even farther out, but in order to reach the central city in a reasonable time—less than an hour at most for workers—its stops must be far apart. The distinction between rail rapid transit and commuter rail is one of service, not ownership or type of rolling stock. Rail rapid transit must operate on a one- to five-minute headway to be effective during rush hour. Suburban commuter lines can operate on a ten-minute to an hour headway.

Another point of view is provided by the user: walking is the best way to get around in a high-density center, providing there are not too many cross-street interruptions where vehicular traffic hampers the pedestrian. This is the way a shopping center or an air terminal operates. The effective radius of a pedestrian area is about a quarter of a mile, which is somewhat limiting. Shuttle buses, as are now in operation in downtown Washington, D.C., can extend this distance.

Driving is the best means of circulation for the myriad of special trips anywhere at odd times—in the absence of other convenient means, and until congestion or parking becomes an inconvenience itself. In the suburbs and in low-density areas roads can handle the random movements. In the crowded center we must have supplementary means to attract as many people away from their cars as we can, to reduce congestion. Driving to suburban mass-transit stations is also quite workable, again largely dependent on convenience and good public transportation. The private car best serves weekend and leisure trips, from which commuter railroads once drew large amounts of revenue.

Public transportation works where there are concentrations of passengers in space and time. People living at low density justify a mass-transit line and stations, if enough come to use it at the same time. A high-density area justifies mass-transit facilities even though people use it at different times of the day.

Finally, the passenger elevator permits high concentrations of people, and works well for them. We often take it for granted as a means of public transportation because it is privately owned and free to the public. The elevator *is* a kind of public service facility. It allows a large building to function. The building owner accepts its costs as part of the operation of his building.

We should think of the cost of all public transportation this way. In its development stages public transport was a profit-making operation. Now it must be thought of as a necessary public utility —like a sewer or a water system or the fire department. Its costs must be measured not in terms of profit as a business venture, but as part of the cost of operation of a social venture—the city. The city once required concentration because means of circulation were highly limited. The apparent potential urban limitlessness created by our modern means of circulation does not imply the dissolution of the city, but the creation of the metropolis—and that still needs one or more concentrated centers.

The "Modal Split"

The discussion of downtown "survival" brings up a major issue currently being debated in transportation planning circles: the optimum balance between private and mass transportation. The proportion is called the "modal split" and cannot be determined by considering urban transportation in isolation—for example, apart from such factors as land use and density. In part, size is

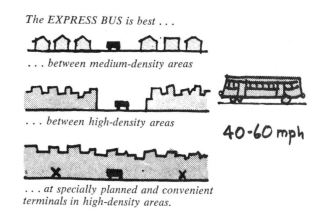

The EXPRESS BUS is best . . .

. . . between medium-density areas

. . . between high-density areas

40-60 mph

. . . at specially planned and convenient terminals in high-density areas.

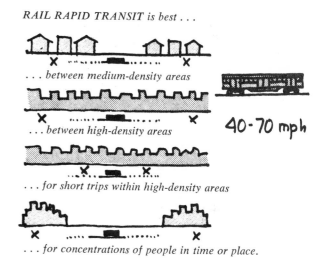

RAIL RAPID TRANSIT is best . . .

. . . between medium-density areas

. . . between high-density areas

40-70 mph

. . . for short trips within high-density areas

. . . for concentrations of people in time or place.

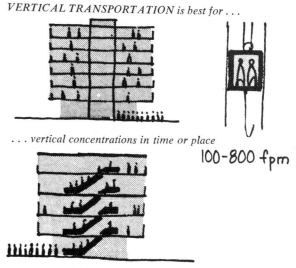

VERTICAL TRANSPORTATION is best for . . .

. . . vertical concentrations in time or place

100-800 fpm

. . . mass vertical movements over short distances.

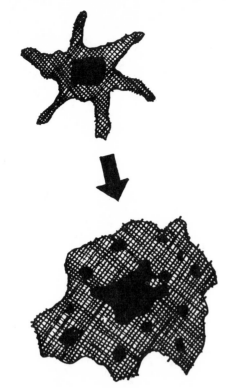

CIRCULATION AS SERVANT OF LAND USE:

Circulation patterns which serve only to continue the pattern of enlargement of a city may be shortsighted.

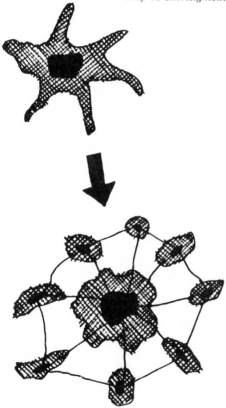

CIRCULATION AS CREATOR OF LAND USE:

Circulation patterns should be regarded as major instruments for achieving better urban forms— forms which are discernible, flexible, amenable, in key with their landscapes, and feeding a variety of urban sectors.

influential. A city must have at least 1 million people moving in and out of its center before rail rapid transit is feasible. The changing character of the city center and the willingness of the community to commit itself is also a factor; an express bus system on a separate right-of-way could be more feasible than a rail rapid-transit system. The commitment to any proportion must be based on the larger purpose and social values which a city aims to achieve. Another two-sided question recognized by urban transportation experts—often discussed independently of modal split but part of the same problem—is whether a transportation system should be designed to accommodate existing conditions or be employed as a creative tool to develop new urban form. The question is usually posed thus: Should circulation *serve* or *create* land use?

In a special issue on transportation *Architectural Forum* mentioned two major studies which are based on these two opposite views. A transportation plan for Chicago (CATS) was based on the propagation of the presently existing pattern—circulation would serve existing and likely land use. A transportation plan for the Pennsylvania–New Jersey–Delaware (Penjerdel) region was premised on the idea that the placement and design of the circulation system creates new urban forms, and thus desired land use.

The idea of the CATS concept is an extension of the familiar origin-and-destination concept of transportation planning. Certainly, it is important to improve the means of circulation for those areas of the city that are in need of improvement. The magnitude of the job for most cities, however, is so great that the very act of improving an existing origin-and-destination situation is decidedly creative. The problem of this approach is that an existing city form and its likely extension may not be good at all. It may be that a better design is possible than the one which enlarges upon an existing pattern. Frequently, this problem occurs in times of change, as, for example, when plumbing came into general use.

Many old buildings without original plumbing and other utilities can now be found with plumbing stacks on the outside, fastened to an exterior wall with many branch connections. To erect a building today in such a manner would be unthinkable. Plumbing is now completely integrated into the design. One cannot help but see a parallel in the new transportation systems we are tacking onto our old cities.

The central question in remodeling our cities on so vast a scale is how and to what extent can our remodeling become positive creation? To what extent *do* we owe allegiance to a past form when we are rebuilding so large a proportion of our cities? Should we not be thinking of a best possible new form, even though we arrive at it piece-by-piece over the years and even though we do not have all the answers now? This question lies at the heart of transportation planning because transportation routes are major determining elements. As we build them we largely fix the form of the city for a long time, even though we build piece-by-piece. In short, should we not discard the attitude of remodeling and adopt instead an approach of new creation—this in recognition of the task as an unprecedented opportunity?

It is clear that any design for the future city must be based on an idea of the way we want to live in the future, a picture that has not yet been sufficiently portrayed. Even before the vision of the future city can be portrayed we must commit ourselves to debate. Here, urban design in its formulative role enters the deliberations.

Formulating the Future City

Current circulation planning is based on the factors we have discussed so far. The plans vary between extensions of existing form and proposals for creating new form. It is very common, therefore, to see plans for improving the star shapes or radio-centric forms of cities, or for proposing new satellite or linear patterns. Two recent plans illustrate the summation of current thinking. The first of these is a plan for the greater metropolitan area of Copenhagen; the second is a plan in its initial stages for the Twin Cities area of Minnesota.

The Copenhagen plan was developed in two stages: the first is called the "finger" plan; the second, the "open space" plan. The first part of the Copenhagen plan is to be an extension of the city into the countryside in the form of five "finger" corridors. Copenhagen is a seacoast city and, therefore, the direction for growth is fixed. The five fingers are to extend inland in the most advantageous directions. All five fingers will be centered on rail rapid-transit lines. The numbers of people in these finger corridors, their development, and the distance between house and station were carefully calculated to insure the workability of the transportation system. In addition to the rail rapid-transit system, a public surface-transportation system and a new road system were planned. The Danes recognized fully the upswing in car use in their country. The land between the five fingers will be left open as recreational space.

The second part of the Copenhagen plan encompassed a much larger area. It considered the entire peninsula of which Copenhagen is the center, and indicated two giant corridors for the city's redevelopment even beyond the five fingers. This plan considered all the possibilities for growth, land use, and circulation in the entire peninsula. The corridors will extend from the edge of metropolitan Copenhagen southwestward. One of these corridors will follow the coast; a new harbor is proposed for its center. Two large corridors will extend some thirty miles out from the center of downtown Copenhagen. These corridors will be mainly industrial sites and places of residence for workers. Commuter railroads and highways will connect them to central Copenhagen. Internal circulation will be by car, bus, and foot. The Copenhagen metropolitan plan sums up our knowledge of travel habits and transportation means and applies it to a positive and creative plan.

The plan for the Twin Cities area of Minnesota amounted to a series of studies that look far beyond the problems and the developments of the Twin Cities themselves. These studies were largely the work of Norman Day on the staff of the Twin Cities Metropolitan Planning Commission. The major cities of the world were studied to discern their patterns of growth. Day's studies suggest the forms that the Twin Cities area might take through the adoption of various transportation concepts. This kind of investigation gives insight to the citizens and officials who will make decisions about them. The studies also show that transportation can be used as a positive tool in creating urban form. Such studies could well be made for all cities.

How, then, does urban design fit into such endeavors? It must start with detailed considerations of a transportation plan and proceed to understanding the transportation system as a whole, with its total effects on the metropolis. Ultimately, the role of urban design is to furnish ideas and goals for urban life, thus

The center of Cumbernauld, a multilevel vehicular-pedestrian separation design for a new town in Scotland.

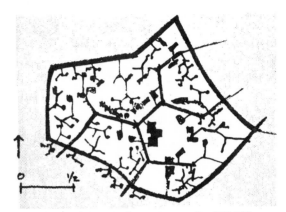

Road plan of Le Mirail, a new town for 100,000 people near Toulouse, France. Basically a concept of branching arteries and precincts.

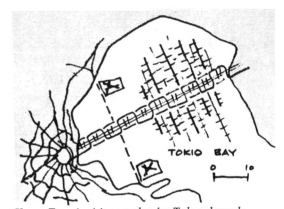

Kenzo Tange's visionary plan for Tokyo depends on a unique automobile circulation system operating along a linear spine.

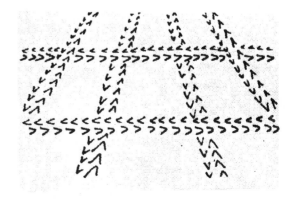

Louis Kahn's method of showing a traffic plan. Circulation conceived as an architecture of motion.

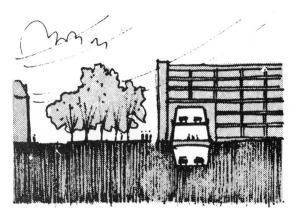

Lawrence Halprin's suggestion for integrating architecture and an urban expressway.

Sequence of views of the city from an urban expressway as envisioned by Appleyard, Lynch, and Myer. (From "A View from the Road.")

Alvar Aalto's three-terraced parking garage for cultural facilities on Töölö Bay in central Helsinki.

giving transportation planning a sound direction.

Modern circulation design can benefit greatly by applying the present techniques and ideas to a number of details. All roadways and bridges should be designed with the imagination and high standards expressed in the best of our modern architecture. Landscape architect Lawrence Halprin suggests, in a series of recent sketches, that the urban expressway can be designed with far greater imagination. Too often treated as a rural expressway finding its way into the city, an urban expressway is actually quite different. Halprin's sketches show how the expressway can be designed in conjunction with urban buildings, using more fully the valuable space it occupies, and integrating it more successfully into the city. Kevin Lynch has pointed out that the expressway can be designed to fit the city far more advantageously from a visual standpoint. He proposes that the views of the various parts of the city seen from the road should be taken into account in the process of expressway design. The pattern and form of the city can be unfolded to the driver. This would not only be esthetically pleasing but also very practical. At expressway speed it is difficult to know where to turn off; a visually-oriented urban expressway can tell the speeding driver where he is and so clarify the system for the driver.

We can also improve our systems by redesigning the traffic signs lining highways and streets. We may be forced to adopt a purely graphic system of signs because pictures are easier to decipher than words. Architects can help design them. They can also be instrumental in open space design, for the access to open country-side afforded by highways carries responsibility for the land's proper development. Since an understanding of open space pervades the history of our profession, architects can clarify its various roles. But there are still larger problems that we must face.

A recent revision of the Highway Act specified that all federally financed roads shall be developed along with "planning processes" by July, 1965. In effect, this means that our major road systems have to become part of a general community plan. This is a major step forward. At this time, however, there are few communities which have developed any ideas of community goals—ideas which should lead transportation planning. This recent amendment of the Highway Act should promote better community planning, compelling communities to think about what they want. The architect must help them for it may open the door to better urban design.

Great architects have always pondered the larger concepts of community design. Frank Lloyd Wright's architecture must be understood in the context of his large-scale thinking—so too the designs of Le Corbusier and Alvar Aalto. Basic to the thinking of these men have been the concepts of circulation.

Frank Lloyd Wright, in his Broadacres plan, foresaw the almost universal adoption of the automobile in this country. Alvar Aalto distinguishes carefully between types of routes in his community plans. Aalto has also been very imaginative in the design of particular details of transportation systems. His proposals for a cultural center for Helsinki built along the city's lake include a parking garage with several levels, forming a three-terraced "fan." The arriving driver will be able to look out over the terraces to the shoreline buildings across the lake. Here, arrival is made a positive experience. In another plan of Alvar Aalto's (a little-known competition design for a group of government buildings in

170

Gothenburg, Sweden) an ingenious entrance ramp was proposed as a forecourt for the group. An expressway and car parking area were designed as *part of* the entrance ramp. On the ramp itself pedestrians and motorists emerging from their cars would meet, to proceed through this grand entrance court to the various government buildings.

Certainly, the architect with the greatest vision in modern times is Le Corbusier. His earliest plans for the modern city were based on new modes of circulation. His plan for Paris, published in the twenties, was sponsored by one of the major automobile interests of France. Le Corbusier early recognized the advantages of the linear city, which derived from transportation, perhaps taking his cue from the work of Soria y Mata. Le Corbusier is also noted for his principle of the "Seven Routes," a refinement of a system long in existence in France. The seven routes are the types of surface circulation paths. They are designated V1, V2, V3, etc. The V1 route, for example, connects city to city. It is the equivalent of our interstate system. The progress of routes leads ultimately to the V7, a pedestrian pathway. A clear expression of the seven routes of Le Corbusier is found in his plan for Chandigarh. Somewhat less known is Le Corbusier's transportation plan for the whole of France. He was also quick to notice the potential of the route system developing in the United States when he visited this country in the thirties. Le Corbusier showed that circulation planning cannot be done without broad vision.

These leading thinkers necessarily based many of their concepts on intuition, which has often been prophetic. Today we have a large body of knowledge derived from careful observation. These scientific studies, gathered and correlated for us, should be taken as further points of departure for our thinking, to supplement the keen intuition of a Le Corbusier, Wright, or Aalto. Knowledge gained includes the different forms the modern city is taking.

It is well to consider again at this point the various urban forms which Kevin Lynch identifies—here viewed with respect to their circulation implications.

The first is the *sheet form,* akin to our spreading suburbs—like the shape of Los Angeles. It is a spread of undifferentiated growth without focal centers, without major routes or particular relief in form. Second is the *core*—a city as a dense and vital center with surrounding development. Most of our cities of a million population are such forms. Third, the *galaxy* is a series of cores arrayed in the landscape at functional distances from one another. The urbanized areas of our country delineated by the census are made up of such galaxies. The *satellite* form is a variation of the galaxy—a galaxy with a predominant central core. Most of our older cities that are spreading out and enveloping what were independent townships represent satellite forms. A variation of the satellite is the *linear* form. A megalopolis is a linear form, as are the cities from Springfield, Massachusetts, southward along the Connecticut River and the cities of the east coast of Florida. The *ring* is a linear form which closes on itself. The cities of the San Francisco Bay area and the principal cities of Holland form rings. The *star* is a core city with linear radials. Boston, St. Louis, and San Antonio are, or have been at certain stages of growth, star forms. Finally, the *polycentered net* is a widely spread city with differentiated foci, dominant and minor routes, built-up and open spaces—the whole an articulated spread.

All these forms have special implications. The sheet lacks vital

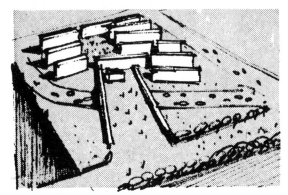

Aalto's concept for a group of government buildings in Gothenburg, Sweden. Roadway and parking are under the entrance ramp.

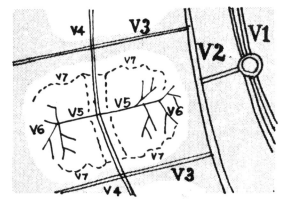

Le Corbusier's road classification. VI cross country; V2 branch to city; V3 sector dividers; V4 sector connectors; V5 local spines; V6 to buildings; V7 pedestrians.

The SHEET form. Los Angeles, Tokyo.

The CORE form. Dallas, Tulsa.

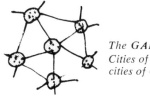

The GALAXY form. Cities of North Germany, cities of Ohio.

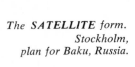

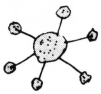

*The **SATELLITE** form.*
Stockholm,
plan for Baku, Russia.

*The **STAR** form.*
Copenhagen,
Washington, D.C.

***The LINEAR** form*
Megalopolis
Stalingrad

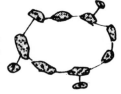

*The **RING** form.*
Cities of Holland,
San Francisco Bay.

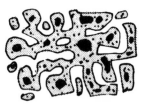

The
POLYCENTERED NET.
Detroit,
New Orleans.

hubs and is limited to automobile circulation. The core becomes congested when occupied by over a million people, but it can support public circulation. The galaxy and satellite have cores, open space, and can support public transit. The linear city can have open space close at hand, it can easily be expanded in any part by adding lateral arms and it can support public transit. The star can enjoy the same amenities—it is a combination of several linear cities intersecting at a core. The ring has a large open space in its center. The polycentered net can have all these advantages plus the major advantage of being most adaptable to changing functions and varying landscapes. With all these forms we must recognize the new scale of design with which we are working. We are no longer dealing with the streetscape or cityscape, but with the *metroscape* and perhaps *regionscape*—an enormous urban environment which we experience through time and motion.

The overall population density of the United States is now about 60 persons per square mile. We could continue our present practices of urban sprawl for some time, despite the increasing problems of congestion that would result. The population density of Japan is over 600 persons per square mile and in Holland it is even higher—some 900 persons per square mile. By Dutch standards our land could hold 2.6 billion people. Clearly, the problem is not one of capacity. It is a problem of the quality of life which our increasing population will have. The ultimate role of urban design, when addressed to problems of circulation, is to help formulate the concepts of life which we can realize in the years to come. Our new circulation systems have the potential to give us a greater freedom of access to land than we have ever had before. They can enable us to use more facilities, to visit more places, and to enjoy more of the opportunities that this country presents. There is no doubt that we will have to mature as a people in the understanding and appreciation of our landscape in order to do this properly. The increasing concern for open space and for the preservation of natural land gives promise that we are awakening to the problem. The pressing task for urban design is, therefore, to wisely implement the new circulation techniques and to help develop the means by which our increasing population—150 million more people in our professional lifetimes—will come to live.

Regulation and Control

For most architects, regulations and controls are a nuisance, because they sometimes prevent us from building our best designs. In our profession the foremost regulations and controls are restrictive building codes and zoning ordinances. Of course, a moment's reflection reveals several more restrictions: our client's tastes, mortgage money, budget, property taxes, climate, site, and mechanical equipment.

In this maze of architectural and urban complexity we have lost sight of what should be foremost among the regulators: the fulfillment of human aspirations and purpose in our surroundings. The overall implications of this problem are not limited to our profession. Indeed, here we face one of the major social and political issues of our times—the interlocking problems of public and private rights, of public and private responsibility, and of the best in individual and public initiative. Increasingly, the seemingly anonymous and growing forces which regulate these areas of action seem to multiply, to become more indifferent and less manageable.

In this chapter we shall examine the factors that control and regulate our work. We shall discuss the roots of our current system of controls, their origins, problems, shortcomings, appropriateness, and application.

County map of central and lower Florida. Four regulatory codes are in effect in the different counties. Within the counties numerous city codes also operate.

173

In early settlements the demands of nature and the settlers' capabilities regulated form.

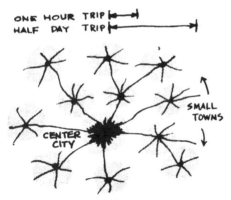

In early towns military necessity often regulated siting.

Practical travel distances between towns and regional centers regulated regional pattern.

ONE HOUR TRIP
HALF DAY TRIP

SMALL TOWNS

CENTER CITY

A simple building technology regulated urban appearance.

The Background of Controls and Regulations

The landing of the Pilgrim settlers marked the encounter of two mighty resources: the abundance of the land and the energy of the immigrants. Unlike the Indians who regarded themselves as caretakers of the land, Europeans brought with them the idea that land was the sole property of its owners, to be used any way they saw fit. Further, as much as nature was a provider, it was also cruel. Its forests were an obstacle to be overcome. The new settlers quickly came to regard land as a resource to be exploited.

The Europeans could not have been more different from their Indian predecessors, whose attitude toward land was one of reverence. Over the centuries the American Indians had achieved an ecological balance between themselves and the land. The pioneers upset that balance in their early zeal, and since that time our country has been searching for a new balance. Scientific technology further complicated this search, revealing even more resources to exploit and less time to reflect upon the whole dynamic experience. As Robert Frost said, "The land was ours before we were the land's." These problems reveal themselves in both our urban and rural life.

Stewart L. Udall, in his book *The Quiet Crisis,* poignantly relates just how we went about exploiting the land. Of particular interest is the way we divided our Western territory. It was ruled off as a series of squares to facilitate distribution and settlement. However, the land west of the 98th meridian was limited in water supply and required careful planning for water usage. It was proposed that this land be allocated on the basis of water resources, the minimum portion being that optimum area which could support an individual farm family. Our sixth President, John Quincy Adams, while serving in the Congress in his later years, proposed apportionment of land based on river basin areas rather than geometric division. With land rights were to go riparian or water rights. This was not done, and the settlers of those relatively dry lands were harassed, if not actually ruined, by the water problem. The climax was the dust bowl of the 1930s. Farm reclamation programs of the Federal and state governments have been working on such land problems ever since.

The development of regulatory measures in our cities is not so easily described, for it evolved from a series of developments not easily summarized. However, we know of the effects of certain events. At one time, for example, civic defense required the construction of a defensive wall, which gave physical limits to the city. Some cities owned their land and so could sell it, according to their charters. The control of city land usually resulted in a simple grid layout of properties. There were no restrictions on the actual use of land before the nineteenth century, and well into it. No one could compel a city landowner to remove a pig or cow from his backyard.

As the city developed and intensified, the lines between the public right-of-way and the private domain became very important. Maintenance of the right-of-way for traffic, the operation of a police and fire system, sewage disposal, water supply, and public schooling emerged as government tasks by the middle of the nineteenth century. The political and social dialogue of the time evolved a system of private rights operating hand-in-hand with public responsibilities to ensure that those rights endured. Social requirements began to be major regulators.

174

At the outset the laws of man and nature regulated both rural and urban land. In the case of rural land, the man-made regulator was the rudimentary system of land apportionment. In the case of urban land, rudimentary agreement between private citizens in collective action established the rules. As technology and the waves of immigration advanced, the urban problem was compounded, and the nineteenth century saw the inception of many public regulatory measures. Laws were drafted for fireproof building construction after fires leveled extensive portions of several crowded cities. Measures were established for obtaining drinking water and for carrying away sewage when the dangers of polluted water were recognized. Franchises were issued to public transportation companies to keep the city moving. When living conditions in crowded areas became intolerable and the public at large was aroused by inhuman slum conditions, housing codes were adopted, forerunners of zoning. The city government itself, having surrendered its landholdings to the public, and with them its source of revenue, began to tax landholders and revenue-producing enterprises. Land taxes replaced land rents. Municipal revenue regulated municipal service in accord with the public's approval.

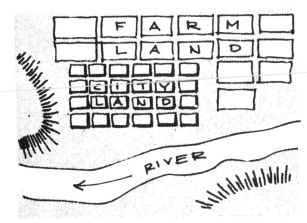

The gridiron plan became a major regulator of town form.

We must not forget that our government's regulating powers originate from our wishes as private citizens. So it was in 1916 when New York City adopted its zoning ordinance—the forerunner of the kind of zoning that cities and towns all over the nation were to adopt. Zoning in New York was necessitated by the threat to property values posed by the unregulated erection of tall buildings. The forty-story Equitable Building rose from the ground as a solid prism. Because it cut off light and air from its neighbors it depressed their value. Overcrowding and overdevelopment had long been of concern to New Yorkers. Sensing the danger to health and property, the public adopted zoning ordinances to stave off further threat. Safeguarding adequate light and air was basic to public health, and zoning was therefore in the public interest. This concept was legally validated in 1925 in the Supreme Court case of *Euclid v. Ambler*. Euclid was a suburb of Cleveland, which had adopted zoning prescribing land-use districts, lot size and setback, and billboard restriction. The features of Euclid's zoning were typical, embodying the new concept of public health, welfare, and safety—the accepted basis of public regulation.

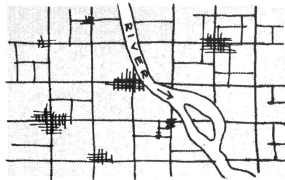

The gridiron land division became a major regulator of regional form.

Even before zoning was taking hold here, Raymond Unwin was pointing out that there was no need to crowd. *Nothing Gained from Overcrowding* was published in 1903 in England, and Unwin's philosophy was widely espoused here. Unwin supported zoning, and by the end of the 1920s the concept of zoning had won general acceptance. It was also agreeable to real estate people because it helped maintain property values and could, with deft manipulation, create value. Clever entrepreneurs could assemble land zoned at a restrictively low density, get the zoning changed, and overnight boost the market value of the land. Similarly, favored communities could restrict undesirable activities and people, to cast that burden on less resourceful neighbors.

The Equitable Building (arrow) in New York exemplified the conditions of overcrowding which led to zoning.

But zoning is not the only regulator which was recognized. Cities were developing the present concepts of eminent domain, taxation, and the enforcement of regulation. Eminent domain did not require the city to compensate private property owners in a restrictive action, but it did require compensation in a taking action. Due process of law in such cases was justified on the basis of the general public's welfare. Compliance with zoning ordinances

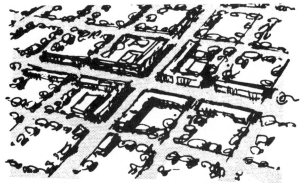

Zoning and grid became the regulators of form in most American towns.

175

There are no regulations to preserve and protect special vistas.

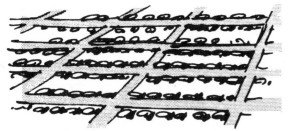

Regulations can produce monotony when used unimaginatively.

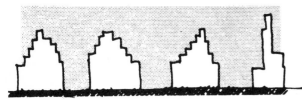

Regulations can set architectural form for better or worse.

No regulations prevent the exposure of ugly rear building facades.

No regulations insist on good sidewalk design, and sidewalks are the basic urban open spaces.

became the responsibility of the police. Meanwhile, private property owners had developed the concept of the restrictive covenant, a means to legally perpetuate their desires for their property.

In the depression it was realized that the homebuilding industry was a key to getting the country back on its economic feet. The Federal government stimulated construction by guaranteeing mortgage loans for housing. Of course, the housing had to meet basic construction standards so that the public's money was spent wisely. Pervading the standards was Unwin's admonition to avoid overcrowding. The standards coincided with the public's predilection to single-family houses on individual lots. Later, proposed modifications to these standards met with objection, for change was seen as a threat to value. *Status quo,* too, can be a regulator.

Regulations and controls exist in the form of laws and powers granted to public officials. In a democracy laws and public powers come into being only after their need has become apparent and proved essential to the public interest. Just as it takes time to create laws and public power, so it takes time to change them when a change is needed. Our history—long-term and recent—has been a history of change. It is not strange, then, that some of our laws are obsolete or at least out of tune. This results in two problems: We have to contend constantly with outmoded regulations and controls; and we are reluctant to adopt new controls or regulatory procedures out of mistrust for the idea of control in general. More specifically, we are slow in adopting techniques more advanced than zoning, such as the public control of land use on a comprehensive scale.

Two events should be noted as landmarks in addition to the *Euclid v. Ambler* decision. One was the drafting of a model document in Washington, D.C., by two attorneys in 1926. At Secretary of Commerce Herbert Hoover's request, Frank Bassett Williams and Edward M. Bassett wrote the "Standard Enabling Legislation." This document was adopted by many states in zoning enabling legislation that empowered their constituent cities and towns to prepare plans, zoning and otherwise. Zoning and planning were made legal on a state-by-state basis over a period of ten to fifteen years.

The second event was more recent, but equally significant. In 1954 the Supreme Court decided that esthetics was a just public concern worthy of support by law. In *Berman v. Parker,* an urban renewal case dealing with the first Southwest urban renewal project in Washington, D.C., the Court ruled that "it was within the power of the legislature to determine that the community should be beautiful as well as healthy, spacious as well as clean, well-balanced as well as carefully patrolled." Many states have followed suit.

The maze of regulations affecting architecture and urban design ranges from requirements of our national economy to building codes. But from this maze one central fact emerges: the controlling factor is our attitude toward what we want from our great productive energy.

Present Regulatory Factors

The Official City Plat

The official city plat regulates urban design directly. It is a legal document showing public streets and private land, with dimensions. It also shows easements on private land—rights of access to alleys or underground utilities. It designates public lands for parks, police stations, hospitals, schools, and libraries. The official city plat is the basis for describing private properties physically for legal documents, such as ownership titles or deeds. Some cities have compiled their plats into official city maps—overall official maps of the city taking in all the separate plat areas.

Once drawn and adopted, the official city plat or map is difficult to change. Actions at the scale of urban expressway building or urban renewal are required to alter it, but even then it is a complicated process. The major difficulty with plats is that anyone can file one, even very poor ones, and once filed, they become indelibly stamped on the land. Their street patterns may run counter to topography, the block size and shape may be ridiculous, but those streets and blocks have legal status. Cities and towns all over the United States are burdened with obsolete and unusable plats. Official plats are the basis for taxation, insurance contracts, and sale. For that reason they have endured as a controlling measure and are difficult to alter at this point. Only through such processes as a public-domain land taking or urban renewal can a plat and street pattern be altered. Historically, of course, street patterns long outlive land-ownership patterns and both outlive the life span of the buildings residing on the whole pattern.

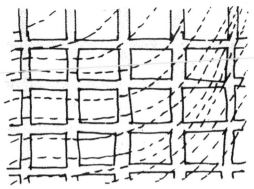

City plats are official city form regulators . . .

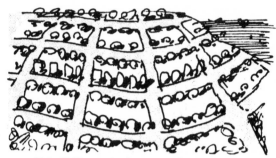

. . . which, if ill-conceived, may produce hardships in later development.

The Zoning Ordinance

Closely allied to the official city plat or map as a regulator of urban design is the zoning ordinance. It specifies the uses to which property may be legally put and the intensity of development allowed, stated in terms of floor area. A zoning plan may often specify off-street parking requirements or off-street truck loading facilities as a ratio of floor area. Zoning designations have become more and more elaborate, with numerous subclassifications to encompass complex variations and combinations. The legal profession has been concerned that the *ad hoc* treatment of zoning problems, as in zoning variance requests, may be undermining zoning because of inept administration and inequity in practice. At the heart of the problem is the lack of a clear public objective —a plan—which would guide judgment in various requests. Our profession must recognize that zoning is no substitute for design and that too often it freezes the design of a city.

Zoning is, by its nature, negative. It can prevent property owners from burdening the public with an ill-suited development. But it cannot plan school locations, traffic movements, or parklands—nor can it create beauty, order, or amenity. Zoning is neither planning nor design. Ideally it is a set of specifications that accompany a plan. Zoning should be regarded like a set of architects' specifications: a binding description of his blueprints. A zoning ordinance is supposed to be a product of a city plan. But city plans are seldom officially "adopted" and, when they are, they have no legal status. They are only guides and descriptions of an idea. Zoning, on the other hand, has legal status.

However, even as a second-best control, zoning serves a purpose. One can readily imagine the chaos that would result if all zoning were abolished. Nevertheless, zoning without a full-blown plan is as silly as a set of building specifications without working drawings or a list of culinary ingredients without a recipe. Zoning falls into proper place as the legal enforcement of an overall urban concept. For the time being we must recognize the powerful role of zoning as a control. As things now stand, it is the single most powerful factor. The appearance of Washington, D.C., and Manhattan are the best evidence of the effects of zoning on the appearance of the

Unnecessarily restrictive height control through zoning can result in dullness as well as uniformity . . .

. . . but most zoning controls cannot prevent disorderly urban form.

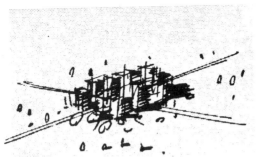

Land values can cause dense cluttering in urban centers . . .

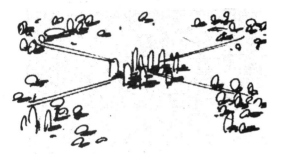

. . . and accelerate outward movement.

Property taxes can destroy a fine old feature building . . .

. . . replacing it with an interim surface parking lot.

city. Zoning ordinances for height and setback in these cities have set their urban design—for better and for worse. In most American cities zoning ordinances have been given a decisive design role by default; that is, out of lack of a city plan.

Land Value

Intimately related to zoning ordinance is land value, as assessed by the city and as determined by the market. Land value is largely controlled by the use to which a property can be put according to the zoning ordinance. Of course, the particular area of a city and its general uses influence land values even more. Critics often point out the flaw that zoning is often adjusted to accommodate the changing circumstances of the market. Hence, it is less a tool for urban design than for speculative enterprise—and fails to maintain order since it can be changed so easily. The problem lies not so much in the restriction of private commerce as in the unreliability of the tool for serving public purpose.

Land value largely determines the uses to which land can be put. Few uses can be tolerated which are not financially feasible. Since land is sold at the highest price obtainable, its market value is usually overstated. Inflated land values are one of the most restricting elements of urban design. Many central city rebuilding projects are therefore impossible without some form of cost "write-down," a process whereby some portion of the cost of land in a project is paid for by the public. The justification for this action lies in the overall return to the city which the project brings, socially, economically, and physically. This can more than repay the public at large, although the return may be difficult to measure. This is the cost to the public of curing an urban disease. In fact, it is somewhat inaccurate to speak of the process as a cost "write-down" since private developers must pay the fair market value of the land—this determined objectively by disinterested appraisers. The public cost, the so-called "write-down," is the cost of urban repair.

The obvious alternative to land value as a capricious determinant of urban design is public control bordering on public ownership, such as is practiced in England. This idea is anathema here. In its place we compensate private owners for their loss in a public taking when a definite program is adopted. This is a cost we have come to accept for the continuance of our attitude toward the rights of private property owners. Legal critics have pointed out that if it is fair to compensate owners for loss in value through public action, we should, by the same reasoning, assess them for value gained through some public action—such as building a new highway along a previously inaccessible property.

Property Taxes

From land and building values tax revenues are computed. *Ad valorem* taxes are based on some fraction of the total assessed value of a property and its building. In real estate language a building is termed an "improvement" since it adds to the value of a piece of property. This value is determined not on the basis of the land and its building in the total community picture, but on its market value. Appraisers (who are professional evaluation experts) determine market value. Profit potential thus becomes the basis of taxation. Critics assail this practice vigorously, some suggesting that cost to the city directly would be a far more equitable basis of taxation. How this would be determined it is not easy to say.

Some formula would have to be developed. Still more complex would be the process of change from the *ad valorem* system to an actual cost system.

Here is an instance of a slowly developed public power now deeply entrenched. The *ad valorem* system was originally adopted because a building's value was easier to determine than its actual cost (or benefit) to the city. The counterproposal—taxation on the basis of actual cost to a city—would require intricate calculations, which we are probably capable of making today through the use of computers. In fact, our knowledge is now sufficient to use taxation policy as a tool of urban design. Taxation is already a tool of economic planning.

A city which functions in fact like this . . .

Municipal Fractionalization

Causing still more difficulties is municipal fractionalization—the division of what is, in fact, a total working organism into separate pieces. This has led to inconsistency in regulations in adjoining communities. The fractionalization of the city into separate political entities is one of the chief obstacles to urban design on the scale of the whole city. At present we are trying to effect urban design programs within the framework of our current mode of operations. A large portion of our taxes goes to our Federal and state governments. They manage funds and develop technical proficiency. Where Federal and state governments supply funds, the local municipalities furnish leadership. This is meant to ensure technical soundness on the one hand and the fulfillment of local objectives on the other. This problem is far from a solution. It will, undoubtedly, require one of the most massive efforts of re-examination which this country has ever contemplated.

. . . may be governed by irrational jurisdictions like this.

Several local programs are aimed at countering the problems of fractionalization. Local planning commissions have voluntarily joined together in regional planning councils for discussion and coordinated decision making. Capital budgeting on a metropolitan basis for police, water, sewage, and parks has been a forward step.

The Federal government's seven-point Workable Program for Community Improvement is a useful guide for overcoming the problems of isolated action. This program shows how to coordinate (1) codes and ordinances, (2) comprehensive community planning, (3) neighborhood analysis, (4) administrative organization, (5) financing, (6) housing for displaced families, and (7) citizen participation. Although this program is intended as a way of organizing a community for HHFA urban renewal funds, some communities have used it as a guide for planning their own action using their own financial resources.

Protective covenants can assure good design in small-scale developments.

Covenants

Restrictive deed covenants are specifications imposed on the use of property in its deed, or statement of ownership. Restrictive covenants have generally been negative in nature to restrict sale to a person of unpopular ethnic or religious background. Yet covenants have been written into deeds to ensure property maintenance, sound use and, hence, community health. Property owners around Louisburg Square in Boston and Gramercy Square in New York agree through covenant to support the cost of their private parks. Suburban residents of Houston, Texas, employ private deed covenants rather than public zoning ordinances. The covenants, however, can only be imposed with the concurrence of the in-

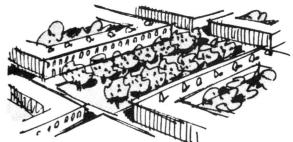

Covenants can maintain small urban neighborhood greens . . .

. . . and common open spaces in surburban developments.

Urban design objectives must be injected into the regulations which form the street . . .

. . . which influence the grouping of buildings . . .

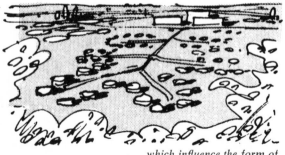

. . . which influence the form of new suburban developments . . .

. . . and which position the highway in relation to the city, functionally and visually (arrow).

dividual property owner, or a developer in the case of a new development project. They can work on a small community basis, but cannot come close to controlling the city as a whole.

Much creative work remains to be done in the positive use of covenants. For example, in the creation of new towns there is a critical period of transition from developer ownership to occupant control. This occurs before the whole community is built—perhaps a third of it is erected—which means that its inhabitants are somewhat homogeneous as a class. They may decide, through legislation, to impose alterations on the original plan which precludes the final development of a socially and commercially balanced "new town." In fact, they may do this out of unwitting shortsightedness. Certainly the inhabitants should have the prerogatives enjoyed by the citizens of other communities. Here is where a new form of covenant might enter in. Covenants could be drafted in the form of development policies that would allow flexibility while assuring that the social rudiments of the new town would be realized more or less as originally planned.

Subdivision Regulations

Subdivision regulations are a physical extension of zoning for forming the character of an area, usually residential. Subdivision regulations state building form and community character more specifically than zoning, specifying the sizes of front and rear yards, minimum lot size, and sometimes minimum house size and materials. Their great weakness from a community design standpoint is that their typical use is to underwrite our suburban sprawl. Subdivision rules may flout good community design. A good house and lot design multiplied ad infinitum over the suburban landscape cannot possibly substitute for the careful design of residential streets, school locations, the siting of business hubs, and the relation between quiet street and busy freeway. Yet it has often been given this role by default.

A most helpful job could be undertaken by local architects in examining their own subdivision regulations and evaluating them on the basis of the products to which they lead. Every subdivision regulation, for example, should have the option of an unspecified alternative. There should always be room for innovation when accompanied by a satisfactory demonstration of proof of validity and the fulfillment of the public's interests.

Building, Housing and Sanitary Codes

To complete the list of regulatory factors, building codes must be added. They ensure the satisfaction of minimum standards to produce sound building. They also affect community design and appearance with their specifications of the use of certain materials and certain mechanical features. Sometimes they may be obsolete. Some plumbing codes, for example, specify elements in such a way as to rule out new advances which would bring cost down to a level where more modest-priced houses could be built in a community. Building codes may specify window-opening areas which do not make sense when considering the relationship between one house and another. Codes are essential in general, but many could well be examined from the point of view of the relation between buildings.

Here, again, allowance must be made for innovation supported by proof of validity. Some building codes do not allow the construction of modest row houses, particularly narrow ones. They also may be so burdened with semantic complexities that the deft and unscrupulous find ways of fulfilling the letter of the law while flouting its intent. One attempt to correct this deficiency has been the use of performance standards which state the *requirements* to be satisfied, leaving the *methods* up to the designer. For example, rather than specifying that the area of a window shall be such-and-such a percentage of a room's floor area, it is sufficient to say that the window shall provide ample light and air.

The Basic Problem

The main regulators of the city's design thus include its official street plats, zoning, land values, taxation plan, municipal fractionalization, covenants, subdivision regulations, and building codes. Within these institutions of regulation and control there are also an array of subordinate regulators. Utility layout, for example, is a by-product of the official city map. Obviously, the city's economic base and sense of civic pride control any actions for civic improvement. Transportation patterns regulate value in urban and suburban land. Fine arts commissions, historical commissions, and *ad hoc* committees regulate the creation and maintenance of the city's higher values.

The missing link in our present regulatory practices is full consideration of urban design. Although our current measures in fact control the city's appearance, we have failed to inject design into the rules of city building. We cannot revolutionize these rules, but we can extend them to incorporate design goals.

Injecting Urban Design into Regulations

Conservation and Upgrading

A major task in building urban America lies in preserving areas that are healthy: physically, socially, and financially. Preservation and rehabilitation of this stock can be achieved through sound housekeeping on an urban scale, accomplished through the judicious exercise of current regulations, while recognizing that all individual buildings are in an environmental context which has a considerable regulatory effect in itself.

In the case of urban housing, for example, almost every city and town has a large proportion of row and semidetached houses two or three generations old. These are the old streetcar suburbs of yesterday, the comfortable houses of the former middle-class suburbanites. Unlike the huge pre-income tax mansions, the old middle-class family dwellings can handily accommodate a contemporary family, or sometimes two. Although the heating and plumbing may not be up-to-date, they are up-to-par. The rooms are often of good size, the gardens ample although not large, and the street trees mature. It is to the interests of the community to ensure that none of its policies in taxing, road building, or other indirect and inadvertent practices threaten these areas, for policy largely regulates their health.

If, for example, municipal finances result in a boost in residential real estate taxes, the owners of these old properties may forsake them for a suburban alternative. The result may be an increase in the city's commuter load, a reduction in public transit passengers, and a decrease in responsible citizenry in the central city. If the quality of local schools in central cities is on the downgrade, one can be sure of an accompanying degree of middle-class exodus. The older areas often endure despite a barrage of insult,

Zoning should protect all views of important historical buildings, such as this church in Charleston, South Carolina.

A height limitation can weld different buildings into a cohesive whole through mass uniformity—K Street in Washington, D.C.

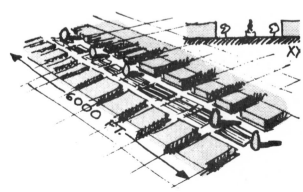

Fine streets like Monument Avenue in Richmond, Virginia, with its five memorials, need protection by regulation.

181

New houses can be integrated into older neighborhoods by continuing the scale of masses and spaces. Regulations can require this.

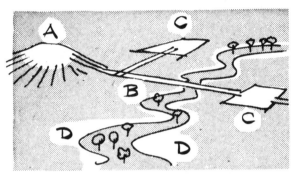

Every city and town should assess and control its special sites: (A) hilltops, (B) grand avenues, (C) special enclaves, (D) the borders of parkland.

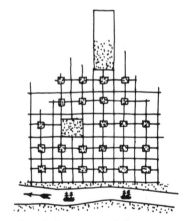

Regulations are needed to protect the old squares of Savannah, Georgia.

Fine views from special promontories should be kept open by regulations.

but there is one blow they can scarcely survive—the transformation of an old residential street into a traffic artery. Robbed of its tranquility, it soon is bereft of neighborly character, and so sentiment for it vanishes. Critics of rough-shod road-building programs who are alarmed at displacement problems should be equally alarmed at the less evident but equally destructive effects of unrelated surface street traffic patterns. They are a main alternative to expressways. Surface street circulation patterns should form precinctual residential islands free of through-traffic flow.

Almost all our old cities have one or two grand avenues lined with old mansions. These were the stately homes of the rich and represent a period of the past that we shall never see again. Usually, these grand old streets indicated the direction of growth for the outward expansion of affluent development. In the majority of cases these streets are in a state of decay, the mansions having been divided up as rooming houses or used as funeral parlors. Some cities have managed to preserve the quality of these streets; East Avenue in Rochester, New York, is one example. There is a case for municipal policy which encourages this type of preservation. Private institutions, citizens' groups, schools, small museum groups, and church groups can use the old mansions. Municipal policy, through tax relaxation, could make this possible. Indeed, it might be shown through careful study that such streets with their old buildings might be the ideal place to divert low tax-yield activities, less supportable economically elsewhere in the city. Such avenues could be attractive linear nuclei for stabilizing in-town residential development.

Some cities have old quarters with a pervading urban scale and character as well as grand Victorian streets. These are precious assets, for such quarters have a human scale that is difficult to reproduce nowadays. Wise communities have established special commissions to oversee these historical quarters. Special historic zoning ordinances such as those of Charleston, South Carolina, New Orleans, and Schenectady, New York, are examples.

Appearance and Design in Zoning

Thus far it has been difficult for zoning ordinances or other regulatory techniques operating through the law to effectuate appearance controls. Courts are reluctant to get into matters which they deem to be "esthetics." Esthetics must be shown to be a real community value, a real basis of property value—a status it does not yet have. Some design elements, however, can be stated in definite terms. Aluminum awnings or fake facade materials may be ruled out of an area because they are specific and not matters of subjective judgment. This suggests that "special-character areas" can be created under zoning administration. Likewise, courts are reluctant to designate historic areas—unless such areas can be shown to have uniqueness of antiquity and tourist attraction value. This limited view needs enlightenment.

Washington, D.C., is one of the few cities which has an appointed body of experts to oversee the appearance of certain major avenues. This body is the Fine Arts Commission, established over a half-century ago. At that time its area of concern was designated—the Mall and certain streets and squares which formed a kite-shape in the center of the city. Recent urban growth and redevelopment has not been accompanied by the extension of this commission's administrative area, however. An example of the result is that the South Capitol Street vista of the Capitol dome is critically marred by a haphazard foreground—much of the foreground being new highway construction. This problem is not unique in Washington.

"Special Site" Controls

Every city has certain special sites and certain special avenues; special in the sense that they serve to embody what is or could be outstanding as features of the city, and thus have a public value. Richmond, Virginia, has its Church Hill. San Antonio has many fine old houses and several fine plazas. New Orleans has been protecting the Vieux Carré with special ordinances and a special commission. Such special places deserve the best we can give them, and one step toward that end is the establishment of groups of experts who can guide their development. Once specified, these special sites can become the objects of public policy through the careful direction of regulatory policies that spur them to realization.

Every city and town with growth potential—and that includes most of them—requires this kind of scrutiny. Dormant now, the possibilities await the rousing of the public's consciousness by the architectural profession, they who are most able to exercise imagination. Once uncovered, ideas must be transferred to the public's trust through the medium of plans and then protected by regulatory techniques that will ensure realization.

Factors Regulating Slum Repair

Charles Abrams once suggested creating a slum surplus by rejecting all policies of slum clearance which cause further crowding. A slum surplus would cause a rent decrease, and so the poor would benefit. Landlords would begin to compete for these tenants on the basis of improved quarters. Raymond Vernon, in a study of New York City, pointed out that the practice of building high-density, high-rise public housing in already crowded areas may also be at fault. Most people, particularly low-income people, prefer small houses of their own in the suburbs, but are often zoned out.

Another program for slum correction is code enforcement—to compel landlords by legal means to bring their properties up to legal standards of decency. Programs of this type are difficult to promote and maintain. Often, they can cause rent increases since the cost of repair is passed directly on to the tenant. This kind of program can be of benefit when applied not to the bottom stratum of low-cost housing, but somewhat above it, where the landlord can bear the cost of repair. An emergency measure is direct rent subsidy to the tenant himself. Special courts to enforce property repair by landlords have proven effective.

Such proposals and criticisms are all valid in themselves, but none of them can succeed in isolation. Necessarily tied as they are to public and market regulatory forces, they cannot operate effectively without a larger public policy—including a design policy. Low-income people cannot be housed in the city without public subsidy. The cost of the land is too great. The private market can only afford to house them where land is relatively cheap— far out in the suburbs—and then only the lower–middle-income groups can be accommodated. Obviously, the answer to poverty is opportunity for employment and betterment. It was along these lines of thought that Clarence Stein, the late Henry Wright, and several other architects in their circle made their New Towns proposals in the twenties and thirties.

Improving the lot of the poor is not accomplished by tearing

Buffers should be placed between expressways and houses.

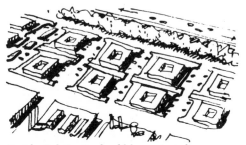
Residential streets should be protected against through traffic by sidewalk improvement.

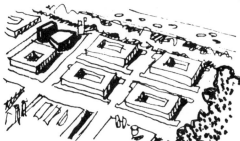
Community facilities—schools and open space— should be added.

Nuisance factories should be replaced or remedied.

Obsolete housing should be removed and replaced concurrently.

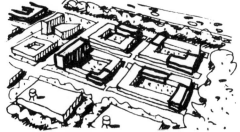
IN SLUM CORRECTION THE FORCES THAT BLIGHT SHOULD BE REPLACED BY REGULATORS THAT CAUSE IMPROVEMENT. PROGRAMS SHOULD BE COORDINATED VERY CAREFULLY TO AVOID DIFFICULTIES OF DISPLACEMENT AND TO ENSURE MAXIMUM BENEFIT FROM EACH STEP.

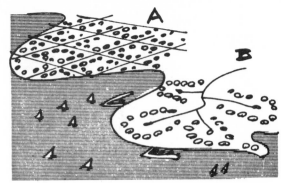

Regulations must not cause senseless monotony (A) but rather sensitive grouping (B).

Regulations must allow responsible innovation in existing communities.

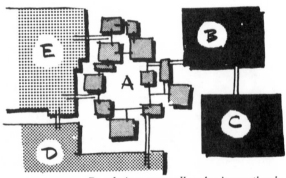

Regulations must allow for innovation in mixture-uses, as in a college campus (A) woven together with a research park (B), an industrial area (C), a commercial center (D), and residential areas (E).

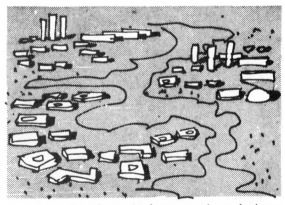

Experiments in cluster grouping and mixture should be allowed in special regulations.

down their dwellings, but by raising their incomes. Likewise, in their housing, it is not simply a matter of applying more regulatory standards, but of providing better total designs. In following the sound steps of Stein and Wright in their work on this problem and hopefully carrying them further, some of our old attitudes will need reexamination.

For example, we are inclined to think that low-income housing is a matter for only the central city, and so we build stark high-rise apartments in the city. It may well be that a concerted effort of creating employment opportunity and new housing out in the far suburbs or in new towns would be far more effective. But we are reluctant to promote the movement of the poor out to the domain of the affluent. It might also be that a reexamination of the minimum property standards of the suburbs would allow lower-income people to afford dwellings there. Many of their jobs are now located out of the city. A constructive regulatory measure might be the allowance of modest houses on modest lots when done in accordance with an open space or common parkland plan.

Regulatory Measures in New Development

Today we have an array of regulatory and disciplining factors which control the building of our communities. But they are not quite the right ones, because they are obsolete in terms of today's problems. They may assure the maintenance of property value and more livable individual houses, but they are not producing sounder community values or more livable cities. It would be impossible in most of our communities, under their existing regulatory laws, to re-create another Bath Crescent, Place des Vosges, or central Edinburgh. It would even be difficult to re-create a New England village green because of "mixed use." How many innovations could we succeed in building into our communities, let alone re-creating the better examples of the past? Current zoning, setback, and minimum lot size regulations, in fact, dictate design. They prevent artful grouping, rhythmic spacing, clustering, and relief—the essence of artful site design. How can we obtain such designs? What new slant is needed in the practice of regulatory design?

It is difficult to alter the regulatory factors governing the existing city on a piecemeal basis, but we have right now an unprecedented opportunity to write new rules for creating truly livable new communities.

We must assess all the factors which regulate community design. We must understand all the regulatory forces at work and their real effects. We must propose concepts for creating new communities. From these concepts we develop regulatory techniques, not vice versa. We can then proceed to single out the regulatory forces most relevant. We can develop new ones based on design where needed. These together become the principal regulatory tools we employ.

Pervading this approach to establishing relevant and helpful regulatory techniques must be the goal of coordinating presently isolated community building programs. A single part of a community should not be designed in isolation, out of context, just as the mechanical system of a building should not be designed apart from its structure or function. The single most important thesis to follow is that we must direct our regulatory programs around community-building lines rather than individual-house or single-building lines.

The typical operative builder knows that he must sell his house to an individual customer. The rules and regulations governing his work all revolve within this context. The typical practicing architect also works with individual buildings but the good architect, of course, takes careful account of his site and neighboring buildings. He reaches into the environs of his site to keep his work in proper relationship. It would be interesting to experiment with new types of covenants on an individual building basis. It is possible that they could instill requirements on upkeep that would be a community— or urban design—contribution. Urban renewal projects must be part of a thorough city plan. Requiring all federally financed urban expressways to be designed within the framework of a local planning activity is a sound step to ensure that all such projects are related to their total settings.

We must recognize that every major element of a community building tangibly affects certain other areas of the community. Road-building programs are the prime examples, and they should be required to relate to all the aspects of the community which they affect. In the case of road building we know that improved access means increased pace of development and that we cannot easily predict the exact nature of that development. It has to be given an arena in which to develop—an arena opened by the road system. We also know that we use land at very low densities—that roads lead to development and development involves great areas of sprawl.

It is in our interest, then, to require the creation of open space commensurate with an accompanying highway construction. Open spaces will largely relieve whatever rash development the highway spawns. State and Federal governments created many of our splendid large parks. What will we now add to this stock? The public should, of course, pay for this, but how often does public leadership propose, for example, a bond issue for open space acquisition? Political leaders may be reluctant to put forward such "extravagant" ideas. Perhaps an assist from the architectural professions would help remove that stumbling block.

A real forward step would be to adopt on a large scale and in many communities a new regulatory concept proposed by Carl Feiss in the Bratenahl suburb of Cleveland. In redrafting the zoning ordinance of Bratenahl, Feiss proposed design districts—designated areas where developers could make special design proposals which would be judged on the basis of merit by qualified experts, architects foremost among them. If no developers made proposals, the land would be developed according to the standard zoning controls applicable to other parts of the town.

These examples show that there are many parts of the city where the accepted regulatory controls now in practice are valid as preservatives. We hope they illustrate, too, that the wise application and sometimes the extension of these techniques can also serve as powerful constructive tools, but we must recognize that these tools do not entirely meet present needs. Most important of all, we must understand that while no regulation can ever substitute for good design, good design on a city-wide scale is impossible without sound regulations.

Current Architectural Techniques

The ever-present question for architects is just how design can be controlled in the city. There are several techniques.

Highway construction which gives access to large extents of land should be accompanied by the creation of open-space reserves by regulation.

Innovation in regulation should allow us further experiments with air rights.

Regulations should never exclude lively pockets of vitality woven into urban centers.

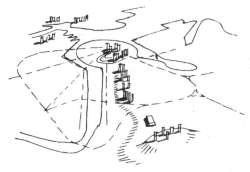

Certain regulations should control the form and location of high buildings when they affect the appearance of the skyline—sketch from the "Architects' Plan" for Boston.

185

Eye-level studies should be made as part of the initial bulk studies . . .

. . . to determine the degree of allowable tolerance and variation in designs.

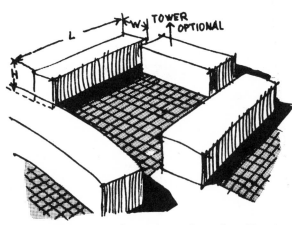

Design control at project scale can be achieved through a plan specifying building bulks and positions, public open space, and circulation . . .

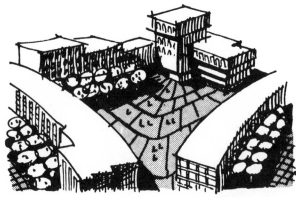

. . . which individual architects can later translate into individual designs.

The first of these techniques is a very old one. It works at project scale, that is, in a finite area where full development can be expected to take place in a definite period of time. The controls involved are minimal—simply the specification in a general design plan of the public spaces and building bulks. This kind of plan becomes in fact a series of separate deed covenants. The builders of each building must keep within the bulk limits set for them. Thus they fill a prescribed building envelope. They are given a latitude of variation of perhaps ten feet in any direction. They may be required to subscribe to roof profile and possibly entrance-location specifications, although the latter is usually not necessary if the public spaces are properly designed.

Intrinsic to the success of that kind of public design plan is the soundness of the public open space and private-building design relationship. The open spaces must be most competently designed, not so monumentally large that they act as inconveniences which discourage private developers. The building bulks must also be well chosen so that they can be realistically filled by other architects working for their private clients. If some of the buildings are public and some private, the uses of the buildings and their interrelations must be carefully studied so that the different uses complement each other.

This practice has been in effect for many years in Stockholm and in Amsterdam on a city-wide basis as we have already mentioned. In this country it has worked successfully on a project basis, starting in the last century with Commonwealth Avenue in Boston and, more recently in that same city, in the Government Center Project. The design of the public open space itself is of key importance, and that may justify the design of all public open space by one very competent architect. The proper design of the public open space gives "address" to the project. It gives an air of distinction which can positively attract private developers.

A key to understanding the nature of this concept is that the concept itself must consist of elements which can easily be built, based as they are on sound market demands and current building vernacular. In the context of this chapter the Government Center Project of Boston went one step further.

Because the clients for many of the buildings comprising that center were numerous, and because there was no assurance that all clients would subscribe to the design plan, the plan itself was designed to tolerate a certain amount of abuse. Because some of the builders of peripheral buildings might choose to build high, as they later did, the central building and those forming the central open space were kept low as the minimum design plan.

This type of design control plan can operate, then, on a project basis. The design elements it specifies are open space and building mass or building surface (as a substitute in some cases). As yet is difficult to specify materials, colors, appearance, or details in component buildings. It is sounder policy to design in detail the public open spaces and, in questions regarding the appearance of private buildings, establish an *ad hoc* design review board. The design review board may be paid by the various developers on an advisory basis. This can be written into the development plan and the separate land titles.

An interesting concept for giving visual order to the generally confusing urban scene was proposed several years ago by architect I. M. Pei, FAIA. Finding the sites of his projects to be often utterly lacking in an urban design motif, he designed his buildings as simple prismatic towers. These acted as visual rallying points for their surroundings. In his Society Hill development in Philadelphia, Pei employed three such towers especially placed for their relevance to the city's skyline. This was, in fact, a fulfillment of the general design plan of Philadelphia, and so illustrates the notion of establishing key sites of great urban design importance.

Architect-planner David Crane carries this concept much further in his "City of a Thousand Designers." Crane would build all those urban elements which are the essentials of urban design, allowing the private pieces to fill in later. The public pieces are utilities, key public buildings and sites, circulation and open spaces.

Crane and others like him who have proposed the techniques we have been mentioning are ingenious in their ability to wrest design control elements from a situation that seems to offer little but chaos. Yet there is one city-building procedure that requires design planning by law—urban renewal. No other procedure we have goes so far in demanding good design in individual buildings and in plan. Urban renewal projects, however, admirable as they are in this respect, do not rebuild entire cities. The real question before us is how we can bring design to bear upon the city as an overall whole, to practice design as cities in our times require. In answer to this we must turn to a very recent speech of a thoughtful colleague.

I. M. Pei, FAIA, proposes distinctive towers at strategic points in the city . . .

. . . to act as visual rallying points on the skyline.

Tomorrow's Regulatory Techniques

At the April 1964 meeting of the American Society of Planning Officials, Professor John W. Reps of Cornell University delivered a paper entitled "Requiem for Zoning." Professor Reps' paper concisely summarizes the inadequacies of zoning. Not only is his paper a critique of the tools we now employ, it is also a proposal for some forward steps.

Professor Reps prefaces his remarks with the reminder that our present methods of trying to shape cities amount to advice, controls, inducements, and development. Early planning agencies assumed an *advisory* role. Many still function that way, their power being limited. *Controls* followed—the controls we have been discussing—but they are negative instruments with limited usefulness. *Inducements* came as the city held out attractions to developers. Public *developments*—roads, utilities, public facilities —recently have been suggested as the urban coordinates for shaping urban form, the basis of Crane's thinking. Public development agencies try to abide by this concept. Professor Reps proposes that these latter tools be expanded greatly, and that zoning, although a minor tool in the scheme of implementation, needs replacement by much sounder means.

Professor Reps criticizes zoning because of its poor compensatory procedures; because it is haphazardly applied; is parochial in the hands of its local administrators; attempts to answer controversial and difficult questions before they arise; because zoned areas have little if any rational relationship to each other; because zoning is not related to any community plan; is administered by ill-equipped officials; because regulation review is by judicial appeal only; and because courts are ill-equipped to make technical decisions in cases of appeal.

He answers these problems by categorical proposals: to introduce a better system of compensation and a system of betterment charge; to compel all communities to enact a system of land reg-

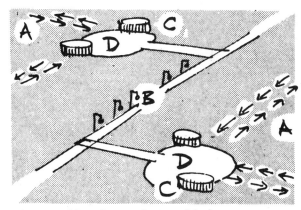

The "capital bones" network of municipal improvements, (A) circulation, (B) utilities, (C) parking, (D) clearance, etc., . . .

. . . establishes a framework for private development projects.

187

*The Bloomsbury area of London.
Regulators: squares, building vernacular,
materials, height, and streets.*

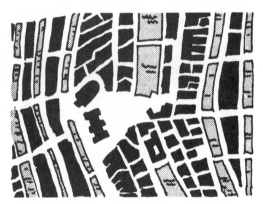

*Central Amsterdam. Regulators: a main square,
building vernacular, height, canals, and streets.*

*The Ile de la Cité, Paris. Regulators:
the site, view factors across the river,
building vernacular, and street pattern.*

*IT IS HELPFUL TO PONDER THE MAIN
REGULATORS OF URBAN FORM
IN THE PAST. THE THREE AREAS SHOWN
ABOVE ARE AMONG THE MOST
INTERESTING URBAN AREAS
IN THE WORLD—A FACT SCARCELY
EVIDENT FROM THEIR PATTERNS
SEEN IN THE PLAN.*

ulation; to place responsibility for zoning or its equivalent at metropolitan or state level; to have a regulatory system which could deal with special situations when they arose; to do away with malfunctioning districts and compatible-use districts which do not work; to consolidate all regulating agencies into one coordinated and efficient agency; to base all statutes on a community plan; to give informed expert judgment a more important role; to institute more equitable control over larger areas; and to create state-administered appeal tribunals staffed with experts.

Professor Reps proposes that a system of "Development Regulations" replace zoning. Actually they would incorporate all regulatory tools into a fairer and more rational package. He also proposes official plans for community development with comprehensive objectives and standards to guide officials. Such plans would be mandatory and would show land use, circulation, density, and public facilities—thus lending planning new importance. Professor Reps envisions a larger geographical jurisdiction for planning than is currently used. In fact we have such bodies working on an *ad hoc* basis, as metropolitan commissions and authorities. He would relate them. Responsibility for land use can be handled rationally only on a metropolitan scale.

A main point of Professor Reps' suggestion is the drafting of a comprehensive plan in graphic form along with descriptive statements of objectives and policies. Here lies the most potential tool for urban design which we can yet imagine. An "Office of Development Review" would administer this plan. In partially developed areas vestiges of the old systems of control would be retained, but in new areas the slate of old regulations would be erased. Developments would be judged afresh according to the large plan, as in urban renewal.

Professor Reps contends that his system would reduce the great uncertainty involved in present regulatory practices. He fears little that his plan is radical, pointing to 1916 as a date when zoning seemed radical. He concludes his remarks with a series of questions, asking whether we are even prepared to assume so large a role: Are we indeed ready to produce the kinds of plans he describes as necessary? Is urban design thinking and knowledge up to its task?

The best cure for the restrictive regulations we shun is to replace them with positive and creative design concepts to which the public can enthusiastically respond. The public's respect and confidence in the design of the community has to be earned. To a large extent the public's confidence has been earned in the field of architecture and in many branches of engineering. The other side of the coin is that the public has to *want* urban design and has to be willing to pay for it.

The problems of the city have to be accepted by controlling authorities at all levels. Every architect can do his part by developing physical design concepts to arouse the public and illustrate the potential.

The architect's role, then, is to lay forth the prospects as realistic yet appealing ideas, and to understand always the relations between the controlling forces and the results, so that regulations are never adopted which prevent getting the best results. If restrictive regulations have temporarily overshadowed us, it is because the initiative has not been taken to establish good community design as the forerunner of regulatory tools. This opportunity awaits us now.

11

Government Programs

Only through the coordination of government and private enterprise at all levels can we rebuild our American cities and towns. Only with coordinated public and private efforts will we be able to build well for the future. This partnership has been developing since the day our country started but its details have become increasingly complex.

An explanation of our city-building programs is a statement of the principal *tools* of urban design. Although these tools came into our hands slowly, we are quickly learning to handle them and we must develop them further.

Architects have an influential role to play in forging these tools because all city building projects end up as architecture in one form or another. Today, complex as our government and lives are, we are better equipped with means to rebuild our cities than ever before.

To present this subject we shall make it personal by inventing a typical American town called "Middletown." We hope it approximates your own city. We are going to describe its history as city and as design—in relation to the people, acting through government, who built it. We shall take it from its founding up to its present, and lay forth the problems it currently faces.

189

Middletown's History

Early Days

Any child in Middletown can tell you the story of its founding, for it is taught in school. Originally it was a fur trading post, established by trappers who chose a river site with good access to overland trails. The original settlement was near a river crossing above flood water. For many years it was a raw camp, sometimes at war with the Indians. Later, under a military governor, a stockade was erected. The first impetus to growth was the opening of the West to settlement when the land became American territory. Middletown then became a major provisioning town for the Western trails.

The territory was surveyed as a series of 6-mile squares according to congressional ordinances enacted from 1784 to 1787. Middletown was thus platted as a grid of streets running north-south, east-west. This gave the land its pattern in both city and country, a system ready-made for land division and sale. When statehood and admission to the Union were achieved, Middletown became the county seat and was a town of some renown. The original trappers' choice of site proved fortunate, for the land and water routes turned out to be major ones. Middletown was destined to become a transportation hub and a center for manufacturing, cattle processing, and farming.

As the city prospered, a land-grant college, a private hospital, and a religious seminary were founded. A state road system was started, financed by 5 per cent of the proceeds from the sale of public lands, this the result of an early Federal act. Middletown set up its municipal government as a corporation according to enabling legislation in the state constitution. This charter was modeled after the charters of other states. Middletown then built a fine courthouse and town hall on a square in the center of town. It had its own public fire department, schools, and a waterworks up-river. People were beginning to talk of such wonders as paved streets and sewers.

Middletown's seemingly golden future was marred by a series of disasters. One spring the river flooded, carrying away some poor houses on the lowland and ruining the riverside docking facilities. In another section of town a fire leveled eight city blocks of wooden houses. The flood prompted thoughts of a flood control system—dikes along the banks. The fire led to legislation forbidding the erection of nonfireproof buildings in a specified central area. The dock problem resulted in the creation of a river commission which issued bonds for the construction of a large common river-ramp docking facility. The commission also erected a dike along with the dock, the cost of both being paid by a tax on ship tonnage. A few shipping companies built their own facilities in accordance with the commission's plan. Middletown was learning how to organize its resources for civil action.

Private Companies for Public Service

A gas company was created to supply gas for lighting. Because of some serious accidents in other cities, the mayor formed a committee to oversee the work of the gas company. A telephone company was organized and telephones installed in the major offices and banks. Long-distance telephones were as yet unknown —telegraph was used for long-distance communication.

At this time Middletown was beginning to feel the pressure

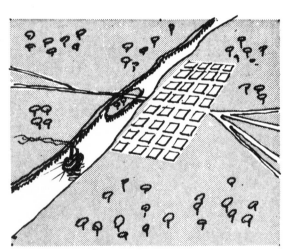

Middletown was originally a fort at the crossing of a river and land routes.

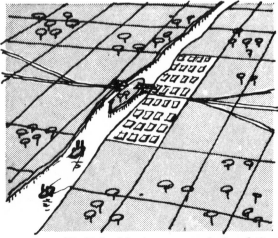

The city's first plat gave it its early form.

The Federal land survey was the foundation of future regional form.

of circulation problems. Many American cities had electric street railways but Middletown had none, for it had not yet developed a source of electric power. The city issued a franchise to the City Power and Light Company, whose first job was to provide electric lighting for the central part of the city. Later the utility company was to extend its lines to provide electricity for residents. An electric street railway company was formed and franchised; then another, for a different route. The street railway companies, eager to exploit their enterprises, bought up land along the streetcar routes for subdivision. At the end of one route they built an amusement park to promote the lots for sale along the way.

The streetcar line construction was accompanied by the paving of streets, some of it done by the traction companies as part of their agreement with the city. The city also embarked on a street improvement program—paving and sewers—supported by tax revenue on the sale of new development tracts.

Middletown was developing its public utilities and learned, in the process, to coordinate private action and public responsibility.

Dike and dock facilities were results of early municipal action.

Civic Beauty Comes to Middletown

Thoughtful citizens of Middletown looked deeper. Was Middletown to be only a place of commerce? Other cities were developing beautiful parks and well-landscaped residential areas which proved to be good speculative ventures. A corporation was formed and a leading landscape architect brought to Middletown to lay out a new residential section on land bought by the corporation. He proposed a city-wide park system, pointing out that outlying lands and stream valleys could be cheaply bought for such a network and tied into the residential section.

When one of the town's wealthy citizens offered to pay half the cost of the parkland, the town voted for a long-term bond issue to pay the rest. Although most people thought the parkland unnecessary—for a short walk in any direction led to open land—the bond issue was passed because landholders felt that the reduction in salable land would raise its value. Also, only the landowners were being taxed to pay off the bond. And the voters who held no land were certainly willing to vote for a "free" park.

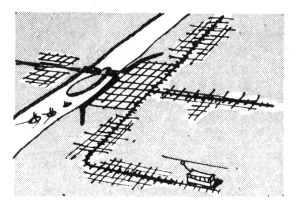

Utility and trolley lines set the pattern of suburban growth.

Debt and Growth

Middletown was empowered by the state to put itself in debt with float bonds, according to a formula based on the value of its real property. Since the city was expanding, this presented no great problems. Indeed, small outlying towns were only too willing to be annexed, for that meant better municipal services.

But some of the growth was haphazard and before the turn of the century a local newspaper carried a small item about a Federal investigation into slum areas. Middletown workingmen's houses were a far cry from the tenements of a city like New York, where conditions were so bad that tenement laws had to be passed requiring minimum construction features, like windows in all bedrooms.

The economy was such that dwellings could be built for low-income workers. But World War I changed that, and more.

Telephone and electric lines were the early symbols of municipal progress.

Effects of World War I

World War I proved to be a boom for Middletown. Its opportune location for shipment, its resources and skilled workers rendered it a prime manufacturing center. Many people came to

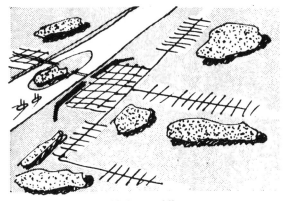

A park system was added to Middletown.

191

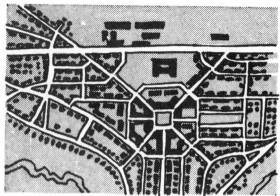

Yorkship Village in Camden, N.J. An example of a workers' residential community built by the U.S. War Shipping Board.

The Denver Civic Center concept—from the 1917 AIA book City Planning Progress.

Proposed river-front improvement in Milwaukee—from the 1917 AIA book City Planning Progress.

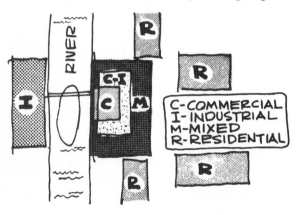

Middletown's zoning map allocated land uses. This was the legal statement of the city's plan.

Middletown to work in its plants. Consequently, housing became a critical problem.

Had Middletown been a shipbuilding town it might have been one of the first cities in the nation to have a federally sponsored housing program. The Emergency Fleet Corporation was building housing for shipyard workers under the U.S. Housing Corporation and was producing residential towns of some distinction. The design concepts were similar to those of Middletown's old landscaped residential areas. Architects mused on the possibilities of extending this notion to the outlying areas of Middletown, which would surely be developing after the war.

Their premonitions were an indication of the generally optimistic turn of mind throughout America. The postwar years were to be boom years. If America could win a world war, what could it not do? The American Institute of Architects sensed this too but was somewhat doubtful of the results. The AIA knew what our towns could be at best, but they had seen too often what they were becoming at worst.

A town planning committee was formed at the national AIA level. In 1917 the AIA published an illustrated book which listed every proposal and accomplishment in town planning in the country. In the early 1920s this committee published a series of articles on town planning by Nils Hammarstrand in the *AIA Journal.* Among the contributors to this effort were Lewis Mumford, Clarence Stein, and Henry Wright.

Many notable works in civic design were built in the twenties. Cities were eager to outdo each other in handsome public works —new municipal buildings, parks, bridges, civic centers, and schools. Speculative builders built notable residential neighborhoods, some on private cul-de-sac streets with attractive entrance gates. Businessmen dreamed of skyscrapers. In Middletown, the city commissioned an elaborate "plan"—an impressive document which showed what Middletown might become at its best. It was a practical, if not ambitious, plan, and all looked on it with pride.

But Middletown's picture was not all rosy. For every conscientious builder there were ten whose sole interest was speculative profit, with no concern for the long-term value of their work. Many people were investing in real estate who had little building experience. These speculators used a land-platting system that was made to measure for transaction, the simple and unimaginative grid subdivision.

A Zoning Ordinance and a Building Code

This haphazard growth alarmed many people in Middletown. They had carefully read a section in the city's plan on zoning, a new system for controlling development. Indeed, at the Division of Building and Housing of the U.S. Department of Commerce, model state-enabling legislation was written, for states to use and modify as they might wish. The states had to allow their constituent cities to adopt zoning. Model zoning ordinances were also drafted for the cities themselves, and experts were available to write a zoning ordinance for Middletown.

When, at the insistence of the real estate interests, the state approved the enabling legislation and Middletown adopted a zoning ordinance, some lawyers questioned the legality of the measure. It seemed too much like an infringement of private property rights. Others questioned the Federal government's involvement in such a local matter. A Supreme Court decision in Ohio set the precedent for settling the legal question and it was pointed out that the Federal government had merely made the zoning enabling legislation and the model zoning ordinance available. Hadn't the government also offered agricultural knowledge? It was for those who wanted it to use as they would. The Federal Bureau of Standards also had written model building codes and outlined methods for establishing and operating a municipal building inspection department. Middletown adopted this as well. The model building codes and zoning ordinances were based on the experience of cities which had developed them independently. The government merely made this experience available to all cities.

Zoning and the building code were regarded by some architects as the legal means for enforcing Middletown's plan. But that plan was advisory only and, even supported by zoning, had no status in the day-by-day process of building the city. It could not persuade developers to build where and how the plan specified. It had no program for replacing the worn-out sections of the city. On the other hand, the plan did guide the city in such questions as the placement of schools, parks, public buildings, the enlargement of the water and sewer system, and in planning for traffic.

The Traffic Problem

Traffic was becoming very complicated, particularly to the police force which had the task of unsnarling rush-hour jams. But traffic concern was not limited to the city. The state was actively engaged in a state road program at the insistence of farmers who were using trucks to get their produce to the market. Better state roads meant wider markets.

A new and expanded state road program was initiated in response to a Federal program matching state funds fifty-fifty. The Federal government again took its cue from existing state programs but wanted to make sure that the several state road systems were connected at state lines. The Federal government also prepared standards for road design and construction based on practices agreeable to states that had pioneered in highway design. Behind the Federal program was the deep-rooted tradition of stimulating interstate commerce. A state highway commission and a local traffic bureau were set up in Middletown, the latter a section of the police department.

New Ideas

The nucleus of architects who, in the twenties, had been active in the AIA's early city planning programs now saw the possibility to plan on a statewide basis. Middletown's architects followed the ideas of Henry Wright and Clarence Stein with great interest. The prospects of integrating statewide highway networks and regional planning were exciting concepts. Moreover, Wright and Stein were working within the established context of our free enterprise system. Theirs was no utopian dream but a real life demonstration for achieving excellence in their time and with America's means.

In the early days of Middletown, urban design had been simply a matter of deciding where to put the next building. Subsequently private groups learned how to adjust their undertakings to the public's rudimentary demands. In the early 1900s a note of civic beauty was introduced. But after World War I and before the depression, our energies to build and exploit, quickened by an expanding technology, outran our ability to design our cities.

It might be interesting to speculate on what would have hap-

Zoning was instituted to prevent incompatible and economically unsound land use like this . . .

. . . but it would often result in overly uniform development like this.

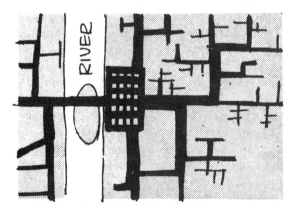

A map of Middletown's traffic volumes portrayed increasing core congestion.

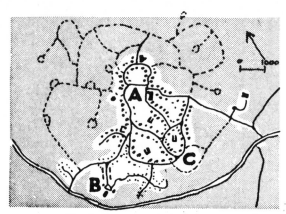

Norris, Tenn., a principal new town in TVA, was planned in 1936 for growth over hilly terrain. (A) Community center; (B) Construction camp; (C) Industrial buildings.

Radburn, N.J., was envisioned as a self-sufficient satellite community in the New York area.

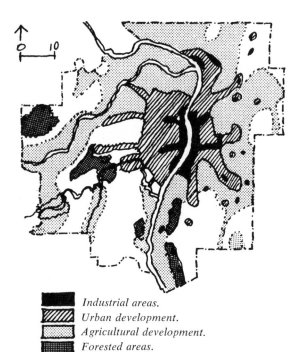

- ■ *Industrial areas.*
- ▨ *Urban development.*
- ░ *Agricultural development.*
- ▦ *Forested areas.*
- ☐ *Pasture areas.*

Diagrammatic plan of the 1930s of the probable organization of the St. Louis region—an example of National Resources Planning Board work. This was a fundamental study in developing a regional plan for a large industrial city with surrounding agricultural areas.

pened to our Middletowns had not the depression occurred. Would our ability to design cities have matched their growth? One can only guess, for that was not to be Middletown's story.

The Depression and National Recovery

Local Crisis and Federal Action

When the depression struck, many homeowners were unable to meet their monthly mortgage payments. Mortgages were foreclosed and homes were taken over by the savings and loan banks. The banks found themselves with unsalable houses and diminishing cash funds. In 1932 the Federal government set up the Home Loan Bank System to relieve the banks directly.

Since this action proved inadequate, the Home Owners Loan Act was passed in 1933 to give relief directly to the homeowners. This enabled many Middletown families to keep their homes and also gave the banks ready cash. The Federal government was beginning to reform an inefficient system of savings and loan institutions.

In 1933 the National Planning Board (later called the National Resources Planning Board or NRPB) was set up to study the entire country as a series of regional areas and to encourage planning at all levels of government. This activity had lasting effects on Federal policies for national development. Studies were made of Middletown in relation to the state. For the first time the economic role of Middletown was accurately understood in terms of its natural resources and productive equipment. Plans drafted to improve that role helped allocate public expenditures.

The architects of Middletown, as well as its citizens, debated the merits of TVA and the new greenbelt towns that resulted from the regional studies. Some felt that any program that could produce such wondrous results were worthwhile, sponsor aside. Others saw in these accomplishments not architectural or planning merit but a threat to our free enterprise system. Their argument was countered by the suggestion that the day of *laissez faire* was over and that government had a leadership role at all its levels. Social reformers saw in the New Deal an attempt to bring the benefits of our industrial technology and social system to all classes. One architect wryly commented that all of the town and regional planning programs employed by the Federal government had been developed a decade or more earlier by private and local (state) government groups. The Federal government was applying the ideas of an individualist society that had faltered.

Aside from the merits of any of these arguments or their rebuttals several things were clear. Middletown and towns like it were subject to forces far beyond the city limits. The role of government at all levels was about to enter into a period of change and evolution. Further, the factors that ruled city growth and development were subtle. The depression spurred a reexamination of the forces that control a city's well-being and its construction activity. Numerous ideas for stimulating these forces were offered and many were tried. The Federal government was to put our Middletowns back on their feet by policy directives, seed money, emergency measures, and a host of programs that would change America's political outlook forever. These experiments were also slated to become major determinants of urban design.

In 1934 the National Housing Act extended programs for rebuilding the country's shattered economy by restoring the building

194

industry's activity. This Act established the Federal Housing Administration (FHA). It gave assurance to commercial banks, savings banks, and insurance companies to lend money, opening the way for investment capital to flow more freely around the country. The Federal National Mortgage Association (FNMA or Fanny May) administered mortgage programs. Construction standards were adopted for the homes insured, reassuring lenders and protecting public funds.

The Federal government also sought to put people to work through civic projects, for which the Public Works Administration (PWA) was set up. Middletown took advantage of their programs to attack unemployment. Fortunately, it had the experience to use the opportunity well. Roads, public buildings, and parks were built. The PWA tried a modest program of moderate income housing in 1933, which resulted in but a few homes around the country. In 1934 PWA introduced a program for low-rent housing in slum areas. Middletown took advantage of this program and built one good "project." The execution of this project, however, created several administrative problems.

In 1937 the U.S. Housing Act was passed. This established the Public Housing Administration (PHA), providing a program to be administered by local agencies. Enabling legislation was required for any state to avail itself of Federal funds. Again, the Federal government drew on the experience of several states which had initiated their own programs. Middletown established the Middletown Housing Authority. To be eligible for Federal grants, it had to make its public housing projects tax exempt. It could then build low-rent public housing with low interest-rate loans and direct Federal grants.

The Federal government, through trial-and-error techniques, had tried to get building construction back in operation as one major key to general employment and economic activity. In doing that, it had tested a mechanism which was to be the basis for more comprehensive urban programs after World War II. FHA remains a basic tool for home construction and PHA for low-income housing. The slum clearance operations of the late thirties were to be models for programs to rebuild our cities after the war, and NRPB at least had set the example for metropolitan planning.

Groundwork for Postwar Growth

During the war a National Housing Agency (NHA) was established to try to ameliorate the housing problems of war workers. The architects who had designed public housing and new towns in the thirties began to design military posts, defense factories, and defense-worker housing, much of it of distinction.

In 1944 the Veterans Administration (VA) was set up to handle the problems of the returning GI—schooling, retraining, hospitalization, and housing. The VA established a program for a 100 per cent GI home mortgage with a 4 per cent interest rate and no insurance fee. Lacking organization to administer construction and working under duress, some scandals occurred. The GIs got their houses, American suburban sprawl got a boost, and some speculators became very rich.

The postwar years opened the door to large-scale suburban building around Middletown's periphery, across and beyond the city limits into the surrounding counties. The majority of houses were built with FHA-insured loans. The minimal standards set by FHA resulted in houses on lots which, multiplied by the

The Carl Mackley Houses in Philadelphia (1935) were an early example of PWA housing.

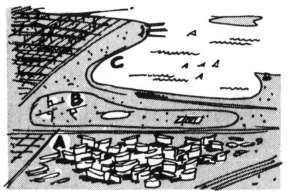
Old Harbor Village in Boston (A) was a 1937 PWA project. The sports field (B) and beach development (C) also were public works projects.

Orchard Beach in the Bronx was created in 1936 under the New York City Department of Parks. (A) Beach; (B) amusement park.

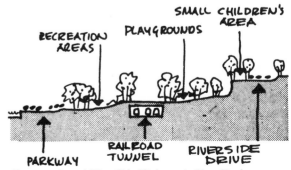
Cross section of West Side Highway in New York City. This project involved Federal, state, city, and railroad authorities in 1937.

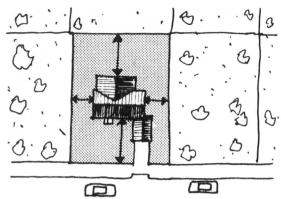

Subdivision regulations, underwriten by VA and FHA loan requirements, assured standards for the individual house on its own lot . . .

. . . but these regulations, applied over extensive areas, . . .

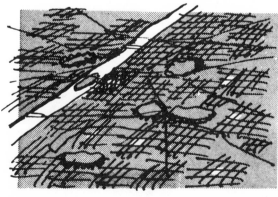

. . . produced monotonous and ill-designed residential communities.

thousands, added much to our suburban monotony. FHA loan programs lacked the ingredients which build sound, well-designed communities.

The demands on Middletown increased as never before. There was a lack of trained personnel and a considerable backlog of civic work as a result of the war. Special districts and authorities were created to circumvent various limitations. Some thought the answer to administrative difficulties lay in hiring a city manager. The universities started holding forums on city administration and planning.

The core of Middletown was beginning to lose population to the suburbs. Old buildings which should have been replaced or extensively remodeled were now obsolete, and people were leaving the old suburbs for the newer ones further out. As the old housing in the city decayed into slums, Middletown's municipal burdens were increasing but its revenue decreasing. Its bond limits were strained, and the city was unable to help itself. Worst of all, the state legislature, being of rural outlook, was unwilling to put money into the city or allow Middletown to develop new sources of revenue. Middletown could no longer annex land and could enter into but few metropolitan compacts.

In the face of their problems, Middletown's public officials showed great ingenuity. They set up municipal agencies to deal with the new situation, rather than increase the operations of existing agencies. Metropolitan commissions were established for water, sewers, parks, police, and traffic. Some problems, however, were made more complex by compounding responsibilities. Circulation problems, for example, became the responsibility of the police, the traffic department, the parking authority, the bridge authority, the public transit authority, the department of streets and highways, and the department of public works. The planning department had made good traffic studies but could not inject these studies into the city's operation.

Thus, the increasing problems of Middletown were met with a fractionalization of responsibilities locally, at metropolitan level, and at state level. In this atmosphere the city could only grow chaotically. More effective programs were needed.

In 1947 the National Housing Agency became the Housing and Home Finance Agency, coordinating housing and community facilities operations. But 1949 was the landmark year which ushered in the first step toward resolving the difficulties of Middletown and many towns like it.

Middletown became the victim of this "design" as it sprawled into the countryside in its postwar growth.

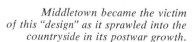

Present Programs of the Federal Government

The Housing Act of 1949: Urban Redevelopment

The Housing Act of 1949 provided Federal assistance to arrest the spread of blight and slums. It set forth as its goal "a decent home and a suitable living environment for every American family." With permission of their states, cities could establish a local redevelopment agency through enabling legislation. The redevelopment authority would buy slum properties, help relocate the people displaced, clear the land, and then offer it for redevelopment on the private market. Because the reuse value was less than the cost of acquisition, two-thirds of the net loss would be paid by the Federal government. This was justified, as we mentioned earlier, as the cost to the public of correcting an unhealthful urban condition—the cost to the public of slum clearance. The Act also authorized a certain amount of public housing. The amount of public housing was, in the eyes of many experts, far too meager. The design of the public housing was also criticized as severely institutional. Some observers felt that it was erroneous to build public housing as projects, preferring to create the opportunity for poor people to afford better housing, even if that meant a client subsidy. Another point of criticism came as a suggestion that projects be broken up and the separate units be deployed in a slum area. All proposals had difficulties, to be sure. The only thing that was not lacking was a healthful and resounding arena of debate.

Public housing, in fact, had become a political stumbling block and still is. It is not the only remedy to the housing problems of the poor but we have yet to develop programs that can resolve this unfinished business of our society. The lack of adequate low income housing is symptomatic of much of our housing production—the fact that choice in housing types is extremely limited for all income groups. Of course the limitations are more and more severe as one examines progressively lower rungs on the income ladder.

The 1949 Act specified that public land-taking action had to be accompanied by the relocation of the people displaced. This was a first in public domain land-taking legislation. Ironically this problem came to be one of the main points of criticism leveled at redevelopment and renewal programs—ironic because highway building programs had been displacing people *without* relocation help for years. It was a long time before the fault was recognized by the public.

The Act also introduced the principle that the most profitable use of land to a private owner was not necessarily the most advantageous use to the city, neither from a tax nor a social viewpoint. Redevelopers were to be selected on the basis of "highest and best" reuse of the cleared land, thus opening the door to a broad spectrum of community interests—monetary, social, industrial, special interest, and soon, good design.

The financial logic behind redevelopment was that the city and the government would regain their outlay in increased taxes. City welfare and management services would also be lessened. The reconstructed area would be able to pay for the services the city provided and would be redeveloped for residential, commercial, or industrial use. Redevelopment would also generate new economic activity. Unfortunately, one early restriction in clearing land was that it had to be originally in residential use. The 1949 Act was

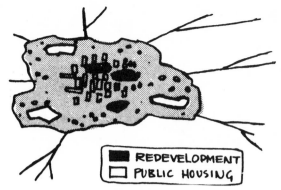

A typical city's concept for redevelopment subsequent to the 1949 Housing Act . . .

. . . cleared sites were redeveloped for such uses as industrial or middle- to upper-income residential . . .

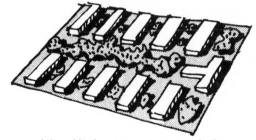

. . . while public housing projects were built for the relocation of displaced people.

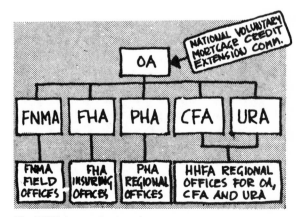

The HHFA organization chart.

197

Federal programs allow the rehabilitation of still useful old structures . . .

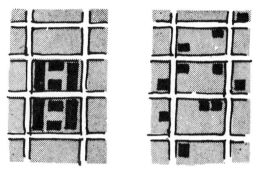

. . . rather than concentrate public housing in a single location, it can be dispersed and blended in a community . . .

. . . housing for the elderly can be arranged as groupings in the community . . .

. . . needed college dormitories can be financed . . .

far from perfect in actual operations, especially in regard to the relocation problem—and that is still a major consideration. In essence the objective of the 1949 Housing Act was the *redevelopment* of portions of the city; hence the term *urban redevelopment.*

The Housing Act of 1954: Urban Renewal

Because all programs thus far had been products of Democratic administrations, the Republican administration of 1953 reviewed existing legislation and studied alternate possibilities. Not only was the existing program confirmed. It was greatly expanded. Government's role in housing and community building thus became bipartisan and broader in objectives.

Starting in 1953 HHFA was reorganized to include five major units: the Federal Housing Administration (FHA); the Public Housing Administration (PHA); the Urban Renewal Administration (URA); the Federal National Mortgage Association (FNMA); and the Community Facilities Administration (CFA). All operate under an Office of the Administrator.

The Housing Act of 1954 enlarged the concept of urban redevelopment to include rehabilitation, conservation, and other blight-preventing measures, thus providing a comprehensive program for renewing cities—hence, the term *urban renewal.* Again the Federal government had drawn upon the experiences of cities already at work—Baltimore, Chicago, and Philadelphia. To develop broad local responsibilities, a seven-front program was conceived. This was called the "Workable Program for Community Improvement" (WPCI), composed of the following seven elements:

1. Enforced housing codes and zoning
2. A comprehensive community development plan
3. A neighborhood analysis to determine treatments needed
4. An effective administrative organization under state law to carry out programs
5. Local financial capability to pay the local share of expenses
6. Provision of suitable housing for displaced families
7. Active citizen participation and support

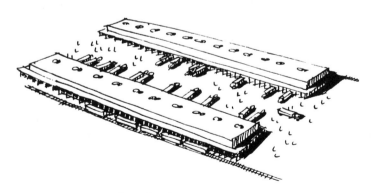

. . . through urban renewal new urban trucking terminals can be created . . .

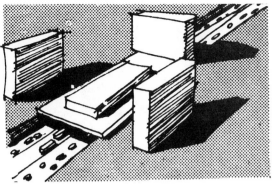

. . . air-rights projects can be developed through cooperation of private enterprise and local authorities, in effect creating new sites . . .

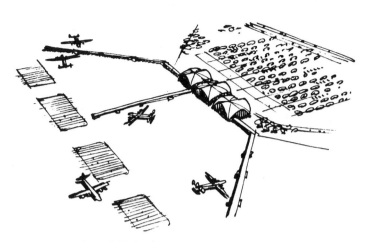

. . . through Federal programs municipal airports can be improved.

These seven points were to be a framework for local action. The 1954 Housing Act also provided numerous loans and grants to help finance these efforts. To be eligible for aid funds, a city had to adopt and follow the seven-point Workable Program.

Two types of planning programs were initiated, one for general *comprehensive* planning and the other for planning the *renewal* projects themselves. The 701 Planning Assistance Program, so designated because it was Section 701 of the 1954 Housing Act, provided funds on a matching basis for metropolitan or city planning. On the metropolitan scale the 701 program is the descendant of NRPB programs.

Subsequent to the 1954 Act, complementary measures were instituted over the years establishing a Community Renewal Program (CRP) to handle the planning of neighborhood improvement programs on a city-wide basis. The General Neighborhood Renewal Plan (GNRP) was devised to draft a renewal plan for a particular neighborhood for execution under a ten-year program. Aids for student and faculty college housing were made available, as well as community facilities loans, loans for advance planning for public works, and a program for demonstrating urban renewal techniques.

The 1956 Highway Act

During World War II a Federal act initiated a national system of interstate highways, 40,000 miles of roads criss-crossing the country. This was enlarged in 1956 to a 41,000-mile network to be completed by 1969. Like housing and community development, federally-aided road construction has a long history of step-by-step programs. The system has two main parts—the primary (interstate) system and the secondary system. In 1956 the primary system was designated as the "National System of Interstate and Defense Highways." Ninety per cent of its cost is paid by the Federal government, ten per cent by the state. The secondary system is financed on a fifty-fifty matching basis. In the haste to expedite the Highway Act, local communities and their planning operations were overlooked, thus causing much difficulty and destroying urban tissue which should have been served. Only after

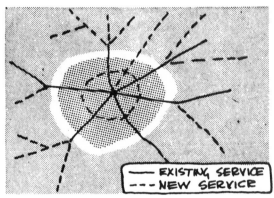

EXISTING SERVICE
NEW SERVICE

. . . funds are available for extension of mass-transit lines . . .

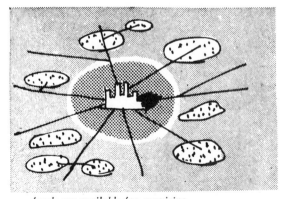

. . . funds are available for acquiring recreational open spaces . . .

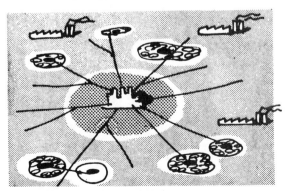

. . . programs are still needed for creating new towns and communities well related to the metropolis and places of work.

*The public's awareness of urban problems was
aroused by numerous examples of deterioration,
such as the progression of blight
along an old street . . .*

*. . . the replacement of downtown fringe buildings
by parking lots . . .*

. . . the general condition of the central city . . .

. . . and ever-increasing urban sprawl.

years of criticism are attempts being made to correct this fault. This problem highlights one of the essential difficulties of programs administered at many levels. Some blame the Federal government for poor decisions and red tape. In fact many problems and poor decisions were products of the state highway departments. No small matter in vast undertakings is the need for local organizations which can avoid such difficulties.

A frequent difficulty of the federally-sponsored highway program was that there were no plans for states and municipalities which could be used as the bases of a highway layout. Ostensibly this was the job of a state for the overall network and of a city at municipal level. But too often the cities had no plans to which the state highway planners could refer. Where local plans existed they were often overlooked, but the overall fault was lack of co-ordination. The 1962 Highway Act corrected this shortcoming by stating that after July 1, 1965, no Federal highway funds will be advanced to cities unless the highway plans are tied into "planning processes"—viable planning operations. The Housing Act of 1961 extended the use of 701 funds to transportation planning. The 701 planning funds and highway planning funds can now be used in joint programs.

The money for our road system comes from its users. We pay for it every time we purchase a gallon of gasoline. The justification for this procedure is based on a cost-benefit concept—the idea that it is justified to tax the highway-using public to pay for better roads. While this policy is sound in itself, critics of the highway programs have suggested that it is not necessarily wise to put all of the money into highways. They argue that some portion of these funds should go into public transit systems to alleviate problems of automobile congestion. However, the congressional lobbies that support highway construction are far from willing to agree to such a diversion of funds. And the cost-benefit analysis supports the idea that a dollar spent on roads is a greater benefit to more people than any other form of subsidy for the public's transportation.

FHA home mortgage insurance programs, PHA low-income housing, the BPR road-building program—these are but a few of the programs through which government, acting on all levels, helps build the community. To these programs must be added a host of others: the Hill-Burton Act which extends aid to hospitals; the works of the Corps of Engineers in flood control, navigation, and harbor installations; the Department of the Interior's park systems; and the Federal Aviation Administration which aids airport construction. At state and local level there are programs for school construction, hospital systems, public housing, recreational districts, and city and state university and college construction.

The 1961 Housing Act: Planning

The cities that engaged in urban renewal programs were testing the elements of the 1954 Housing Act. In 1961 another Housing Act was passed to make needed improvements based on the experience gained. The 1949 Act had stressed spot redevelopment. The 1954 Act had enlarged the concept of redevelopment to renewal, a more comprehensive approach stressing the prevention of blighting conditions that make clearance and redevelopment necessary. The 1961 Act went even further—from correction and prevention to forward-looking planning.

Among the improvements in the 1961 Act were more liberal loan conditions for homebuilding and home repairs, mortgage arrangements for moderate-income families and families displaced by renewal, further programs for experimental housing, condominiums, housing for the elderly, and nursing homes. More urban renewal funds were authorized; 701 planning funds were enlarged in scope and purpose—with coordinated highway planning, for example, as pointed out above. Small business loans were made available through the Small Business Administration (SBA) to displaced businessmen. HHFA provided more technical assistance, and planning grants for public works were improved.

Important new features were grants for open space acquisition and mass transit. The Federal government would contribute 20 per cent of the cost of acquisition for parcels of open space—30 per cent if the open spaces were part of an overall area plan. Funds for test demonstrations in mass transit were made available. For example, a commuter railroad could reduce fares to see the effects on patronage. Two-thirds of the loss in revenue would be reimbursed. FHA housing programs by now had begun to address themselves to the problems of moderate-income families. Three-quarters of the urban renewal projects were residential. It was also evident that the Federal programs had generated a great amount of activity in the private economy. The programs were stimulants; the funds were seed money.

The 1961 Area Redevelopment Act

In 1961 the Area Redevelopment Act (ARA) came into being, designed to solve unemployment problems in economically depressed areas. It consisted of a whole series of programs—industrial loans, public facility loans, grants, technical assistance, and job retraining. The programs of HHFA and BPR were incorporated as principal tools in the ARA program, consolidating much of what we already had in operation.

The 1964 Mass Transit Act

In the spring of 1964 a major step was made toward revitalizing the mass transit systems of our cities. The Federal government allocated funds for transit agencies at the local level to improve public transit facilities. New tracks can now be laid for existing subway or commuter rail systems; new cars and buses can be purchased. Companies can plan their transit for the future, build new stations, and replace obsolete equipment. Small and medium-sized cities, in particular, need this aid. Some have no public transit facilities at all. Although the sum of money authorized is relatively modest when compared to our highway expenditures, it begins to recognize a neglected aspect of transportation planning.

Through Federal programs historic architecture can be restored . . .

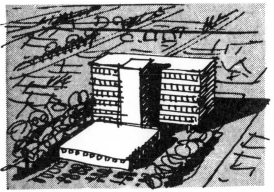

. . . through the Hill-Burton act funds are provided for community hospitals . . .

. . . The federally supported Interstate Highway system is moving rapidly toward completion . . .

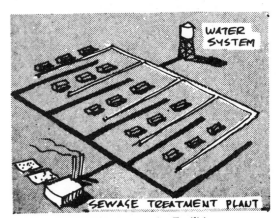

. . . and, through the Community Facilities program of the Urban Renewal Administration, communities can plan and build public facilities.

Further Ideas for Improving Programs

Several new ideas were introduced in 1964 to improve our current programs which are now being considered in Congress. They represent the status of Congressional thinking and, let us hope, will find their way into programs of various sorts.

The 1964 Housing Bill proposes improvements in housing programs, stressing aid to low income, minority, elderly, and rural people. Requests are being made for more urban renewal funds, greater financial help to persons displaced from their homes, and for displaced small businessmen. Funds are recommended to institute a training program for municipal facility managers.

The most important measures concern means allowing communities to plan further growth effectively. A "new communities" program would establish financing programs for building satellite towns around existing urban hubs. Other programs would allow the acquisition of undeveloped land and the planning and placement of certain key public facilities to fix the main elements of future communities—main utilities, roads, and open space. The underlying significance of the 1964 Act is its emphasis on metropolitan planning and development.

It is also proposed to establish a "Department of Housing and Community Development." This was earlier referred to as a "Department of Urban Affairs" and would give recognition to the actual role that all our programs play.

The most recently proposed advances in Federal programs involve a "War on Poverty" and the protection of scenic America. One of the interesting facts in the constant evolution of Federal programs is their reflection of our national values and concerns. Let us hope that they do more than reflect a current focus of attention and keep a constant eye on future needs whose manifestations are less apparent.

The Actual Programs

The detailed programs of local, state, and Federal government would require treatments too extensive to deal with here. There are several government publications which describe them: *The Urban Renewal Manual, Urban Renewal Notes,* various technical bulletins, etc. In addition, there are the publications of the American Society of Planning Officials (ASPO), the National Association of Housing and Redevelopment Officials (NAHRO), the American Institute of Planners (AIP), the American Council to Improve Our Neighborhoods (ACTION), the Urban Land Institute (ULI), the National Housing Conference (NHC), and *Urban America.* These organizations have often served as the voice of the public in evaluating congressional legislation. There are also numerous books and published studies sponsored by foundation grants to leading universities. Everyone committed to the design of the city owes it to himself to familiarize himself with these programs and organizations.

Let us outline these efforts by returning to the story of Middletown and describing what happened there as a result of these programs.

Middletown Helps Itself

When the 1949 Housing Act was passed the state adopted enabling legislation. Within its housing authority Middletown established a redevelopment agency which delineated slum clearance areas after careful study and consultation with the city's planning commission. Public housing projects were started and slum sections razed. A relocation branch was set up in the housing authority to help find new homes for displaced people, about a quarter of whom went to the public housing projects. Overall, 80 per cent of them were better housed than they were before the slum clearance projects began, reflecting the national average.

Middletown's citizens were much alarmed by the sweeping effects of land clearance. They agreed that the slums could not remain but were disturbed by the displacement of slum dwellers and the small businesses. When they saw the nature of the redevelopment—often rather luxurious buildings erected by large corporations—they sensed inequities in the program. The more perceptive among them were equally alarmed at the displacement problems caused by state highway construction which made no provision at all for displaced people. They learned, through long thought, that luxury buildings were the only financially feasible prospects for the in-town residential areas. It was a complex issue involving land cost, market, and habit. Middle income housing meant one thing: the suburbs. The problem was not a fault of renewal but rather a fact of building financing.

In time a group was formed to study the problems of the downtown area. Its members consisted of bankers, store owners, realtors, newspaper owners, and other businessmen. They examined the declining downtown sales picture and increasing urban expansion. Major downtown department stores were losing customers; one closed after building two suburban branches. An arrangement was worked out with the parking "industry" whereby shoppers' parking fees were partially paid by the stores patronized. There was talk of a general downtown fix-up campaign.

At that time urban redevelopment legislation could not cover areas other than residential. The downtown committee thought that it should. Certain vacant downtown properties could be developed as commercial and parking structures. It was impossible to buy many of these properties, since they were in the hands of owners whose agreement to sell could not be easily obtained. Others had complex deed restrictions. Urban renewal was to help in such situations.

An economics expert was consulted to study the potential of the downtown area. His conclusion, based on study of the downtown in relation to the city and region, was that downtown had a major role in the expanding metropolis—depending on accessibility, diversity, facilities, and attractiveness. His calculations took into account the growth of suburban commercial cores.

The local AIA chapter prepared a plan showing what this meant in terms of the region's network and what the downtown could become. The main shopping street could be a pedestrian mall with limited local traffic and parking garages flanking the commercial core. Surrounding the downtown could be new apartment houses, a riverfront park with a museum and an expanded college campus, to mention only the principal possibilities.

This plan provided a vision for Middletown. Newspapers and local television gave considerable coverage to the plan but in actual

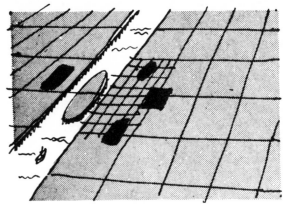

Middletown embarked on a series of redevelopment projects (black areas).

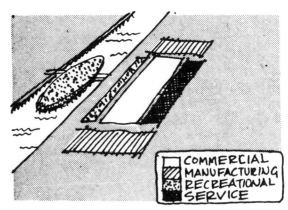

COMMERCIAL
MANUFACTURING
RECREATIONAL
SERVICE

A downtown committee prepared a downtown plan.

TRAFFIC
PARKING
PEDESTRIAN AREA

The downtown plan's circulation system tied into the metropolitan system and raised important questions in metropolitan planning.

The AIA chapter designed a pavilion and exhibit in the heart of the city to display these planning proposals.

203

Middletown prepared a Community Renewal Program (CRP) for general improvement.

A General Neighborhood Renewal Program (GNRP) was composed of three elements.

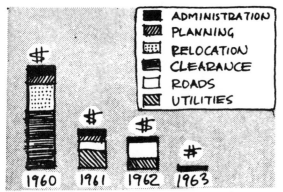

Capital budgeting for individual projects was adopted by Middletown. Above is an example of municipal budgeting for a project.

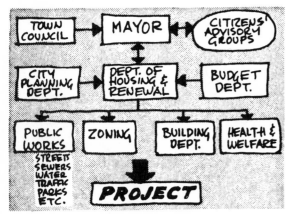

Middletown's municipal organization for redevelopment followed these general lines.

fact it had no visible means of support. Although the city traffic department, the parking authority, and all the other agencies concerned supported the proposal, the machinery of the government was not tooled to carry the plan through except in certain minor details—a change in a one-way street, or the installation of pedestrian crossing signals.

It was this situation coupled with the growing concern for urban redevelopment that led to the formation of Citizens For Middletown, Inc., a nonprofit private group that was free to inquire into a number of civic affairs. What was more, CFM Inc. could prod the legislature, support measures to improve Middletown and act as watchdog, devil's advocate, and *vox populi*. It was financed by private funds and subscriptions.

CFM Inc. inaugurated its founding by holding a national conference on the American City. The conclusions of that conference were: (1) Middletown needed a mayor dedicated to rebuilding the city, (2) Middletown needed an up-to-date city plan and a strong city planning staff, (3) planning at metropolitan level was essential, (4) the needs of individual groups, organizations, and institutions had to be assessed, and all groups who could contribute to building a better Middletown had to be mobilized. The local AIA chapter was delighted with this, feeling it had played a large part in stimulating interest in a major way—as it definitely had.

Two immediate results were an increase in the city's budget for a city planning staff and the formation of a Metropolitan Council of Governments. A major early recommendation of the city planning studies was that all municipal expenditures should be reviewed by the Middletown City Planning Commission as a means of coordinating expenditures for improvements—capital budgeting thus came into being in Middletown. Through studies, the planning commission saw numerous shortcomings in Middletown's transit system and lack of coordination between state road building and city streets. CFM Inc. and the local AIA were able to point out these deficiencies.

In the face of these concerns the National Housing Act of 1954 became law. Its chief benefits to Middletown were to coordinate its several programs into one conjoined effort to rebuild the worn parts of the city. An overall Community Renewal Plan was started, and the areas of the city most in need of rehabilitation were determined. The proposal to review municipal budgeting through the planning commission was adopted, for these expenditures could thus better be tied to redevelopment projects and then be counted as part of the city's share in the cost of renewal.

In addition, numerous neighborhood rehabilitation efforts were undertaken. CFM Inc. worked to help develop neighborhood organizations to work with the redevelopment authority in drafting plans. The nearby college gained needed land through a redevelopment plan, and campus housing for faculty and students was built with the aid of HHFA's Community Facilities Administration.

A program of housing for elderly people was also started, again through Federal funds. One of the rundown areas slated for rehabilitation contained fine old buildings dating from the city's early days. The local AIA chapter made a survey and selected those that should be saved, also suggesting ways for new buildings to harmonize with the old.

When the Middletown Redevelopment Agency wished to hold a redevelopment competition based on design, it contacted the AIA chapter which, in turn, proposed an architectural jury of colleagues from other cities. When a state highway plan was released, revealing serious errors in road and ramp placement, numerous citizen groups rose up in protest and the plan was altered. These citizens had acquired the organizational skill to render effective criticism.

Middletown also learned from its own experience and that of other cities that redevelopment competitions could not be decided on the basis of the developer's offered price for land *and* design together. These had to be separated because a decision based on price invalidates a decision based on design—and some low-bid designs can return more to the city over the long run.

Zoning controversies added further to Middletown's experience and judgment. Middletown learned that the best argument against an inappropriate variance request was a sound plan. Zoning could become a helpful enforcement tool. In redevelopment projects zoning could be relaxed—its protective role being transferred to the redevelopment program. On the one hand, this gave the developer latitude; on the other, it protected the interests of the city.

Middletown's architects gained firsthand knowledge of the HFA's mortgage insurance programs: Section 207 for multifamily rental housing; Section 213 for co-ops; Section 220 for urban renewal housing; Section 221 for low-cost relocation housing; Section 231 for housing the elderly; Section 233 for experimental housing; and Section 234 for condominiums.

The local AIA acted as adviser and architectural overseer. When it was proposed to replace some fine street lamps—highly sculptured cast-iron standards of the City Beautiful days—the local AIA rose up in protest. The lamps were saved. The local AIA was always helpful in preparing models and other visual exhibits, helping to choose architectural juries and setting up competitions. Individual members were employed to make design studies of special study areas. Most recently the AIA chapter proposed a total visual survey of Middletown as the physical basis for all planning. Their real contribution, overall, was to inject urban design thinking into all operations affecting the city's physical appearance.

In time a demonstration grant was obtained to develop techniques for rehabilitating old neighborhoods through conservation and through open space improvements. Acquisition for the open space began shortly after 1961, when partial funds for it became available. A mass transit demonstration grant tested the effects of better bus service on commuter patronage. State highway planning was related to local planning using BPR funds and HHFA planning funds. Middletown began to plan the improvement of its transit lines and equipment in anticipation of the 1964 Mass Transit Act. It was wise to do so because the application for funds was ready for submission when the bill was enacted.

In this unfolding panorama of programs a new range of clients and "designers" was becoming evident. The local housing agency was in effect a client of local architects. In road building, contracted engineers were the designers for state and city road departments, their work subject to review. In redevelopment projects, developers contracted architects, the client in effect being the city's redevelopment agency.

Middletown had firmly established the beginnings of a municipal program for reconstruction and enlargement. It had begun to inject good design into many of its programs. Even in so complex an area as highways, Middletown's architects were speaking of alignment designed to reveal special vistas in careful sequence, to integrally fit the road to topography.

Middletown constructed a number of public facilities—an airport, bridges, a municipal incinerator, an athletic stadium, and parks.

Public housing projects of various designs were built.

The downtown plan's circulation system was influential in locating urban expressways.

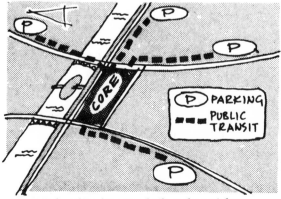

Municipal parking lots were built at the periphery of Middletown to intercept commuter traffic.

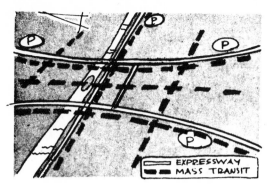

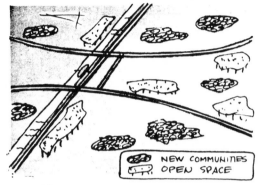

Middletown must now work toward a balanced transportation system— automobiles and public transit.

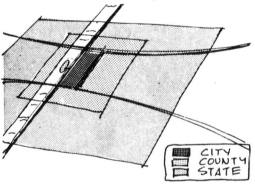

Middletown must also have the means to control land use in the face of increased demands for land. Middletown needs land for open space, new communities, and new industries.

Middletown and its surrounding communities must equip their numerous governments to meet the new problems of a rapidly forming region.

Conclusion

The new frontier of design for Middletown is now its metropolitan area, indeed its entire physical and economic region. On that frontier all our Middletowns now labor, dealing with administrative complexes far more intricate than those of an individual city. Air pollution, a form of refuse, can only be disposed of on a metropolitan basis. It is also evident that the control of the metropolis is needed to protect its public and private investments.

There are also numerous technical matters to be comprehended and added to the general public's knowledge. It is relatively easy for the public to understand urban design when illustrated with models and drawings. It is relatively easy to present a municipal budget and a municipal program. But as yet the whole field of taxes and mortgage operations as they affect our cities are but crudely understood.

The lesson of our history is that the tools of urban design are increasingly the tools of government operating through appropriate local bodies. Because of circumstances it was Federal and state government which gave us our current programs—which, in turn, were developed by local efforts.

Urban Renewal Notes, a bimonthly publication of URA, presented many ingenious applications of the newfound means. Grady Clay, speaking at the 1962 ASPO conference, summed up the lessons learned from over a decade of experiments. His advice was: avoid overly large projects; merge all projects with the cityscape; design projects to have a beneficial effect on their surroundings; design open spaces (the cheapest urban building material) very carefully; try new circulation concepts; design each particular area for the maximum diversity of use; incorporate old elements into projects; select project boundaries that will meld rather than separate urban tissues (project boundaries best run through the middle of a block rather than the center line of the street); and design richly in detail for the pedestrian's or even the child's scale.

Every program affecting the physique of the city is of concern to the architectural profession because it is a tool of urban design. We take rightful pride in the imaginative urban concepts we envision—the Radburn idea, the pedestrian way, the greenbelt concept or the multilevel city. We must now be just as imaginative and perceptive in grasping the means to realize urban design which government offers us. For more and more, it is through the programs of government that our concepts become the living city.

A Comprehensive Role
for Urban Design

Every society in history has faced the problem of shaping the environment it inhabited. Some rose magnificently to the occasion and produced works which rank among the fine arts. Very many more produced less sophisticated but completely livable and enjoyable countrysides, villages, towns, and cities. The more sophisticated efforts in time gained such descriptive names as architecture, landscape architecture, and town planning.

So clearly did some societies recognize this social task that they developed terms for it in their languages. The French, for example, speak of *urbanisme* and *paysage*. The Germans refer to *Stadtbaukunst* and the Italians to *urbanistica*. In some ways it is a pity that we have had to devise so many separate categories for the ways we now try to design our environment and that we had to add "urban design" to our vocabulary. This occurred because of a fractionalization of approach which too often has led us to divisions of thought and action. Because of these divisions, the concept of urban design had to be established—not to create a new or separate field, but to prevent this essential environmental concern from being ignored and lost.

In this final chapter we shall present a comprehensive role for urban design in the United States. Let us remember that many great social ideas in history were embodied in urban design concepts, just as they have been in architectural concepts. Thomas Jefferson, for example, saw an image of a future America that was as much a physical as a social vision. His abilities as architect and town planner were not incidental, nor were his visions ethereal. They were the design ideas consequent to his social precepts. At present we lack a consensus of what our future might be at its best. We sorely need vision of the quality that Jefferson gave us.

The Job We Face

Every twelve seconds there is a net population gain of one person in the United States, which amounts to an increase of 2,620,800 people per year. At this writing our present population stands at well over 190,000,000, and it is not difficult to find frequent comment on our "population explosion" on the editorial pages of newspapers or in special articles in popular magazines. The implications of this growth affect every aspect of our daily life. It creates problems in education, medical care, recreation, resources, government, and jobs. It also presents opportunities for industry, commerce, distribution, building, and artistic creation.

Accompanying this explosion of population is an ever improving standard of living. Indeed, for many of us, it is not a standard of living which we measure, but a standard of affluence. If the population were not growing but remained fixed in number, we would have a considerable job merely improving our present physical environment—a task involving the upkeep of a healthy building and urban inventory, new building for the replacement of the worn stock, and the removal of obsolete areas. But our multiplying population compounds these problems and adds a further burden —the creation of totally new urban areas to house our increasing numbers.

We find great difficulty in designing for this growth because it is taking place around existing urban centers whose long-standing problems we have scarcely begun to solve. Although we Americans have built splendid communities in the past, we are now unable to put a sufficient number of our ideas to work. How unfortunate for a nation that has been among the foremost in history as an innovator of rural, of urban, and of architectural form.

We cannot blame our shortcomings on a lack of technical knowledge. The United States has more people developing more ideas and advancing more theories than any other country. Most of these ideas are understandable to the lay public. The relationship between land use and transportation routes is quite obvious. The effects of property and building taxes on real estate development are comprehended by the average businessman. Most people are quite aware of urban redevelopment and its problems, as well as some of the alternatives to urban sprawl. Popularized visions of the future city draw crowds at fairs and readers' attention in magazines. Increasingly, "letters to the editor" on these subjects appear in the daily newspapers. More and more, foreign colleagues come to the United States to observe our methods firsthand. The growing number of books and articles by experts has long passed the point where even professionals can keep abreast of them. Computers are being used to assimilate statistics, draw maps, and even make perspective drawings.

Yet the application of our current store of ideas for improving cities is seen in but a handful of our own cities, and then only in isolated sites. Altogether these concepts have been more broadly

The illustrations in this last chapter are aerial photographs of the American landscape and cityscape—seen in their frank reality from a broad perspective. These pictures are meant to emphasize the importance of the suggestions for a comprehensive urban design program offered in this chapter.

realized and are more evident in the cities across our northern border. Toronto and Montreal have in operation many of the ideas long espoused here. Toronto has a modern subway and a sensible system of off-street parking just behind Yonge Street, its main shopping spine. Montreal has a large "greenbelt" along its southern edge. Across the ocean the reconstructed cities of Europe are living encyclopedias of the modern concepts of urbanism, many of which were developed by us. To anyone observing these differences of accomplishment comes the insistent question: "Why have we not done as much if not more?" One of the first answers likely to be given is that our individual units of government (some 90,000 of them at present in the United States) are ill-equipped, if not obsolete, in the face of this difficult job.

Urban problems do not respect city, county, or state lines. They traverse them. But governments must respect those lines. In many cases local governments zealously enforce their significance. This difficulty will not easily be resolved, although it is clearly recognized as an obstacle to city improvement and is becoming more and more a main subject of political deliberations. However, it would be inaccurate to lay the blame on our governments, which, after all, represent the will of the people—or at least of the most forceful among us. And certainly we must acknowledge a great amount of ingenuity on the part of our governments. The urban renewal programs have been an important step forward. Our special authorities to deal with particularly pressing problems have been quite imaginative and helpful.

Fundamentally, the major fault may lie in our total outlook toward rural and urban life, as well as rural and urban land use, and, subsequently, in the many ways this outlook finds outlet. Our objectives have largely been the betterment of life through the profits of commerce, industry, and the quick use of natural resources. This is not to say that we are insensitive as a people. Our finer products include the New England village, the Southern plantation, the Spanish-Mexican village, the clipper ship, the jet passenger plane, and many poetic bridges. The growing concern over the preservation of the finer environmental works of the past is further testimony of an underlying passion we are somewhat reluctant to acknowledge fully and fairly. Too often we relegate our sensitivity to a second- or third-rate slot in our scale of values. The Americana of Disneyland or the numerous "Freedomlands" around the country symbolize the popular appreciation of the better values of our past.

Our emphasis on the immediate and tangible, coupled with our relegation of higher values, has gotten us into no small difficulties. In too many city plan reports, the mention of design, if it exists at all, is treated as a cosmetic added to two-dimensional function diagrams. Too many leisure pursuits—the opera, the symphony, and the theater—are regarded as quasi-commercial and have to bear the burden of business taxes. And now it appears that buildings in New York City will have to carry a tax increase based on their beauty, as a result of the Seagram case. But one of the most unfortunate and revealing errors of all is the program for road building, which has upset cities as much as it has served them.

In his review of *Traffic in Towns*, the British study of automobile transportation and its effects by Colin Buchanan (published by Her Majesty's Stationery Office), Frederick Gutheim evaluated our urban highway programs. In this review, published in *Architectural Record*, June, 1964, Mr. Gutheim points out that our urban high-

Bitterroot Range, Idaho.

Texas plains.

209

Colorado plains.

A town in the state of Washington.

way program was put into the hands of a retired army general to expedite it. Expedited it was, to the neglect of mass transportation, which could have solved many urban transportation problems more cheaply and effectively. Moreover, mass transit in many instances would not have cut away large swaths of city as do the urban highways.

Buchanan and his group started their study by acknowledging the increasing role and popularity of the automobile and recognizing its superiority for many types of trips. But, in contrast to the American approach, they saw that the values of the city as an institution and servant of society are paramount to the benefits brought by the automobile. Thriving cities have a limited capacity for automobile traffic. Any attempts to overburden the capacity of streets in a tightly woven cityscape come at the cost of destruction of the shops, schools, houses, offices, nurseries, and hospitals along those streets—the delicate fabric of city life woven over the years. Traffic capacities are limited by the existing abilities of a street, and the traffic volume of a whole city must be restricted to the capacity of all its streets together.

This comparison illustrates that the approaches to urban problems which are so widely considered practical may not be practical at all. Our urban programs cannot succeed if they are founded on anything but the best interests of a city as a social institution. Our attempt to solve circulation problems is the best example to take because it has so far been the greatest single urban effort upon which we have embarked—with all other projects far behind. If we have made mistakes in our urban traffic efforts, we can learn from them as we enlarge other endeavors. We can learn that the most practical goals of all in the short run and the long run are programs whose foremost objective is the improvement of the *quality* of the life we lead, both in the city and the country—those two areas which must be considered as one in the face of our mobility and daily pursuits.

Could it not be that the most comprehensive role of urban design is the specific articulation of social objectives, in specific programs of action in specific areas of city building which we have in hand?

It has been argued that the great examples of building in other places and other times were quite often the results of happy accidents. This attitude we can dismiss by ascribing it to frustration with our own limited approach. Who can seriously conclude that a Gothic stonemason or a Cape Cod carpenter could fail to notice every effect and aspect of appearance of his handiwork as he trod toward it each morning and gazed at it over his shoulder each evening? Similarly, it has been argued that only absolutist societies could produce fine cities. Those critics have failed to ponder seventeenth-century Amsterdam, eighteenth-century London, nineteenth-century Vienna—let alone the accomplishments in our own country around the turn of the century. Further, they fail to see that past societies, no matter how centralized they may appear to us now, were in fact controlled by numerous competing interests. True, the great works of the past were the results of powerful individuals and groups, but a large portion of the credit is due to the men of art and intellect who furnished the ideas and models. If the number of individuals of power was small in past times there is without question a modern parallel. For our public undertakings are results of the urgings of articulate groups of businessmen, of the spokesmen of industry, of real estate people, of the representatives of commerce and trade. What models are being held up for them?

We have in these few lines lapsed into a recitation of difficulties. Such recitations are tolerable to the creative person only when they are a preface to proposals for resolute action. By way of resolution, let us list and describe every area of community design which can become action now. Let us propose a full-fledged program of urban design for cities and towns throughout the United States. Then let this list be the architect's statement of the comprehensive role of urban design.

Urban Design on a National and Regional Scale

In 1956 a collection of essays was published under the title *Man's Role in Changing the Face of the Earth*. Covering such topics as the deforestation of Europe, the great grasslands of the world, and the climate of towns, this book stands as the largest single work on man's endeavors and the alterations he has made on the world's geography. It has undergone four editions. In discussing these changes, the authors have laid the groundwork for what could well be a natural sequel—a visionary book which might be called "Man's Role in *Designing* the Face of the Earth."

No matter how powerful his tools, man's choices of action have been shaped largely by the character of the land he attempted to transform. Some lands were totally unfit for any cultivation or habitation. Others could support only marginal cultivation and hence scant population. Others produced so abundantly that they posed questions as to their best use. Today, however, we can base our choice of action on an extremely wide range of possibilities. We can now transform deserts, level mountains, carve harbors, and convert salt bays to fresh-water lakes. Within broad limits we can redesign the earth—and by design we mean knowing what to leave alone as well as how to use intelligently the lands we inhabit.

The United States has a geography of great variety and hence abundant design possibility. We have already established the major uses of land according to the natural resources of various regions. Iowa and portions of its neighboring states comprise one of the richest farmland areas in the world. Our grasslands are among the world's finest cattle grounds. The various regions of the nation, distinguished by their climate, topography, and verdure, have developed their appropriate uses and subsequent physical characteristics.

These regions of their characterizing differences are one of the chief design assets of our country and must be regarded as the major design subdivisions of the United States. We have already begun to tend to some of them, usually because of engineering necessity. Many rivers and river basins traversing several state lines are cases in point—the Mississippi River, the St. Lawrence Seaway, and the Tennessee Valley.

Program: Regional Design

The entire United States should be studied to determine its significant and integral physical sections. These should be delineated according to their characteristic topography, climate, and culture. Many of the regions will traverse our northern and southern national boundaries.

We propose the formation of groups of persons, representing all walks of life and all professions, to study and lay forth a future

A town in the state of Washington.

Cincinnati, Ohio.

211

South San Francisco, California.

Chicago, Illinois.

vision of what these areas could become at their best. We propose that architects of broad vision be foremost in these groups. Most appropriately these groups would be supported by a large foundation. Not only would the participants prepare design plans showing the overall region and its land use, but numerous studies of the appropriate appearance of all man-made objects in this landscape —from telephone poles to cities—would also be made. The character of the land would be the basis for the design of cities and towns. A road and its overpass and cloverleaf appurtenances would be designed for its appearance *in* the landscape as well as for the appearance of the landscape *from* it.

These studies would maximize diversity of choice in the various regions, while at the same time assuring the protection of land character. Our new mobility and increase of leisure time is fast leading to a very intense use of land in, around, and beyond the city. That land will either be desecrated or enhanced, depending on what we envision now for its future use.

Program: Recreational Area Design

Discussion of land use beyond the city immediately suggests recreational activities. As a rule it should not take more than an hour to reach areas of natural terrain from the center of a city. Many cities now enjoy this convenience, but unless it is protected it will soon be lost.

We propose a study of the potential recreation areas around all cities as a basis for conceiving a complete panorama of many types and sizes of recreation places. Of particular concern should be the coastal areas of the entire United States. Thoughtless and insensitive development is too quickly ruining some of our finest shorelines, which is neither necessary nor economically wise.

Each state should formulate a plan for the use of its main recreational resources, along with private land development. The quality of recreation areas is bound to occupy an increasingly important role in a state's well-being. Our people now choose their place of residence on the basis of its ability to offer the good life as much as they choose places with economic and job opportunities. Programs on a state level could designate recreational areas —lakes, beaches, mountains—and plan the most desirable resort towns and resort homesites. This would maintain a proper and sensitive balance between untouched wilderness and developed land. Indeed, the wilderness areas could have lodges, trails, and other appropriate facilities at certain places. The towns would have a main street, a variety of shops to form a spine for the evening promenade, and perhaps a bit of carnival, like the boardwalk resorts of the nineteenth century.

Several prototype studies and accomplishments now exist. The state of Wisconsin recently completed a comprehensive report called *Recreation in Wisconsin* with a supplement of sketches and design principles. Recreation is a main source of income in Wisconsin. In Europe, the entire coast of Yugoslavia is being carefully designed for recreational use. Ernesto Rogers, editor of Italy's *Casa Bella* magazine, recently devoted two special issues to the problems of Italy's shore areas. Rogers urgently proposes a landscape plan for Italy at national scale. Our American national parks and the concession facilities developed in them generations ago are still good models, and so are the many resort towns built near large cities in the last century. Connecticut has completed a study of its natural characteristics as a basis for statewide development and resource planning. It is urgent for us to apply these and other new techniques not only to recreation areas but to all regions in our country prone to rapid expansion.

Program: Developing Regions

In many regions development is only a matter of time—indeed, is fast proceeding. Among these are subareas within the east-west "megalopolis" described by geographer Jean Gottmann, large portions of the St. Lawrence Seaway, the San Francisco Bay area, the interrelated complexes of the Pacific Northwest and shore areas along the Great Lakes.

We propose as a start that rapidly growing regions be designed as exemplary physical developments, coupling private initiative with public regulating control. This practice would encourage the flow of investment capital, maintain development interest and, above all, create fine places to live. Dominant in this program would be the role of creative design.

Highschool and suburbs.

A large triangular portion of Florida is one of the most interesting areas now being studied—the section roughly defined by Orlando, Cape Kennedy, and Daytona Beach. A group of officials and private citizens recently commissioned a design and planning study for this area. Seemingly, it was one of the most featureless terrains in the entire country—a flat, and often swampy, coast. Because the physical and hence visual development is of prime concern, a survey of the visual impact of the land on its inhabitants was made. Personal interviews revealed a surprising number of subtleties in land character and development—far more intricate and differentiated than suspected. Although many of the inhabitants were not sophisticated in their tastes because of their predominantly rural experience, there is no question that well-designed improvements of a fairly sophisticated nature would become meaningful to them. If this seemingly featureless landscape has such visual appeal, how much have those areas whose physical distinctions are more obvious?

As our country expands, many regions become obsolete, just like old buildings and roads. The poverty-stricken Appalachian region around West Virginia is the most obvious case in point. In recent studies of these depressed areas under the Area Redevelopment Act, proposals for new recreational activities are being given very serious consideration. Sheer imagination of the kind the architect can exercise may furnish some of the most helpful ideas.

Program: Wilderness Areas and Old Preserves

As our urban centers enlarge and as more land is consumed, the value of untouched sections becomes even more important. So does the value of the older rural areas which have acquired a character we look back upon with deep pride and admiration.

Lake Barcroft, northern Virginia.

We propose that these two kinds of areas—wilderness and the "old preserve"—receive special attention in every region of the country. The selection standards to follow could be the degree to which the area in question expresses its regional character. Both the wilderness and the old preserves could readily be judged on this basis. For example, the valleys of the Rocky Mountains contain old mining towns strung along the valley stream. Many of the towns have fine Victorian buildings which make some of the towns worthy of preservation in their entirety. Certainly they deserve protection from the intrusion of garish roadhouses as close neighbors.

213

The older towns of Vermont and New Hampshire with their farms and farm buildings constitute a landscape so dear to us that we often depict it on calendars. These areas are examples of our old preserves in building and in cultivated land. The wilderness areas are those parts that were beyond the reach of cultivation. Let us organize programs to anchor the prevalence of this way of life, for it brings beauty to the land and is living evidence of our continuing traditions and values.

We must present our proposals with these broad brush suggestions for design at the overall scale of America because we live and use our country as a whole. As a whole we shall improve or ruin its beauties. If it is necessary to begin on a large scale, it is equally necessary to progress to the domain with the most problems and therefore with the greatest opportunities. We shall now turn to proposals for urban design at the metropolitan scale.

Urban Design at the Metropolitan Scale

Little need be added to the list of problems encumbering the metropolis, where our greatest population growth is occurring. The emerging metropolis of the United States is a new urban form— or at least an urban form more extended than anything previously seen.

Much must be added to the store of ideas pertaining to the design of metropolitan areas. While problems of government, economics, taxing, and transportation receive due consideration, there is no surplus of thought on the city as a design and on the quality and variety of life in it. Some assert that the physical appearance of the metropolis is of no consequence. This attitude can only be met with shock by the architect. It would deny the value of the advances made in the whole history of architecture. Others have suggested that our society is too mobile and too much in transition to be nailed down to any fixed design ideas. This is to deny our obligation to provide continuity and quality in the course of urban expansion.

We are definitely able to control many areas of design, if we recognize the forces now at work in our cities. These forces can be redirected by the following programs.

Program: Design for Metropolitan Structure

Design plans of entire metropolitan areas should be undertaken at once. According to the Bureau of the Census, there are now over 200 metropolitan areas, not all of which are conducting planning activities that can be considered adequate. The 1962 Highway Act will increase this activity considerably but only for land-use and transportation planning—transportation usually being interpreted as automobile transportation. Many of these metropolitan areas have established commissions to discuss the common problems of their governments. Numerous *ad hoc* commissions have proven effective in dealing with specific problems. These commissions are concerned with land use, transportation, administration, development, schools, utilities, air pollution, water supply, stream pollution, and recreational green space. Rarely do official planning studies seriously commit themselves as primarily artful design efforts. At the metropolitan scale we are *building* but not *designing* the urban landscape—the new-forming environment where so many spend the major portion of their time.

We propose a program of design studies of the total form and

Atlanta, Georgia.

Suburbs.

appearance of all our metropolitan areas. The basis for perceived urban form at the metropolitan scale is the relation between natural and man-made shapes. These together proclaim to the eye of the moving observer the hierarchy of urban parts, their relative importance to each other and their relative sizes. A prominence here is an important element to be balanced with a flat area there. Various accents disposed about the skyline give orientation and are clues to functions. Highways demarked by identifying lamps or accompanying greenery trace paths through the complex metropolis, acting as visual guides within, around, and about. Open spaces surrounded by cityscape give relief and vista to urban clusters. All of this is arranged in a vastly complex series of patterns and relationships. All of it is seen and perceived and must be designed as a total design structure—which is just as important to the city as planning the capacity of expressways.

In Philadelphia Edmund Bacon has woven a design structure, first for the central city and then for the entire metropolis. It consists of major functional and visual axes connecting various hubs of activity, some of special purposes, some of highly diverse purposes—all of them related to the entire metropolitan complex. These hubs are the sites of the many new urban developments in Philadelphia.

In Detroit Charles A. Blessing, FAIA, is in the process of devising a metropolitan design structure as a clear statement of direction for all planning. Detroit's city form is flat, bounded on one side by the Detroit River. Its street pattern is the gridiron, with radial and circumferential routes. Its "flats" are the large stretches of subdivision houses. Its "peaks" are one dominant cluster of office towers in the center and numerous outlying vertical clusters at great distances. This cityscape-in-the-making can best be compared to Monument Valley—a great flat desert characterized by large rock mesas. Detroit's extensive urban flats are the counterpart to the desert of Monument Valley, and its skyscraper clusters are the counterpart to Monument Valley's mesas.

So powerful is the connection between these "landscapes," that Blessing is able to show slides of both simultaneously without a word of explanation. An application of this design approach is seen in Detroit's Lafayette Park redevelopment area, which is a short distance from central Detroit. The towers of central Detroit are readily seen from within Lafayette Park because the slots of space between its towers were intentionally designed to frame the views of the center. Here is the Renaissance principle of "reciprocity of view" restored in modern context.

Detroit will become increasingly important to watch as its design structure evolves. It is surpassed only by Los Angeles as a city shaped by the automobile. But unlike Los Angeles, Detroit may pave the way in showing how the forces of automobile transportation can properly reshape a city—this through the conscientious location of freeways and building clusters for their physical and visual effects. (Design studies of the central city, prepared by Detroit architects through their AIA chapter, were published in the September, 1959, *AIA Journal*.)

A metropolitan design structure is essential to every architect working at the scale of a building group or a single building. Since it reveals the situation of his building functionally and visually, it furnishes important clues to the way each building is approached, seen, and used. It gives the city an essential skeleton within which special buildings and clusters are the vital organs and in which the

Cincinnati, Ohio.

Central Park, New York City.

lesser buildings are the flesh. A design structure is the framework for foreground and background architecture working together.

Program: Metropolitan Form and Pattern

Urban design at metropolitan scale involves study of total metropolitan form. Our metropolitan areas are fast becoming undifferentiated and haphazard, whereas they could become works of art. At the metropolitan scale, planning is now inadequately limited to land use and transportation relations. It is therefore necessary to combine all the elements of metropolitan form into a total approach in order to state the case for design on a metropolitan scale.

We propose that all our metropolitan areas be studied to discern their evolving form and that, subsequently, designs be made exploring the likely alternative forms which could be perfected through present techniques—transportation planning, land-use designation, open space, new satellite towns, and new urban corridors.

Form and pattern constitute an armature for urban organization. Both derive from topography, function, and transportation. Particular forms have particular implications. Dependent on form and pattern are proximity to green space, mixture of parts, choice, opportunity, accessibility of various facilities, obsolescence, and stability. Form is fundamental to climatic orientation as well as each person's sense of where he is in the city.

The Year 2000 Plan for Washington, D.C., deals with alternate forms for growth and has become a focus of planning discussion in Washington's metropolitan area. The San Francisco Bay metropolitan area is a large circle geographically. Recent studies of its future possibilities strongly connote variations of pattern. The finger and open space plans of Copenhagen involved considerable study of metropolitan forms. Metropolitan planning studies for the Minneapolis–St. Paul area likewise required an examination of alternate possible forms. A metropolitan form and pattern plan proposes in broad terms the physical design possibilities of a city and their implications. In so doing, it consolidates all elements of urban design at a very large scale into one easily understood concept.

Program: A Metropolitan Open Space System

A corollary to a metropolitan design structure and form is a metropolitan open space plan. Although it is inherently part of a large-scale urban design structure, it is so important a design element that it must be considered independently.

We propose that every metropolitan area prepare a master plan for open spaces, that the open space plan be envisioned as a total structure complementary to the built-up areas of the city, and that all possible means be brought to bear on the establishment of open space reserves. There is nothing new about this concept. It was developed and proven right here in the United States.

About ninety years ago a father suggested to his energetic son that an interesting day's excursion would be to take a commuter train out of the city, get off at an outlying town, walk circumferentially along wooded trails to a neighboring town and then return at day's end via another commuter train. The young man took his father's advice and recorded perhaps fifteen or twenty such excursions in his diary.

The father was Charles W. Eliot, President of Harvard University; the son was Charles Eliot, later to become one of America's

Kansas City, Missouri.

Washington, D.C.

216

great landscape architects. From his early excursions he conceived a metropolitan park system for Boston. He envisioned a ring of outlying park reserves connected by a series of green routes penetrating the city. This concept is not unique for American cities. Kansas City and Minneapolis developed such park systems, and the smaller parks of many other cities were based upon Eliot's system.

Although Eliot concentrated on the landscaped treatment of open spaces, his designs reveal almost the entire category of types of open spaces. Open spaces range in size from the vast reserves of natural land, to the urban park, to the urban plaza, and down to the street. Indeed, it is the sidewalk that is the elementary open space of a city. In use, open spaces range from completely passive, almost unused spaces, to highly active urban spaces—the city's outdoor salons and playrooms. All these are found in Eliot's model green space system for Boston.

Kansas City, Missouri.

We must now regard open space as an essential land use equally as significant as the complex designations of land use found in zoning. Architect-planner S. B. Zisman has proposed that an open space framework in the city can serve as a lone land-use control. A good open space system will act as a complement to a variety of land uses. Poorly built city areas can always be rebuilt later but are more tolerable in the interim because of open space. It is crucial to set aside land for open space before it is needed, since it is difficult, if not impossible, to create it by razing built-up areas, whether in, or far beyond, the reaches of the metropolis. Today the basic urban distance is the area the average person can readily traverse. That covers considerable territory and should determine the upper limits of the open space systems we must now create—the modern counterparts to Eliot's concept of nearly a century ago.

Program: Design for Metropolitan Transportation

Road building for the automobile is the largest single urban reconstruction program today. It has forced planning in every metropolitan area, but the type of planning it is fostering is limited. Often it is misapplied. Seeking to increase mobility it has often destroyed vital urban tissue, its uncertainties placing many urban areas in a state of limbo while route and construction schedules are debated. Urban expressways made their debut as landscaped parkways a half century ago. The roads, often the product of the landscape architect's skill, were aligned for artful sequences of vista—urban and rural. The green axis of the landscaped parkway wove a path through the city, its landscaping accompanying the driver from the green countryside into the heart of a city. Its bridges accented the progress of the route. If the roads were prose, the bridges were poetry. These elements of roadway design have not only been relegated and forsaken but, worse, the emphasis on roads themselves has been exaggerated beyond proportion.

Queens, Long Island, New York.

We propose a program of urban design for transportation which puts the city first as an institution to be served. We propose that all means of transportation be examined as a prelude to any transportation improvement programs. The design of the roadway and its appurtenances is but one aspect of proper road design: the consideration and design of every means of urban transportation must be made basic to all transportation design. The current preoccupation with automobile travel is an adolescent stage in circulation planning. Rail rapid transit has been unfairly neglected in our automobile era. For over fifty years rail rapid transit has received almost no share of the kind of design attention given to the auto, the airplane, even the elevator or the truck.

Advocates of rail rapid transit can give only hesitating estimates of the expected patronage of a proposed subway system because the design of the subway is so meanly inadequate. Architect Don Emmons and others are now developing designs for the San Francisco Bay area subway that will make it as attractive as, if not more attractive than, the automobile for the trip to work. Emmons' studies included on-site inspection of newer subways of the world. Recently he saw a prototype car in Hamburg, Germany, which matches a Mercedes in comfort and appeal. In Paris one train runs on rubber tires to prevent the deafening roar and clack so familiar in the old subway. In Stockholm each station has murals, color, benches, and is light and airy. The Toronto subway stops are connected under shelter to bus terminals. Again, in Paris each station has its own stationmaster—one on each platform—to control operations.

Boston, Massachusetts.

If we exercised the design ingenuity lavished on airplane travel we would introduce advances making these examples seem minor in comparison. Imagine, for example, a subway train in which a light breakfast is served, where the morning newspapers could be read in comfort, where the morning news is presented on TV, where the frequency of trains assures adequate seating for all. A short while after the workers' journey, school children could use the same trains, giving them a place for homework comparisons on their way to school, or even presenting televised lessons for the more studious. A metropolitan school system could be devised to give children a city-wide choice of schools, perhaps encouraging again the specialized high schools once prevalent in older cities. During the day the housewife could conveniently travel to shopping centers. The train could post advertising pages of the daily newspapers, as well as shoppers' guides. Packages could be delivered to subway stations via a special service, as they are on intercity bus systems. Architect Louis Justement, FAIA, is currently conjecturing on the possibilities of preplanned high-density developments at outlying subway stations in the Washington, D.C., area. These could be new nuclei for office and business clusters and could help balance the subways' outbound and inbound loads.

Charlotte Amalie, St. Thomas, Virgin Islands.

Critics of subway systems decry their fixed location and hence their purported inflexibility. Subway routes are no less permanent than the automobile expressway and certainly take up less space. Further, they do not elbow existing urban areas out of existence. But before the subway can be expected to present its credentials to the public, it must be given a fair chance to compete for attention. The time has long passed when road construction was approved through public referendum. We pay for our roads every time we purchase gasoline. We pay for a proposed public transit system only when we agree to pass on a bond issue. To the surprise of many, San Franciscans did just that in recent years. They agreed to tax themselves for this subway. Yet the capital outlay for their entire system is surpassed by California's total budget for roads in the coming year alone.

Program: Approaching the City

The first sight of a city leaves a lasting impression. When cities were smaller their entrances were clearly marked by a gate, statue, bridge, or some other feature. The entrances to most cities are now generally obscure. They are more a progression of undifferentiated views rather than distinct movements of revelation. The need for clarity in entrance is as strong as it ever was—even more so, since the city is more complex.

We propose a program for designing the entrance sequence to each city. We now approach cities over land, through air, and across water. The various parts of the city must be articulated as one enters them. So, too, must be the sights of places one sees and passes when departing.

Many existing approaches are quite good and serve as illustrations. For example, the air approach to Salt Lake City from the east takes its passengers on a thrilling ride over the Rocky Mountains, then swoops over Salt Lake City to the airport. Arriving passengers never lose sight of the mountains and the city together, even when driving in the airport limousine to the city's central hotels. Kansas City's municipal airport places arriving passengers at the foot of the central city. The location of Boston's airport gives its arriving passengers a fine view of the central city towers across Boston harbor. San Francisco's Golden Gate Bridge is the portal to the United States from the Pacific—a poetic counterpart to the Tori gates of Japan. The Statue of Liberty in New York harbor is one of the most meaningful symbols of all at the entrance to a city. The approach to Dallas from the west across a branch of the Trinity River was carefully designed a half century ago; so was the approach to Manhattan on the West Side Highway and the approach to Boston down the Charles River embankment.

A well-designed entrance to the city heightens anticipation, alerts acute powers of sight, aids orientation, and sharpens the eye for the full observation of the things ahead—which brings us to the consideration of views and vistas.

Cleveland, Ohio.

Program: Metropolitan Views and Vistas

Every city is characterized by certain key vistas. Some of these vistas embrace either the entire city or a substantial part of it, while other major views cover only a small but nevertheless telling portion of the city. These views need the formal recognition, protection, and enhancement of a design plan.

We propose that every city survey and evaluate its important vistas and draw up a map with the objects and angles of view, to serve as a basic document against which related construction can be checked. On the vista map necessary corrections of elements marring the view, as well as unsightly parts which need screening, would be indicated. Also, the many dormant views in the city can be noted—views which, if opened up, could play a major visual role.

A basic category of views would include such differentiation as the extent of the panorama, its symbolic importance, the distance from which it is perceived, the degree to which it is seen, and its correspondence to the city's hierarchy of values. Too often today, a minor view is overplayed and major objects lack sufficient prominence.

The Columbia River, dividing Oregon and Washington.

The sequence of views would have to be given special attention. The approach experience is essentially a sequence of views. So, too, is the movement through and around a city. Special studies could single out particularly important movement-vista sequences in order to yield definite design suggestions. An example will illustrate these points:

The entrance approach to Washington, D.C., from the north passes over New York Avenue, which is the extension of a rather pleasant landscaped highway. When that highway ends to enter the city (becoming New York Avenue), it reveals a chaotic disarray of urban miscellany—hardly an appropriate first impression of the nation's capital. Further along, the road rises to offer a long vista of the Capitol dome at the center of the city, about a mile and a half away. That distance is just about correct for a first long-distance view of the Capitol dome, but it is badly marred by a haphazard foreground of truckyards and wholesale warehouses. With careful land shaping, however, the immediate foreground could be blocked from sight. The middle distances of the panorama would then be far enough away to mute its discordances, and the Capitol dome could stand out in unimpaired dignity.

No less important than the views *of* the city are the views *from* it. Steen Eiler Rasmussen has commented on the characteristic American grid layout which gives an almost infinite view of the sky to every street, for each street frames a piece of sky at normal eye level. For a European this is a treat. For us it is perhaps too frequent to be desirable. The eye needs points of reference in the city, well placed as distinct objects seen in silhouette against the sky. But Rasmussen's observation suggests an important role for vista design.

Just as nature is the best setting for a city when seen from afar, the city itself can act as a picture frame for viewing nature. Photographers know this very well. Often the most modest of architectural elements exploit this possibility. The old bay window in a series of row houses on a grid street allows people to get a long axial vista of the street. On Boston's Beacon Hill this design provides a fine sweeping view of the Charles River or the Boston Common. In San Francisco it affords long views of the bay. The bay window serves an effective role in relieving the closeness of a street of row houses. It can be credited with helping to make the high-density row house areas livable.

Other designs for the out-looking vista include the skyscraper rooftop observatory, the shoreline promenade, the hilltop park, the bridge into the city, and the parkway as it passes over high ground. A day's study of your own city would reveal many more.

Program: The Metropolitan Skyline

Closely allied to views and vistas is the urban skyline—indeed, it is a chief component of vista. The late Henry Churchill, FAIA, noted that we do not see three-dimensional objects in plan but by vertical definition. Albert Mayer, FAIA, spoke in some detail about the current anarchy of our contemporary skylines in his address before the 1964 AIA convention.

In colonial days the accents of skylines proclaimed a hierarchy of values. Characteristically, the skyline consisted of church steeples at high point with a domed building, usually a seat of government, as the focus. Fire watch towers, shot towers, or signal towers had distinct profiles and did not add confusion—neither did a cluster of ships' masts in the harbor, for they were thin, almost lacelike. All of these secondary skyline features had secondary visual roles which complemented the one or two prime skyline accents.

Our contemporary skylines cannot be read in such a simple way, for theirs is an order proclaiming multiplicity of values and goals. Almost any American city serves as an indication of a raw skyline order we have fast been developing. The center is a cluster of many shafts. Few, if any, correspond with each other. They are distinguished primarily by apparent age or newness when seen in com-

Cincinnati, Ohio.

Cleveland, Ohio.

220

parative juxtaposition. Almost never is there an intentional balance or design correspondence between facades and masses. Visually they act as a group because they are a group and because the eye does not choose to see fine details of difference when too many details are offered simultaneously.

As the city grows, tower buildings are built at prominent peripheral junctions. Sometimes they are minor clusters, as in Detroit. Sometimes they are handsome single shafts like the B. M. A. Building in Kansas City. In any case, here are certainly the major new elements of skyline design. Since the central cluster of the city is the outstanding profile of the metropolis, expressways should be artfully aligned to give drivers views of it as they approach the city. Likewise, the outlying clusters or single shafts act as peripheral skyline verticals for the outgoing driver. Thus the various verticals of the city form a new reciprocity of view.

Preserving fine old skylines, particularly low ones with historic and symbolic accents, is especially vital. In some cities laws have been passed to restrict building height as a means to protect the skyline. This must be done with caution, for a continuous stretch of squat low buildings can be dull. Unless it is effected through a vista plan, some major features of the skylines are likely to be blocked off inadvertently. In addition, unavoidable urban appurtenances such as smokestacks, TV masts, mechanical penthouses, billboards, and telephone relays begin to assume more important visual importance than they deserve. Simple rules do not work in complex situations.

We have underlined the need for a careful skyline plan for each city, commensurate with its particular physical condition. This plan must, of course, be made in conjunction with the groups of people who can control the skyline—private builders and developers together with city officials who can exercise control through zoning. Guiding these decisions must be a sound and realistic design plan, whose major emphasis is the development of a handsome urban skyline.

Program: Special Sites

A skyline plan would quickly begin to specify sites of special vertical prominence, but not all the special sites of a city are high. Some low-lying sites also have fine vistas from them. There are others with an historical connotation, others containing particularly fine old buildings, and still others which contain important public buildings. These make up the special sites of the city.

We propose that every city designate its outstanding sites, selected by a number of criteria which measure their value to the city and the public at large. The special sites plan could also outline programs for improvement where necessary. In addition, the plan would be influential in shaping the metropolitan design structure, for these sites could be significant hubs and nodes, distinguished by character as well as use.

Society Hill in Philadelphia, an old historic quarter of the city, has been improved by rehabilitation and the addition of carefully placed towers and new row houses. La Villita in San Antonio represents an historic area which is carefully protected and actively used. The Los Angeles Chapter AIA recently made a study showing how hillsides could be beautifully developed for a variety of house types—in effect treating the whole design of hillside and buildings as a work of art. This they proposed as an alternative to the too frequent and too wanton bulldozer terracing.

Chicago, Illinois.

Cleveland, Ohio.

221

The approaches and settings of major public buildings should be designated as special sites. Many river banks and urban shorelines, no longer used for industrial operation, can become interesting in-town enclaves for mixed residential-commercial-recreational use. Old market areas, once chief provisioning centers, can still function as suppliers to in-town hotels, hospitals, restaurants, and institutions. In addition, they can thrive as specialty restaurant and gourmet centers. They need designation as special places to prevail in the face of uncaring development.

Countless opportunities for private developers will thus be supplied. Indeed, there are many projects private developers cannot undertake without the provisions which designation as a special area gives. This official designation should also facilitate lending money for unusual types of buildings and development. The HHFA experimental housing programs and numerous air-rights designs in cities around the country hint at the need for greater innovation.

Las Vegas, Nevada.

Santa Fe, New Mexico.

Urban Design at the Scale of the City

The programs we suggest for metropolitan areas are, of course, equally applicable to the smaller and more familiar urban entities, the city, the town, and the village. We address our proposals to the metropolis because that is the critical urban entity of our day. Discussions of the city versus the country or the city versus the suburb miss the real issue entirely. The principles of urban design at the metropolitan scale hold for smaller types of cities because the problems of design are essentially the same; of course, differences of scale introduce vast differences of emphasis and treatment. However, we can now proceed to some individual elements of design. In these programs, working at a more familiar scale, we are likely to achieve the first steps toward our larger objectives.

Program: Plan for Urban Open Space

In current city plans open spaces are designated for use as parks, playgrounds, schoolyards, beaches, and athletic stadiums. There are many more types and sizes of open spaces, however.

We propose a design plan for urban open spaces containing a category of open spaces with more intricate classifications of size and type. A proper classification would begin with the sidewalk, the basic but most neglected of all open spaces. The classification would continue with small plazas, malls, large plazas, boulevards and avenues, small and large parks, bodies of water and their shorelines. It would merge with the urban open space system of the metropolis. An urban open space system must be considered along with the metropolitan system. Individual counties and cities in a metropolis each have a role to play in creating the larger open space system.

Classification of size and use alone, however, is inadequate. Open spaces must not be designed as isolated islands of space but as a connected network of spaces, in relation to the areas they serve. The public open spaces serving a neighborhood of row houses are quite different from the small plazas of a busy city center or around a school, or indeed in an area of detached houses. In addition, the uses of open spaces differ from season to season. So, also, do the kinds of landscape treatment appropriate to various types of parks.

222

Program: Pedestrian Circulation

Automobile and bus traffic planning has reached a nearly scientific stage of engineering. Streets are classified according to the types and volumes of traffic they carry. This engineering technique should be extended to the pedestrian. Pedestrian counts have been made in busy urban areas and pedestrian malls have succeeded where they are tied into a total traffic plan. However, plans principally for pedestrian circulation do not exist.

We propose that plans for pedestrian movement be drafted in each city and that every city establish a Department of Pedestrian Circulation. The techniques of capacity and flow applied to autos would be helpful in doing this, but they should be extended to include the artistic approach to designed movement which the architect can bring. Architect Phillip Thiel has done significant work in this direction, and landscape architect Lawrence Halprin has been developing thoughts on what he calls "urban choreography."

A proper pedestrian circulation plan would knit the movement of the pedestrian into a city-wide network. It would be connected to the major generators of pedestrian traffic—parking garages, bus and subway stations. This plan would also be based on the principles of artful processional movement as was done in Renaissance buildings and baroque towns. It could as well be based on the more casual movement sequences found in medieval towns. Designed as formal or informal walks, city streets could be furnished with artful accents, events, pauses, transitions, intersections, and points of arrival. A pedestrian circulation plan would guide developers in locating certain types of shops, garages, and subway stations, as well as the functional and symbolic hubs.

Dallas, Texas.

Program: Municipal Trees

It is a sad commentary that a nation which once led the world in planting and caring for street trees now neglects this most welcome urban feature. A few generations ago a municipal street-tree program was a prerequisite of civic pride. We seldom attend to our street trees now except when it is too late or else to remove dangerous branches. We seldom shape them to proper form to keep them healthy. Many new street trees are too small and are planted in places where their size makes them easy prey to the normal abuses of city life.

We propose that every city reestablish a dedicated street-tree planting program. Trees can do more to beautify and humanize a street than any single element alone. Street trees must be chosen on the basis of beauty and practicality and be supervised under an ample care program.

Studies show that it is less expensive for a city to take care of its trees than to allow them to deteriorate. City trees must be trimmed to diminish water loss by evaporation. Their roots must be generously fed by water. The typical dirt pockets found at the base of city trees are mean to view and hardly ample for nourishment. Beyond its practical aspects, a municipal tree program is a rich field for imaginative design.

San Francisco, California.

Program: Electric Lighting

One of the most breathtaking sights in the world is that of an American city at night. From the air the patterns and colors of the lights read like an X ray. The illumination of cities is one of the great untapped reservoirs of modern urban design possibility.

223

Unfortunately our interest in street lighting is restricted merely to the output of candlepower, when it could strive for selective and beautifying illumination.

We propose urban design plans for city illumination, starting with the most practical areas of improvement. First of all, we could clarify the pathways of urban expressways by distinct types of light. We could then illuminate special junctions and, last, treat the lesser arteries and slow-speed streets with appropriate lighting that would read like a code.

We could develop special types of lights for pedestrian streets. In our zeal to get the maximum candlepower per square foot, we have first installed overly bright lights, then reduced the number of lights to a minimum, and finally resorted to huge poles completely out of scale. We have also overused mercury-vapor lamps on pedestrian streets. Pedestrian streets require a more delicate lighting. In shopping streets the light from shop windows often provides adequate illumination by itself. On such streets, lighting has an esthetic role—to unify the street by receding dotlike lights. Having completely neglected pedestrian lighting for forty years, we must remember that it is not only a matter of a fine pole and lamp—it is a matter of the total appearance of the street or road and its lights seen together.

San Juan, Puerto Rico.

Program: Street Furniture

Street lighting is one element of a whole category of objects which we have come to call street furniture. While there has been much thought given to this subject there have been few results.

We propose a program of street furniture design and an arrangement among manufacturers to make better designed products available. These include street benches, advertising kiosks, lamps, pavilions, bus and cab shelters, canopies, and planting boxes.

Shopping center malls have given much attention to these details, and other urban developments show promise. Charles Center in Baltimore, Constitution Plaza in Hartford, and Zeckendorf Plaza in Denver display the kinds of furniture our streets should abound in.

Program: Street Hardware

While street furniture serves people directly, street hardware pertains to the outfittings of utility and mechanical systems, including parking meters, utility poles, traffic signals, transformers, overhead wires, traffic signs, direction signs, curbs, manhole covers, sewer covers, police and fire call boxes.

San Juan, Puerto Rico.

We propose a program to improve the design of all street hardware. As with street furniture, it is the manufacturer who can effect the biggest changes—if the cities throughout the country request them. Cities will want better-designed street fixtures—furniture as well as hardware—if the superiority of better design can be shown. This is a job for architects in general, to be accomplished through their local AIA chapters.

Advertising signs would be emphasized particularly in this program. The street advertising or billboard industry is one of the biggest and best organized in the country, exercising considerable political power in many communities. It should launch a research program to improve this striking component of modern city life, for in some areas advertising signs constitute 50 per cent of the visual scene, or even more. The recent contributions to visual theory by modern art should be incorporated in the design of street signs. Let some of the creative energy devoted to the galleries be diverted to the art of the street! The billboard industry is certainly more than able to sponsor such a movement.

Program: Urban Sculpture and Art

The outfittings of the street need not all be utilitarian. In the world of design there surely is room for objects that lift the spirit on the one hand and delight the sense of humor on the other. Nothing does this better than art and sculpture in the streets.

We propose that every city resume the time-honored traditions of civic art; that budgets be set aside for sculpture, outdoor murals, pavement designs, fountains, bells, and commemorative plaques. In fact, well-designed street hardware is a kind of sculpture.

But there must be room in our cities and provisions in our civic budgets for art for art's sake. Statues placed at key points of the city proclaim the sense of place. They also indicate an important direction, commemorate a citizen or a noteworthy event, and offer the eye a point of reference. The city needs reminders of human values for its hurrying throngs, and those values must surely include humor. We do little to provide for this and so it is no surprise that people will often furnish their own. A Southern visitor to Washington said that he had no trouble finding his way around. He simply referred to the frequent equestrian statues, all of whose behinds, he observed, faced north. On Commonwealth Avenue in Boston there is a statue of a Viking, arm upraised to shade his eyes as he scans new lands. The recess formed by his arm, shoulder, and head perfectly accommodates a cardboard beer carton. An irresistible tradition thus exists among the nearby college fraternities: every Monday morning a beer carton rests on the Viking's shoulder.

In our terribly serious world these bits of merriment constitute a case for urban decorations that make us laugh. For those city councils not yet prepared to stick their necks out so far, we suggest a look at the many works of Carl Milles in this country. For those with smaller budgets, we recommend some thinking about the ubiquitous blank walls exposed so frequently when buildings are razed. These walls are usually stuccoed. They offer superb opportunities for temporary large-scale murals. On a more sober note we might erect modest glass cases for display of paintings in the street, as is done in many small Danish towns.

Boston, Massachusetts.

Program: Sculpturing the Landscape and Cityscape

Speaking of art in the street, it is fitting to speak of art on the ground. Many cities have flat areas which would welcome relief in topography. Low hills at certain strategic points of view can block out irrelevant and distracting objects.

We propose programs, where appropriate, for the artificial sculpturing of the urban landscape to enhance views, complement landform, and correct visual errors. Land sculpturing offers many possibilities.

First of all, earth from highway or building excavation furnishes ample material for little hills in otherwise flat playgrounds. This has been tried successfully in Detroit. The many marina developments along coastal areas are superb opportunities for creative land-and-water sculpture. Unusable hill sites can be reshaped as sites for buildings or for vista-promontories. Berms can block unsightly views from the highway and be effective shields against

Dallas, Texas.

225

glare from oncoming headlights. Carefully sculptured earth banks along a highway can help to divert sound waves from residential areas. The work of Thomas Jefferson reminds us of artful earth excavation. He dug a shallow ditch or "ha-ha" around his house at Monticello to keep cattle from wandering into the gardens—the "ha-ha" avoiding obstruction of his scenic vistas.

Program: The Visual Survey and the Parts of the City

Assessing the visual qualities of a site is a familiar aspect of architecture, whether the site be urban or rural. In the third chapter we outlined an elementary approach to making a visual survey on an urban scale. Perhaps it would be better to think of such a survey as an urban design survey, for not all the conditions of a site are visual.

We propose that every city be surveyed and assessed for its quality and amenity as environment. Assets and liabilities will be discerned and evaluated, the resulting data serving as a basic reference for formulating urban design action plans.

The visual or urban design survey will detect sections of the city distinguished by use, character, quality, mixture, form, pattern, and mood. Among the more commonly recognized *urban parts* which should receive attention are those discussed below.

Program: The Downtown

Downtown areas have received the most attention because they are the vital hubs of our cities and have the most articulate spokesmen. So far, successful designs for downtown rejuvenation have been those tied to sound traffic, business, and financing studies.

We propose an expanded program of downtown rejuvenation, stressing urban design. Downtowns will continue to be the nuclei of our cities. The objectives of these programs are: to make downtowns easy to reach through all transportation media; to make them worth frequenting because of their facilities, diversity, and attractions; and to develop a resident population to keep them alive at all times.

AIA chapters have contributed many successful downtown rejuvenation programs. Little Rock and Salt Lake City are outstanding examples of their advantageous application.

Program: Rehabilitating Old Neighborhoods

Urban renewal is now emphasizing rehabilitation of old areas, using a method that seeks to prevent and reverse the effects of blight in old neighborhoods. In the short and long run, this scheme will be less costly and more successful in producing better neighborhoods than even the most ambitious redevelopment programs.

We propose special programs for examining and planning the improvement of old neighborhoods, along with action to assure the soundness of existing neighborhoods. Such efforts call for careful survey and analysis work to disclose these elements stabilizing and those blighting a neighborhood. They also require design plans for the removal of blighting influences and the introduction of stabilizing elements.

Good shopping, schools, parks, accessibility to roads and public transit; good churches and neighborhood institutions; good houses and streets; good jobs and municipal services—these are the stabilizing elements in a neighborhood. Deteriorating houses, poor schools, traffic congestion, poor access, poor shopping, poor public services, noxious air, nuisance uses, unemployment, ghetto char-

A town on the Columbia River.

A town at a river junction.

226

acter—these are elements of destruction.

Every city must assess its neighborhoods and embark upon action programs to correct their problems. The scheduling and budgeting of these corrections requires ingenuity in order to stimulate the greatest amount of individual initiative. Official labeling of areas destined for rehabilitation and explicit plans will encourage property owners and investors, once the rehabilitation idea has proved itself.

Program: Historic Preservation

The preservation of historic buildings is by now firmly established and accepted. Accompanying preservation efforts is the art of restoration—using the sound parts of an old building and restoring the unsound. Restoration and remodeling of an urban area is equally important.

We propose programs for the restoration and remodeling of historic areas of the city. The objective is to develop interesting and unique enclaves of the city as well as to add to the sum of useful city parts.

It is not enough to recreate the scale, atmosphere, and character of the older areas—they should also be carefully blended with neighboring areas and extended in sympathetic modern terms. In some cases it may be wise to relocate old buildings to more appropriate settings. A group of them can be collected to recreate an old type of village, like Mystic, Connecticut. In other cases a group of historic buildings on historic sites can undergo a careful restoration program which *adds* harmonious new buildings to fill the voids between the old.

Houses in Ohio.

Program: Suburban Centers

As our road networks grow, the number of suburban centers increases, which embody, almost without exception, the most haphazard growth possible. It is a pity that they cannot learn from the well-planned industrial park the benefits of good design. But the new centers are usually at highly accessible crossroad intersections and the land is in many hands. The townships and counties in which they lie have little experience in planning and administration.

We propose programs for the careful and practical design of suburban centers. Plans for these developments should include circulation of vehicles and pedestrians, parking, landscaping, functional grouping of shops, careful placement of pedestrian traffic, ample entrances and location for office towers and medical groups, interspersal of recreation buildings, and location of public buildings.

Kansas City, Missouri.

Planning in these areas should be required by law. The interests of the public are to be protected. Indeed, the interests of the developers themselves surely are at stake. In many cases responsible developers are willing to plan soundly but are unable to do so in the face of unscrupulous competitors. AIA chapters can and have taken leading positions toward these ends, because they can best show the benefits to be gained from carefully designed suburban centers—which are, after all, a new form of town center. Too often the roads straddled by the suburban centers are main auto routes. Expressways should not cut through, but should bypass them, with convenient connector roads branching off to the centers. A ring of reserve land should surround the center as buffer between commercial buildings and houses. Through careful plan-

227

Chicago, Illinois.

Plains of the state of Washington.

ning of the pedestrian ways, the center can be connected to nearby schools, old-age homes, public buildings, etc., thus being tied to a variety of functions.

Program: New Suburbs and New Towns

The many new suburbs springing up around our cities present the finest opportunities to build new residential communities. But too often they are simply dull subdivision layouts—one class, one type, undifferentiated housing. Experience has shown that diversity of house type and essential community facilities are basic guarantees for stabilizing neighborhoods.

We propose programs for the shaping of suburban residential developments into viable new communities, utilizing all the techniques that can be brought to bear. Among the programs are the creation of open space reserves; preplanning of major utility lines to direct growth; zoning provisions which allow developers to submit their own plans for new towns in accordance with a county master plan; the requirement that subdivisions be well designed as communities; and the cooperation of individaul developers in joint enterprises. Most desirable would be the creation of design plans for entire suburban areas of new communities with a variety of building types. Certain key open spaces, facilities, vistas, and features could be specified while the balance of the design could be designated as density alone—thus paving the way for flexibility in development.

Some Not-So-Incidental Incidentals

Our comprehensive list of urban design programs is, of course, incomplete. It always will be. As long as we put our minds to it we shall uncover new problems needing urban design attention. A moment's thought readily suggests even further programs than those discussed—the restoration of despoiled town sites; the improvement of focal buildings like churches and schools by reshaping their settings; the design of special enclaves like hospital areas, high schools, and college campuses woven into the community; the creation of places of fun in the city; and innovations in housing, particularly low-cost housing.

This task emphasizes the role of our professionals and citizens throughout the country as it has never been emphasized before. Leadership will, of course, always come from individuals but even the best of individuals work more effectively when reinforced by strong organizations. The AIA, for example, is a ready-made organization at city, state, and regional level. Its immediate obligations at these levels include the arousing of interest and contact with the public and private groups which build our cities. The AIA should establish a Mayor's Urban Design Advisory Committee in every city and a Governor's Urban and Regional Design Advisory Committee in every state. These committees could explain the importance of urban design at all levels of public undertakings; make suggestions to improve public policies of action; be a vehicle for transmitting ideas; act as ambassadors between the planning commissions of the cities, counties, and states, and private developers. Local AIA publications could serve as major publications for presenting urban design ideas. The Utah Chapter AIA did this very well in publicizing Salt Lake City's downtown plan.

There are a number of special urban design problems which can best be tackled by AIA chapters: the question of design controls;

sign designs; urban design education in nearby universities; urban design consideration in all public works; preservation of historic buildings and areas; contact with the local press (the Sunday art and local news sections are woefully lacking in articles on urban design); examination of local codes and building ordinances; parking plans for downtown areas—the list is indeed long.

These professional obligations in no way transfer the duties of architecture from the individual practitioner to his AIA chapter. Instead, it means the obligations of both are increased together. We have been adding to the vocabulary of architecture in these last years at a rate more rapid than anything history has ever seen. But our advances have focused on the individual building alone. We must broaden our design vocabulary to include the urban scene, to better relate buildings to their neighbors. In our facade designs we must recognize that the eye pauses at edges and accents. This is true, of course, when we see clothing, a garden, or a building. The eye is wearied by a too-continuous run of features unless they are fashioned by a master designer, and even then, they should only be applied to particularly important buildings.

Our facades and masses are becoming larger and larger and it is increasingly difficult to keep them in scale. We must remember that the eye delights in probing objects which do not reveal themselves in their entirety at first glance. The eye needs the enticement to look more, to discover more, to be surprised by the unexpected and held by the sublime. It would be well to get a bit of tasteful décolleté into our designs. We also have more opportunities to create enclosed urban spaces between buildings as we design groups of buildings together. A handsome enclosed space can give more distinction to buildings than the best possible mass or facade design alone. That is one of the many old lessons of urban design we are beginning to relearn. In short, our urban design outlook will add as much to the improvement of individual works of architecture as to the city as a whole. To speak of such effects in the design of a single building is not at all strange. We expect such things of architecture. Why, then, should we not expect such subtleties in our cities in their entirety, or in geographical regions?

Fundamentally the question before us is simple and it is posed when we design a single building or address our thoughts to an entire region. The question is how we want to live on this land of ours, and whether we wish to care for it as our dearest asset or exploit it carelessly. It is as simple as that. Architects see this concern as urban design and this book is their contemporary statement of the problems of design facing our country. But this book is only an initial statement which we hope will sharpen debate and stimulate action. No generation of architects at any time in history has had as promising and inspiring an opportunity as we do now. And no generation of Americans ever had so great a responsibility.

Bibliography

The bibliography consists of material that is readily available to the reader for further reference. Each item is listed only once, under the chapter heading where it was first used as a primary or secondary source. Reports and plans cited in the text but not readily available through normal channels have not been listed in the bibliography.

Chapters 1 and 2

Butterfield, Roger: *Ancient Rome,* The Odyssey Press, Inc., New York, 1964.

Churchill, Henry Stern: *The City Is the People,* Harcourt, Brace & World Inc., New York, 1945.

Cole, John Peter: *Geography of World Affairs,* 2d ed., Penguin Books, Inc., Baltimore, 1963.

Cottrell, Leonard: *The Anvil of Civilization,* Mentor Books, New American Library of World Literature, Inc., New York, 1963.

Fortune (eds.): *The Exploding Metropolis,* Doubleday & Company, Inc., Garden City, N. Y., 1958.

Geddes, Sir Patrick: *Cities in Evolution,* Ernest Benn, Ltd.—Benn Bros., Ltd., London, 1949.

Gutkind, Erwin Anton: *Our World from the Air,* Doubleday & Company, Inc., Garden City, N.Y., 1952.

———: *The Twilight of Cities,* The Free Press of Glencoe, New York, 1962.

Hilbersheimer, Ludwig: *The Nature of Cities,* Paul Theobald, Chicago, 1955.

Hiorns, Frederick R.: *Town-Building in History,* George G. Harrap & Co., Ltd., London, 1956.

Howard, Sir Ebenezer: *Garden Cities of Tomorrow,* Faber & Faber, Ltd., London, 1946.

Lavedan, Pierre: *French Architecture,* Penguin Books, Inc., Baltimore, 1956.

———: *Histoire de l'Urbanisme,* 4 vols., H. Laurens, Paris, 1952–1959.

Le Corbusier: *When the Cathedrals Were White,* Harcourt, Brace & World, Inc., New York, 1947.

Lowdermilk, W. C.: *Conquest of the Land through 7,000 Years,* U.S. Department of Agriculture Information Bulletins, no. 99, Soil Conservation Service, Washington, D.C., 1959.

Lubove, Roy: *Community Planning in the 1920's,* The University of Pittsburgh Press, Pittsburgh, 1963.

———: *The Progressives and the Slums: Tenement House Reform in New York City, 1890–1917,* The University of Pittsburgh Press, Pittsburgh, 1963.

Millon, Henry A.: *Key Monuments of the History of Architecture,* Harry N. Abrams, Inc., New York, 1964; text ed., Prentice-Hall Inc., Englewood Cliffs, N.J., 1964.

Mumford, Lewis: *The City in History,* Harcourt Brace & World, Inc., New York, 1961.

———: *The Culture of Cities,* Harcourt Brace & World, Inc., New York, 1938.

Pinkney, H.: *Napoleon III and the Rebuilding of Paris,* Princeton University Press, Princeton, N.J., 1958.

Rasmussen, Steen Eiler: *London, The Unique City,* The M.I.T. Press, Cambridge, Mass., 1959.

———: *Town and Buildings,* Harvard University Press, Cambridge, Mass., 1952.

Reps, John W.: *The Making of Urban America: A History of City Planning in the United States,* Princeton University Press, Princeton, N.J., 1965.

Rodwin, Lloyd: *The British New Towns Policy,* Harvard University Press, Cambridge, Mass., 1956.

Saarinen, Eliel: *The City: Its Growth, Its Decay, Its Future,* Reinhold Publishing Corporation, New York, 1943.

Sitte, Camillo: *The Art of Building Cities,* Reinhold Publishing Corporation, New York, 1945.

Summerson, John N.: *Georgian London,* Charles Scribner's Sons, New York, 1946.

Tunnard, Christopher: *The City of Man,* Charles Scribner's Sons, New York, 1953.

———— and Henry Hope Reed: *American Skyline,* Houghton Mifflin Company, Boston, 1955.

Udall, Stewart L.: *The Quiet Crisis,* Holt, Rinehart and Winston, Inc., New York, 1963.

Willets, William: *Chinese Art,* 2 vols. in 1, George Braziller, Inc., New York, 1958.

Wright, Frank Lloyd: *The Disappearing City,* William F. Peyson, New York, 1932.

————: *The Living City,* Horizon Press, Inc., New York, 1958.

Wycherly, Richard Ernest: *How the Greeks Built Cities,* St Martin's Press, New York, 1962.

Zucker, Paul: *Town and Square from the Agora to the Village Green,* Columbia University Press, New York, 1959.

Chapter 3

American Institute of Architects, Georgia Chapter: *Visual Survey and Design Plan,* Atlanta, 1962.

————, New York Chapter: *The State of the City,* New York, June, 1964.

————, American Institute of Planners, and American Society of Landscape Architects, Georgia chapters: *Improving the Mess We Live In,* Atlanta, 1963.

Casson, Sir Hugh Maxwell: "The Temple of Heaven," *Architectural Review,* 118:400–401, December, 1955.

Gibson, James J.: *The Perception of the Visual World,* Houghton Mifflin Company, Boston, 1950.

Goldfinger, Erno: "The Elements of Enclosed Space," *Architectural Review,* 91:5–8, January, 1942.

————: "The Sensation of Space," *Architectural Review,* 90:129–131, November, 1941.

————: "Urbanism and Spatial Order," *Architectural Review,* 90:163–166, December, 1941.

Hall, Edward T.: *The Hidden Dimension,* Doubleday & Company, Inc., Garden City, N.Y., 1965.

Jacobs, S. W., and B. G. Jones: *City Design Through Conservation: Methods for Evaluation and Utilization of Aesthetics and Cultural Resources,* 2 vols., University of California, Berkeley, Calif., 1960.

Kepes, Gyorgy: *The Language of Vision,* Paul Theobald, Chicago, 1944.

Lynch, Kevin: "The Form of Cities," *Scientific American,* 190:20, 54–63, April, 1954.

————: *The Image of the City,* Harvard University Press and The M.I.T. Press, Cambridge, Mass., 1960.

———— Donald Appleyard, and Students: *The Form of a Metropolitan Sector: Washington and the Maryland Peninsula,* The M.I.T. Press, Cambridge, Mass., 1962.

———— Donald Appleyard, and Students: *Signs in the City,* study by graduate students in urban design of the Department of City and Regional Planning, The M.I.T. Press, Cambridge, Mass., 1963.

Meltzer, Jack, and Associates: *Aspects of Environmental Design,* prepared for the Chicago Community Renewal Program, Chicago, 1963.

Nagy, L. Mohrly: *Vision in Motion,* Paul Theobald, Chicago, 1947.

Nairn, Ian: *The American Landscape: A Critical View,* Random House, Inc., New York, 1965.

Rasmussen, Steen Eiler: *Experiencing Architecture,* The M.I.T. Press, Cambridge, Mass., 1959.

State of Wisconsin, Department of Resource Development: *Lake Superior South Shore Area,* Landscape Analysis, no. 1, Madison, Wis., 1963.

Thiel, Phillip: "Processional Architecture," *AIA Journal,* 16:23–28, February, 1964.

————: "A Sequence Experience Notation for Architectural and Urban Spaces," *Town Planning Review,* 32(1):33–52, April, 1961.

Chapter 4

Bacon, Edmund N.: *Design of Cities,* The Viking Press, Inc., New York, 1965.

Blumenfeld, Hans: "On the Concentric Circle Theory of Urban Growth," *Land Economics,* May, 1949.

————: "Scale and Civic Design," *Town Planning Review,* April, 1953.

————: "Scale in the Metropolis," *Canadian Architect,* September, 1957.

————: "Theory of City Form, Past and Present," *Journal of the Society of Architectural Historians,* 8(3 and 4):7–16, July–December, 1949.

Chapin, F. Stuart: *Urban Land Use Planning,* The University of Illinois Press, Urbana, Ill., 1965.

Doxiadis, Constantinos A.: *Dynapolis: The City of the Future,* Doxiadis Associates, Athens, Greece, 1960.

Gallion and Eisner: *The Urban Pattern,* D. Van Nostrand Company, Inc., New York, 1963.

Gibberd, Frederick: *Town Design,* 3d ed. revised and enlarged, Frederick A. Praeger, New York, 1960.

Haar, Charles M.: *Land-use Planning: A Casebook on the Use, Misuse and Reuse of Urban Land,* Little, Brown and Company, Boston, 1959.

Hegemann, Werner, and Elbert Peets: *Civic Art: The American Vitruvius,* Architectural Book Publishing Company, Inc., New York, 1922.

Holford, William: "The Tall Building in the Town," *Journal of the Town Planning Institute,* 45(4):78–86, March, 1959.

Le Corbusier: *Concerning Town Planning,* Yale University Press, New Haven, Conn., 1948.

———— and De Pierrefeu: *The Home of Man,* The Architectural Press, London, 1958.

Lynch, Kevin: *Site Planning,* The M.I.T. Press, Cambridge, Mass., 1962.

Opperman, Logan, and Tucker: *Environmental Engineering and Metropolitan Planning,* Northwestern University Press, Evanston, Ill., 1962.

Peets, Elbert: "Studies in Planning Texture for Housing in a Greenbelt Town," *Architectural Record,* 106:130–137, September, 1949.

Rapuano, Michael, P. P. Pirone, and Brooks E. Wigginton: *Open Space in Urban Design,* report prepared for the Cleveland Development Foundation and sponsored by the Junior League of Cleveland, Inc., The Spiral Press, New York, 1964.

Sanders, Spencer Edward, and A. J. Rabuck: *New City Patterns,* Reinhold Publishing Corporation, New York, 1946.

Sert, José Luis: *Can Our City Survive?* Harvard University Press, Cambridge, Mass., 1942.

Sharp, Thomas: *Dreaming Spires and Teeming Towers: The Character of Cambridge,* Liverpool University Press, Liverpool, 1963.

Stamp, L. Dudley: *Applied Geography,* Penguin Books, Inc., Balt.,1960.

Tunnard, Christopher, and Boris Pushkarev: *Man-made America: Chaos or Control?* Yale University Press, New Haven, Conn., 1963.

Chapter 5

American Institute of Architects, Southern California Chapter, Urban Design Committee, 1963–1964: *Land Development Control in Hillside and Mountain Areas,* Los Angeles, 1964.

Auzelle, Robert: *Encyclopedie de l'Urbanisme,* Vincent Fréal et Cie., Paris, 1950.

Chicago Department of City Planning: *Basic Policies for the Comprehensive Plan of Chicago,* Chicago, 1964.

Copenhagen Regional Planning Office: *Preliminary Outline Plan for the Copenhagen Metropolitan Region,* Copenhagen, 1961.

Cullen, Gordon, and Richard Matthew: *A Town Called Alcan,* Alcan Industries, Ltd., London, 1964.

Cumbernauld Development Corporation: *Cumbernauld New Town: Preliminary Planning Proposals* (with 1st and 2nd Addendum Reports), Glasgow, Scotland, 1958, 1959, 1962.

Dahir, James: *Region Building,* Harper & Row, Publishers, Incorporated, New York, 1955.

Detroit City Planning Commission: *Urban Design Study,* Detroit, 1964.

Downtown Planning Association and American Institute of Architects,Utah Chapter, *Official Report, Downtown Salt Lake City 2nd Century Plan,* Salt Lake City, Utah, 1962.

Grebler, Leo: *Europe's Reborn Cities,* Technical Bulletin, no. 28, Urban Land Institute, Washington, D.C., 1956.

Lower Colorado River Land Use Advisory Committee: *The Lower Colorado River Land Use Plan,* U.S. Department of the Interior, Washington, D.C., 1964.

McHarg, Ian, and David Wallace: *Plan for the Valleys,* Greenspring and Worthington Valley Planning Council, Inc., Baltimore, 1964.

Meyerson, Martin, and Associates: *The Face of the Metropolis,* Random House, Inc., New York, 1963.

Millspaugh, Martin (ed.): *Baltimore's Charles Center, A Case Study of Downtown Renewal,* Technical Bulletin, no. 51, Urban Land Institute, Washington, D.C., 1964.

Office for Regional Development: *Change, Challenge, Response: A Development Policy for New York State,* Albany, N.Y., 1964.

San Francisco Bay Conservation Study Commission Report, report to the California Legislature by the San Francisco Bay Conservation Study Commission, San Francisco, 1965.

Scott, Mel: *The San Francisco Bay Area: A Metropolis in Perspective,* University of California Press, Berkeley, Calif., 1959.

Technical Report, University City, Unit 3, Urban Renewal Area, prepared by the Group for Planning and Research of Philadelphia for the Redevelopment Authority of the City of Philadelphia, Philadelphia, 1964.

Chapter 6

Bowra, Sir Maurice: *Golden Ages of the Great Cities,* introduction by Sir Ernest Barker, Thames Hudson, London, 1952.

Crowe, Sylvia: *The Landscape of Power,* The Architectural Press, London, 1958.

————: *Tomorrow's Landscape,* The Architectural Press, London, 1956.

Cullen, Gordon: *Townscape,* The Architectural Press, London, 1961.

De Wolfe, Ivor: *Italian Townscape,* The Architectural Press, London, 1963.

Eaton, Leonard K.: *Landscape Architect in America: The Life and Work of Jens Jenson,* The University of Chicago Press, Chicago, 1964.

Eliot, Charles William: *Charles Eliot, Landscape Architect,* Houghton and Mifflin, Boston, 1902.

Halprin, Lawrence: *Cities,* Reinhold Publishing Corporation, New York, 1963.

Simonds, John Ormsbee: *Landscape Architecture: The Shaping of Man's Natural Environment,* McGraw-Hill Book Company, New York, 1961.

Chapter 7

Blumenfeld, Hans: "Alternative Solutions for Metropolitan Development," in *Planning 1948,* American Society of Planning Officials, Chicago, 1948, pp. 15–24. (Proceedings of the Annual National Planning Conference in New York City, October 11–13, 1948.)

————: "Are Land Use Patterns Predictable?" *Journal of the American Institute of Planners,* 25:61–66, May, 1959.

————: "The Conceptual Framework of Land Use," *Ekistics,* 14(85): 259–263, December, 1962.

————: "Form and Function in Urban Communities," *Journal of the Society of Architectural Historians,* 3(1 and 2):11–21, January–April, 1943.

————: "The Metropolitan Region," *Canadian Art,* no. 77, January–February, 1962.

————: "The Tidal Wave of Metropolitan Expansion," *Journal of the American Institute of Planners,* 20:3–14, Winter, 1954.

————: "The Urban Pattern," *Annals of the Academy of Political and Social Science,* 352:74–83, March, 1964.

Boley, Robert E.: *Industrial Districts Restudied: An Analysis of Characteristics,* Technical Bulletin, no. 41, Urban Land Institute, Washington, D.C., 1961.

Clawson, Marion: *Land for the Future,* The Johns Hopkins Press, Baltimore, 1960.

Downtown Planning Association and American Institute of Architects, Utah Chapter, *Official Report, Downtown Salt Lake City 2nd Century Plan,* Salt Lake City, Utah, 1962.

Gist, N. P., and L. A. Halbert: *Urban Society,* Thomas Y. Crowell, New York, 1950.

Gruen, Victor, and Larry Smith: *Shopping Towns USA,* Reinhold Publishing Corporation, New York, 1960.

Hoover, Edgar M., and Raymond Vernon: *Anatomy of a Metropolis,* Doubleday & Company, Inc., Garden City, N.Y., 1962.

Horwood, Edgar M., and Ronald R. Boyce: *Studies of the Central Business District and Urban Freeway Development,* University of Washington Press, Seattle, 1959.

McKeever, J. Ross: *Shopping Centers Restudied,* part I: "Emerging Patterns," part II: "Practical Experiences," Technical Bulletin, no. 30, Urban Land Institute, Washington, D.C., 1957.

Planned Industrial Districts: Technical Bulletin, no. 19, Urban Land Institute, Washington, D.C., 1952.

Rannels, John: *The Core of the City: A Pilot Study of Changing Land Uses in Central Business Districts,* Columbia University Press, New York, 1956.

Space for Industry: Technical Bulletin, no. 23, Urban Land Institute, Washington, D.C., 1954.

Tyrwhitt, Jacqueline et al. (eds.): *The Heart of the City: Towards the Humanization of Urban Life,* Farrar, Straus & Giroux, Inc., New York, 1952.

Vernon, Raymond: *Metropolis 1985,* New York Metropolitan Region Study, no. 9, Harvard University Press, Cambridge, Mass., 1960.

————: *The Myth and Reality of Our Urban Problems,* Harvard University Press, Cambridge, Mass., 1962.

Von Eckardt, Wolf: *The Challenge of Megalopolis,* based on the original study by Jean Gottmann, The Macmillan Company, New York, 1964.

Weber, Max: *The City,* Collier Books, New York, 1962.

Chapter 8

Abrams, Charles: *Forbidden Neighbors: A Study of Prejudice in Housing,* Harper & Row, Publishers, Incorporated, New York, 1955.

Blumenfeld, Hans: "Comments on the Neighborhood Concept," *Journal of Housing,* December, 1948.

————: "Residential Densities," in *Planning 1957,* American Society of Planning Officials, Chicago, 1957, pp. 119–122. (Selected papers from the National Planning Conference in San Francisco, March, 1957.)

Chermayeff, Sergius I., and Christopher Alexander: *Community and Privacy,* Doubleday & Company, Inc., Garden City, N.Y., 1964.

The Community Builder's Handbook, Urban Land Institute, Washington, D.C., 1961.

Innovations vs. Traditions in Community Development: A Comparative Study in Residential Land Use. Technical Bulletin, no. 47, Urban Land Institute, Washington, D.C., 1963.

Lovelace, Eldridge, and William L. Weismantel: *Density Zoning: Organic Zoning for Planned Residential Developments.* Technical Bulletin, no. 42, Urban Land Institute, Washington, D.C., 1963.

Mead, Margaret: "Contributory Papers to the Delos Symposium," *Ekistics,* 16(95):255, October, 1963.

Nash, William W.: *Residential Rehabilitation: Private Profits and Public Purposes,* McGraw-Hill Book Company, New York, 1959.

New Approaches to Residential Land Development, Urban Land Institute, Washington, D.C., 1961.

Osborn, F. J.: *The New Towns: The Answer to Megalopolis,* Doubleday & Company, Inc., Garden City, N.Y., 1962.

Perry, Clarence: "The Neighborhood Unit," vol. III, *Regional Survey of New York and Environs,* Regional Plan of New York, New York, 1929.

Planned Unit Development with a Homes Association. Land Planning Bulletin, no. 6, Federal Housing Administration, Washington, D.C., 1963.

Rapkin, Chester, and E. W. Grigsby: *Residential Renewal in the Urban Core,* University of Pennsylvania Press, Philadelphia, 1960.

Stein, Clarence S.: *Toward New Towns for America,* rev. ed., Reinhold
    Publishing Company, New York, 1957.
Suggested Land Subdivision Regulations, Housing and Home Finance
    Agency, Washington, D.C., 1962.
Whyte, William H.: *Cluster Development,* American Conservation Associ-
    ation, New York, 1964.
Winnick, Louis: *Rental Housing: Opportunities for Private Investment,*
    McGraw-Hill Book Company, New York, 1959.

Chapter 9

Appleyard, Lynch and Myer: *The View from the Road,* The M.I.T. Press,
    Cambridge, Mass., 1964.
Blumenfeld, Hans: "Transportation in the Modern Metropolis," *Queens
    Quarterly,* Winter, 1961.
Buchanan, Colin et al.: *Traffic in Towns,* Her Majesty's Stationery Office,
    London, 1963.
Chinitz, Benjamin: *Freight and the Metropolis,* Harvard University Press,
    Cambridge, Mass., 1960.
City of Philadelphia, Mayor's Transit Study: *The Public Transit Authority:
    A Study of Five Cities,* Philadelphia, 1964.
City of Toronto Planning Board: *The Pedestrian in Downtown Toronto,*
    Toronto, 1959.
Crowe, Sylvia: *The Landscape of Roads,* The Architectural Press, London,
    1960.
Drew, Kent, and Charles McCafferty: *Detroit Freeway Esthetics,* Com-
    munity Renewal Urban Design Study, Detroit City Planning Commis-
    sion, 1964.
Federal Aid for Highways: What It Is, How It Works, National Highway
    Users Conference, Washington, D.C., 1959.
Goldschmidt, C.: "Windshield Vistas: Who Cares?" *Journal of the Amer-
    ican Institute of Planners,* 24(3):158–166, 1958.
Historic Preservation Through Urban Renewal, Housing and Home Finance
    Agency, Washington, D.C., 1963.
Mitchell, Robert B., and Chester Rapkin: *Urban Traffic: A Function of
    Land Use,* Columbia University Press, New York, 1954.
New Highways: Challenge to the Metropolitan Region, Technical Bulletin,
    no. 31, Urban Land Institute, Washington, D.C., 1957.
Owen, Wilfred: *Cities in the Motor Age,* The Viking Press, Inc., New
    York, 1959.
Pushkarev, Boris: "The Esthetics of Freeway Design," *Landscape,* 10(2):
    7–15, Winter, 1960–1961.
Ritter, Paul: *Planning for Man and Motor,* Pergamon Press, London, 1964.
Twin Cities Metropolitan Planning Commission, Joint Program: "The In-
    fluence of Transportation on the Form of Urban Growth," St. Paul,
    Minn., 1963. (Mimeographed.)
Warner, Sam B., Jr.: *Streetcar Suburbs: The Process of Growth in Boston,
    1870–1900,* Harvard University Press, Cambridge, Mass., 1962.

Chapter 10

Babcock, Richard F., and Fred P. Bosselman: "Suburb Zoning and the
    Apartment Boom," *University of Pennsylvania Law Review,* June,
    1963.
Codman, John: *Preservation of Historic Districts by Architectural Control,*
    American Society of Planning Officials, Chicago, 1956.
Density Zoning: Organic Zoning for Planned Residential Developments,
    Technical Bulletin, no. 42, Urban Land Institute, Washington, D.C.,
    1961.
Fagin, Henry, and Robert Weinberg (eds.): *Planning and Community Ap-
    pearance,* Regional Plan Association, New York, 1958.
Jacobs, Stephen K.: *Historic Preservation in City Planning and Urban Re-
    newal,* National Trust for Historic Preservation, Washington, D.C.,
    1959.
Los Angeles County, Regional Planning Commission: *A Guide to Parking
    Lot Requirements,* Los Angeles (no date).
Margolis, Alfred L.: "Esthetic Zoning: The Trend of the Law," *Western
    Law Review,* March, 1956.

Model Zoning Ordinance, 2d ed., American Society of Planning Officials, Chicago, 1960.

Planning Advisory Service Reports, American Society of Planning Officials, Chicago.

    No.   6, *Architectural Control,* September, 1964.

    No. 37, *Minimum Requirements for Lot and Building Size,* April, 1952.

    No. 38, *Installation of Physical Improvements as Required in Subdivision Regulations,* May, 1952.

    No. 46, *Public Open Space in Subdivisions,* January, 1953.

    No. 86, *Land Development Ordinances,* May, 1956.

    No. 96, *New Developments in Architectural Control,* March, 1957.

    No. 102, *Subdivision Design: Some New Developments,* September, 1957.

    No. 124, *Subdivision Manuals,* July, 1959.

    No. 135, *Cluster Subdivisions,* June, 1960.

Strong, Ann Louise: *Urban Growth Techniques for Guiding Development in the Philadelphia Region,* Philadelphia Housing Association, Philadelphia, March, 1964.

Chapter 11

American Council to Improve Our Neighborhoods: *Organization in Renewal: A Program Aid,* Series in Housing and Community Development, Harper & Row, Publishers, Incorporated, New York.

Ascher, Charles S. et al.: *Urban Redevelopment: Problems and Practices,* edited by Coleman Woodbury, The University of Chicago Press, Chicago, 1953.

Bauer, Catherine et al.: *The Future of Cities and Urban Redevelopment,* edited by Coleman Woodbury, The University of Chicago Press, Chicago, 1953.

City of Philadelphia, Planning Commission: *Capital Program, 1963–1968,* Philadelphia, 1962.

City and County of San Francisco, Department of City Planning: *Capital Improvement Program, 1963–64, 1968–69,* San Francisco, 1963.

Colean, M. L.: *Renewing Our Cities,* The Twentieth Century Fund, New York, 1953.

Fiser, Webb S.: *Mastery of the Metropolis,* Prentice-Hall, Inc., Englewood Cliffs, N.J., 1962.

Fisher, Robert M.: *Twenty Years of Public Housing: Economic Aspects of the Federal Program,* Harper & Row, Publishers, Incorporated, New York, 1959.

Haar, Charles M.: *Federal Credit and Private Housing: The Mass Financing Dilemma,* American Council to Improve Our Neighborhoods Series in Housing and Community Development, McGraw-Hill Book Company, New York, 1960.

Meyerson, Martin, and Edward C. Banfield: *Politics, Planning and Public Interest: The Case of Public Housing in Chicago,* The Free Press of Glencoe, New York, 1955.

————, Barbara Terret, and William L. C. Wheaton: *Housing, People, and Cities,* American Council to Improve our Neighborhoods Series in Housing and Community Development, McGraw-Hill Book Company, New York, 1962.

Millspaugh, Martin, and Gurney Breckenfield: *The Human Side of Urban Renewal,* Fight-Blight, Baltimore, 1958.

Municipal Manpower Commission: *Governmental Manpower for Tomorrow's Cities,* McGraw-Hill Book Company, New York, 1962.

Rouse, James Wilson: *No Slums in Ten Years,* report to the Commissioners of the District of Columbia, D.C. Redevelopment Land Agency, Washington, D.C., 1955.

Sears, Roebuck and Company: *ABC's of Urban Renewal.*

Strong, Ann Louise: *Preserving Urban Open Space,* Urban Renewal Administration, Washington, D.C., 1963.

U.S. Department of Commerce: *Handbook of Federal Aids to Communities,* Area Redevelopment Administration, Washington, D.C., 1963.

Van Huyck, Alfred P., and Jack Hornung: *The Citizen's Guide to Urban Renewal,* Chandler-Davis, West Trenton, N.J., 1962.

Von Eckardt, Wolf: *Bulldozers and Bureaucrats: Cities and Urban Renewal,* The New Republic, Washington, D.C., 1963.

Webster, Donald H.: *Urban Planning and Municipal Public Policy,* Harper & Row, Publishers, Incorporated, New York, 1958.

Wood and Almendinger: *1400 Governments,* Harvard University Press, Cambridge, Mass., 1961.

Chapter 12

The Ad Hoc Committee on the Triple Revolution: *The Triple Revolution,* Santa Barbara, Calif., 1964.

Aronovici, Carol: *Community Building: Science, Technique, Art,* Doubleday & Company, Inc., Garden City, N.Y., 1956.

Blumenfeld, Hans: "A Hundred Year Plan: The Example of Copenhagen," *Ekistics,* 17(99): February, 1964.

Carter, Edward: *The Future of London,* Penguin Books, Inc., Baltimore, 1962.

Commission of Regional Planning: *The Case for Regional Planning, with Special Reference to New England,* Yale University Press, New Haven, Conn., 1947.

Doxiadis, Constantinos A.: *Architecture in Transition,* Hutchinson & Co., London, 1963.

————: *Ekistics, An Introduction to the Science of Human Settlements,* Hutchinson & Co., London (to be published).

————: "The Science of Ekistics," *Ekistics,* 19(110):4–38, January, 1965.

————: *Urban Renewal and the Future of the American City,* 2 vols., prepared for the National Association of Housing and Redevelopment Officials, Doxiadis Associates, Athens, Greece, 1962.

Futterman, Robert A.: *The Future of Our Cities,* Doubleday & Company, Inc., Garden City, N.Y., 1961.

Galbraith, John Kenneth: *The Affluent Society,* Houghton Mifflin Company, Boston, 1958.

Hall, Gordon, and Simon Eisner: *The Peninsula Tomorrow: Research and Forecast,* Monterey Peninsula Area Planning Commission, Monterey, Calif., 1961.

Heckscher, August: *The Public Happiness,* Atheneum Publishers, New York, 1962.

Le Corbusier: *The City of Tomorrow and Its Planning,* translated from the 8th French edition of *Urbanisme,* with an introduction by Frederick Etchells, Payson & Clarke Ltd., New York, 1929.

Lord, Russell: *The Care of the Earth,* New American Library of World Literature, Inc., New York, 1962.

MacKaye, Benton: *The New Exploration: A Philosophy of Regional Planning,* The University of Illinois Press, Urbana, Ill., 1962.

Ministry of Housing and Local Government: *The South East Study, 1961–1981,* Her Majesty's Stationery Office, London, 1964.

Norton, Perry L. (ed.): *Urban Problems and Techniques,* Chandler-Davis, West Trenton, N.J., 1959.

The Planning of a New Town, data and design based on a study for a New Town of 100,000 at Hook, Hampshire, London County Council, London, 1961.

Reissman, Leonard: *The Urban Process: Cities in Industrial Societies,* The Free Press of Glencoe, New York, 1964.

Rodwin, Lloyd (ed.): *The Future Metropolis,* George Braziller, Inc., New York, 1961.

Thomas, William L., Jr. (ed.): *Man's Role in Changing the Face of the Earth,* an international symposium under the co-chairmanship of Carl O. Sauer, Marston Bates, and Lewis Mumford, The University of Chicago Press, Chicago, 1962.

Town Planning Institute of Canada: *Regional Planning in Plan,* June, 1960.

Twin Cities Metropolitan Planning Commission, Joint Program: Part I: "Comparative Studies, Theoretical Proposals and Sketch Alternatives for the Twin Cities," part II: "Proposals for Ideal Systems of Urbanization," St. Paul, Minn., 1963. (Mimeographed.)

U.S. Department of Agriculture: *A Place to Live: The Yearbook of Agriculture, 1963,* Washington, D.C., 1963.

Whyte, William H.: *Securing Open Space for Urban America: Conservation Easements.* Technical Bulletin, no. 36, Urban Land Institute, Washington, D.C., 1959.

Index

Index of Illustrations